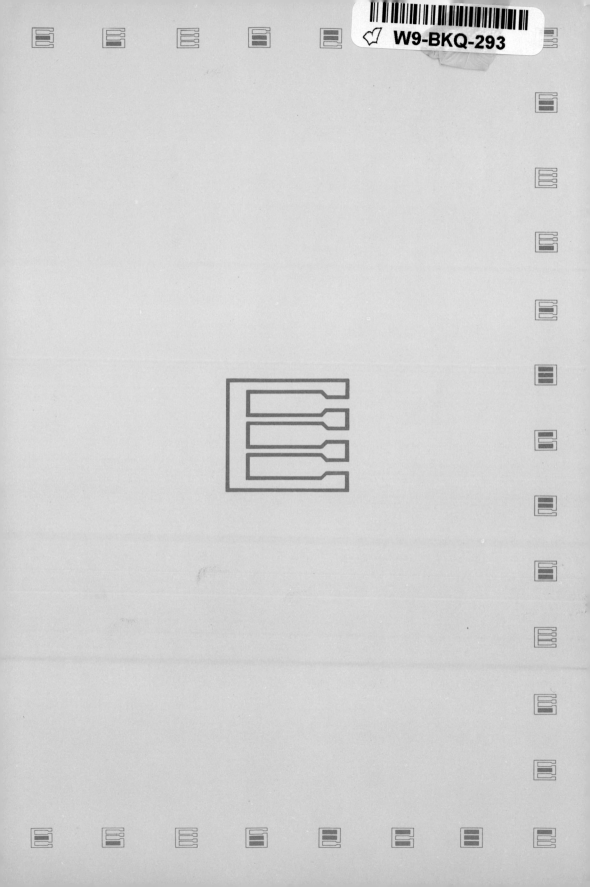

An Introduction to Database Systems

Volume II

C. J. DATE

IBM Corporation

 ADDISON-WESLEY PUBLISHING COMPANY
Reading, Massachusetts · Menlo Park, California
London · Amsterdam · Don Mills, Ontario · Sydney

This book is in the
Addison-Wesley Systems Programming Series
Consulting editors: IBM Editorial Board

Library of Congress Cataloging in Publication Data

Date, C. J.
    An Introduction to Database Systems
    Vol. II

    Includes bibliographies and index.
    1. Data base management. I. Title.
QA76.9.D3D367   001.64   80-17603
ISBN 0-201-14474-3   AACR2

Reprinted with corrections, June 1983

ISBN 0-201-14474-3
CDEFGHIJ-HA-89876543

This one is for Fanny

THE SYSTEMS PROGRAMMING SERIES

*Published

Foreword

The field of systems programming primarily grew out of the efforts of many programmers and managers whose creative energy went into producing practical, utilitarian systems programs needed by the rapidly growing computer industry. Programming was practiced as an art where each programmer invented unique solutions to problems with little guidance beyond that provided by immediate associates. In 1968, the late Ascher Opler, then at IBM, recognized that it was necessary to bring programming knowledge together in a form that would be accessible to all systems programmers. Surveying the state of the art, he decided that enough useful material existed to justify a significant codification effort. On his recommendation, IBM decided to sponsor The Systems Programming Series as a long term project to collect, organize, and publish those principles and techniques that would have lasting value throughout the industry.

The Series consists of an open-ended collection of text-reference books. The contents of each book represent the individual author's view of the subject area and do not necessarily reflect the views of the IBM Corporation. Each is organized for course use but is detailed enough for reference. Further, the Series is organized in three levels: broad introductory material in the foundation volumes, more specialized material in the software volumes, and very specialized theory in the computer science volumes. As such, the Series meets the needs of the novice, the experienced programmer, and the computer scientist.

Taken together, the Series is a record of the state of the art in systems programming that can form the technological base for the systems programming discipline.

The Editorial Board

ABOUT THE AUTHOR

Mr. Date is an Advisory Programmer with IBM General Products Division, San Jose, California.

On graduating in mathematics from Cambridge University (England) in 1962, Mr. Date joined Leo Computers Ltd., London, as a programmer and programming instructor. He moved to IBM in 1967 as an instructor to help develop and teach a comprehensive training program in computer system fundamentals, System/360 assembler language, and PL/I. Subsequently he helped to establish the IBM European Laboratories Integrated Professional Training Program (ELIPT), a cooperative education scheme intended for computer professionals in the IBM development laboratories in Austria, England, France, Germany, the Netherlands, and Sweden. This involved developing and teaching several new courses, covering such topics as system programming techniques and Operating System/360 (both externals and internals).

In 1970, Mr. Date worked on a database language project in IBM (UK). Since that time he has been more or less continuously active in the database field, both inside and outside IBM. In particular he designed and taught a highly successful course on database concepts in the IBM ELIPT program mentioned previously. The present book's predecessor, *An Introduction to Database Systems: Volume I,* was a direct outcome of experience gained in teaching that course. Mr. Date is also responsible for the design of a proposed database programming language known as UDL (Unified Database Language). In addition Mr. Date has lectured widely on database topics—particularly on relational database—both in the United States and in many other countries. He is a member of ACM and the ACM Special Interest Group on Management of Data (SIGMOD). For some time he was actively involved in a British Computer Society working group on relational database. He is the author/coauthor of several technical papers.

Preface

As its title indicates, this book is a sequel to my earlier book *An Introduction to Database Systems* (henceforth referred to simply as *Volume I*). Its overall objective is to describe a somewhat miscellaneous collection of "further database topics"—topics that, despite their importance, had to be omitted from Volume I for a variety of reasons. One of those reasons was that the topics in question did not fit well into that book's overall structure, which was built around what might be termed a "data models" view of database management (all the chapters of that book were related to a greater or lesser degree to a single underlying theme, the theme of data models, and the book thus possessed a reasonably coherent and self-contained structure). The topics of Volume II, by contrast, are much less closely interconnected (as will be made clear below), and in most cases they have little to do with data models per se. In addition, of course, some of these new topics could not reasonably have been included in Volume I at all when that book was first written (about 1972), because they simply had not reached an adequate level of definition or development at that time. Distributed database and database machines are cases in point.

It follows from the foregoing that Volume II does not have such a close-knit structure as Volume I. There is no underlying or unifying theme comparable to the data models theme of Volume I. But in one significant respect Volume II does resemble Volume I—namely, in its general style and level of exposition. The book is still intended more as a textbook than as a work of reference, and it therefore still possesses an introductory or tutorial flavor. On the other hand, of course, it does assume more background knowledge on the part of the reader than did Volume I. To be specific:

■ Readers are expected to have at least a general appreciation of the overall structure, concepts, and objectives of a database system.

■ Readers should also be familiar with the major aspects of the relational model, including in particular the relational algebra, and preferably including also a specific relational language such as SQL.

This background material can be found in Parts 1 and 2 of Volume I. Certain comparatively minor sections of Volume II also require specific knowledge of IMS and DBTG, but such sections can simply be ignored if the reader has no interest in the details of those systems; again, the background material can be found in Volume I, this time in Parts 3 and 4.

As suggested above, a specific objective of Volume I, in addition to the overall objective of serving as an introduction to database systems in general, was to describe—compare and contrast—the three best-known data models, namely the relational, hierarchical, and network data models. When Volume I was first written, there did not appear to be any existing book that brought all that material together into a single publication and treated it in a uniform and tutorial style. Now, some ten years later, the situation seems to be similar with respect to the more recent (and/or more advanced) developments in the field: There does not currently seem to be any single book that covers more than one or two of those newer topics, either in a tutorial manner or in technical depth, let alone in both. A major goal of Volume II, then, is to attempt to fill that gap. This fact accounts for the scope of the book, which is as follows. There are eight (long) chapers, each devoted to a single major topic:

1. Recovery
2. Integrity
3. Concurrency
4. Security
5. Data models
6. The extended relational model RM/T
7. Distributed databases
8. Database machines

Since as already explained these eight topics are only loosely interconnected, each chapter stands on its own to a large extent. However, Chapters 1, 2, and 3 (and, to a lesser extent, Chapter 4) do form a loose-knit unit and should preferably be read in sequence. Chapters 5 and 6 also go together and should be read in order. Finally, Chapters 7 and 8 are also somewhat interrelated, and Chapter 7 in particular depends to some extent on material first presented in Chapters 1 and 3. But in all cases the links between chapters are slight at best.

Chapter 5 perhaps requires a little extra justification, since I have already said that the subject of that chapter (data models) is the primary topic of Volume I, and the reader may be wondering why it is necessary to deal with it again. In fact, however, there is almost no overlap between that chapter and Volume I. The chapter can perhaps best be characterized as "a discussion of data models for people who already know what they are." It consists of a number of more or less independent subsections, each covering some specific aspect of data modeling:

- a discussion of the general concept of a data model;
- a formal treatment of the relational model (Volume I provided an informal treatment only);
- a brief description of several data models not covered in Volume I (the binary relational, irreducible relational, and functional data models);
- an examination of the problem of "null values" (that is, the problem of missing information);
- an introduction to the topic of "semantic modeling" (which serves as a lead-in to the next chapter).

One further point concerning subject matter: This book, like its predecessor, contains numerous references to the relational prototype System R, originally developed at the IBM San Jose Research Laboratory in California. Many readers will be aware that IBM is now actively marketing a relational product, called SQL/DS (SQL/Data System), that makes extensive use of the System R technology. Certainly the database aspects of the two systems are essentially identical, except for a few minor details (aspects that depend on the system environment are different, however; in particular, SQL/DS runs under the DOS/VSE operating system and uses CICS as its Data Communications manager, whereas System R ran on VM and used CMS for its terminal access). Since this book is of course primarily concerned with database aspects, most of the points made in the text with respect to System R apply equally to SQL/DS.

As in Volume I, most of the chapters (actually all except the last) are followed by a set of exercises. Answers to most of the exercises are also included, and in many cases they give additional information about the subject of the question. Each chapter is also followed by a list of references, many of them annotated. References are identified in the text by numbers in square brackets. For example, [6.1] refers to the first item in the list of references at the end of Chapter 6, namely, a paper by E. F. Codd published in the *ACM Transactions on Database Systems (TODS)*, Vol. 4, No. 4 (December 1979).

Finally, it is a great pleasure to acknowledge the help I have received in writing this book. I am grateful, first of all, to numerous friends and colleagues for their help over various technical questions and for their many valuable comments and suggestions on early drafts of one or other of the chapters (in some cases more than one): Marilyn Bohl, Paula Capello, Ted Codd, Bob Engles, Ron Fagin, Jim Gray, Bill Kent, Bruce Lindsay, Bill McGee, Dennis McLeod, Walt Roseberry, Pat Selinger, Phil Shaw, Herb Swain, and Irv Traiger. I would especially like to mention Bill Kent's contribution to Chapter 5. A special acknowledgment is also due to Mike Stonebraker, whose informative and frequently entertaining seminar on database machines [8.1] enabled me to impose some structure on my previously rather confused thoughts in that area. I would also like to thank the Association for Computing Machinery (ACM) for permission to quote short extracts from certain papers (references [4.12], [4.23], and [4.34]) for which ACM holds the copyright, and W. H. Freeman and Company, publishers of Scientific American, for permission to base one of the exercises in Chapter 4 (Exercise 4.9) on material that originally appeared in the issue of that journal dated August 1977. I am also pleased to thank IBM for supporting me in this work (I must stress, however, that, as with Volume I, the content of the book is entirely my own responsibility; the views expressed are my own and in no way represent an official statement on the part of IBM). And last but not least, of course, I would like to express my gratitude to Addison-Wesley, and to do that I cannot do better than paraphrase my remarks from the preface to Volume I: It is a real pleasure to express once again my appreciation of the friendliness, cooperation, and professionalism shown by everyone involved in the production of this book. I would especially like to thank Bill Gruener, Sponsoring Editor for the Systems Programming Series, and Marion Howe, Production Editor for this volume, for their cheerful and untiring efforts on my behalf.

Saratoga, California   C.J.D.
June 1982

Contents

1
Recovery

1.1 INTRODUCTION

Nothing ever works perfectly 100 percent of the time. This simple observation, trite though it is, has far-reaching consequences for the design of computer systems in general and database systems in particular. Such systems must incorporate, not only a variety of checks and controls to reduce the likelihood of failure, but also, and more significantly, an extensive set of procedures for recovering from the failures that will inevitably occur despite those checks and controls. In System R, for example, approximately 10 percent of the code is devoted to recovery; moreover, that particular 10 percent was quite difficult to write [1.4]. The figure for IMS is even larger. In this chapter we consider the question of recovery in a database system in some detail.

Recovery in a database system means, primarily, recovering the database itself: that is, restoring the database to a state that is known to be correct after some failure has rendered the current state incorrect, or at least suspect. (Recovery also has implications for the handling of messages, as we shall see later.) There are many possible causes of such failure—programming errors in an application or in the operating system or in the database system itself, hardware errors on the device or the channel or the CPU, operator errors such as mounting a wrong tape, fluctuations in the power supply, fire in the machine room, even sabotage; the list is endless. In all cases the underlying principles on which recovery is based are quite simple, and can be summed up in a single word: *redundancy*. That is, the way to protect the database is to ensure that any given piece of information in it can be reconstructed from some other information stored redundantly somewhere else in the system. In outline (omitting a *lot* of detail), what happens is the following.

1

1. Periodically, say once a day, the entire database is copied or *dumped* to archive storage (typically tape).

2. Every time a change is made to the database, a record containing the old and new values of the changed item is written to a special data set called the *log*. (For an insertion, of course, there will be no old value; likewise, for a deletion there will be no new value.)

3. If a failure occurs, there are two possibilities:

   a) The database itself is damaged (for example, a head crash occurred on the disk). In this case the database is restored by loading it from the most recent archive copy and then using the log to *redo* all changes made since that archive copy was taken.

   b) The database is not damaged but its contents are unreliable (for example, a program terminated abnormally somewhere in the middle of performing a sequence of logically related updates). In this case the database is restored to a correct state by using the log to *undo* all "unreliable" changes. The archive copy is not needed in this case.

We stress, however, that the outline just given is *very* incomplete. In fact, as our opening paragraph suggests, the topic of recovery is rather complex at the detail level, even though the basic principles are comparatively straightforward. Some of the reasons for this complexity will become apparent in the remainder of this chapter. We do not claim, however, that our treatment of the subject is in any way exhaustive. Moreover, we do not suggest that any system actually behaves in exactly the way we describe; rather, we are concerned with recovery problems in general and with *conceptual* approaches to their solution. We ignore many implementation issues, including in particular various possibilities for optimization. For a description of the recovery features of specific systems, see Section 1.7 and the Bibliography at the end of the chapter.

Before beginning our detailed explanation of the recovery procedure outlined above, we offer the following comments on the possibility of *duplexing*. Our earlier remark to the effect that all recovery is based (in the final analysis) on redundancy suggests that one obvious approach to recovery is simply to "duplex the database"—that is, keep two identical copies, and apply all updates to both simultaneously. Duplexing does have its advantages, including both increased reliability and, surprisingly, improved performance [1.11], and is employed in some systems (for example, ENCOMPASS [1.10]). But the approach also has its drawbacks, among them the following. First, of course, it requires twice as much storage. Second, the two copies should as far as possible have independent "failure modes" (for example, they should be on different channels), to reduce the chances of a single malfunction causing both copies to fail simultaneously;[1] unfortunately, such in-

---

1. Of course, even in a recovery scheme not based on full duplexing, it is desirable for the database and the recovery information to have independent failure modes as far as possible.

dependence cannot be totally achieved—for example, both copies will have to depend on the same CPU (assuming there is only one CPU in the system). Third, the approach is inadequate as it stands; there is still a need to be able to *undo* changes, which implies the need for a log giving old as well as new values. Fourth, the log may be needed anyway for auditing, performance analysis, and other reasons, quite apart from its use in recovery (though some systems use a separate log for these purposes).

One final introductory remark. In practice, there may well be portions of the database for which the cost of providing recoverability—in particular, the overhead of maintaining the log—outweighs the potential benefit. As a concrete example, a program might create a temporary, private file within the database, use it briefly, and then destroy it, all within the confines of a single "transaction" (see the next section for a discussion of transactions). There is little point in making such a private file recoverable, in the sense of this chapter. Ideally, therefore, the system should allow the user (or more likely the database administrator) to specify where recoverability is required and where it is not, on (say) a file-by-file basis within the total database. But for simplicity we assume for most of this chapter that the entire database *is* required to be fully recoverable, and do not discuss nonrecoverable data any further.

1.2 TRANSACTIONS

The fundamental purpose of the database system is to carry out *transactions*. A transaction is a *unit of work*. It consists of the execution of an application-specified sequence of operations, beginning with a special BEGIN TRANSACTION operation and ending with either a COMMIT operation or a ROLLBACK operation. COMMIT is used to signal *successful* termination (the unit of work has been successfully completed); ROLLBACK is used to signal *unsuccessful* termination (the unit of work cannot be successfully completed because some exceptional condition has occurred—for example, a needed record could not be found). Note clearly that "termination" here refers to transaction termination, not necessarily program termination; one program execution may correspond to a sequence of several transactions, one after another (see Fig. 1.1). In practice, however, one program execution very commonly does represent just one transaction, rather than several.

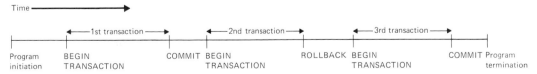

Fig. 1.1 Transactions and program execution (example).

Transactions cannot be nested; that is, BEGIN TRANSACTION can be executed only when the application currently has no transaction in progress. Conversely, COMMIT and ROLLBACK can be executed only when a transaction *is* in progress. All *recoverable operations* must be executed within the bounds of a transaction. A "recoverable operation" is an operation that may have to be undone or redone in the event of a failure (in other words, an operation for which an entry must be made in the log). Database updates and message I/O transfers are recoverable operations.

Note: It is convenient to assume that transactions are always explicitly bounded by BEGIN TRANSACTION and COMMIT/ROLLBACK operations (that is, BEGIN TRANSACTION and COMMIT/ROLLBACK statements appear explicitly where necessary in the original source program). In practice these operations may often be implicit. For example, program initiation may cause an implicit BEGIN TRANSACTION, normal program termination an implicit COMMIT, and abnormal program termination an implicit ROLLBACK. This is the situation in UDL [1.7], for example; in fact, UDL does not include a BEGIN TRANSACTION statement at all—the first transaction of the program is begun automatically at program initiation, and subsequent COMMIT and ROLLBACK operations not only terminate the current transaction but also initiate the next.[2] (More accurately, an implicit BEGIN TRANSACTION actually occurs at execution of the first recoverable operation *following* program initiation or COMMIT or ROLLBACK.) All coding examples in this chapter will be based on the PL/I version of UDL; explicit BEGIN TRANSACTION statements will therefore not be shown. But the reader should understand that the *effect* of BEGIN TRANSACTION (and COMMIT and ROLLBACK) still occurs at appropriate points.

Figure 1.2 gives an example of the source code for a banking transaction that transfers a dollar amount from one account to another. The transaction is invoked by entering an *input message* at a terminal, specifying the name of the program (TRANSFER), the two account numbers, and the amount; for example,

```
TRANSFER $100 FROM 4732166 TO 9940103
```

(Note that to the user entering this message—presumably a bank clerk—the input message looks like a *command* that instructs the system to perform some function.) The TRANSFER program is then called and the input message is made available to it, in a manner to be explained. The code in the example has deliberately, and rather unrealistically, been written to decrement the FROM balance before testing it, in order to illustrate the need for the ROLLBACK statement. Declarations are omitted for simplicity. Also, we assume that AMOUNT is positive.

It is important to note that, from the point of view of the end-user, transactions are *atomic.* In the TRANSFER example, for instance, the bank clerk is not inter-

---

2. No commercial implementation of UDL is available at the time of writing.

```
TRANSFER: PROC;

    GET (FROM, TO, AMOUNT);    /* input message */
    FIND UNIQUE (ACCOUNT WHERE ACCOUNT# = FROM);
    /* now decrement the FROM balance */
    ASSIGN (BALANCE - AMOUNT) TO BALANCE;
    IF BALANCE < 0
    THEN
        DO;
            PUT ('INSUFFICIENT FUNDS');    /* output message */
            /* undo the update and terminate the transaction */
            ROLLBACK;
        END;
    ELSE
        DO;
            FIND UNIQUE (ACCOUNT WHERE ACCOUNT# = TO);
            /* now increment the TO balance */
            ASSIGN (BALANCE + AMOUNT) TO BALANCE;
            PUT ('TRANSFER COMPLETE');    /* output message */
            /* commit the update and terminate the transaction */
            COMMIT;
        END;

END /* TRANSFER */ ;
```

Fig. 1.2 The TRANSFER transaction (source code).

ested in the fact that two distinct updates must be made to the database; to that user, "transfer *x* dollars from account A to account B" is a single, atomic operation, which either succeeds or fails. If it succeeds, well and good; if it fails, then *nothing should have changed* (the effect should be as if it had never started). Specifically, the database must not be left in a state in which the FROM account has been decremented but the TO account has not been incremented.

We see, therefore, that transactions are an all-or-nothing proposition. The user must be guaranteed that (in effect) each transaction is either executed in its entirety or not executed at all. Moreover, the user must also be guaranteed that, if the transaction *is* executed, then it is (in effect) executed *exactly once*. (As suggested in Section 1.1, there are situations in which transactions have to be redone, that is, executed more than once. But the net effect should always be as though they were executed just once.) In other words, the requirement is that the system, considered as a transaction processor, should be *reliable:* Transactions should not be lost, or partially done, or done more than once. Acceptance of the input message should be a guarantee that the transaction will be run exactly once, that any database updates produced by the transaction will be applied exactly once, and that any output messages produced by the transaction should be transmitted exactly once. The *Recovery Manager* is the system component that is responsible for providing this reliability.

Now let us examine the TRANSFER transaction (Fig. 1.2) in a little more detail.[3] The code starts by obtaining (GET) the input message that provides it with its parameters (FROM, TO, and AMOUNT). It then locates the FROM account and reduces the balance of that account by the specified amount. (Note that the UDL ASSIGN statement actually updates the record in the database, *not* just a retrieved copy of that record in main storage [1.7].) Having performed the update, the code then tests to see whether the balance is now negative; if so, the FROM account did not have sufficient funds, and the transfer cannot be successfully completed. The transaction therefore sends an "INSUFFICIENT FUNDS" message back to the terminal (PUT) and issues a ROLLBACK. The ROLLBACK operation represents "unsuccessful transaction termination"; it has the effect of *undoing all the updates* made by the transaction (that is, all updated records are restored to the value they had at the start of the transaction). After the ROLLBACK, control is returned to the program, which (in the case at hand) then terminates also, via the final END statement.

If, on the other hand, the FROM account does have sufficient funds, then the code goes on to locate the TO account and updates the balance of that account accordingly. It then sends a "TRANSFER COMPLETE" message to the terminal (PUT) and issues a COMMIT (representing *successful* transaction termination, also known as a *commit point*). At this point all updates made by the transaction are "committed"—that is, COMMIT guarantees the updates and "makes them permanent." (Prior to COMMIT all updates are best thought of as tentative only, since until that point they are always subject to possible rollback.) After the COMMIT, control returns to the program, which (again in the case at hand) then terminates also.

Messages

As we have hinted several times already, recovery has various implications for messages as well as for the database. Let us consider the message-handling aspects of the TRANSFER example. The TRANSFER transaction not only updates the database, it also sends messages to the end-user (INSUFFICIENT FUNDS or TRANSFER COMPLETE). If the transaction reaches its *planned* termination (the explicit COMMIT or ROLLBACK statement), then clearly it is appropriate that the relevant one of these messages be displayed at the terminal. But if the transaction fails, that is, does not reach its planned termination because of an error such as overflow, then, as

---

3. It would be more accurate to say that Fig. 1.2 represents an entire class of similar transactions, rather than one specific transaction; individual transactions in that class correspond to specific executions of the code. The distinction is the familiar one of procedure (static source code) versus process (dynamic execution of that code). It is common to blur the distinction in informal discussion.

explained in the next section, *the system will automatically roll it back*. The effect in this case will be as if the transaction had never started; its database updates will be undone, and *neither* message will be displayed. (A system-generated error message—for example, "OVERFLOW OCCURRED AT STATEMENT such-and-such"—might perhaps be displayed instead.) Thus we see that, in general, *output messages should not be transmitted until (planned) end-of-transaction*. In other words, the effect of PUT should be, not to transmit the output message directly, but to place it on a pending queue; on planned termination (that is, application-issued COMMIT or ROLLBACK), all messages on the queue can be transmitted, on a transaction failure such as overflow they can simply be discarded.[4] A striking example of the need for such a rule is provided by the case of a "message" that triggers some irrevocable external action, such as a payment from a cash-issuing terminal —either the payment is made *and* the account in the database gets updated, or nothing should happen at all.

The component responsible for handling messages and message queues is the *Data Communications Manager* (DC Manager). Thus it is the Data Communications Manager that receives the original input message (giving FROM, TO, and AMOUNT in the TRANSFER example). On receipt of this message, the Data Communications Manager (a) writes a log record containing the text of the input message and other details, and (b) places the message on the *input queue*. A GET operation can then be used to retrieve a copy of the input message from the input queue. Conversely, PUT (as explained before) is used to place an output message on an *output queue*. (Input and output queues may be held in main storage or on secondary storage or both. It is probably advisable from the point of view of understanding to think of them as being on secondary storage. Each queue can contain any number of messages.)

The other operations that affect queues are COMMIT and ROLLBACK. COMMIT and (explicit, planned) ROLLBACK cause the Data Communications Manager (a) to write a record on the log for the messages on the output queue, (b) to arrange for the actual transmission of those messages, and (c) to remove the input message from the input message queue (since it has now been processed). Transaction failure such as overflow causes the Data Communications Manager to cancel the output messages. (The purpose of the log records, for both input and output messages, is to support transaction redo, not undo. See Section 1.4.)

---

4. It should be pointed out that many systems do not in fact behave as recommended by this paragraph. Typically, application-issued ROLLBACK is *not* treated as a planned termination; thus, the effect of such an explicit ROLLBACK is to discard output messages, not to send them. This state of affairs is unfortunate; it means that, in the case of TRANSFER (for example), the INSUFFICIENT FUNDS message has to be issued *after* the ROLLBACK (that is, by a subsequent transaction), and this in turn means that there is no guarantee that the message will actually be sent (that subsequent transaction may fail for reasons beyond its own control, as explained later).

In passing, we remark that, just as the DBMS provides data independence, so the Data Communications Manager should provide what we might call "message independence." In other words, messages should look just like logical records to the application; the details of their format on the screen or external document are irrelevant and should be handled by a mapping process that is outside the program per se. For example, a program that prints an airline ticket should not have to be aware of the precise layout of that ticket, only of the information that the ticket contains. An example of a system that provides such independence is provided by the Message Format Services facility of IMS [1.12]. We effectively assumed such a system in the code for our TRANSFER example.

For additional background material on data communications, see reference [1.3].

Transaction Structure

The logical structure of the TRANSFER example may be considered as typical of transactions in general. That is, we can generally assume that all transactions fall into the same simple pattern, namely:

accept input message;

perform database processing;

send output message(s).

Note that a single input message might give rise to multiple output messages. Of course, the generation of these messages may be interleaved with the "perform database processing" step, although, as we have seen, the messages will not actually be transmitted until the end of the transaction.

More complex "conversations," in which there are multiple communications in each direction between the end-user and the program, can be handled in two ways: Either they can be subdivided into a sequence of simple transactions, each having the structure shown above, or they can be treated as one big transaction that repeats the input-process-output cycle many times and *then* issues COMMIT or ROLL-BACK. Neither approach is totally satisfactory, however. The first suffers from the drawback that the database may be updated in the interval between two consecutive interchanges in the "conversation," thus potentially causing the end-user to act on incorrect information; the second requires the ability to transmit messages directly (that is, without any intermediate queueing and without waiting for end-of-transaction), and also suffers from the drawback that at any time the end-user must be prepared to receive a message that says (in effect) "ignore all messages since the start of the conversation, a failure has occurred." (Observe, incidentally, that in the latter case it is the application, not the system, that is responsible for generating such a message if necessary.) In this book we shall usually assume that messages are *not* transmitted directly, and that "conversations," if required, are handled by the first approach.

Types of Failure

The TRANSFER example illustrates how an explicit ROLLBACK statement can be used to ensure that a failure does not corrupt the database in the case where the transaction itself discovers the failure condition. Unfortunately, of course, many failures are not so easily anticipated and cannot be left for the application programmer to handle in this way. In fact, we can conveniently categorize the various types of failure that can occur as follows:

- Transaction-local failures that are detected by the application code itself (for example, the INSUFFICIENT FUNDS condition in the TRANSFER example).
- Transaction-local failures that are not explicitly handled by the application code (for example, arithmetic overflow).
- System-wide failures (for example, CPU failure) that affect all transactions currently in progress but do not damage the database.
- Media failures (for example, disk head crash) that damage the database, or some portion of it, and affect all transactions currently using that portion.

We have seen by example how the first of these cases is handled (Fig. 1.2). The other three cases are discussed in the next three sections.

1.3   TRANSACTION FAILURES

In what follows we use "transaction failure" to mean a failure caused by unplanned, abnormal program termination—an ABEND, in IBM parlance. Conditions that may cause abnormal program termination include arithmetic overflow, division by zero, storage protection violation, and the like. As a specific example, consider the case of a program coded in PL/I, and suppose that the program attempts to divide by zero. (The following explanation is slightly simplified.)

1. Division by zero raises the ZERODIVIDE "ON-condition" in PL/I. The programmer has the option of explicitly providing a ZERODIVIDE "ON-unit" (procedure) to handle this condition. If no ON-unit is provided, then "system action" for ZERODIVIDE is taken.

2. System action for ZERODIVIDE is to raise another ON-condition, called ERROR (a catchall); again the programmer has the option of providing an ON-unit for ERROR or of allowing system action to be taken.

3. System action for ERROR is to cause abnormal program termination; and it is only if this point is reached—that is, if system action for ERROR is taken—that we say that "transaction failure" has occurred.

In general, then (and regardless of whether the language concerned is PL/I), "transaction failure" occurs if and only if the program terminates *in an unplanned fashion*—that is, if and only if an error occurs for which no explicit exception-handling code is provided in the application. Execution of an explicit ROLLBACK statement is not considered as a transaction failure, but rather as a planned abnormal termination (of the transaction, not of the program).

As an aside, we note that the PL/I philosophy of exception-handling via ON-units allows errors to be handled at a variety of levels, and provides the user with a great degree of freedom in the amount of control that can be exercised over that exception-handling. The same philosophy applies to UDL. Thus, for example, if the UDL FIND statement fails to locate a record, the user can deal with that condition in-line, via the NOTFOUND clause of the FIND statement itself. If no NOT-FOUND clause is specified, the NOTFOUND ON-condition is raised, and can be handled via a NOTFOUND ON-unit. System action for the NOTFOUND condition is to raise DBERROR, a database catchall condition, which can again be handled via an ON-unit; and system action for DBERROR is to raise ERROR. For more details on UDL, see Volume I or reference [1.7].

Transaction failure means that the transaction has not reached its planned termination (COMMIT or explicit ROLLBACK). It is therefore necessary for the system to *force* a rollback—that is, to undo any changes the transaction has made to the database and to cancel any output messages the transaction has produced, to make it as if the transaction had never started. The rollback procedure is coordinated by the Recovery Manager. Canceling messages is achieved by simply discarding them from the output queue. Undoing changes involves working backward through the log, tracing through all log records for the transaction in question until the BEGIN TRANSACTION record is reached.[5] If the log is kept on disk rather than tape, then each log record can include a pointer to the previous one for the same transaction in order to facilitate this process (see the subsection "On-Line Log," later). For each log record encountered, the change represented by that log record is undone by replacing the new value in the database by the old value from the log.

The procedure just outlined raises a number of further points, which we discuss in the following paragraphs (although some of them are only remotely connected with transaction failure per se).

Undoing Changes

First, we consider the process of actually undoing a change. There are three basic types of change—updating an existing record, deleting an existing record, and inserting a new record. We may imagine the DBMS as including three components —an Update component, a Delete component, and an Insert component—to perform these three types of change. Each of these components should include, not only a "DO" entry point, which is used to perform the appropriate action in the first place, but also an "UNDO" entry point, which is used to undo the effects of any such action at a later time. When the Recovery Manager encounters a particular

---

5. BEGIN TRANSACTION, COMMIT, and ROLLBACK operations each cause records to be written to the log.

log record in its backward trace, it simply invokes the UNDO entry point of the corresponding component, passing it appropriate parameters, and it is that component
that actually undoes the change.

On-Line Log

From the description of the rollback procedure given earlier, it can be seen that the
Recovery Manager needs to be able to access log records in a selective fashion, instead of purely sequentially. It is therefore convenient if the log can be kept on a direct access device. However, as Gray suggests in [1.3], a (large) operational system
might easily generate of the order of 200 million bytes of log data every day. It is
thus clearly infeasible (and in any case it would also be undesirable) to keep the
entire log permanently on-line. Instead, a possible approach is as follows.

First, the *active* log is indeed written as a direct access data set. When that data
set is full, the Log Manager (another component of the DBMS) switches to another
such data set and dumps the first to archive storage, usually tape.[6] Of course, the
dumping process can be performed in parallel with on-line usage of the second data
set. The total log thus consists of the currently active on-line portion, on direct access, plus an arbitrary number of earlier portions on archival storage.

Actually the switch to the second data set is not quite so straightforward as the
previous paragraph suggests. If it is to be possible to rollback an active (but failing)
transaction without human intervention, all log records for all active transactions
must reside in the on-line portion of the log. For this reason, the second data set
should be brought into use (opened) as soon as the amount of data in the first passes
some threshold, say 95 percent of the data set capacity. Thereafter, newly started
transactions have their log records written to the new data set; transactions that were
active at the time of the switch continue to have their log records written to the old
data set. Eventually one of two things happens: Either the first data set overflows,
or all transactions using that data set terminate with space to spare. In the first case
transactions that are still using the first data set are abnormally terminated (failed by
the system) and rolled back. In either case the first data set (which thus contains log
records for completed transactions only) can now be closed and passed to the archiving process.

UNDO Logic

The process of rolling back a transaction is of course itself subject to failure (that is,
a *system* failure might occur before the rollback is complete). As we shall see in the
next section, such a failure will subsequently cause the rollback procedure itself to be
restarted from the beginning. In other words, the Recovery Manager must be prepared to handle the situation where it is trying to undo an update that has already
been undone in a previous (incomplete) rollback. All this means is that the UNDO

---

6. System R employs a variation on this technique [1.4], in which the switch is not to a second data set but back to the beginning of the first (that is, System R has just one on-line log
data set, which it uses in a wraparound fashion).

logic in the Update, Delete, and Insert components must be such that undoing a given change any number of times is the same as undoing it exactly once. Gray [1.3] expresses this requirement by saying that UNDO must be *idempotent*—that is, UNDO(UNDO(UNDO . . . (*x*))) = UNDO(*x*) for all *x*.

Long Transactions

It is clear from our discussions so far that a transaction is a *unit of recovery* as well as a unit of work. This fact suggests that transactions should be short, in order to reduce the amount that has to be undone, and perhaps subsequently redone, in the event of a failure (also to reduce the likelihood of the transaction failing because of log overflow). If the application is intrinsically long-running (involving, for example, mass update of a large sequential file), then it is a good idea to subdivide it into multiple transactions by means of explicit COMMITs. As an example (oversimplified), consider a payroll application that is written to deal with all the A's, then all the B's, then all the C's, and so on, each as a single transaction. The program would have to include logic to cater for the fact that any given execution is potentially a restart; for example, it could maintain a restart record in the database (containing the single field LETTER) indicating which letter of the alphabet it should start on this time. Successive values of LETTER would then serve as the "input messages" for the transactions. Outline logic for this program is sketched in Fig. 1.3. (Note: ALLOCATE and FREE are the PL/I-UDL versions of INSERT and DELETE. The DO-loop DO EMPLOYEE . . . END iterates over all EMPLOYEE records satisfying the condition "initial letter = TEMP".)

A technique similar to that of this example could be useful in communicating from one transaction to the next within a "conversation" (see the discussion of this topic in Section 1.2).

```
PAYROLL: PROC;
   FIND UNIQUE (RESTART_REC)
   FOUND   /* OK - restart in progress */ ;
   NOTFOUND   /* not a restart - so create restart record */
      ALLOCATE RESTART_REC INITIAL ('A');
   DO TEMP = each letter in turn
                 from RESTART_REC.LETTER to 'Z';
      ASSIGN TEMP TO RESTART_REC.LETTER;
      DO EMPLOYEE WHERE initial letter = TEMP;
         perform payroll processing for this EMPLOYEE;
      END;
      PUT ('LETTER '||TEMP||' PROCESSED');
      COMMIT;
   END;
   FREE RESTART_REC;   /* destroy restart record */
   COMMIT;
END /* PAYROLL */ ;
```

Fig. 1.3 Dividing a long program into multiple transactions (example).

Log Compression

It is not necessary for the archive version of the log to be identical to the on-line version as originally written. On the contrary, it is convenient to apply various compression techniques during the archival process (or subsequently), in order to reduce storage requirements and speed up any later use of the archive version for recovery. First, it is clearly unnecessary to retain log records for transactions that failed to COMMIT, since those transactions have *already* been rolled back. Second, transactions that did COMMIT will now never have to be undone, so old data values are no longer needed (new values are still needed in case the transactions have to be redone). And third, changes can be consolidated (that is, if a given object was updated several times [by several transactions], only the final value needs to be retained).

We note also that archive log records can be sorted by physical address of the corresponding records within the database, making any subsequent recovery using the archive a fast sequential process.

1.4   SYSTEM FAILURES

We use "system failure" to mean any event that causes the system to stop and thus requires a subsequent system restart: The contents of main storage—in particular, the contents of all I/O buffers—are lost, but the database is not damaged. Transactions that were in progress at the time of the failure must be rolled back, since they did not complete.

The question arises, how does the Recovery Manager know at restart which transactions to roll back (that is, which transactions were in progress at the time of the failure)? In principle, this question could be answered by searching the entire log from the very beginning, identifying those transactions for which there is a BEGIN TRANSACTION record but no termination (COMMIT or ROLLBACK) record. But of course such a search would be very time-consuming. We can reduce the amount of searching dramatically by introducing the notion of the *checkpoint*.

The checkpoint principle is essentially very simple. At certain prespecified intervals (say every five minutes, or whenever some given amount of log data has been written), the system "takes a checkpoint." Taking a checkpoint consists of the following steps:

Step 1: Forcing the content of the log buffers out to the log data set (that is, force-writing any log records that are still in main storage out to the actual log);

Step 2: Forcing a "checkpoint record" out to the log data set;

Step 3: Forcing the content of the database buffers out to the database (that is, force-writing any updates that are still in main storage out to the actual database);

Step 4: Writing the address of the checkpoint record within the log data set into a "restart file."

(Note: A refinement of this procedure and the corresponding recovery procedure will be described at the end of this section.)

The notion of "force-writing" requires a little explanation. The point is basically that performing a log write or database update is not an atomic operation at the system level. Rather, it involves (a) moving the output record into a buffer in main storage, and then (b) writing the content of that buffer out to secondary storage. To reduce the number of physical I/O operations and to improve the utilization of secondary storage space, it is normal to batch up records in the buffer, with the result that step (b) is usually performed some considerable time after step (a)—namely, when the buffer becomes full. Force-writing is the operation of forcing a write to secondary storage to occur even if the buffer is not yet full.

We are not yet in a position to explain the checkpoint procedure in detail—in particular, to explain exactly why the force-writing is necessary. But to give some indication: Step 3 is included to eliminate the possibility of having to redo work that completed prior to the checkpoint, and Steps 1 and 2 are required to comply with the write-ahead log protocol. The write-ahead log protocol is explained later in this section. The rationale for Step 3 is given below.

Before we can amplify the foregoing explanations, it is first necessary to describe the checkpoint record itself.[7] Each checkpoint record contains

- a list of all transactions active at the time of the checkpoint; together with

- the address within the log of each such transaction's most recent log record.

At restart time, the Recovery Manager obtains the address of the most recent checkpoint record from the restart file, locates that checkpoint record in the log, and proceeds to search forward through the log from that point to the end. As a result of this process, the Recovery Manager is able to determine both the transactions that need to be undone *and* the transactions that need to be redone in order to restore the database to a correct state. In order to explain this statement, we show first that, for the purposes of restart, transactions can be classified into five distinct categories. See Fig. 1.4.

Figure 1.4 is interpreted as follows:

- A system failure has occurred at time *tf*.

- The most recent checkpoint prior to time *tf* was taken at time *tc*.

- Transactions of type T1 were completed before time *tc*.

- Transactions of type T2 started prior to time *tc* and completed after time *tc* and before time *tf*.

- Transactions of type T3 also started prior to time *tc* but did not complete by time *tf*.

---

7. Different systems assign different meanings to the terms "checkpoint" and "checkpoint record." In particular, it is common to find them both used to mean what we refer to as an archive dump—that is, a copy of the entire database, or some portion thereof. In this book, however, we will generally use the terms in the sense defined in this chapter.

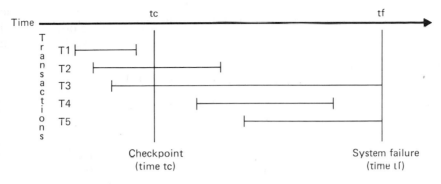

Fig. 1.4 The five transaction categories.

- Transactions of type T4 started after time *tc* and completed before time *tf*.
- Finally, transactions of type T5 also started after time *tc* but did not complete by time *tf*.

It should be clear that, at restart, transactions of types T3 and T5 must be undone.[8] What is perhaps less obvious is that transactions of types T2 and T4 must be redone (this fact was not mentioned in the outline recovery procedure sketched briefly in Section 1.1). The reason is that, although the transactions did complete before the failure, *there is no guarantee that their updates were actually written to the database* (the failure may have occurred after the updates were placed in the database buffers but before those buffers were actually written to secondary storage). So the Recovery Manager must be able to identify all transactions of types T2–T5; note, however, that type T1 transactions do not enter into the recovery process at all (because their updates were forced out to the database at the time the checkpoint was taken).

We can now describe the algorithm by which the Recovery Manager determines which transactions must be undone and which redone. It starts with two lists, an undo-list and a redo-list; the undo-list initially contains all transactions listed in the checkpoint record, the redo-list is initially empty. It then searches forward through the log, starting from the checkpoint record.

- If it finds a BEGIN TRANSACTION record for a given transaction, it adds that transaction to the undo-list.
- If it finds a COMMIT record for a given transaction, it moves that transaction from the undo-list to the redo-list.

---

8. If the system is truly to satisfy the reliability requirement discussed in Section 1.2, it should then go on to *restart* those transactions (types T3 and T5) without any involvement on the part of the user.

When it reaches the end of the log, the undo-list and the redo-list identify, respectively, those transactions that must be undone and those that must be redone. As the next step of the recovery process, the Recovery Manager works backward through the log again, undoing the transactions in the undo-list; finally, it goes forward again, redoing the transactions in the redo-list. No new work can be accepted by the system until this process is complete.

Note that, in redoing a transaction of type T2 (see Fig. 1.4), it is necessary to redo only those changes that occurred after time tc. This is because we are guaranteed by Step 3 of the "take checkpoint" procedure that all changes prior to time tc were actually recorded in the database. (For the same reason, however, it will be necessary when *undoing* a transaction of type T3 to undo work that occurred *before* time tc.)

Once again, the recovery procedure as we have outlined it raises a number of additional points.

Redoing Changes

Just as the Update, Delete, and Insert components of the DBMS must include an UNDO entry point, as described in Section 1.3, so they must also include a REDO entry point. The REDO entry point is of course used to redo some change previously made by means of the DO entry point. The Recovery Manager is thus able to redo a transaction by tracing forward through the log records for that transaction and invoking the REDO entry point of the appropriate component for each log record it encounters.

REDO Logic

REDO, like UNDO (and for effectively the same reasons), is required to be "idempotent"—that is, REDO(REDO(REDO . . . (x))) = REDO(x) for all x. In other words, the effect of redoing a given change any number of times must be the same as that of doing it once; for if the system were to fail again during the REDO process, then the next attempt to recover may call for some changes to be redone that in fact have been redone already.

Log Write-Ahead

So far we have tended to gloss over the fact that writing a change to the database and writing the log record representing that change are two distinct operations. Unfortunately they *are* distinct. This fact introduces the possibility of a failure occurring in the interval between the two. Suppose that in fact such a failure does occur, so that only one of the writes, the first one, survives and the other is lost. If the survivor is the *database* write, we are now in the position of having made a change to the database that is not recorded in the log *and so cannot be undone*. It follows that, for safety, the log record should always be written first. This observation is the basis of the *Write-Ahead Log Protocol* [1.3]. In detail:

- A transaction is not allowed to write a record to the physical database until at least the undo portion of the corresponding log record has been written to the physical log.
- A transaction is not allowed to complete COMMIT processing until both the redo and the undo portions of all log records for the transaction have been written to the physical log.

An implication of the write-ahead log protocol is that, if a failure occurs, a change may be recorded in the log and not in the database. On restart, then, the UNDO/REDO entry points of the Update, Delete, and Insert components must be prepared for a request to undo/redo a change that in fact was never done in the first place.

System Startup

There are three types of system startup, commonly known as cold start, warm start, and emergency restart (though these terms are not used consistently across systems).

- Emergency restart is what we have previously been calling simply "restart"; it is the process that is invoked (via the operator command RESTART) after a system failure has occurred. It involves the recovery procedures (undo and redo) that we have been describing. It may also involve reloading the database from archive storage (see Section 1.5).
- Warm start is the process of starting up the system after a *controlled* system shutdown—that is, a shutdown initiated by a SHUTDOWN command from the operator. On receipt of a SHUTDOWN command, the system refuses any further attempts to initiate transactions, waits for all active transactions to terminate, and then terminates itself. The subsequent warm start does not involve any undo or redo operations at all. From the system's point of view, however, warm start is typically treated as a special case of emergency restart; the fact that there is no undo/redo work to be done is discovered by inspecting the log (the last record in the log will be a checkpoint record listing no active transactions).

  It is crucial to warm start (or emergency restart) that the Recovery Manager be able to locate the most recent checkpoint record in the log. The address of that record was placed in the "restart file" when the checkpoint was taken. In order to reduce the risk of losing the restart file, it is common to duplex that file (which of course is not very large) and to alternate writes to the two copies, so that, in general, one copy points to the most recent checkpoint record and the other to the next most recent.

- Starting the system from scratch is a cold start. The term is also, and more commonly, used to refer to the process of starting the system after some disastrous failure (such as losing the restart file) makes a warm start impossible. This latter process involves starting again from some archive version of the database (see Section 1.5); work done since that version was created will probably be lost and will probably have to be redone (that is, resubmitted by the operator or user). *Ideally* cold start should be performed exactly once, when the system is first installed.

Messages

Just as the need to be able to *undo* transactions has certain implications for the handling of messages, so too does the need to be able to *redo* transactions. First, if the system is to be able to reschedule transactions of types T3 and T5 automatically, as suggested in Footnote 8, then it must force-write input message log records to the log as soon as those messages are received, since the input parameters provided by those messages are needed to redo the transactions. Second, if a transaction is re-done from the log (types T2 and T4), then output messages should *not* be retransmitted; the user has already seen them, and should not be interested in the fact that the system has had to redo the work. (Actually the messages may not yet have been sent—the system may have failed between the completion of the transaction and the actual message transmission—but the fact that output message log records were force-written in accordance with the write-ahead log protocol guarantees that they *will* eventually be transmitted.)

A Refinement of the Checkpoint/Recovery Procedure

The checkpoint/recovery procedure presented at the beginning of this section is workable but unduly pessimistic. In effect, it assumes that *all* of the updates for types T3 and T5 transactions (since time *tc*) have actually been written to the physical database, and that *none* of those for types T2 and T4 have been so written (see Fig. 1.4). That is, it "undoes" T3/T5 updates even if they were never done in the first place, and it "redoes" T2/T4 updates even if they have in fact already been done. We can improve matters as follows. Step 3 of the checkpoint procedure, force-writing the database buffers, is not really necessary. The purpose of including it was to establish a point *t* (actually time *tc*, the time of the checkpoint) such that no work done prior to that point need ever be redone, and thus to put a bound on the amount of recovery processing needed. (Recall, however, that it will still be necessary to *undo* work done prior to that point, if any transactions in progress at that point were still active at the time of the failure.) What we now do instead is incorporate logic into the recovery procedure itself to determine such a point as and when necessary (namely, when the recovery procedure is actually invoked), thus avoiding the overhead of force-writing the database buffers at every checkpoint. The cost of this strategy is that we will have to go slightly further back in time if and when recovery is actually performed. However, the recovery procedure itself will be more efficient, in that it will not blindly undo/redo changes that are already undone/redone (particularly important if, as is not unlikely, another system failure occurs during recovery and the recovery process itself has to be restarted). The technique is as follows.

First, we arrange for each log record to be assigned a unique log sequence number (LSN) at the time it is written. LSNs are assigned in ascending sequence. Second, each time an updated page (block) is written to the physical database, we place in

that page the LSN of the log record corresponding to that update. Consider a particular log record R, with LSN r say, representing an update to database page P. Let
the LSN recorded in P in the database be p. (In general, of course, there will be
many log records for a given page.) Then a key observation is that, if $p >= r$, then
the update represented by R did get written to the physical database; and if $p < r$, it
did not. (Exercise: Do you agree with this statement?)

Now we modify the checkpoint procedure to eliminate Step 3 and to incorporate into the checkpoint record (Step 2) the value m, where m is the LSN of the log
record corresponding to the oldest page in the database buffer (that is, m is the minimum of all LSNs for unwritten database pages; note that these LSNs are all known,
by virtue of Step 1 of the checkpoint procedure). The log record with LSN m corresponds to the furthest point back in time that the recovery procedure need go to *redo*
work. Note, however, that some type T1 transactions (see Fig. 1.4) may now have to
be considered "active at the time of the checkpoint" (because their updates may not
yet have been written), and may thus now have to be listed in the checkpoint record.
The recovery procedure is as follows.

■   The undo-list and redo-list are established as before.

■   Work backward through the log.

```
do for all log records from end of log
    until BEGIN TRANSACTION records have been found for
                        all transactions in the undo-list;
    if log record is for a transaction in the undo-list
    then
        do;
            let r be the LSN of the current log record;
            let p be the LSN in the corresponding
                                    database page;
            if p >= r
            then undo the change;
        end;
end;
```

■   Work forward through the log.

```
do for all log records from LSN m to end of log;
    if log record is for a transaction in the redo-list
    then
        do;
            let r be the LSN of the current log record;
            let p be the LSN in the corresponding
                                    database page;
            if p < r
            then (re)do the change;
        end;
end;
```

1.5   MEDIA FAILURES

A media failure is a failure in which some portion of the secondary storage medium is damaged. As the outline in Section 1.1 suggests, the recovery process in this case consists essentially of restoring the database from an archive dump and then using the log to redo transactions run since that dump was taken. Let us examine this process in slightly more detail.

Consider first the operation of taking a dump of the database. In general, this will be a fairly lengthy process, much more time-consuming than the operation of taking a checkpoint. Moreover, it is desirable that the dump be taken when the system is in a *quiesced state* (that is, when no transactions are currently active, and all updates have been forced out to secondary storage), for otherwise the dump might contain uncommitted changes that will have to be undone if the dump is ever used in recovery. Dumps are therefore normally taken only at very carefully chosen times, such as immediately after a database reorganization or at the time of a controlled system shutdown—unlike checkpoints which, as we have already seen, may be taken quite frequently during normal transaction processing. (However, some systems —for example, the Fast Path feature of IMS—do provide facilities for dumping just selected portions of the database while other portions remain available to active transactions. Other systems support the dumping of just those pages [blocks] that have been updated since the last dump [*incremental dumping*]. Such facilities are essential if the database is very large or if normal transaction processing occupies all available time.)

Now suppose a media failure occurs. All transactions in progress at the time of the failure will be abnormally terminated. (Again, it may be possible in some cases just to terminate those transactions that are using the portion of the database that has failed. For simplicity we ignore this refinement.) The operator is informed of the failure and is responsible for allocating a new device to replace the one that failed. A utility program is then run which (a) loads the database on to the new device from the most recent archive dump, and then (b) uses the log to redo all transactions that completed since that dump was taken. Note that we are using "log" here to include not only the on-line active portion but also all necessary archive log files. Ideally the system should have a record of the serial numbers of those log files, to reduce the risk of operator error during the recovery process.

So far we have tacitly assumed that the *log* does not fail. In practice, of course, a media failure is just as likely to occur on a log device as on any other. However, it should be obvious from everything that has been said in this chapter so far that such a failure is potentially much more serious. It is therefore a good idea to duplex the log. If the log is destroyed then it will be necessary to perform a cold start.

1.6   TWO-PHASE COMMIT

We have not yet discussed exactly what is involved in the process of executing a COMMIT operation itself, except to point out (in the discussion of log write-ahead) that when a transaction COMMITs, the system should at least force all log records for that transaction (including the log record for the COMMIT itself) out to the log data set. This will guarantee that the Recovery Manager will be able to redo the transaction in the event of a subsequent system or media failure. Corresponding database changes themselves may or may not be forced out to secondary storage at this time.

In practice the situation may be a little more complicated than the previous paragraph indicates. So far in this chapter we have for the most part assumed that transactions deal with a single "resource manager" (namely, the DBMS)—that is, we have generally considered transactions as involving just one "recoverable resource" (the database), though we have touched on one other such resource in our discussions of message-handling (where the resource manager is of course the Data Communications Manager). More generally, a given transaction might require any number of distinct recoverable resources and might thus interact with any number of such resource managers. As a concrete example, we could imagine a transaction T that updates information in both a System R database and an IMS database; the two resource managers would then of course be System R (the System R run-time control system) and IMS (the IMS control program).

Now, remember that transactions are an all-or-nothing proposition—their effect on the system should be as if they executed either in toto or else not at all. In the example above, for instance, if transaction T terminates normally, then its updates must be guaranteed in both the System R database and the IMS database; and if it fails, then its updates should be rolled back in both. However, the two resource managers in this example are *autonomous*—they have independent recovery mechanisms, and in particular independent logs; and this fact makes achievement of the required "all-or-nothing" objective rather difficult. To make the example very concrete, we can imagine the transaction T executing a SQL END TRANSACTION operation (thus committing the updates to the System R database) and then failing before it has a chance to execute a DL/I SYNC operation (to commit the updates to the IMS database). Considerations such as these lead to the requirement for a protocol known as *two-phase commit*.

Aside: System R and IMS do *not* actually cooperate in the sense of the following paragraphs. We took the example we did merely to illustrate the need for such cooperation in general. We note that such cooperation is particularly necessary in "distributed" systems, in which distinct resource managers reside at distinct sites in a communications network and individual sites or links may spontaneously fail at any time. Distributed systems will be discussed in detail later in this book (Chapter 7).

Two-phase commit is required in principle whenever a transaction is able to invoke multiple independent resource managers. In outline it works as follows: A new system component is introduced called the *Coordinator*. Let us agree to refer to the resource managers involved as "participants." Then transactions do *not* issue separate COMMIT-type requests to each participant as in our example earlier, but instead issue a single "global" COMMIT to the Coordinator. On receipt of such a request, the Coordinator goes through the following two-phase process.

- Phase 1

  The Coordinator requests all participants to get themselves into a state in which they can "go either way" on the transaction (that is, either commit it or roll it back, as far as that participant's local resources are concerned). In practice, this means that each participant must force all log records involving the transaction and that participant's local resources out to that participant's local log. If the participant succeeds in reaching this state, it replies "OK" to the Coordinator, otherwise it replies "NOT OK" (or a timeout occurs, in which case the Coordinator assumes "NOT OK").

- Phase 2

  If all replies are "OK", the Coordinator then broadcasts the command "COMMIT" to all participants; all participants then complete their local COMMIT processing (that is, commit the transaction, forcing a COMMIT log record to their local log). Otherwise, the Coordinator broadcasts the command "ROLLBACK" to all participants; all participants then undo all local effects of the transaction, using their local log. The net effect is thus that *either* all participants commit the transaction *or* all roll it back; the transaction cannot be committed by some participants and rolled back by others.

Following Gray [1.3], we can make the protocol a little more precise by giving possible pseudocode procedures for the Coordinator (Fig. 1.5) and a typical participant (Fig. 1.6). The procedures must be understood to execute asynchronously (in different processes), and on different *processors* in a distributed system. Notice the timeout check in Phase 1 of the Coordinator procedure. This is included to force a rollback if any participant does not respond (which will occur if the participant is on an independent CPU and that CPU, or the link to it, has failed). Timeout checks are also included in Phase 2 of the Coordinator procedure to guarantee that the broadcast command does eventually get through. Observe in the participant procedure that local resources must remain allocated to the transaction until the "genuine" (global) termination of the transaction.

    To see that the two-phase commit protocol does indeed guarantee that all participants commit or rollback the transaction in unison, it is also necessary to consider what happens if a failure occurs at any point in the foregoing procedures. First consider the Coordinator:

1. If a failure occurs at any point before the "broadcasting" record appears in the log, the restart procedure must broadcast ROLLBACK to all participants.

2. If a failure occurs after the "broadcasting" record appears in the log, the restart procedure must (re)broadcast COMMIT or ROLLBACK (whichever is applicable) to all participants.

```
COORDINATOR: PROC;
   ASSIGN 'OK' TO VOTE;
   DO for all participants WHILE VOTE = 'OK';
      ASSIGN ' ' TO REPLY;
      send "get ready to commit" message to participant,
          wait for reply or timeout;
      IF REPLY ¬= 'OK'
      THEN ASSIGN 'NOT OK' TO VOTE;
   END;
   IF VOTE = 'OK'
   THEN /* broadcast COMMIT command */
      DO;
          force "broadcasting COMMIT" record to Coordinator log;
          DO for all participants;
             DO UNTIL acknowledgment received;
                send "commit" message to participant,
                    wait for acknowledgment or timeout;
             END;
          END;
      END;
   ELSE /* broadcast ROLLBACK command */
      DO;
          force "broadcasting ROLLBACK" to Coordinator log;
          DO for all participants;
             DO UNTIL acknowledgment received;
                send "rollback" message to participant,
                    wait for acknowledgment or timeout;
             END;
          END;
      END;
END /* COORDINATOR */;
```

Fig. 1.5 Coordinator procedure.


```
PARTICIPANT: PROC;
   wait for "get ready to commit" message;
   force undo/redo log records to local log;
   force "agree to COMMIT" record to local log;
   IF no errors occurred
   THEN send "OK" message to Coordinator;
   ELSE send "NOT OK" message to Coordinator;
   wait for broadcast command from Coordinator;
   IF command is "COMMIT"
   THEN commit changes to local resources;
   IF command is "ROLLBACK"
   THEN undo changes to local resources;
   release local resources;
   send acknowledgment to Coordinator;
END /* PARTICIPANT */;
```

Fig. 1.6 Participant procedure.

Now the participant:

1. If a failure occurs before the "agree to COMMIT" record appears in the log, the restart procedure should send a NOT OK reply to the Coordinator. (Actually this is not essential, since the timeout will cause the Coordinator to assume NOT OK anyway.)
2. If a failure occurs after the "agree to COMMIT" record appears in the log, the restart procedure must ask the Coordinator to retransmit its broadcast message (COMMIT or ROLLBACK), and then redo or undo the transaction locally, as appropriate.

For a more detailed discussion of two-phase commit (and particularly of ways to reduce the communication overhead of the procedures as we have presented them), reference [1.3] is recommended. Further details are also given in Chapter 7.

1.7   DATA MANIPULATION LANGUAGE RECOVERY OPERATIONS

We conclude this chapter by sketching very briefly the recovery operations provided in various data manipulation languages (DMLs), namely, SQL, DL/I, DBTG, and UDL. The reader is expected to be familiar with the general characteristics of these languages; background material can be found in Volume I. The purpose of this section is to serve as a reference summary rather than as a detailed description of the various language facilities. The discussion of DL/I in particular, which covers a lot of ground, is especially terse.

SQL (System R)

Embedded SQL as implemented in System R provides the operations BEGIN TRANSACTION, END TRANSACTION (successful termination), and RESTORE TRANSACTION (unsuccessful termination). Program initiation does *not* cause an implicit BEGIN TRANSACTION and normal program termination does *not* cause an implicit END TRANSACTION; in fact, program termination, normal or abnormal, might be considered as causing an implicit RESTORE TRANSACTION, since any database changes made after the last END TRANSACTION or COMMIT (see below) will eventually be backed out.

END TRANSACTION and RESTORE TRANSACTION both have the effect of closing any open cursors, thus causing all database positioning to be lost.

As just indicated, SQL also provides a COMMIT operation. However, it is END TRANSACTION that corresponds to "commit" as we have been using the term in this chapter; the SQL COMMIT may be thought of as an END TRANSACTION immediately followed by a BEGIN TRANSACTION, except that it does not close cursors. The SQL COMMIT is used to divide a long transaction into "subtransactions'' (not a SQL term), without losing database position at the end of each of those subtransactions. Note, however, that a subtransaction *is* a transaction: RESTORE TRANSACTION (or a system-initiated rollback) will undo a transaction only back to the last COMMIT or to BEGIN TRANSACTION, whichever was more recent.

DL/I (IMS)

In order to understand the DL/I recovery operations it is first necessary to have some understanding of the various categories of application program in IMS. We therefore start with an outline explanation of this categorization. The major categories are

- batch programs,
- batch/message processing programs (BMP),
- message processing programs (MPP),
- Fast Path, non-message-driven programs (NMD),
- Fast Path, message-driven programs (MD).

First, a *batch* program is one that executes under its own private copy of IMS and makes no use of the IMS message processing facilities (by contrast, all other types of program execute under the control of a central, shared copy of IMS). Such a program is typically long-running. The private IMS copy is loaded into main storage immediately prior to execution of the batch program in question and is deleted immediately after that execution; it has no knowledge of any concurrent execution of any other IMS applications, batch or otherwise. Databases accessed by a batch program are not available for concurrent access from any other program (except in the special case where all programs involved are performing retrieval access only). A batch program cannot access a Fast Path database. Batch programs are invoked by the operator via appropriate JCL commands (actually specifying IMS as the job to be run and passing the name of the batch program as a parameter to IMS).

A batch/message processing program (BMP) is in effect a ''batch'' application, typically long-running, that needs access to a database that is shared by other applications. Like all program types except pure batch, it runs under a central, shared copy of IMS; all databases are considered as belonging to that shared IMS copy, rather than to individual programs, and are thus available for shared access from multiple concurrent programs. The batch/message processing program may or may not use the IMS message processing facilities; if it does, it is said to be ''transaction-driven'' (TD), otherwise it is said to be ''non-transaction-driven'' (NTD). (The term ''transaction'' in IMS is generally used to refer to the input message rather than to the program execution.) Batch/message processing programs are invoked via JCL, like batch programs.

A message processing program (MPP), by contrast, is invoked by entering an appropriate message at the terminal (as in the TRANSFER example of Section 1.2), and certainly does make use of the IMS message processing facilities. A message processing program may operate in either *single message mode* or *multiple message mode:* That is, a transaction (in our sense of the term rather than IMS's) may correspond either to a single input message or to a sequence of several. (Note: Transaction-driven batch/message processing programs may also operate in either single or multiple message mode. In fact, a transaction-driven batch/message processing program is very similar to a message processing program.)

Fast Path programs are programs that access Fast Path databases—that is, Main Storage databases (MSDBs) or Data Entry databases (DEDBs). They may or may not access ordinary IMS databases in addition to the Fast Path databases. Fast Path programs come in two varieties, message-driven (MD) and non-message-driven (NMD). A message-driven application definitely does perform message processing; each input message corresponds to a single transaction (and thus a message-driven application is analogous to a message processing program operating in single message mode). A non-message-driven application may not perform message processing; such an application is thus analogous to a non-transaction-driven batch/message processing program. Both message-driven and non-message-driven applications are invoked via JCL.

Batch/message processing programs and message processing programs are also allowed to access Fast Path databases.

Finally, we observe that message processing programs and Fast Path message-driven applications are not allowed to use ordinary OS/VS access methods such as QSAM or VSAM; and message processing programs and Fast Path applications (message-driven or non-message-driven) are not allowed to use the special IMS access method GSAM.

Now we turn to a discussion of the DL/I recovery operations. First we note that the first recoverable operation causes an implicit BEGIN TRANSACTION (our terminology) in all environments. Normal program termination causes an implicit COMMIT (our term) in all environments, *except* for the case of a non-message-driven Fast Path application; such an application must issue SYNC or CHKP (or ROLL or ROLB)—see below—before it terminates. Abnormal program termination (ABEND) causes an automatic ROLLBACK (our term) in all environments, except in the case of batch where a special backout utility must be used [1.6]. The ABEND causes the program to be deleted from main storage; in the case of a message-driven Fast Path application, however, the program is then reloaded and given control again.

Rollback, planned or unplanned, always discards output messages generated by the transaction, except for messages transmitted via a PCB designated as EX-PRESS. EXPRESS messages are never placed on a pending queue but are transmitted directly.

An implicit COMMIT (or BEGIN TRANSACTION, on the first execution) is caused in message-driven Fast Path applications, message processing programs (single message mode), and batch/message processing programs (single message mode) by the DL/I operation that gets a new input message ("get unique from message queue").

Apart from the special case of "get unique from message queue," the DL/I calls that are relevant to recovery are CHKP, XRST, SYNC, ROLL, and ROLB.

■   CHKP

CHKP ("program checkpoint"—not to be confused with "checkpoint" as we have been using the term) is used to establish an explicit commit point (the IMS term is "synchronization point" or *synchpoint*). It can be used in all environments. For message-driven Fast Path applications and single message mode message processing programs, however, there is no need to use it, since its effect is *exactly* the same as that of "get unique from message queue" (see earlier). For multiple message mode message processing programs, CHKP provides the only means of establishing an explicit synchpoint; note, however, that its function also *includes* that of "get unique from message queue"—that is, it obtains the next input message. For non-message-driven Fast Path applications, its effect is the same as that of SYNC (see later). For batch/message processing programs, it establishes an explicit synchpoint and (for transaction-driven batch/message processing programs) it also does a "get unique from message queue." Last, for batch and batch/message processing programs, CHKP also allows selected program variables to be written out to the log; these variables can be restored on a restart by means of the XRST call (see below). All database positioning is lost after a CHKP call, except for GSAM databases.

■   XRST

XRST applies to batch and batch/message processing programs only. If such a program includes any CHKP calls (and is therefore subject to restart at a checkpoint), that program must execute XRST as its first DL/I call. If no restart is in progress, the XRST is effectively a no-operation. If a restart is in progress, XRST causes IMS to restore the program variables that were saved at the time the checkpoint was taken and to supply the keys of the database records that were current at that time (placing those keys in the appropriate PCBs). Reestablishment of current position within those databases is the application's responsibility, except for GSAM.

■   SYNC

SYNC applies to non-message-driven Fast Path applications only. It establishes an explicit synchpoint.

- ROLL

ROLL does not apply to batch programs. For other environments a rollback to the last synchpoint occurs. The program is deleted and reloaded and reentered at the beginning, so that it may begin to process the next transaction.

- ROLB

ROLB does not apply to batch programs, multiple message mode message processing programs, or multiple message mode batch/message processing programs. For other environments a rollback to the last synchpoint occurs, as with ROLL; unlike ROLL, however, control returns directly to the executing application. Database positioning is lost unless PROCOPT=P is specified in the PCB (in which case the positioning as of the last synchpoint is restored). For message-driven Fast Path applications, ROLB will optionally repeat the most recent "get unique from message queue."

Figure 1.7 is a summary of the different IMS application program categories and the operations that apply to them.

Finally, we note that updates to Fast Path databases are never written out to secondary storage before the transaction reaches a synchpoint. (This fact is concealed from the programmer in the case of a Data Entry database but is exposed in the case of a Main Storage database; see Volume I.) In consequence, it is never necessary to write "undo" log records for a Fast Path database; "undoing" changes to such a database consists simply of not writing those changes out. For all other types of database, IMS force-writes the buffers out to the database at each synchpoint, so that it is never necessary to redo changes to those databases after a system failure.

DBTG

DBTG provides two recovery statements, COMMIT and ROLLBACK. Both mark the end of the current transaction and the start of the next. Both set all currency indicators to null. Program initiation is an implicit "BEGIN TRANSACTION"; program termination, normal or abnormal, is an implicit *abnormal* end of transaction.

UDL

UDL, like DBTG, provides two recovery statements, COMMIT and ROLLBACK. Again both statements mark the end of the current transaction and the start of the next.[9] Both set all cursors to null. Program initiation is an implicit "BEGIN TRANSACTION"; program termination is an implicit end of transaction, normal or abnormal according as the program termination is normal or abnormal. UDL

---

9. Loosely speaking. See the remarks on UDL in Section 1.2.

	batch	BMP		NTD	MPP		NMD	MD
		TD		NTD				
		single message mode	multiple message mode		single message mode	multiple message mode		
message processing	N	Y	Y	N	Y	Y	N	Y
OS access method	Y	Y	Y	Y	N	N	N	N
GSAM	Y	Y	Y	Y	Y	Y	N	N
Fast Path	N	Y	Y	Y	Y	Y	Y	Y
normal termination ⟶ commit	Y	Y	Y	Y	Y	Y	N	Y
ABEND ⟶ rollback	N	Y	Y	Y	Y	Y	Y	Y
ABEND ⟶ reload program	N	N	N	N	N	N	N	Y
GU message ⟶ commit	N	Y	N	N	Y	N	N	Y
CHKP	Y	Y (2)	Y (2)	Y	Y (1)	Y (2)	Y (3)	Y (1)
XRST	Y	Y	Y	N	N	N	N	N
SYNC	N	N	N	N	N	N	Y	N
ROLL	N	Y	Y	Y	Y	Y	Y	Y
ROLB	N	Y	Y	Y	Y	N	Y	Y (4)

Notes:
  (1) Same as "get unique from message queue"
  (2) Includes "get unique from message queue"
  (3) Same as SYNC
  (4) Optionally repeats last "get unique from message queue"

Fig. 1.7 Summary of IMS program categories and DL/I operations.

also allows the program to declare its dependence (if applicable) on the recoverability or nonrecoverability of a given "baseset" (set of all records of a given type). Incorporation of support for savepoints [1.4] is under consideration.

EXERCISES

1.1 Explain why data manipulation languages do not allow a given transaction to COMMIT changes to one database (or file or relation or . . .) and not to another.

1.2 Why is it not possible to nest transactions inside one another?

1.3 Why is it undesirable for application-issued ROLLBACK to be treated as an unplanned transaction termination?

1.4 Describe the two approaches to dealing with "conversations." What is involved on the part of the system in each of the two approaches in carrying information from one user/system exchange to the next?

1.5 Design a log record structure to support the recovery operations (both database and message) discussed in this chapter.

1.6 Define the write-ahead log protocol.

1.7 What are the recovery implications of (a) force-writing buffers to the database at COMMIT; (b) never physically writing buffers to the database prior to COMMIT?

1.8 Define the two-phase commit protocol.

REFERENCES AND BIBLIOGRAPHY

1.1 C. T. Davies, Jr. "Recovery Semantics for a DB/DC System." *Proc. 1973 ACM National Conference.*

1.2 L. A. Bjork. "Recovery Scenario for a DB/DC System." *Proc. 1973 ACM National Conference.*

> These two companion papers [1.1, 1.2] represent some of the earliest theoretical work in the area of recovery.

1.3 J. N. Gray. "Notes on Data Base Operating Systems." IBM Research Report RJ2188 (February 1978). Also published in R. Bayer, R. M. Graham, and G. Seegmuller (eds.), *Operating Systems: An Advanced Course.* Springer-Verlag (1978).

> The major subject of this paper is transaction management (over two thirds of the paper, some 70 pages, are devoted to this topic). Data structures and data communications are also discussed. Under the heading of transaction management there are good discussions of concurrency and locking (see Chapter 3), recovery, and log management. The present chapter draws heavily from this source. Strongly recommended.

1.4 J. N. Gray et al. "The Recovery Manager of the System R Data Manager." *ACM Comp. Surv.* **13,** No. 2 (June 1981).

> Describes the recovery features of System R. Most of the concepts discussed in the present chapter are supported in one form or another in System R, with the exception of message handling. System R uses a differential file technique for the writing of updates, which simplifies restart after a system failure. (It also uses a recovery log in the usual way, however.) When a page (block) is updated, that page is not changed in secondary storage; instead, a new copy of it (incorporating the update) is written elsewhere on the device, and the database directory is updated to point to this new page. The old copy is referred to as a *shadow*. At system checkpoint, updated pages become part of the current database and shadow pages are discarded. As work proceeds, new updated pages and corresponding shadow pages are created. If a system failure occurs, the first step of the recovery process then involves discarding pages updated since the last checkpoint and reinstating the corresponding shadow versions, after which the log is used to redo forward from that checkpoint all processing for transactions that completed before the failure and to undo backward from the checkpoint all processing for transactions that did not. For more details of this scheme, see [1.5].

System R also provides a feature known as *savepoints*. Savepoints go part way (arguably as far as it is feasible to go) toward supporting the requirement for transaction nesting. Briefly, the idea is as follows: Two additional recovery operations, SAVE and RE-STORE, are provided (however, these are internal operations only—they are not supported at the SQL interface, although there is no reason why they should not be). SAVE establishes a savepoint by recording the current transaction state (positioning information, etc.) on the log. RESTORE rolls the transaction back to a specified savepoint (note therefore that SAVE does *not* commit changes, since it is possible to restore the transaction to any previous savepoint). By convention, BEGIN TRANSACTION is savepoint one. Now suppose that procedure A includes a CALL for procedure B. Procedure A can guarantee that the behavior of procedure B is atomic (all or nothing) as far as its effect on the database is concerned, by issuing SAVE before the CALL and (if B returns an error code) issuing the corresponding RESTORE afterward. Similarly, B can guarantee that a lower-level procedure C is atomic, and so on. (Output messages could be handled similarly, in principle, but System R does not support messages at all.) Note, however, that the entire set of nested procedures is still a single transaction, and they must all COMMIT or ROLLBACK together.

Savepoints can also be used to reduce the amount of rollback necessary in the event of a deadlock (see Chapter 3).

1.5 R. A. Lorie. "Physical Integrity in a Large Segmented Database." *ACM TODS* **2**, No. 1 (March 1977).

Describes the shadow page mechanism of System R in detail.

1.6 IBM Corporation. IMS/VS Version 1 Recovery/Restart. IBM Form No. GG24-1515.

IMS also supports most of the concepts discussed in this chapter, including (for example) on-line and archive versions of the log, selective dumping and selective recovery after a media failure, the log write-ahead protocol, and also (unlike System R) integrated message recovery. For reference we give a brief description of the major IMS recovery utilities, since they may reasonably be regarded as typical.

- Image copy

Used to take an archive dump ("image copy") of a database data set. Note that an IMS database usually consists of several data sets.

- Change accumulation

Used to construct a database change accumulation file, containing database changes in chronological order within data set within database. For each database segment (record), only the most recent change is retained. The utility takes as its input a previous version of the change accumulation file, together with log tapes written since that previous version was created.

- Database recovery

Uses an image copy, the change accumulation file, and subsequent log tapes to recover (specified data sets within) a specified database after a media failure.

- Backout

Used to undo the effects of a specified batch program, either in toto or back to a specified program checkpoint. To restart a batch program, the operator must first use the backout utility to undo changes back to some specified checkpoint, then initiate the program via IMS in the usual way, naming that checkpoint as the restart point.

1.7 C. J. Date. "An Introduction to the Unified Database Language (UDL)." *Proc. 6th International Conference on Very Large Data Bases* (October 1980).

1.8 J. S. M. Verhofstad. "Recovery Techniques for Database Systems." *ACM Comp. Surv.* **10,** No. 2 (June 1978).

A tutorial survey.

1.9 N. J. Giordano and M. S. Schwartz. "Data Base Recovery at CMIC." *Proc. 1976 ACM SIGMOD International Conference on Management of Data* (June 1976).

A detailed description of the implementation of a specific recovery package.

1.10 TANDEM Computers Inc. ENCOMPASS Distributed Data Management System.

1.11 J. N. Gray and J. H. Howard. "Duplexed Disk Performance." Private communication (June 1980).

1.12 IBM Corporation. IMS/VS Message Format Services User's Guide. IBM Form No. SH20-9053.

ANSWERS TO SELECTED EXERCISES

1.1 Such a feature would conflict with the objective of transaction atomicity. If a transaction could COMMIT some but not all of its updates, then the uncommitted ones might subsequently be rolled back, whereas the committed ones of course could not be. Thus, the transaction could not be regarded as all-or-nothing. (Note: This is in fact precisely the situation when transactions are allowed to update "nonrecoverable data," since updates to nonrecoverable data are implicitly committed as soon as they occur. See the remarks on this topic at the end of Section 1.1.)

1.2 Again, such a feature would conflict with the atomicity objective. For consider what would happen if transaction B were nested inside transaction A, and the following sequence of events occurred:

transaction A begins (start of transaction A)

transaction A updates record R1

transaction A invokes transaction B (start of transaction B)

transaction B updates record R2

transaction B issues COMMIT (end of transaction B)

transaction A issues ROLLBACK (end of transaction A)

If record R2 is restored to its pre-A value at this point, then B's COMMIT was not in fact a COMMIT at all. Conversely, if B's COMMIT was genuine, then record R2 cannot be restored to its pre-A value, and hence A's ROLLBACK cannot be honored.

For further discussion of transaction nesting, see the annotation to reference [1.5].

1.3 See the subsection "Messages" in Section 1.2, especially Footnote 4 on page 7.

1.4 See the subsection "Transaction Structure" in Section 1.2. In the first approach, since each exchange is treated as a separate transaction, carrying information from one exchange to another will have to be done by means of a (recoverable) intermediate file on secondary storage. In the second case, such information can be kept in main storage.

1.5 We give an outline design for a "database record update" log record (with acknowledgments to reference [1.3]). Other types of log record will follow the same overall pattern.

```
DCL 1 DB_REC_UPD_LOG_REC,
      2 TYPE                       /* indicates "DB rec upd log rec"     */,
      2 LOG_REC_SEQUENCE_NO        /* identifies this log record         */,
      2 TRANSACTION_ID             /* identifies updating transaction    */,
      2 ADDR_PREVIOUS_LOG_REC      /* ptr to prev log rec for this trans */,
      2 DATABASE_ID                /* identifies updated database        */,
      2 RELATION_ID                /* identifies updated relation        */,
      2 RECORD_ADDR                /* address of updated record          */,
      2 #_OF_UPDATES               /* no of fields updated               */,
      2 UPDATES (#_OF_UPDATES)     /* details for each updated field     */,
        3 FIELD_ID                 /* identifies an updated field        */,
        3 OLD_VALUE                /* value before update                */,
        3 NEW_VALUE                /* value after update                 */;
```

1.7 (a) REDO is never necessary following system failure. (b) Physical UNDO is never necessary, and hence UNDO log records are also unnecessary.

2
Integrity

2.1 INTRODUCTION

The term *integrity* is used in database contexts with the meaning of *accuracy, correctness,* or *validity.* The problem of integrity is the problem of ensuring that the data in the database is accurate—that is, the problem of guarding the database against invalid updates. Invalid updates may be caused by errors in data entry, by mistakes on the part of the operator or the application programmer, by system failures, even by deliberate falsification. The last of these, however, is not so much a matter of integrity as it is of *security;* protecting the database against operations that are actually illegal, as opposed to merely invalid, is the responsibility of the *security subsystem* (to be discussed in Chapter 4). In this chapter we assume that the user is at least authorized to attempt the update in question, and we consider what is involved on the part of the *integrity subsystem* in checking that update for validity and preventing it if it turns out to be invalid.

Another term that is sometimes used for integrity is *consistency.* But it seems preferable to reserve this term for the special case in which two or more values in the database are required to be in agreement with each other in some way (that is, mutually consistent). Examples of this type of consistency requirement are: (a) The DEPARTMENT# field in an EMPLOYEE record must be equal to the DEPARTMENT# field in some DEPARTMENT record; (b) the TOTAL field in a SUMMARY record must be equal to the total of the BALANCE fields in some set of ACCOUNT records. In this book we shall generally use the term "consistency" only in this latter, more specialized (though imprecise) sense.

One final note on terminology: The term "integrity" is also very commonly used to refer just to the special situation that arises in a multiuser system, in which it is possible that two concurrently executing transactions, each correct in itself, may interfere with each other in such a manner as to produce incorrect results. However, systems that provide "integrity" in this sense typically guarantee merely that such interference cannot occur; they do not concern themselves with the question as to whether individual transactions are correct when considered in isolation. In other words, such systems guarantee merely that errors will not be *introduced* by the fact that transactions run concurrently. While this level of protection is obviously important, and indeed difficult to achieve reliably, it seems desirable to recognize that the problem of integrity is wider than just the problem of interference. Indeed, it has been suggested [2.30] that, in principle, the specification of integrity rules could account for as much as 80 percent of a typical database description (conceptual schema). But the reader should be warned that, whereas many systems do currently provide protection against interference, almost no systems other than experimental ones provide more than the most rudimentary validation of individual transactions.[1] Some of the reasons for this state of affairs will become apparent as we proceed.

The material in this chapter should thus be seen primarily as a framework for research, rather than as a description of the way systems work today. (Some indication of the facilities provided in existing systems is given in Section 2.7.) The question of concurrency and interference is deferred to Chapter 3; for the present chapter we assume, without loss of generality, that we are dealing with a single-user system. We note that there are strong similarities between the ideas presented in this chapter and the *abstract data type* notion of programming languages [2.31]. But we do not assume any familiarity with abstract data types on the part of the reader.

Most examples will be based on the usual suppliers-and-parts database (see Volume I). For reference we show in Fig. 2.1 a set of sample values for this database. (As usual, we adopt the relational approach as a convenient basis for our discussions. A few comments on other approaches appear in Sections 2.5 and 2.7.)

2.2 INTEGRITY RULES

As a starting point, we assume the existence of an *integrity subsystem* (a component of the DBMS) with the following responsibilities:

- monitoring transactions (specifically, update operations) and detecting integrity violations;

- in the event of a violation, taking appropriate action (for example, rejecting the operation, reporting the violation, perhaps even correcting the error).

---

1. There are obvious limitations on the extent to which such validation is even possible; for example, there is probably no way of detecting the fact that an input value of 35 for "hours worked" should really be 33 (on the other hand, a value of 350 would obviously be in error).

S	S#	SNAME	STATUS	CITY
	S1	Smith	20	London
	S2	Jones	10	Paris
	S3	Blake	30	Paris
	S4	Clark	20	London
	S5	Adams	30	Athens

SP	S#	P#	QTY
	S1	P1	300
	S1	P2	200
	S1	P3	400
	S1	P4	200
	S1	P5	100
	S1	P6	100
	S2	P1	300
	S2	P2	400
	S3	P2	200
	S4	P2	200
	S4	P4	300
	S4	P5	400

P	P#	PNAME	COLOR	WEIGHT	CITY
	P1	Nut	Red	12	London
	P2	Bolt	Green	17	Paris
	P3	Screw	Blue	17	Rome
	P4	Screw	Red	14	London
	P5	Cam	Blue	12	Paris
	P6	Cog	Red	19	London

Fig. 2.1 The suppliers-and-parts database (sample values).

In order to be able to perform these functions, the integrity subsystem must be provided with a set of *rules* that define what errors to check for, when to do the checking, and what to do if an error is detected. An example of such a rule is given in Fig. 2.2.

The rule in Fig. 2.2 (rule SIR1—"supplier integrity rule #1") consists of three parts: an AFTER clause, a predicate, and an ELSE clause. The AFTER clause indicates when the check is to be applied (namely, after field S.STATUS is updated[2]); the predicate (S.STATUS > 0) indicates the nature of the check (namely, the new value of S.STATUS should be greater than zero); and the ELSE clause indicates

```
SIR1 : AFTER UPDATING S.STATUS :
            S.STATUS > 0
        ELSE
            DO ;
                set return code to "rule SIR1 violated" ;
                REJECT ;
            END ;
```

Fig. 2.2 Example of an integrity rule.

---

2. In practice, of course, it would be preferable to apply the check *before* actually doing the update. See note (9) following Fig. 2.7, later.

what should be done if the check fails (namely, reject the update with a return code indicating the reason for rejection). We shall assume that integrity rules always have this three-part structure (at least approximately, though as we shall see later there are actually two types of rule with slightly different structures; also it may be possible to omit some parts in certain cases). In general we shall refer to the three parts as the *trigger condition* (or conditions—there may be more than one), the *constraint,* and the *violation response,* respectively. Note in particular that we use this last term to refer to the response to an *attempted* violation; we do not mean to imply that the violation should be allowed to occur.

It can be seen, therefore, that what we are suggesting is a system in which integrity rules can be expressed in a high-level language, perhaps a language akin to UDL or SQL.[3] Such rules are compiled and stored in the system dictionary by a special component of the integrity subsystem (the integrity rules compiler). Once entered into the system, the rules are then enforced from that point on. (We assume that a new rule may be defined at any time. The definition should be rejected if the new rule is violated by the current state of the database.) The major advantage of this approach is, of course, that validation is handled by the system instead of being left to individual applications (the prevailing situation today). Corollary advantages are that the rules are concentrated into a single central location (the dictionary) instead of being scattered across applications, and that they are thus easier to understand in their totality and easier to change if necessary. There is also a better chance of detecting contradictions or redundancies within those rules, and a possibility of getting the overall validation process to perform more efficiently.

Note, incidentally, that since the rules are stored in the system dictionary, it should be possible to use the normal system query language to make inquiries concerning them, just as it is possible to query other portions of the dictionary. Examples of such inquiries might be "What integrity rules pertain to employee salaries?" "What data is affected by integrity rule SIR1?" and "What happens to a supplier's shipments if the supplier is deleted?"

We note too that a means of deleting and modifying rules would also be needed in a working system.

Integrity rules can be divided into two broad categories: domain integrity rules and relation integrity rules. Domain rules concern the admissibility of a given value as a candidate value for a given attribute (field), considered in isolation—that is, independent of its relationship to other values in the database. Relation rules concern, for example, the admissibility of a given tuple as a candidate for insertion into

---

3. Numerous proposals have been made for languages for specifying integrity rules [2.1–2.3, 2.5, 2.9, 2.10, 2.13, 2.14, 2.18, 2.19]. As already indicated, however, little has been done in the way of implementation for any of them. In this chapter we therefore take the liberty of using a language of our own (very loosely based on the PL/I version of UDL—see Volume I or reference [1.7]).

a given relation, or the relationship between tuples of one relation and those of another. We consider domain rules in Section 2.3 and relation rules in Section 2.4. Also, in Section 2.5, we briefly consider the effect of introducing fansets as another permissible data construct, over and above the domains and relations already considered.

2.3 DOMAIN INTEGRITY RULES

Every attribute of every relation has an underlying domain, identified in the definition of the relation in question. Let attribute A of relation R (that is, attribute R.A) be defined on domain D. Then any value v submitted as a candidate value for R.A (via either an INSERT operation or an UPDATE operation for some tuple t of R) must belong to D. The definition of domain D (which either explicitly or implicitly specifies all values in D) thus constitutes a simple but important integrity rule, which should be checked on all inserts or updates involving any attribute defined on D. The domain integrity rule for a given domain is thus nothing more than the *definition* of that domain. According to McLeod [2.1], violations of domain integrity rules (or domain definitions) occur sufficiently often to justify a special facility to handle them. (Our discussions in this section are heavily influenced by the proposals of [2.1].) Domain integrity rules also play a leading role in Fagin's work on "domain/key normal form" [2.24], which we discussed briefly in Volume I. But we should warn the reader that few existing systems provide very much in the way of domain support at all.

Every domain is assumed to be a subset of one or other of the "base domains" (namely, the set of all character strings, the set of all fixed-point numbers, and the set of all floating-point numbers), and inherits an ordering (lexicographic or numeric) from that base domain. Figure 2.3 gives a possible BNF syntax for domain definitions (derived from a syntax presented in [2.1]). Figure 2.4 gives a set of possible domain definitions for the suppliers-and-parts database, based on this syntax.

```
domain-definition    ::=   DCL domain-name [ PRIMARY ] DOMAIN
                           constraint
                           terminator

constraint           ::=   data-type [ predicate ]

terminator           ::=   ;  | ELSE violation-response

violation-response   ::=   executable-unit
```

Fig. 2.3 Domain definition syntax.

```
DCL S#         PRIMARY DOMAIN CHARACTER (5)
               SUBSTR (S#,1,1) = 'S'
               AND IS_NUMERIC (SUBSTR (S#,2,4) )
               ELSE
                  DO ;
                      set return code to
                      "S# domain rule violated" ;
                      REJECT ;
                  END ;
DCL SNAME      DOMAIN CHARACTER (20) VARYING ;
DCL STATUS     DOMAIN FIXED (3,0)
               STATUS > 0 ;
DCL LOCATION   DOMAIN CHARACTER (15) VARYING
               LOCATION IN ('LONDON','PARIS','ROME','ATHENS') ;
DCL P#         PRIMARY DOMAIN CHARACTER (6)
               SUBSTR (P#,1,1) = 'P'
               AND IS_NUMERIC (SUBSTR (P#,2,5) ) ;
DCL PNAME      DOMAIN CHARACTER (20) VARYING ;
DCL COLOR      DOMAIN CHARACTER (6)
               COLOR IN ('RED','GREEN','BLUE',
                         'YELLOW','BROWN','PURPLE') ;
DCL WEIGHT     DOMAIN FIXED (5,1)
               WEIGHT > 0 AND WEIGHT < 2000 ;
DCL QTY        DOMAIN FIXED (5)
               QTY >= 0 ;
```

Fig. 2.4 Sample domain definitions.

Figure 2.4 is interpreted as follows.

■   First note that domains S# and P# are designated as PRIMARY. We defer discussion of this point to Section 2.4.

■   Note also that no trigger conditions are stated. The reason is that the trigger conditions for a domain rule are always the same—namely, UPDATE of a field, or INSERT of a record containing a field, that is defined on the domain in question.

■   Domain S# consists of all character strings of length 5 in which the first character (that is, the substring starting at position one and of length one character) is the character 'S', and the remaining characters (that is, the substring starting at position two and of length four characters) are all numeric. (For the sake of the example, we assume the existence of an IS_NUMERIC built-in function, which returns the value *true* if and only if its argument is a character string in which each character represents a valid decimal digit.) If an attempt is made, via an INSERT or UPDATE operation, to introduce an S# value into the database that does not conform to this pattern, the operation is rejected and a code indicating violation of the S# domain rule is returned to the user. Note that the rule needs no independent name of its own, since it is uniquely identified by the name of the domain.

The particular form of violation response shown here (reject the operation with a return code) is likely to be so common that we take it as the default if the ELSE clause is omitted. No violation responses are specified explicitly for the remaining domains in the example, but in general the possibilities include the following:

simple rejection (as in the example);

correcting the invalid value (for example, replacing a numeric value by zero, or replacing an invalid character by '?');

failing the transaction (that is, forcing a rollback).

- Domain SNAME consists of all character strings of length not more than 20.

- Domain STATUS (data type FIXED, with three digits of precision and no digits in the fractional part) consists of all positive integers of three decimal digits or less. If the predicate were omitted, negative integers (and zero) would also be valid STATUS values. (Of course, if the predicate is included, there is no need for the integrity rule SIR1 of Fig. 2.2.)

For data type FIXED we take the number of digits in the fractional part as zero if nothing is specified; for an example, see domain QTY (later). Floating-point numbers are specified with data type FLOAT(n), where n is the number of decimal digits of precision.

- Domain LOCATION consists of an enumerated set of character strings ('LONDON', 'PARIS', etc.). This domain will be used as the domain for the CITY attributes of relations S and P (we have deliberately used a domain name other than CITY to stress the distinction between attributes and domains). Different LOCATION values are of different lengths—hence the VARYING specification.

- Domain P# is defined analogously to domain S#.

- Domain PNAME is defined analogously to domain SNAME.

- Domain COLOR is defined analogously to domain LOCATION, except that all strings are the same length (values are considered to be padded at the right with blanks if necessary).

- Domain WEIGHT is defined analogously to domain STATUS, except that (purely for the sake of the example) we show weight values not as integers but as decimal numbers of five digits with an assumed decimal point just before the rightmost digit. Also values are constrained to be positive and less than 2000.

- Domain QTY is also defined analogously to domain STATUS, except that a value of zero is permitted.

The basic concept of domain definition as described above is open to a number of extensions and improvements, some of which we discuss below. Not all are directly relevant to domain integrity per se.

Null Values

We assume that each of the base domains includes a null value, different from all other values in the domain, and hence that each defined domain also includes a null value (barring explicit constraints to the contrary). However, the question of null values raises a host of subsidiary questions, some of them of a fairly nontrivial nature. We defer detailed discussion of null values to a later chapter (Chapter 5); for the purposes of this chapter, however, we assume the existence of a built-in function IS_NULL(x), which returns the value *true* if and only if its argument x is null.

Data Types

Other data types are of course possible in addition to those illustrated so far. BOOLEAN is one obvious instance. A PICTURE data type might simplify the expression of constraints such as those for domains S# and P# in our example.

Composite Domains

McLeod [2.1] proposes a scheme for (in effect) defining composite domains. For example, domain DATE may be defined as the concatenation of DAY, MONTH, and YEAR. In addition, we could impose the constraint that DAY is in the range 1–31 and MONTH in the range 1–12 (or even the constraint that if MONTH is 4, 6, 9, or 11, then DAY is in the range 1–30, etc., etc.). Assuming that the decomposition carries over into attributes defined on the composite domain, this notion has obvious applicability—and implications—in the area of data manipulation languages (DMLs) also.

Ordering

The ordering rule for a domain D is of course what gives meaning to comparisons such as "$d1 < d2$" (where $d1$ and $d2$ are values in D). Earlier we stated that each domain inherits its ordering from the underlying base domain. However, the inherited ordering may not always be what is required; consider domain DATE in the example above, where we would at least like to be able to state that the ordering is ascending by DAY *within* MONTH *within* YEAR. More complex orderings can easily be imagined, including orderings that must be defined procedurally rather than declaratively. It should therefore be possible to override the inherited ordering with an explicit ordering specification, which could conceivably even be expressed in terms of a user-written procedure. McLeod [2.1] suggests that it should also be possible to state "ORDERING NONE," meaning that only equality and inequality comparisons are valid, but it is difficult to think of a domain where ordering *never* makes sense. Perhaps the most satisfactory approach would be to support a specification of "ORDERING NONE," but also to provide a DML option to allow the user to override it at need.

User-Written Procedures

As just indicated, user-written procedures have a part to play in the specification of ordering. Other points at which they might be incorporated are in the predicate (the constraint specification) and in the ELSE clause (the violation response). Apart from this possibility, incidentally, domain constraint predicates are likely to be fairly simple, in particular involving no variables other than the one representing the candidate value to be tested (represented by the domain name).

Interdomain Comparisons

In the absence of any specification to the contrary, comparisons such as "$d < e$", where d and e are values from distinct domains D and E, are generally considered to be in error. For example, it makes little sense to compare a color and a city, even though both are represented as character strings.[4] However, there are examples when it does make sense to compare values from different domains, particularly when the major difference between those domains is just the units in which values are represented. For example, two distinct domains may both contain distances, but one may give values in kilometers and the other in miles. Accordingly, it should be possible to provide *conversion rules* (procedures) for converting values from either domain into equivalent values in the other. Given the existence of such a rule for domains D and E, comparisons such as "$d < e$" may no longer be in error.

We conclude this section with an example of a possible definition for the part relation P, showing how that definition might identify the underlying domains (Fig. 2.5). The PRIMARY KEY clause will be discussed in Section 2.4. We remind the reader that it is a common convention that if "DOMAIN (domain-name)" is omitted from an attribute definition, then the attribute is assumed to be defined on a domain having the same name as that attribute.

```
DCL  P  RELATION
         ATTRIBUTES   ( P#       DOMAIN (P#),
                        PNAME    DOMAIN (PNAME),
                        COLOR    DOMAIN (COLOR),
                        WEIGHT   DOMAIN (WEIGHT),
                        CITY     DOMAIN (LOCATION) )
         PRIMARY KEY ( P# ) ;
```

Fig. 2.5 Sample relation definition.

---

4. Little sense, maybe, but not no sense at all. The reader is invited to think of a counter-example. Again the DML should provide an option to allow the prohibition to be overridden if necessary.

2.4 RELATION INTEGRITY RULES

Rule SIR1 (Fig. 2.2) is an example of a relation integrity rule. A comprehensive set of examples is given in Fig. 2.6. We shall discuss each of those examples in detail later in this section; before then, however, we give in Fig. 2.7 a BNF syntax for the language in which those examples are expressed, together with some notes on the interpretation of that syntax. We observe that the syntax could do with refinement in some areas if it were to be seriously considered for implementation. However, it is adequate as it stands for our purposes.

The following notes (1)–(12) explain the syntax of Fig. 2.7 in detail. They are intended primarily for reference. It is probably a good idea to skip them on a first reading.

1. The trigger-condition-commalist, if specified, consists of either the single clause WHEN COMMITTING, or a list of BEFORE clauses and/or AFTER clauses separated by commas. If a trigger-condition-commalist is specified, it must be followed by a colon.

2. All parameters (record-parameters or field-parameters) mentioned in a given trigger-condition-commalist must have the same explicit or implied qualifying cursor. (See note (5) below for an explanation of implicit cursor qualification.) This rule ensures that all BEFORE and/or AFTER clauses within a given integrity rule refer to [fields within] the same record, and hence that references to [fields within] that record in the predicate or violation-response are unambiguous.

3. If the FROM clause "FROM structure-name" or "FROM structure-name.element-name" is specified within a before-change, the structure designated by "structure-name" is assumed to have the same internal structuring and naming as the record designated by the record-name, or record-name portion of the parameter, immediately preceding that FROM clause. This rule allows us to refer to fields of the FROM structure within the predicate and/or violation-response.

4. If multiple FROM clauses are specified within a given trigger-condition-commalist, then (a) all such FROM clauses must include a structure-name, either in isolation or as the explicit qualifier of an element-name, and (b) those structure-names must all be the same. If an element-name within a FROM clause is explicitly qualified by a structure-name, then that element-name must be identical to the field-name in the field-parameter immediately preceding that FROM clause. These rules ensure that all BEFORE clauses within a given integrity rule refer to [fields within] the same FROM structure, and hence that references to [fields within] that structure in the predicate or violation-response are unambiguous.

5. A cursor in UDL is an object whose value is (normally) the address of some specific record in the database. The cursor is said to *point to* the record concerned.

```
SIR1  : S.STATUS > 0 ;

PIR2  : P.CITY = 'LONDON'  OR
        P.CITY = 'PARIS'   OR
        P.CITY = 'ROME' ;

SPIR3 : SP.QTYSHIP ¬> SP.QTYORD ;
        /* assuming additional fields - "quantity shipped" */
        /* and "quantity ordered" - in relation SP          */

SPIR4 : BEFORE DELETING SP :
                SP.QTY = 0 ;

SPIR5 : BEFORE UPDATING S.STATUS FROM NEW_STATUS :
        NEW_STATUS > S.STATUS ;

SPIR6 : AFTER INSERTING SP,
        AFTER UPDATING  SP.S# :
          EXISTS (S WHERE S.S# = SP.S#) ;
SIR6  : BEFORE DELETING S,
        BEFORE UPDATING S.S# :
        ¬ EXISTS (SP WHERE SP.S# = S.S#) ;

EIR7X : AFTER INSERTING E1->EMPLOYEE,
        AFTER UPDATING  E1->EMPLOYEE.MGR# :
          EXISTS (E2->EMPLOYEE WHERE
                    E2->EMPLOYEE.EMP# = E1->EMPLOYEE.MGR#) ;
EIR7Y : BEFORE DELETING E2->EMPLOYEE,
        BEFORE UPDATING E2->EMPLOYEE.EMP# :
        ¬ EXISTS (E1->EMPLOYEE WHERE E1 ¬= E2 AND
                    E1->EMPLOYEE.MGR# = E2->EMPLOYEE.EMP#) ;

SPIR8IU : AFTER INSERTING SPC1->SP,
          AFTER UPDATING  SPC1->SP.QTY :
            SPC1->SP.QTY <= 1.05 * SETAVG (SPC2->SP.QTY) ;
SPIR8D  : AFTER DELETING SPC1->SP :
            ¬ EXISTS (SPC3->SP WHERE SPC3->SP.QTY >
                            1.05 * SETAVG (SPC2->SP.QTY)) ;

SIR9 : BEFORE INSERTING S     FROM NEW_S,
       BEFORE UPDATING  S.S# FROM NEW_S.S# :
       ¬ EXISTS (S WHERE S.S# = NEW_S.S#)
         AND ¬ IS_NULL (NEW_S.S#) ;

SIR10 : AFTER INSERTING SC1->S,
        AFTER UPDATING  SC1->S.SNAME :
        ¬ EXISTS (SC2->S WHERE SC2->S.SNAME  = SC1->S.SNAME
                      AND    SC2->S.S#    ¬= SC1->S.S#) ;

IR11 : BEFORE INSERTING SJT FROM NEW_SJT,
       BEFORE UPDATING  SJT FROM NEW_SJT :
       ¬ EXISTS (SJT WHERE
                    SJT.T  = NEW_SJT.T AND
                    SJT.J ¬= NEW_SJT.J) ;

IR12 : WHEN COMMITTING :
       SETSUM (ACCOUNT.BALANCE) =
                    UNIQUE (SUMMARY.TOTAL) ;
```

Fig. 2.6 Relation integrity rules (examples).

```
relation-integrity-rule
   ::= label : [ trigger-condition-commalist : ]
                 constraint
                 [ ; | ELSE violation-response ]
trigger-condition
   ::= WHEN COMMITTING
       | BEFORE before-change
       | AFTER  after-change
before-change
   ::= INSERTING record-name [ FROM structure-name ]
       | UPDATING record-parameter [ FROM structure-name ]
       | UPDATING field-parameter
                   [ FROM [ structure-name . ] element-name ]
       | DELETING record-parameter
after-change
   ::= INSERTING record-parameter
       | UPDATING record-parameter
       | UPDATING field-parameter
       | DELETING record-parameter
record-parameter
   ::= [ cursor-name -> ] record-name
field-parameter
   ::= [ cursor-name -> ] record-name . field-name
constraint
   ::= predicate
violation-response
   ::= executable-unit
```

Fig. 2.7 Relation integrity rule syntax.

The expression "C→R" refers to the specific instance of record-type R that cursor C is currently pointing to; similarly, the expression "C→R.F" refers to the specific instance of field-type F within that specific record. Each cursor is constrained to point to records of one particular record-type. Each record-type has exactly one *default* cursor (named in the declaration of that record-type). If "cursor-name→" is omitted from a record-parameter or field-parameter, the default cursor for the record-type designated by the record-name is assumed. (See [1.7] or Volume I for more details of cursors and cursor-qualification in UDL. Note: Cursors used in the expression of integrity rules are *system* cursors [cursors defined by the DBMS], and are independent of any cursors defined in user programs.)

6. The constraint can include parameter references, that is, cursor-qualified references (to a record and/or to fields within that record) in which the qualifying cursor is that nominated in the (explicit or implicit) trigger-condition-commalist. It can also include references to the FROM variable (either the designated element variable, or elements within the designated structure variable), if a FROM clause is specified. It can also include bound records and fields (see Examples 2.4.6–2.4.12). It cannot include any other variable references.

7. The trigger-condition-commalist can be omitted if and only if the constraint includes at least one cursor-qualified reference. Assuming that the constraint does include one or more such references, let C be the qualifying cursor in those references,
and let the corresponding record-type be R. (C is well-defined by virtue of note (2),
and R is well-defined by virtue of note (5).) Then the following trigger-condition-
commalist is assumed if none is explicitly specified:

```
AFTER INSERTING C->R,
AFTER UPDATING  C->R :
```

8. The integrity rule

```
L : BEFORE change : predicate ELSE response
```

is logically equivalent to the sequence of statements

```
L : PROC ;
        IF change is about to be executed
        THEN IF ¬ ( predicate )
             THEN execute response ;
    END ;
```

If *response* is executed and includes the operation REJECT, then *change* is not executed; otherwise *change* is executed on return from application of the rule. In either
case, references to C→R and C→R.F within *predicate* and *response* (where C is the
qualifying cursor in the BEFORE clause) are interpreted on the basis that *change* has
not (yet) occurred.

9. The integrity rule

```
L : AFTER change : predicate ELSE response
```

is logically equivalent to the sequence of statements

```
L : PROC ;
        execute change ;
        IF ¬ ( predicate )
        THEN execute response ;
    END ;
```

If *response* is executed and includes the operation REJECT, then *change* is undone
at that point. References to C→R and C→R.F within *predicate* and *response* (where
C is the qualifying cursor in the AFTER clause) are interpreted as follows: Prior to
the execution of REJECT, *change* has occurred; after the execution of REJECT,
change has been undone (the effect is as if it was never done in the first place).

Aside: The explanation just given should not be construed as implying that, in the
case of AFTER, the implementation always has to perform the change before checking the constraint, and then has to undo it again if the constraint is violated. It will

obviously be possible in some cases (not all) to detect the violation without making the change in the first place. The key phrase is *"logically* equivalent."

10. An integrity rule containing multiple BEFORE clauses and/or AFTER clauses is a shorthand for a corresponding set of distinct rules containing one BEFORE clause or AFTER clause each.

11. For an explanation of WHEN COMMITTING, see the discussion of Example 12, later.

12. Relation integrity rules can involve more than one relation (by contrast, domain integrity rules always involve exactly one domain). For this reason, relation rules are generally specified in a separate statement of their own, rather than as a part of some relation definition.

Examples

We now discuss the examples of Fig. 2.6 in detail. For the purposes of these examples, we assume that SC, SC1, SC2, . . . are cursors for relation S; PC, PC1, PC2, . . . are cursors for relation P; and SPC, SPC1, SPC2, . . . are cursors for relation SP. We also assume that the *default* cursors are SC, PC, and SPC, respectively.

2.4.1 For the first example, we assume once again that we wish to constrain values of S.STATUS to be greater than zero, and we assume also for the sake of the example that such a constraint is *not* specified in the definition of the STATUS domain. Then we can specify

```
    SIR1 : S.STATUS > 0 ;
```

(trigger conditions and violation response both omitted). This rule is interpreted as follows. First, let use make the default cursor explicit:

```
    SIR1 : SC->S.STATUS > 0 ;
```

Now let us make the trigger conditions explicit:

```
    SIR1 : AFTER INSERTING SC->S,
           AFTER UPDATING  SC->S :
           SC->S.STATUS > 0 ;
```

Now it can be clearly seen that the expression S.STATUS in the constraint is a reference to the value of the field *after* the record has been inserted or updated. Note that *deletion* of an S record cannot possibly cause the constraint to be violated (nor can update of any other field of S apart from STATUS; the implementation should recognize that it need not check the rule on update of any other field).

Last, omitting the violation response is equivalent to specifying "reject the operation with a return code," as with domain integrity rules (but see the discussion of EXCEPTIONS below). Thus the complete expansion of SIR1 is

```
SIR1 : AFTER INSERTING SC->S,
       AFTER UPDATING   SC->S :
       SC->S.STATUS > 0
       ELSE
          DO ;
              set return code to "rule SIR1 violated" ;
              REJECT ;
          END ;
```

We remark that one reason for stating the trigger conditions explicitly is that different conditions for the same constraint might require different violation responses. For example,

```
SIR1U : AFTER UPDATING S.STATUS :
        S.STATUS > 0
        ELSE
           DO ;
               set return code to "rule SIR1U violated" ;
               REJECT ;
           END ;
SIR1I : AFTER INSERTING S :
        S.STATUS > 0
        ELSE
           DO ;
               change S.STATUS to 1 ;
               set return code to
               "STATUS invalid, set to one" ;
           END ;
```

It is possible that a single update may cause several distinct integrity violations. Simply rejecting the update with a return code is inadequate in such a case. We therefore propose the following mechanism for handling a varying number of return codes. Let EXCEPTIONS be a varying-length character string that is implicitly set to "empty" at the start of each database operation. We assume that the violation response part of an integrity rule is allowed to append a value to EXCEPTIONS. Thus, for example, the violation response of rule SIR1U might be

```
DO ;
   APPEND code meaning "rule SIR1U violated" to EXCEPTIONS ;
   APPEND separator ";" to EXCEPTIONS ;
   REJECT ;
END ;
```

If several distinct errors occur, and if all integrity rules are coded as suggested above, then after each operation EXCEPTIONS will contain a sequence of error codes, one for each error, separated by semicolons. Note the implication that RE-JECT should not take effect until after all applicable rules have been checked.

2.4.2 Suppose that part cities are limited to London, Paris, and Rome (a proper subset of the values in the LOCATION domain):

```
PIR2 : P.CITY = 'LONDON' OR
       P.CITY = 'PARIS'  OR
       P.CITY = 'ROME' ;
```

Or equivalently,

```
PIR2 : P.CITY IN ('LONDON','PARIS','ROME') ;
```

As an exercise, the reader might like to expand PIR2 into its complete form, with all defaults supplied.

2.4.3 For the sake of this example, assume that SP records include two additional fields, QTYORD (quantity ordered) and QTYSHIP (quantity shipped to date). Within any given SP record, QTYSHIP must not exceed QTYORD.

```
SPIR3 : SP.QTYSHIP ¬> SP.QTYORD ;
```

What are the (minimum) trigger conditions here?

2.4.4 Shipment records may be deleted only if the QTY value is currently zero.

```
SPIR4 : BEFORE DELETING SP :
            SP.QTY = 0 ;
```

2.4.5 When a STATUS value is updated, the new value must be greater than the old.

```
SIR5 : BEFORE UPDATING S.STATUS FROM NEW_STATUS :
       NEW_STATUS > S.STATUS ;
```

This example is an instance of a *transition* constraint—that is, a constraint that involves a comparison of the before and after states of the database (conceptually). By contrast, all other rules shown so far have been *state* constraints—that is, they have been concerned purely with the question of whether a given database state is valid, independent of all other states.

2.4.6 Any S# value appearing in relation SP must also appear in relation S, to reflect the fact that only a supplier that actually exists is allowed to supply parts.

```
SPIR6 : AFTER  INSERTING  SP,
        AFTER UPDATING   SP.S# :
            EXISTS (S WHERE S.S# = SP.S#) ;
SIR6  : BEFORE DELETING S,
        BEFORE UPDATING S.S# :
            ¬ EXISTS (SP WHERE SP.S# = S.S#) ;
```

This example is an instance of a *set* constraint—that is, a constraint that involves an entire set of records instead of just the particular record being operated on. (Previous examples have been of *record* (or *tuple*) constraints—that is, constraints that can be evaluated by examining just the particular record in question.) Observe that we need two rules to express the overall situation. The first states that insertion of a new shipment or update of an existing shipment supplier number is permitted only if the new shipment supplier number already exists in relation S. The second states that deletion of an existing supplier or update of the supplier number of an existing supplier is permitted only if that supplier currently has no shipments.

Alternatively, we may wish to replace the second rule by rules stating that operations on S are to "cascade" to the corresponding shipments (if there are any):

```
SIR6D : BEFORE DELETING S :
          ¬ EXISTS (SP WHERE SP.S# = S.S#)
          ELSE DELETE ALL SP WHERE SP.S# = S.S# ;
SIR6U : BEFORE UPDATING S.S# FROM NEW_S# :
          ¬ EXISTS (SP WHERE SP.S# = S.S#)
          ELSE UPDATE ALL SP.S# FROM NEW_S# WHERE SP.S# = S.S# ;
```

(Note that the DELETE and UPDATE in rules SIR6D and SIR6U are set-level operations. We have included the noiseword ALL to emphasize this point.) In these two rules, however, the specification of the constraint (¬EXISTS . . .) is actually superfluous. In fact, we are beginning to move away from the realm of integrity rules as such and into the realm of *triggered procedures*. (It would be more accurate to say that integrity rules are an important special case of triggered procedures.) We shall have more to say on this topic in Section 2.6.

We consider rule SPIR6 again in a little more detail, since it is the first illustration of the use of bound records and bound fields. If we make all default cursors explicit, rule SPIR6 becomes

```
SPIR6 : AFTER INSERTING SPC->SP,
        AFTER UPDATING  SPC->SP.S# :
        EXISTS (SC->S WHERE SC->S.S# = SPC->SP.S#);
```

Within the argument to the EXISTS function reference, cursor SPC is playing its usual role: SPC→SP.S# is a normal cursor-qualified field reference, identifying the S# field within the SP record that cursor SPC currently happens to be pointing to (that is, the SP record just inserted or updated). Cursor SC, however, is not playing its usual role but is acting as a *bound cursor* (and SC→S is a *bound record* and SC→S.S# is a *bound field;* bound records and fields are the UDL equivalents of the tuple variables and domain variables of the relational calculus). Conceptually, cursor SC is being used to run through the entire set of S records, one by one, in the evaluation of the EXISTS argument. For further discussion of the bound cursor notation, see reference [1.7]. Several of our subsequent examples will make use of it, though the cursors themselves will often be implicit (as in the original version of SPIR6).

Rules SIR6D and SIR6U (the "cascading" rules) raise another interesting point. Since the violation response in each of these rules involves making further changes to the database, it is conceivable that another integrity rule will need to be checked during processing of those further changes.[5] It is even possible that the violation response for a given rule R could directly or indirectly invoke rule R again. The implementation must therefore be prepared to handle nested and possibly recursive invocation of certain integrity rules (perhaps appropriately designated). We note in passing that it is also desirable for integrity rules to be reentrant, in order that they may be used concurrently on behalf of multiple transactions in a multiuser system.

Our final point on Example 2.4.6 concerns *usability*. The constraints in this example are typical of a common and very important requirement: namely, the requirement to specify that each record in a given relation *references* (perhaps *is existence-dependent on*) some other record elsewhere. Such a requirement is so common that, for usability reasons, it may well be desirable to introduce some syntactic shorthand to deal with it. Using a special syntax would also help the system to recognize this special class of constraint and thus perhaps to "special-case" its implementation. We do not discuss any such shorthand here; see Exercise 2.3 and reference [2.32] for some concrete proposals.

2.4.7 We leave suppliers and parts for a moment and consider the relation

```
EMPLOYEE (EMP#,...,MGR#,...)
```

where MGR# is the employee number of the manager of the employee identified by EMP# (within any given record). The rule we wish to express here is that every value of EMPLOYEE.MGR# must also appear somewhere as a value of EMPLOYEE.EMP#. This rule is similar to that of the previous example, except that the two relations involved are one and the same.

```
EIR7X : AFTER INSERTING E1->EMPLOYEE,
        AFTER UPDATING  E1->EMPLOYEE.MGR# :
          EXISTS (E2->EMPLOYEE WHERE
                E2->EMPLOYEE.EMP# = E1->EMPLOYEE.MGR#) ;
EIR7Y : BEFORE DELETING E2->EMPLOYEE,
        BEFORE UPDATING E2->EMPLOYEE.EMP# :
          ¬ EXISTS (E1->EMPLOYEE WHERE E1 ¬= E2 AND
                E1->EMPLOYEE.MGR# = E2->EMPLOYEE.EMP#) ;
```

This example illustrates very clearly the role of bound records and bound fields. (For clarity all qualifying cursors have been shown explicitly.) In rule EIR7X, for example, cursor E1 identifies the particular EMPLOYEE that has just been inserted or updated, cursor E2 ranges over the entire set of EMPLOYEEs (the set of EM-

---

5. In fact, as the reader may have noticed, the violation response for rule SIR6U will cause rule SPIR6 to be invoked (in general), and this latter rule will then cause the cascade update to be rejected! Rule SPIR6 will have to be replaced by a deferred rule (see Example 2.4.12) for the cascade in rule SIR6U to work.

PLOYEEs, that is, *after* the INSERT or UPDATE has been performed). Note that rule EIR7X implies that at least one employee must have himself or herself as manager. The condition E1 ¬ = E2 in rule EIR7Y is necessary to allow such an employee to be deleted.

2.4.8 Any QTY value appearing in relation SP must not be more than 5 percent greater than the average of all such values (an example of a "statistical" constraint). Note that INSERT, UPDATE, and DELETE can all affect the average value of QTY.

```
SPIR8IU : AFTER INSERTING SPC1->SP,
          AFTER UPDATING  SPC1->SP.QTY :
             SPC1->SP.QTY <= 1.05 * SETAVG (SPC2->SP.QTY) ;
SPIR8D  : AFTER DELETING SPC1->SP :
             ¬ EXISTS (SPC3->SP WHERE SPC3->SP.QTY >
                              1.05 * SETAVG (SPC2->SP.QTY)) ;
```

This example raises an interesting question of efficiency. In principle the two rules above could be condensed into the single rule

```
SPIR8 : ¬ EXISTS (SPC3->SP WHERE SPC3->SP.QTY >
                       1.05 * SETAVG (SPC2->SP.QTY)) ;
```

(simply stating, in other words, that at no time does there exist a shipment with QTY outside the limit). This constraint must be checked on all INSERTs and DELETEs on SP and all UPDATEs on SP.QTY. But in the case of INSERT and UPDATE it is sufficient to check just the tuple being inserted or updated; only for DELETE is it necessary to check every tuple in the relation (and notice that the checking must be done [conceptually] *after* the DELETE). This is an efficiency consideration that is made explicit in the first formulation above but is concealed in the second. (Of course, the implementation may still be able to *handle* the constraint efficiently, as is shown in reference [2.19].) Note also that the predicate in the second formulation does not include any parameter references—that is, it contains no references to cursor SPC1 (it does include bound records and fields). Our rule for generating a default trigger-condition-commalist (note 7 following Fig. 2.7) therefore needs some refinement.

We note in passing that it would probably be more efficient *not* to check this kind of rule on every update, but instead to run a periodic batch program (or query) that simply scans the data and reports on exceptions. Special action can be taken subsequently to remedy any errors found.

2.4.9 By definition the primary key of every relation in the database (a) has the property of uniqueness—no two tuples in the relation can have the same primary key value at the same time—and (b) cannot accept null values. Thus for relation S we could specify, for example,

```
SIR9 : BEFORE INSERTING S    FROM NEW_S,
       BEFORE UPDATING  S.S# FROM NEW_S.S# :
          ¬ EXISTS (S WHERE S.S# = NEW_S.S#)
           AND ¬ IS_NULL (NEW_S.S#) ;
```

But this formulation is intolerably clumsy, especially for such an important and common case. We therefore choose to "special-case" primary key constraints, specifying them by means of a PRIMARY KEY clause in the definition of the relation concerned (see Fig. 2.5 for an example).

2.4.10 For similar reasons, the fact that SNAME is an alternate key for S, which (if we rely on the fact that we already know that S# is the primary key) *could* be specified as

```
SIR10 : AFTER INSERTING SC1->S,
        AFTER UPDATING  SC1->S.SNAME :
        ר EXISTS (SC2->S WHERE SC2->S.SNAME = SC1->S.SNAME
                         AND   SC2->S.S#   ר= SC1->S.S#) ;
```

is much better specified as

```
ALTERNATE KEY (SNAME)
```

in the definition of S.

2.4.11 If a relation involves any additional functional dependencies (FDs) over and above those that are a consequence of its keys, then those FDs should be specified explicitly. For example, in Volume I we gave an example of a relation called SJT (student-subject-teacher), with primary key the combination student/subject (S,J) and with the additional FD "teacher determines subject." This additional FD can be expressed as

```
IR11 : BEFORE INSERTING SJT FROM NEW_SJT,
       BEFORE UPDATING  SJT FROM NEW_SJT :
       ר EXISTS (SJT WHERE
                      SJT.T  = NEW_SJT.T AND
                      SJT.J ר= NEW_SJT.J) ;
```

Again an argument might be made for special-casing; though if the normalization discipline of (at least) Boyce/Codd Normal Form is used in the design of the database, then the need to be able to define such additional FDs is likely to be rare in practice.

2.4.12 Our last example illustrates the concept of the *deferred* integrity rule. All rules so far have been *immediate,* in that they are applied immediately the INSERT, UPDATE, or DELETE is executed. However, some constraints—specifically, certain of those classified as "consistency" constraints in Section 2.1—cannot by their nature be satisfied at all times. As an example, suppose that the database includes (a) a set of ACCOUNT records, each containing a BALANCE field, and (b) a single SUMMARY record, containing a TOTAL field whose value is supposed to be equal to the total of all the BALANCE fields:

```
IR12 : ... :
       SETSUM (ACCOUNT.BALANCE) = UNIQUE (SUMMARY.TOTAL) ;
```

Now consider the TRANSFER transaction from Chapter 1, which transfers a dollar amount from one account to another and thus updates two separate balances. Clearly, if the constraint above (IR12) is satisfied before TRANSFER is executed, then it will still be satisfied afterward; but during the transaction the constraint is inevitably (but of course temporarily) violated. Since we do not want rule IR12 to be invoked after the first update and before the second, the trigger condition must not be any of the AFTER or BEFORE formats. Instead, what we need is the alternative format WHEN COMMITTING, meaning that the constraint is to be checked at the end of the transaction.

A deferred integrity rule, then, is an integrity rule for which the trigger condition is specified as WHEN COMMITTING. Such rules have no explicit parameters. They are applied as part of commit processing for any transaction that changes any variable that could affect the evaluation of the constraint. The default violation response (and the interpretation of REJECT, if specified for this type of rule) is to roll back the offending transaction.

As an aside, we remark that this example assumes that maintaining the TOTAL field is a user responsibility (that is, a credit or debit transaction, or any other user transaction that updates balances so that the overall total is altered, must update TOTAL appropriately too). It would alternatively be possible to get the system to maintain the TOTAL field, using a triggered procedure (Section 2.6). There are two points to be made if this second approach is used. First, there will now be no need for integrity rule IR12 at all—or, rather, the rule can be *replaced* by the specification of the triggered procedure—because that rule can no longer possibly be violated. Second, there is a performance penalty: If the system adjusts TOTAL every time some transaction changes a balance, then it may execute many unnecessary updates (consider TRANSFER, for example, where there is actually no need to update TOTAL at all). On the other hand, the penalty may be worse if TOTAL is maintained by the user and checked by the system at COMMIT—the check could cause the retrieval of every single balance in the database, instead of just those that have been changed by the transaction in question.

This completes our list of examples. We have introduced the notions of record and set constraints, state and transition constraints, and immediate and deferred constraints. All combinations are possible, though as we shall see in the next subsection they are not all equally useful. We note in particular that our syntax does not permit the expression of the combination "transition + deferred." Examples of deferred transition constraints might be: (1) No transaction may increase the TOTAL field by more than 1000 (a record constraint); (2) no transaction may change the average QTY value by more than 25 percent (a set constraint). The point is that these constraints may be violated during a transaction but must be satisfied by the time the transaction COMMITs. Expression of such constraints requires the ability to reference the values of records and fields as they were prior to execution of the terminating transaction, which in turn implies that the constraint checking mechanism may need access to the log. We feel that this case requires additional investigation.

One form of constraint we have not mentioned at all is *nonupdatability:* It might be considered desirable to specify that field S.S# (for example) is not updatable at all. Our position on this point is that *every* field may require updating at some time, if only to correct some human error, and that control over the updating of critical fields is best exercised through judicious use of the security subsystem, rather than through the integrity subsystem. See Chapter 4.

We conclude this subsection with a description of PRIMARY domains, as promised in Section 2.3. Recall that domains S# and P# were designated as primary in our example. Primary domains have to do with what in Volume I we called *referential integrity* (an integral part of the relational model as defined in that volume). The basic idea of referential integrity is that if one relation includes references to another, as relation SP (for example) includes references to relation S and relation P, then all targets for those references must exist (every shipment must refer to an existing supplier and an existing part). More formally:

■ Let D be a primary domain. (Note that the designation of a domain as primary is optional.) Then:

    a) There must exist at least one relation R in the database having a primary key defined on D.

    b) Let R1 be a relation with an attribute A, not necessarily the primary key of R1, defined on D. Then, at any given time, each value of R1.A must be *either* null *or* equal to k, say, where k is the primary key value of some tuple in some relation R2 with primary key defined on D. R1 and R2 are not necessarily distinct.

Attribute R1.A is an example of a *foreign key*. We note that (b) above is trivially satisfied if A is the primary key of R1.

Now, for the suppliers-and-parts database, the rules given earlier in Example 2.4.6 (either the cascading or the noncascading version), plus analogous rules for relation P and foreign key SP.P#, guarantee that the referential integrity rule will be satisfied; in fact, they are *stronger* (more specific) than the referential integrity rule. In a sense, specification of a given domain D as primary is merely an indication that more explicit relation integrity rules must be specified for each relation having a foreign key defined on D.

The concept of referential integrity is discussed in depth in reference [2.32]. See also Exercise 2.3.

Some Comments

We offer a few comments concerning the different classes of constraint and the problems of their implementation. We remark in passing that one general approach to implementation is to interrogate the integrity rules at compile time and thus to incorporate suitable checks directly into the application object code itself [2.9, 2.10, 2.19], instead of providing a distinct system component to do the checking at run-time.

1. Immediate record state constraints (e.g., Example 2.4.1)

These constraints involve no additional access to the database, only additional CPU activity at the time the record is changed (ignoring the question of finding the integrity rules in the first place). Such constraints are therefore straightforward and cheap to implement, and should generally be supported.

2. Immediate record transition constraints (e.g., Example 2.4.5)

These constraints also involve no additional database access (unless the transaction intends simply to replace the entire record without retrieving it first, which is un-likely and in any case impossible in many systems). The remarks under (1) above therefore apply here also.

3. Immediate set state constraints

This class includes some rather important cases, including key uniqueness (Examples 2.4.9 and 2.4.10), referential integrity (Examples 2.4.6 and 2.4.7), additional func-tional dependencies (Example 2.4.11), and certain "statistical" constraints (Exam-ple 2.4.8). Key uniqueness is crucial and can be supported with an index or a hash. Referential integrity is also extremely important—probably one of the most impor-tant constraints of all—and should definitely be supported (ideally in both cascading and noncascading versions); a double index or a stored fanset structure (for exam-ple, the child/twin pointer structure of IMS) can be used to provide this support (see Exercise 2.4). Additional functional dependencies and statistical constraints are much less significant; they can be supported without any special implementation structures if necessary (it might be possible to support certain statistical constraints by having the system maintain hidden fields representing, for example, the sum and cardinality of a given set). There is a good argument for insisting in these last two cases that the constraints be deferred rather than immediate.

4. Immediate set transition constraints

We conjecture that any "immediate set transition" constraint can always be refor-mulated as some simpler type of constraint (since the only possible "immediate" operation that can change the set is basically an INSERT or DELETE or UPDATE on a single record). For example, the "immediate set transition" constraint that the new average value (in some given set) must be greater than the old average value after an INSERT operation is equivalent to the "immediate set state" constraint that the inserted value must be greater than the old average value before that IN-SERT operation. We do not consider this case any further.

5. Deferred record state constraints

Any record state constraint that is to apply at COMMIT must also have applied at the time of the last update to the record. DEFERRED therefore has little meaning for a record state constraint (though forcing all such constraints to be IMMEDIATE could conceivably have minor repercussions on the way transactions are programmed). In any case deferred checking for a record state constraint is bound to be expensive, because the record in question has to be accessed twice (once for the update and once for the check); for a simple transaction this fact could double the amount of I/O and thereby double the execution time. And note too that the implementation would have to remember which records the transaction has updated, or the constraint will effectively have to be treated as a set constraint.

6. Deferred record transition constraints

As suggested earlier, this type of constraint could be expensive to implement, in that it could involve searching the log for the old value of the changed record.

7. Deferred set state constraints (e.g., Example 2.4.12)

This class is potentially important. See the remarks under (3) above.

8. Deferred set transition constraints

This class would be *very* expensive to implement, since it conceptually requires access to the entire set as it was prior to the transaction (may need assistance from the log) and to the entire set afterward. It is also difficult to think of a practical application.

In conclusion, cases (1), (2), (3) (especially keys and referential integrity), and (7) seem to be the important ones. (Not surprisingly, these are also the ones that were illustrated in our original set of twelve examples.) But we would not claim that this observation is anything more than a starting point for a more searching investigation.

2.5 FANSET INTEGRITY CONSTRAINTS

In a network database the *fanset* construct plays a role in maintaining integrity[6] (in addition to various other roles, such as providing certain preferred access paths). In this section we examine the integrity aspects of the fanset construct. Figure 2.8 shows a network version of the suppliers-and-parts database, with the usual three record-types (S, P, and SP) and with two fansets, S_SP and P_SP. Fanset S_SP has parent S and child SP, fanset P_SP has parent P and child SP. Observe that rec-

---

6. This practice of building integrity constraints into the data structure itself is criticized in Volume I.

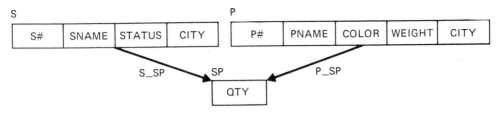

Fig. 2.8 Suppliers and parts as a network database.

ord-type SP does not contain an S# field or a P# field, and that the two fansets are therefore *essential*. (A fanset is *essential* if it carries information that would be lost if the fanset were eliminated. If each SP child record were to include the S# and P# values corresponding to its parent S and P records, then fansets S_SP and P_SP would be *inessential,* and could be eliminated without any loss of information. See Volume I for a thorough discussion of essentiality.)

The major application of fansets in the area of integrity is in the provision of (various flavors of) *referential* integrity. In terms of suppliers and parts, the basic referential constraint we would like to enforce is, of course, that no SP record be allowed to exist in the database without being connected to a corresponding S record (and corresponding P record; for brevity we concentrate on suppliers and ignore parts). Informally, the operations of interest are as follows (using a simplified form of UDL):

- INSERT SP
- DELETE S
- UPDATE S.S#
- CONNECT SP UNDER S [VIA S_SP]
- DISCONNECT SP FROM S [VIA S_SP]
- RECONNECT SP UNDER S [VIA S_SP]

The question of updating an "SP.S#" field does not arise: RECONNECT is the fanset analog of this operation (assuming both old and new values of "SP.S#" to be nonnull). By the same token, the reader may find it helpful to regard CONNECT as the analog of an update that changes SP.S# from a null value to some nonnull value, and DISCONNECT as the analog of the converse operation. We now discuss each operation in turn.

Aside: The VIA options can all be omitted for the suppliers-and-parts database, since there is only one fanset with parent S and child SP. As a reminder, however, we will often show such an option, but will always enclose it in square brackets as shown.

■   INSERT SP

A more complete version of this statement is

        INSERT SP [CONNECT UNDER SC->S [VIA S_SP]] ;

The CONNECT option could be omitted if it were possible to insert an SP record and not have it connected to any S record at the time of the insertion. But this is *not* possible, given the required constraint. Effectively, therefore, the rule we need for INSERT is that the CONNECT option cannot be omitted; the normal run-time checking on the expression "UNDER SC→S" will then ensure that an SP record will be inserted only if its parent-to-be already exists. Note, however, that checking for the presence of the CONNECT option could be done at *compile-time,* if the constraint is expressed as a compile-time declaration. In both UDL and DBTG, specification of an "insertion class" of AUTOMATIC within the definition of fanset S_SP constitutes such a declaration. (The term AUTOMATIC is hardly self-explanatory, incidentally; an explicit statement along the lines of "CONNECT required on IN-SERT" would seem preferable. Similar remarks apply to the subsequent cases also.)

■   DELETE S

The statement is really

        DELETE SC->S ;

If we require the DELETE to cascade, we could in principle write a rule (more accurately, a triggered procedure) as follows:

        FSDC : BEFORE DELETING SC->S :
                DELETE ALL SP UNDER SC->S [VIA S_SP] ;

    In UDL and DBTG the same effect is achieved by means of the "retention class" declaration FIXED in the definition of fanset S_SP. FIXED may be regarded simply as a shorthand for rule FSDC (in this case).

    If, on the other hand, we require the DELETE to fail if any dependent SP records exist, we could (again in principle) specify

        FSDF : BEFORE DELETING SC->S :
                ¬ EXISTS (SP UNDER SC->S) ;

This case is handled in UDL and DBTG by the retention class declaration MANDA-TORY, which may similarly be seen as a syntactic shorthand for the rule FSDF.

    (Note that although FIXED and MANDATORY are both compile-time declarations, the cascade or checking activity they cause is of course still a run-time operation.)

    The third possibility would be

        FSDD : BEFORE DELETING SC->S :
                DISCONNECT ALL SP UNDER SC->S [VIA S_SP] ;

(corresponding to retention class OPTIONAL in UDL and DBTG). In our particular example, of course, this case would not be permitted, since it would violate the required constraint.

■   UPDATE S.S#

This update effectively cascades without any additional specifications at all (since the SP records for the supplier in question do not contain an S# field, and remain connected to the supplier record after the update).

■   CONNECT SP UNDER S [VIA S_SP]

This operation is invalid, since it assumes that the SP record to be connected (a) already exists but (b) is not connected to an S record, contrary to the required constraint. The combinations AUTOMATIC MANDATORY and AUTOMATIC FIXED both cover this case (both imply that (a) CONNECT is not allowed as a stand-alone operation but that (b) the CONNECT option on INSERT is required). MANUAL insertion class and OPTIONAL retention class would both be invalid, since they would both permit CONNECT as a stand-alone operation.

■   DISCONNECT SP FROM S [VIA S_SP]

This operation is also invalid, since its whole point is to break the connection between the SP record and its corresponding S record without simultaneously deleting that SP record. Either MANDATORY or FIXED will cover this case, since each prohibits DISCONNECT operations.

■   RECONNECT SP UNDER S [VIA S_SP]

A more complete form of the statement is

        RECONNECT SPC->SP UNDER SC->S [VIA S_SP] ;

The definition of RECONNECT requires that the SP record already be connected to some S record and that the new target S record (SC→S) already exist; thus the normal run-time checking will ensure that the required constraint is not violated. No compile-time specifications are required or relevant.

To summarize, the fanset version of this example has one advantage over its relational equivalent, namely, the fact that updating S.S# effectively cascades "for free" (that is, without any additional specifications of any kind). Inserting an SP record and deleting an S record involve run-time checks in both versions; reconnecting an SP record also requires run-time checking, as does its relational analog, updating SP.S#. Note, however, that all three of the network operations require additional language constructs here—inserting an SP record requires the CONNECT option, deleting an S record requires the UNDER option in the DML or else additional declarative features (FIXED, MANDATORY), and reconnecting an SP record of course requires the RECONNECT statement itself. CONNECT and DISCONNECT operations are invalid and violations could theoretically be detected at compile time (the additional declarative features—AUTOMATIC MANDATORY or AUTOMATIC FIXED—make this a possibility); the relational version does not have distinct statements corresponding to these operations.

In conclusion, we repeat that the discussions of this section have been solely in terms of *essential* fansets. Some remarks on inessential fansets appear at the end of Section 2.7.

2.6 TRIGGERED PROCEDURES

As already indicated, integrity rules may be considered an important special case of *triggered procedures.* Simplifying matters somewhat (ignoring defaults and the like), the specification of a triggered procedure will take the general form

```
[ label : ] trigger-commalist : executable-unit
```

where "trigger" is

```
WHEN event | AFTER event | BEFORE event
```

(PL/I ON-units provide a simple example, with ON replacing WHEN). If the event occurs (WHEN or AFTER) or is about to occur (BEFORE), the executable-unit is executed. As an example, we give a simplified version of Rule SIR6D from Section 2.4 (Example 2.4.6):

```
TP1 : BEFORE DELETING S :
        DELETE ALL SP WHERE SP.S# = S.S# ;
```

TP1 is intended to preserve the integrity of the database in the light of a deletion against relation S by "cascade-deleting" all shipments corresponding to the S record in question. The BEFORE format can obviously be used only for events that can be detected before they actually occur, not for "out of the blue" events like an external interrupt. The execution of a statement that is issued by a program clearly does fall into the class of events for which BEFORE makes sense.

Triggered procedures cannot be "transparent to the user," in general. Taking TP1 as an example, the user is probably required to know that deleting a supplier will cause all shipments for that supplier to be deleted too as a side effect. The point is, however, that the triggered procedure *can* be transparent to a user who is unaware of the existence of relation SP. If, for example, the database initially contained only relation S and not relation SP, it would be possible to add relation SP subsequently, together with the cascade delete rule (TP1), without affecting existing users who had no knowledge of SP. But users who did know about both S and SP would typically also have to know about TP1.

As another example, consider a triggered procedure that is responsible for maintaining a field called #EMPS (number of employees) within the DEPARTMENT record. (Compare the discussion following Example 2.4.12 of the possibility of having the system maintain the TOTAL field in the SUMMARY record.) Users may be allowed to see this field but they must understand that it is maintained automatically and that they cannot directly update it. The security subsystem may be able to prevent users from updating the field but it cannot conceal the fact that it is being updated by the DBMS.

Triggered procedures do have application in areas other than integrity. Consider the definition of a virtual relation or *view* (see Volume I). Taking System R as a concrete example, the DEFINE VIEW statement could be seen as defining a triggered procedure to be invoked when a SELECT statement is executed against the view in question, in order to materialize that view. (In System R the "triggered procedure" is incorporated into the expansion of the SELECT statement itself.) We can extend this idea to handle the *updating* of views. Recall that it is not possible to build into the DBMS completely general rules for updating an arbitrary view; only if the view is a simple row-and-column subset of a single underlying relation is the effect of INSERT/UPDATE/DELETE well defined in every case. But what *is* conceivable is to allow such operations against any specific view V (say a join of relations R1 and R2) provided there exist triggered procedures to handle them; for example,

```
TP2 : WHEN INSERTING V :
      DO ;
          make desired changes to R1 and/or R2 ;
          rematerialize V if necessary ;
      END ;
```

and similarly for UPDATE and DELETE. References [2.25–2.29] consider this problem in some depth.

Other application areas for triggered procedures include the following:

- Virtual fields (computing fields such as #EMPS on demand, instead of maintaining an actual field in the database);

- Security (enforcing authorization constraints or performing data encryption and decryption);

- Performance measurement (monitoring or tracing various database-related events, or system events in general);

- Program debugging (monitoring references to and state changes in designated database variables, or other variables);

- Controlling stored record formats (for example, compressing and decompressing data on all storage and retrieval operations);

- Exception reporting (for example, "warn me if the quantity in stock of any item goes below the danger level");

and so on. It is not our intention here to investigate triggered procedures in detail. In any case little has been done to date on the implementation of such procedures. The closest that most existing systems come to them is in the provision of "exit routines"; IMS, for example, permits the DBA to supply an exit routine[7] to be invoked whenever a segment is inserted or updated (but not deleted). Typically, however, such routines operate under rather severe restrictions; in IMS, for example, they are not allowed to execute any DL/I operations, which means that they might be used to

---

7. IMS also provides certain additional "triggering" facilities; see Section 2.7.

implement integrity constraints at the segment (record) level but not at the set level (see Section 2.4). For further discussion of triggered procedures, see references [2.6–2.8] and [2.15]. In particular see [2.6] for consideration of the interactions between triggered procedures and other subsystems, especially the security subsystem.

2.7   SOME EXISTING SYSTEMS

We conclude this chapter with a brief survey of the integrity aspects (excluding concurrency considerations) of a number of specific languages and systems: SQL and System R, Query By Example, INGRES, IMS, and DBTG.

SQL and System R

System R offers rather little in the way of integrity in the sense of this chapter; the SQL language as defined in [2.8] includes a number of integrity features that were never implemented in System R. System R does provide (a) field data type checking; (b) enforcement of "nulls not allowed" for designated fields, via the optional NO-NULL specification for fields within CREATE TABLE; (c) enforcement of uniqueness for designated field combinations, via the optional creation of a "UNIQUE" index over the field combination concerned. All these aspects are discussed in Volume I. Features of the SQL language that were not implemented in System R include

- *assertions,* of the basic form

    ```
    ASSERT assertion-name ON table-name : predicate
    ```

    which would allow specification of all the constraints and trigger conditions in the Examples of Section 2.4, more or less (but violation responses cannot be specified); and

- *triggers* (our "triggered procedures"—though the trigger condition is restricted to SELECT, INSERT, UPDATE, or DELETE against a specified base table [not a view], instead of being totally general).

Assertions and triggers are created and destroyed via ASSERT, DEFINE TRIGGER, DROP ASSERTION, and DROP TRIGGER statements (all executable). An ENFORCE INTEGRITY statement [2.7] allows the user to force the evaluation of deferred constraints without having to issue COMMIT or END TRANSACTION.

We give SQL assertions corresponding to Examples 2.4.1 through 2.4.12. In interpreting these examples, we assume that "tuple variables" appearing before the colon (represented by table names or by introduced names such as EMPX in Example 7 below) are considered to be universally quantified within the predicate appearing after the colon. (References [2.7, 2.8] do not fully explain how assertions are to be interpreted.)

```
1. ASSERT SQL1 ON S : STATUS > 0
2. ASSERT SQL2 ON P : CITY IN ('LONDON','PARIS','ROME')
3. ASSERT SQL3 ON SP : QTYSHIP <= QTYORD
4. ASSERT SQL4 ON DELETION OF SP : QTY = 0
```

Note the specification "DELETION OF" in this example. If such a specification is not included (as in the first three examples), the system is presumably intended to decide for itself exactly when to check the assertion.

```
5. ASSERT SQL5 ON UPDATE OF S (STATUS) :
                          NEW STATUS > OLD STATUS
6. ASSERT SQL6 ON SP : SP.S# IN (SELECT S# FROM S)
```

Although this assertion is "ON SP," it has implications for operations on S as well. A formulation that is symmetric in S and SP would omit the ON clause:

```
ASSERT SQL6X : NOT EXISTS (SELECT * FROM SP WHERE
                    NOT EXISTS (SELECT * FROM S WHERE
                                        S.S# = SP.S#))
```

Comments similar to those under Example 4 above apply here also.

```
7. ASSERT SQL7 ON EMPLOYEE EMPX : EMPX.MGR# IN
                                  (SELECT EMP#
                                  FROM   EMPLOYEE)
```

Or perhaps:

```
ASSERT SQL7X : NOT EXISTS (SELECT *
                    FROM    EMPLOYEE EMPX
                    WHERE   NOT EXISTS
                        (SELECT *
                        FROM    EMPLOYEE EMPY
                        WHERE   EMPX.MGR# = EMPY.EMP#))
8. ASSERT SQL8 ON SP : QTY <= 1.05 * (SELECT AVG(QTY)
                                    FROM    SP)
9. ASSERT SQL9 ON S : (SELECT COUNT(UNIQUE S#) FROM S)
                      =
                      (SELECT COUNT(*) FROM S)
                      AND
                      S# IS NOT NULL
```

The predicate shown here is not a valid predicate in System R SQL, though it is allowed in the language of [2.8]. However, the effect of this particular assertion can be achieved in System R by the combination of (a) a NONULL specification for field S# in the CREATE TABLE for table S and (b) a CREATE UNIQUE INDEX over that field.

```
10. ASSERT SQL10 ON S SX : NOT EXISTS (SELECT *
                                       FROM    S SY
                                       WHERE   SY.SNAME = SX.SNAME
                                       AND     SY.S#    ¬= SX.S#)
```

11. Similar to SQL10.

```
12. ASSERT SQL12 DEFERRED : (SELECT SUM(BALANCE) FROM ACCOUNT)
                            =
                            (SELECT TOTAL FROM SUMMARY)
```

Reference [2.8] suggests that all SQL assertions be DEFERRED unless IM-MEDIATE is explicitly specified. The opposite assumption seems more sensible. Note, incidentally, that we have to assume in this example that the second SELECT will return exactly one value (that fact cannot be stated explicitly in SQL).

Query By Example

The basic Query By Example language as implemented by IBM includes both (a) a limited form of domain support (data types CHAR [varying length], CHAR(n), FIXED, FLOAT, DATE, and TIME are supported, and the system is also capable of recognizing that, for example, fields S.CITY and P.CITY are defined on the same domain); and (b) support for primary keys (primary keys are required, must be unique, and cannot be null). In addition, reference [2.18] proposes extensions for the support of relation constraints (not implemented at the time of writing). As with other QBE definitions, the constraints are inserted into the QBE dictionary by filling in entries in blank tables; that is, the user inserts "constraint" rows (specified by "I.CONSTR.", with an optional specification of those operations ["I." and/or "U." and/or "D."] that cause the constraint to be checked), making use of constant elements and example elements in the normal QBE manner. We show in Fig. 2.9 QBE versions of Examples 2.4.1–2.4.6. Violation responses cannot be specified. Note that Examples 2.4.5 and 2.4.6 require more than one row for their complete formulation. Note also that Example 2.4.6 as formulated here is actually too strong (it requires not only that every shipment have a corresponding supplier and corresponding part, but also the converse). For more information see reference [2.18].

INGRES

INGRES does not support domains in the sense of this chapter, except for the "base domains" INTEGER, FLOAT, and CHAR. Nor does it explicitly support the concept of primary keys. Relation integrity rules are specified in INGRES using the language QUEL [2.9, 2.10]. As an illustration we give the QUEL equivalent of Example 2.4.1.

```
RANGE OF SX IS S
DEFINE INTEGRITY ON SX IS SX.STATUS > 0
```

S		S#	SNAME	STATUS	CITY	Examples
I. CONSTR (I., U.).	I.			>0		1
I. CONSTR (U.).	I.	SX		>SS		5
	I.	SX		SS		5
	I.	SY				6

P		P#	PNAME	COLOR	WEIGHT	CITY	Examples
I. CONSTR (I., U.).	I.					[LONDON PARIS ROME]	2
	I.	PY					6

SP		S#	P#	QTY	QTYORD	QTYSHIP	Examples
I. CONSTR (I., U.).	I.				QX	<=QX	3
I. CONSTR (D.)	I.			0			4
I. CONSTR (I., U.).	I.	SY	PY				6

Fig. 2.9 Sample integrity constraints in QBE.

INGRES does not support transition constraints or deferred constraints, nor does it allow the specification of trigger conditions. All other constraints in the examples of Section 2.4—namely, numbers 2.4.1-2.4.3 and 2.4.6-2.4.11—can be specified in QUEL, one way or another. Violation responses cannot be specified.

The interesting aspect of integrity constraints in INGRES is the technique used to implement them [2.9, 2.10].[8] Basically, each user request is modified before execution in such a way as to guarantee that it cannot possibly violate any constraints. We give a single example to illustrate the procedure. For more details see references [2.9, 2.10].

Example

Required: Subtract 10 from STATUS for all suppliers in London.

Original QUEL statements:

```
RANGE OF SY IS S
REPLACE SY (STATUS = STATUS - 10)
          WHERE SY.CITY = 'LONDON'
```

---

8. The current implementation supports only what we called record constraints in Section 2.4—that is, constraints that can be checked by examining just the record concerned.

After modification:

```
RANGE OF SY IS S
REPLACE SY (STATUS = STATUS - 10)
            WHERE SY.CITY = 'LONDON'
            AND  (SY.STATUS - 10 > 0)
```

Hence the status of London suppliers will be decreased only in those cases where the resultant value is still greater than zero.

IMS

There are four features of IMS that can be viewed as mechanisms for handling integrity constraints. The first concerns uniqueness of sequence field values. If a segment (record) is declared in the DBD to have a sequence field, and if M ("multiple-valued") is *not* specified, IMS will guarantee that no two occurrences of the segment (under a given parent, if applicable) will contain the same value for this field at the same time. In other words, it will reject any ISRT operation that attempts to introduce a duplicate (REPL operations are not relevant because IMS does not allow a sequence field to be replaced).

The second feature concerns the so-called "parent-child" constraints (referential constraints) that are built into the data structure itself. In the terminology of Section 2.5, an IMS database (hierarchy) may be considered as a collection of fansets, each with AUTOMATIC insertion class and FIXED retention class. Suppose, for example, that the suppliers-and-parts database is represented by a "physical database" in which parts are superior to shipments, and shipment segments include the relevant supplier details (Fig. 2.10). Then it is not possible for the database to contain a segment showing that a supplier is supplying a nonexistent part, because every shipment segment must be subordinate to some existing part segment. On the other hand, of course, this database involves a lot of redundancy, and two distinct segments for the same supplier could be inconsistent.

In practice it is unlikely that the suppliers-and-parts database would be represented as a single physical hierarchy, partly because of the redundancy involved and partly also because of the corresponding consistency problem (though there could be a performance advantage). A more likely structure, using two physical databases

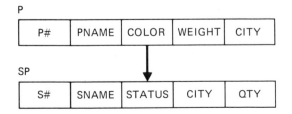

Fig. 2.10 Suppliers and parts as a physical database (IMS).

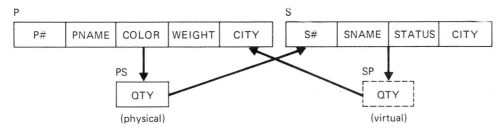

Fig. 2.11 Suppliers and parts as paired databases (IMS).

and "virtual pairing," is illustrated in Fig. 2.11. This structure would allow the user to see a variety of logical databases, including one with suppliers subordinate to parts and another with parts subordinate to suppliers.

Given the structure of Fig. 2.11, a suitable choice of insert and delete rules [2.11] can ensure that every shipment does correspond to both a genuine supplier and a genuine part. (Replace rules are irrelevant to this particular requirement.) For example, we can arrange that deletion of a supplier will cause deletion of all corresponding shipments, even though shipments are in a different physical database and even though the user performing the delete may be unaware of their existence. Also the consistency problem mentioned earlier now no longer arises. Thus the insert and delete (and replace) rules provide a third IMS integrity feature.

Note, incidentally, that these rules serve as a genuine (if limited) example of triggered procedures—that is, they do not restrict themselves to rejecting the operation if a constraint is violated, but in some cases actually perform additional updates. The triggered updates are not "transparent to the user."

The fourth IMS feature that is pertinent to integrity is the exit routine, already discussed briefly in Section 2.6.

DBTG

The features described in this subsection are based on the DBTG DDL as defined in the current ANSI X3H2 working document [2.12].[9] We start by noting that DBTG does support various data types (FIXED, FLOAT, CHARACTER, and BIT), though it has no notion of domains as such.

The next class of constraint we consider is *uniqueness*. Uniqueness constraints are defined in DBTG via the DUPLICATES ARE NOT ALLOWED clause, which can be specified: (a) within a record description, in which case it effectively defines a candidate key for the record-type concerned; (b) within a "set" (fanset) description,

---

9. ANSI is the American National Standards Institute, and X3H2 is the ANSI Data Definition Language Committee. The charter of X3H2 is to develop a proposal for a standard DDL, based on the CODASYL DDL (as of January 1978). The current version of the DDL [2.12] differs quite markedly from the original DBTG version; in particular, a number of features that were originally intended for use in handling integrity requirements have been either eliminated or drastically revised. For convenience we retain the familiar DBTG label, however.

in which case it effectively defines "uniqueness within parent," as in IMS. (Actually, the DUPLICATES clause can appear at various distinct points within a set description, with slightly different meanings in each case. See [2.12] for details.)

Third, again as in IMS, "parent-child" constraints are built into the DBTG data structure itself. In place of the IMS insert/delete/replace rules, DBTG has the concepts of insertion class (MANUAL or AUTOMATIC) and retention class (OPTIONAL or MANDATORY or FIXED). These features were discussed in Section 2.5; see Volume I for additional details. Incidentally, we do not mean to imply that the IMS and DBTG concepts are equivalent—merely that they address somewhat similar problems. Note in particular that the "triggered" updates that DBTG will perform are more limited than those in IMS, being restricted in fact to cascade delete (and then only if the retention class is FIXED).

Last, DBTG provides a CHECK clause for the specification of arbitrary record constraints and also certain interrecord constraints, notably (in the context of an *in*essential fanset) certain referential constraints. CHECK clauses can be specified within a data-item (field) description or a record description or a set description. We consider each of these in turn, with examples based on Fig. 2.8 (interpreted as a data structure diagram for a DBTG database).

Example 2.7.1 (within data-item description)

```
RECORD NAME IS S
   .....
   STATUS ... CHECK IS STATUS > 0
```

At the data-item level the only variable that can be referenced within the CHECK clause is the data-item in question.

Example 2.7.2 (within record description)

```
RECORD NAME IS SP
   .....
   CHECK IS QTYSHIP <= QTYORD
   .....
     QTYSHIP ...
     QTYORD  ...
```

At the record level any data-item in the record can be referenced within the CHECK clause.

Example 2.7.3 (within set description [member subentry])

For this example we need to assume that record-type SP does include an S# field and that set-type S_SP is inessential.

```
SET NAME IS S_SP
OWNER IS S
MEMBER IS P
   .....
   CHECK IS S# IN SP = S# IN S
```

As the example illustrates, a CHECK clause within a set description can include references to data-items in both the owner and the member record-types. The *only* implication of the particular CHECK clause shown is that the system will not permit a database state in which a given SP record is connected to a given S record within set-type S_SP, and those two records have different S# values. The full scope of the interactions between this constraint, on the one hand, and, on the other,

1. insertion class for set S_SP,
2. retention class for set S_SP,
3. the effect of STORE (INSERT) for record-type S,
4. the effect of MODIFY (UPDATE) for data-item S# IN S,
5. the effect of MODIFY (UPDATE) for data-item S# IN SP,
6. the effect of ERASE (DELETE) for record-type S,
7. the effect of CONNECT for record-type SP and set-type S_SP,
8. the effect of DISCONNECT for record-type SP and set-type S_SP,
9. the effect of RECONNECT for record-type SP and set-type S_SP, and
10. SET SELECTION for record-type S and set-type S_SP,

is not immediately obvious. The wisdom of providing such a plethora of interacting features must surely be questioned. Of course, the real culprit is the inessential fanset.

EXERCISES

2.1 The exercises in Volume I made a lot of use of the suppliers-parts-projects database:

```
S    (S#, SNAME, STATUS, CITY)
P    (P#, PNAME, COLOR, WEIGHT, CITY)
J    (J#, JNAME, CITY)
SPJ (S#, P#, J#, QTY)
```

The meaning of an SPJ record is that the indicated supplier (S#) supplies the indicated part (P#) to the indicated project (J#) in the indicated quantity (QTY).

For this database, write a suitable set of

a) domain definitions;

b) relation definitions;

c) referential integrity rules;

d) other integrity rules as seem appropriate.

2.2 The following is an outline relational schema for a simple bill-of-materials database:

```
PART      (P#, DESCRIPTION)
COMPONENT (MAJOR_P#, MINOR_P#, QTY)
```

Write a suitable set of referential integrity rules for this database.

2.3 Design a special-case syntax to handle referential integrity rules. Your syntax should allow for at least all of the following (expressed in terms of suppliers-and-parts): (a) Rejecting a deletion on S or an update on S.S.# if there currently exist any dependent SP records; (b) cascading the delete or update in the same situation; (c) setting SP.S# values to null in the dependent SP records in the same situation (this would be illegal for suppliers-and-parts because SP.S.# is a component of the primary key for SP; but suppose shipments had a separate SHIP# primary key and that (S#,P#) were an alternate key only); (d) rejecting an insertion on SP or an update on SP.S# if there does not exist an appropriate S record. (See reference [2.32] for an extensive discussion of this topic.)

2.4 How would you implement referential integrity?

2.5 How would you implement integrity rules that involve no parameters (such as those of Examples 2.4.8 and 2.4.11)?

2.6 Design a special-case syntax for functional dependencies over and above those that are a consequence of keys.

2.7 Do you think it is necessary to be able to define integrity rules for multivalued dependencies (that is, MVDs that are not also FDs)? Can such rules be formulated in the syntax of Section 2.4? What about join dependencies (that is, JDs that are not also MVDs)?

2.8 Write a suitable set of IMS delete rules for the databases of Fig. 2.11 (see reference [2.11]).

2.9 Write a suitable set of IMS insert rules for the databases of Fig. 2.11. (This is easier than Exercise 2.8.)

2.10 Write a suitable set of IMS replace rules for the databases of Fig. 2.11. (So is this.)

2.11 Repeat Exercises 2.8–2.10 for an IMS version of the suppliers-parts-projects database (see Volume I, Exercise 20.7).

2.12 Design a syntax for the expression of deferred transition rules (see Section 2.4).

2.13 Give deferred versions of the rules of Fig. 2.6, where possible.

REFERENCES AND BIBLIOGRAPHY

2.1 D. J. McLeod. "High Level Expression of Semantic Integrity Specifications in a Relational Data Base." Report No. MIT/LCS/TR-165, Laboratory for Computer Science, Massachusetts Institute of Technology (September 1976).

2.2 D. J. McLeod. "High Level Definition of Abstract Domains in a Relational Data Base System." In *Computer Languages 2:* Pergamon Press (1977). An earlier version of this paper can be found in *Proc. ACM SIGPLAN/SIGMOD Conference on Data: Abstraction, Definition, and Structure* (March 1976): Joint Issue—ACM SIGPLAN Notices 11 (Special Issue)/ACM SIGMOD Bulletin FDT 8, No. 2 (1976).

Basically the material on domain integrity from [2.1].

2.3 M. M. Hammer and D. J. McLeod. "Semantic Integrity in a Relational Data Base System." *Proc. 1st International Conference on Very Large Data Bases* (September 1975).

An early and abridged version of the material from [2.1].

2.4 M. M. Hammer. "Error Detection in Data Base Systems." *Proc. NCC* **45** (1976).

A high-level survey of the problem, not a specific proposal.

2.5 K. P. Eswaran and D. D. Chamberlin. "Functional Specifications of a Subsystem for Data Base Integrity." *Proc. 1st International Conference on Very Large Data Bases* (September 1975).

The classification of constraints in Section 2.4 (into record vs. set, state vs. transition, and immediate vs. deferred) is derived from this paper.

2.6 K. P. Eswaran. "Specifications, Implementations, and Interactions of a Trigger Subsystem in an Integrated Data Base System." IBM Research Report RJ1820 (August 1976).

2.7 M. M. Astrahan et al. "System R: Relational Approach to Database Management." *ACM TODS* **1,** No. 2 (June 1976).

2.8 D. D. Chamberlin et al. "SEQUEL 2: A Unified Approach to Data Definition, Manipulation, and Control." *IBM J. R&D* **20,** No. 6 (November 1976).

2.9 M. R. Stonebraker. "High Level Integrity Assurance in Relational Data Base Management Systems." Memorandum No. ERL-M473, University of California, Berkeley (August 1974).

2.10 M. R. Stonebraker. "Implementation of Integrity Constraints and Views by Query Modification." *Proc. 1975 ACM SIGMOD International Conference on Management of Data* (May 1975).

2.11 IBM Corporation. IMS/VS System Application Design Guide. IBM Form No. SH20-9025.

2.12 American National Standards Institute Data Definition Language Committee (X3H2). Working Document (September 1980).

2.13 R. W. Graves. "Integrity Control in a Relational Data Description Language." *Proc. ACM Pacific Conference,* San Francisco (April 1975), Available from ACM Golden Gate Chapter, P.O. Box 24055, Oakland, California 94623.

Presents proposals for specification of certain classes of integrity constraint in a relational DDL based on the DDL of DBTG. The proposals include the following:

- Data validation: A CHECK clause, with evaluation optionally deferred until AFTER TRANSACTION, which can test the VALUE of an item against an arbitrary expression (which can include quantifiers), or can compare an item to see if it fits a specified EDIT format. Uniqueness can be enforced via a DUPLICATES NOT ALLOWED clause. Reserved words OLDVALUE and NEWVALUE allow the specification of transition constraints.

- Data generation: Permits the definition and automatic maintenance of virtual fields, via a "VALUE IS expression" clause.

- Update implications: Provides triggered procedures, which can be invoked BEFORE or AFTER a designated operation is performed.

- Update restrictions: Controls the update of items and records, via a "REWRITE (or WRITE or DELETE) IS [NOT] ALLOWED IF . . ." clause.

2.14 E. M. Rifkin. "Maintaining the Integrity of a Relational Database with Assertion Tests as Specified by Boolean Expressions." *Proc. 13th Hawaii International Conference on System Sciences* (1978).

> The Boolean expressions of this paper are a Boolean combination of comparisons, where each comparison in turn can involve constants, "assertion variables" (same as bound fields in UDL), expressions representing sets of records, the usual scalar comparison operators (= , > , etc.), and the comparison operators IN and ¬ IN for testing set membership. (The "parameters" of the syntax given in Section 2.4 do not appear explicitly. Our examples 2.4.4, 2.4.5, 2.4.9, 2.4.10, and 2.4.11 cannot be represented as Boolean expressions.) The paper is concerned with the efficient implementation of constraints expressed in this form. It gives an algorithm for deciding which records need to be tested after a given update, and hence places an upper bound on the amount of processing required in performing the checks. It also describes techniques for reducing the amount of computation overhead.

2.15 O. P. Buneman and E. K. Clemons. "Efficiently Monitoring Relational Databases." *ACM TODS* **4,** No. 3 (September 1979).

> This paper is concerned with the efficient implementation of triggered procedures (here called *alerters*)—in particular, with the problem of deciding when the trigger condition is satisfied, without necessarily just evaluating that condition. It gives a method (an *avoidance* algorithm) for detecting updates that cannot possibly satisfy a given trigger condition; it also discusses a technique for reducing the processing overhead in the event that the avoidance algorithm fails, by evaluating the trigger condition for some small subset (a *filter*) of the total set of relevant records.

2.16 D. Z. Badal and G. J. Popek. "Cost and Performance Analysis of Semantic Integrity Validation Methods." *Proc. 1979 ACM SIGMOD International Conference on Management of Data* (May 1979).

> Compares three different approaches to the implementation of integrity rules: compile-time validation (that is, validation by examining database values and the effect of executing the transaction at the time it is compiled); run-time validation (that is, validation at COMMIT but before any writes have been made to the physical database); and post-execution validation (that is, validation after the physical writes). Run-time validation is deemed to give the best performance (based primarily on the number of I/O operations necessary but also taking into account such matters as lock duration).

2.17 G. Gardarin and M. Melkanoff. "Proving Consistency of Database Transactions." *Proc. 5th International Conference on Very Large Data Bases* (October 1979).

> Presents a technique for verifying at compile time that transactions cannot violate any integrity rules. The technique is based on Hoare's axiomatic approach to program correctness. It is suggested that such a technique could form the basis for a generalized compile-time "transaction consistency verifier."

2.18 M. M. Zloof. "Security and Integrity within the Query-By-Example Data Base Management Language." IBM Research Report RC6982 (February 1978).

2.19 M. M. Hammer and S. K. Sarin. "Efficient Monitoring of Database Assertions." *Proc. 1978 ACM SIGMOD International Conference on Management of Data* (June 1978).

An algorithm is sketched for generating integrity checks (given appropriate integrity constraints) that are more efficient than the obvious, "brute force" method of simply reevaluating those constraints after an update has been performed. The checks are incorporated into transaction object code at compilation time. In some cases it is possible to detect that no run-time checks are necessary at all. Even when they are necessary, it is frequently possible to reduce the number of database accesses significantly in a variety of different ways. The ideas of this paper may be seen as an extension of those of Stonebraker [2.9, 2.10] and Buneman and Clemons [2.15].

2.20 G. A. Wilson. "A Conceptual Model for Semantic Integrity Checking." *Proc. 6th International Conference on Very Large Data Bases* (October 1980).

Describes an experimental integrity subsystem called COPE. COPE is intended as a stand-alone, DBMS-independent "front end" to the rest of the system. Integrity rules are stated in terms of a relational description of the database, which maps to another description of the database as supported by the underlying DBMS (for example, as a DBTG-style network). Both these database descriptions must be given in a COPE specific form; the second must presumably map in turn to the underlying DBMS's own description, so that update operations (expressed in the DBMS's own DML) can be translated into equivalent COPE operations at run-time. The current COPE implementation supports interactive users only, not application programmers.

2.21 P. A. Bernstein, B. T. Blaustein, and E. M. Clarke. "Fast Maintenance of Semantic Integrity Assertions Using Redundant Aggregate Data." *Proc. 6th International Conference on Very Large Data Bases* (October 1980).

Presents an efficient method of enforcement for integrity rules of a certain special kind. An example is "every value in set A must be less than every value in set B." The enforcement technique is based on the observation that (for example) the rule just given is logically equivalent to the rule "every value in set A must be less than the *minimum* value in set B." By recognizing this class of rule and automatically deciding to store the necessary minimum value, the system can reduce the number of comparisons involved in enforcing the constraint from n (the cardinality of set B) to one (at the cost of having to maintain the stored minimum value whenever updates are made to the set B).

2.22 H. Weber. "A Semantic Model of Integrity Constraints in a Relational Data Base." In G. M. Nijssen (ed.): *Modelling in Data Base Management Systems.* North-Holland (1976).

2.23 C. Machgeels. "A Procedural Language for Expressing Integrity Constraints in the Coexistence Model." In G. M. Nijssen (ed.): *Modelling in Data Base Management Systems.* North-Holland (1976).

The integrity rules language proposed in this chapter (Section 2.4) is somewhat more procedural than many other proposals. This paper [2.23] presents another procedural proposal, though in less detail.

2.24 R. Fagin. "A Normal Form for Relational Databases That Is Based on Domains and Keys." *ACM TODS* **6,** No. 3 (September 1981). Also available as IBM Research Report RJ2520 (Version 3: May 1980).

2.25 L. A. Rowe and K. A. Shoens. "Data Abstraction, Views, and Updates in RIGEL." *Proc. 1979 ACM SIGMOD International Conference on Management of Data* (May 1979).

2.26 A. L. Furtado. "A View Construct for the Specification of External Schemas." Tech. Report No. 3/78 (Computer Science Monograph Series), Dept. of Informatics, Pontificia Universidade Catolica, Rio de Janeiro, Brazil (February 1978).

2.27 K. C. Sevcik and A. L. Furtado. "Complete and Compatible Sets of Update Operations." Dept. of Informatics, Pontificia Universidade Catolica, Rio de Janeiro, Brazil. Presented at International Conference on Management of Data (ICMOD), Milan, Italy (June 1978).

2.28 A. L. Furtado and K. C. Sevcik. "Permitting Updates Through Views of Data Bases." Dept. of Informatics, Pontificia Universidade Catolica, Rio de Janeiro, Brazil. Also in *Information Systems* **4**, pp. 269–283 (1979).

2.29 S. J. P. Todd. "Automatic Constraint Maintenance and Updating Defined Relations." *Proc. IFIP Congress 1977* (North-Holland 1977).

2.30 G. M. Nijssen. "Towards an Ideal Conceptual Model for Data Base Management" (position paper for panel discussion). In S. M. Deen and P. Hammersley (eds.): *Proc. International Conference on Data Bases,* Aberdeen, Scotland (July 1980). British Computer Society Workshop Series: Heyden (July 1980).

2.31 *Proc. Workshop on Data Abstraction, Databases and Conceptual Modeling,* Pingree Park, Colorado (June 1980). Available from ACM.

2.32 C. J. Date. "Referential Integrity." *Proc. 7th International Conference on Very Large Data Bases* (September 1981).

2.33 A. Walker and S. C. Salveter. "Automatic Modification of Transactions to Preserve Data Base Integrity Without Undoing Updates." State University of New York, Stony Brook, New York: Tech. Report 81/026 (June 1981).

> Describes a technique for automatically modifying any transaction template (transaction source code) into a corresponding "safe" template—safe, in the sense that no transaction instance conforming to that template can possibly violate any declared constraints. The method works by adding queries and tests to the original template to ensure *before* any updating is done that no constraints will be violated. At run-time, if any of those tests fails, the transaction is rejected and an error message is generated.

ANSWERS TO SELECTED EXERCISES

```
2.1 (c) SPJR  : BEFORE INSERTING SPJ FROM NEW_SPJ,
                BEFORE UPDATING  SPJ FROM NEW_SPJ :
                EXISTS (S WHERE S.S# = NEW_SPJ.S#)
                AND
                EXISTS (P WHERE P.P# = NEW_SPJ.P#)
                AND
                EXISTS (J WHERE J.J.# = NEW_SPJ.J#) ;

        SR1   : BEFORE DELETING S:
                DELETE ALL SPJ WHERE SPJ.S# = S.S# ;
```

(and analogous rules PR1, JR1, for P, J)

```
        SR2   : BEFORE UPDATING S.S.# FROM NEW_S# :
                UPDATE ALL SPJ.S# FROM NEW_S#
                       WHERE SPJ.S# = S.S# ;
```

(and analogous rules PR2, JR2 for P, J)

Each of these rules except SPJR is really a triggered procedure.

```
2.2  CIR : BEFORE INSERTING COMPONENT FROM NEWC,
           BEFORE UPDATING  COMPONENT FROM NEWC :
           EXISTS (PART WHERE P# = NEWC.MAJOR_P#)
           AND
           EXISTS (PART WHERE P# = NEWC.MINOR_P#) ;

     PIR : BEFORE DELETING PART,
           BEFORE UPDATING PART.P# :
           ¬ EXISTS (COMPONENT WHERE MINOR_P# >= PART.P#) ;
```

2.3 The following proposal is taken from reference [2.32]. The reader is referred to that paper for further explanations.

```
referential-constraint
   ::= label : dependency [ delete-rule ] [ update-rule ] ;

dependency
   ::= referential-attribute ->> referenced-spec

referential-attribute
   ::= attribute-spec

attribute-spec
   ::= relation-name . attributes

attributes
   ::= attribute-name | ( attribute-name-commalist )

referenced-spec
   ::= primary-key
       | [ quantifier ] ( primary-key-commalist )

primary-key
   ::= attribute-spec

quantifier
   ::= EXACTLY ONE OF | AT LEAST ONE OF | ALL OF

delete-rule
   ::= DELETING effect

effect
   ::= CASCADES | NULLIFIES | RESTRICTED

update-rule
   ::= UPDATING effect
```

Notes

1. The default delete-rule is DELETING RESTRICTED. The default update-rule is UP-DATING RESTRICTED.

2. The default quantifier is EXACTLY ONE OF.

3. The delete-rule defines the effect of deleting (or attempting to delete) a tuple in a referenced relation. It applies to all referenced relations identified (via a primary-key) on the right-hand side of the dependency. CASCADES means that matching tuples in the referencing relation are also deleted. NULLIFIES means that the referential attribute in those tuples is set to null (if the referential attribute is composite, then all components are set to null). RE-STRICTED means that the delete will fail if any such matching tuples exist.

4. The update-rule defines the effect of updating (or attempting to update) the primary key value in a tuple of a referenced relation. It applies to all referenced relations identified (via a primary-key) on the right-hand side of the dependency. CASCADES means that matching tuples in the referencing relation are updated correspondingly. NULLIFIES means that the referential attribute in those tuples is set to null (if the referential attribute is composite, then all components are set to null). RESTRICTED means that the update will fail if any such matching tuples exist.

5. No syntax is provided for specifying any rules concerning the insertion of a tuple into a referencing relation or the update of a referential attribute within such a tuple. Instead, such operations are always governed by the following rule. On completion of any transaction that includes such an operation (that is, at commit time for such a transaction), the referential attribute in question must satisfy the following constraint (otherwise the transaction is rejected).

- Let the referential attribute, which for generality we assume to be composite, consist of simple attributes B1, B2, . . . , Bn, and let the values of these attributes in the inserted or updated tuple (that is, after the insert or update) be b1, b2, . . . , bn. These values must either all be null or all nonnull (in some cases, of course, nulls will not be allowed).

- Let each referenced relation corresponding to the referencing relation have attributes C1, C2, . . . , Cn corresponding (in order) to B1, B2, . . . , Bn. (The combination (C1, C2, . . . , Cn) constitutes the primary key in each such relation. We assume without loss of generality that all such primary keys have the same attribute-names.)

- Then, assuming that b1, b2, . . . , bn are all nonnull: If the applicable quantifier is EXACTLY ONE OF, there must exist a tuple in exactly one of the referenced relations having C1 = b1, C2 = b2, . . . , Cn = bn. If the applicable quantifier is AT LEAST ONE OF, there must exist a tuple in at least one of the referenced relations having C1 = b1, C2 = b2, . . . , Cn = bn. If the applicable quantifier is ALL OF, there must exist a tuple in each of the referenced relations having C1 = b1, C2 = b2, . . . , Cn = bn.

Examples

```
RX1 : SP.S# ->> S.S# ;
```

This constraint may informally be read as "Given an SP tuple with value x for SP.S#, there exists an S tuple having that value x for S.S#." Deleting an S tuple or updating an S.S# value is allowed only if there are no corresponding SP tuples. Inserting an SP tuple or updating an SP.S# value is allowed only if an S tuple exists (by commit time) with S# value equal to the new SP.S# value.

```
RX2 : SP.S# ->> S.S#
        DELETING RESTRICTED
        UPDATING CASCADES ;

RX3 : SP.P# ->> P.P# ;
```

Let us now suppose for the sake of the example that relation S is split into a set of supplier relations L_S, P_S, R_S, A_S (one for each of the supplier cities London, Paris, Rome, Athens).

```
RX4 : SP.S# ->> EXACTLY ONE OF
                 (L_S.S#, P_S.S#, R_S.S#, A_S.S#) ;
```

As another example, suppose that relation S is replaced by its projections SN(S#,SNAME), ST(S#,STATUS), and SC(S#,CITY).

```
RX5 : SP.S# ->> ALL OF (SN.S#, ST.S#, SC.S#) ;
```

The next two examples are based on a relation

```
EMPLOYEE ( EMP#, ..., MGR#, ... )  .

RX6 : EMPLOYEE.MGR# ->> EMPLOYEE.EMP# ;

RX7 : EMPLOYEE.MGR# ->> EMPLOYEE.EMP#
        DELETING NULLIFIES
        UPDATING CASCADES ;
```

The next two examples are based on the following relations:

```
COURSE   ( COURSE#, ... )
OFFERING ( COURSE#, OFF#, ... )
STUDENT  ( COURSE#, OFF#, EMP#, ... )

RX8 : OFFERING.COURSE# ->> COURSE.COURSE#
        DELETING CASCADES
        UPDATING CASCADES ;

RX9 : STUDENT.(COURSE#,OFF#) ->> OFFERING.(COURSE#,OFF#)
        DELETING CASCADES
        UPDATING CASCADES ;
```

For a final example, assume that we have two relations:

```
EMPLOYEE   ( EMP#, ..., DEPT#, ... )
DEPARTMENT ( DEPT#, ..., ADVISOR#, ... )
```

where the ADVISOR# attribute identifies an employee (by employee number) who is the advisor to the department in question. We thus have a *cycle*:

```
RX10 : EMPLOYEE.DEPT# ->> DEPARTMENT.DEPT# ;
RX11 : DEPARTMENT.ADVISOR# ->> EMPLOYEE.EMP# ;
```

2.4 We offer the following comments on the suitability of *stored fansets* as an implementation mechanism for referential constraints in a relational database. (Naturally we assume that any such fansets would not be visible at the relational interface.) We assume that the constraints are expressed in a language such as that sketched in the answer to Exercise 2.3 above.

- The most significant point is that stored fansets *are* a suitable mechanism for many of the most commonly occurring cases, but that there are also quite a number of situations that they cannot handle well (or at all).

- In general, the stored fansets may be either essential or inessential (see Section 2.5, also Volume I, for a discussion of essentiality). Each approach has its own performance advantages and disadvantages.

- There is no convenient correspondence between the insert/update/delete rules of the language of the answer above (to Exercise 2.3) and the various CODASYL insertion-class and retention-class options. In other words, most of the insert/update/delete rules would have to be implemented via procedural code, rather than by simple declarations, if the relational system in question were being implemented on top of a CODASYL system.

- If parent and child in the stored fanset are required to be different stored relations (as is normally the case), then there is a problem in supporting constraints in which the referencing relation and the referenced relation are one and the same. An example is

      EMP (EMP#, ..., MGR#, ...)

  with

      EMP.MGR# ->> EMP.EMP#

- Fanset support for the quantifiers EXACTLY ONE OF and AT LEAST ONE OF is not straightforward.

- Fansets are not a very suitable implementation for constraints that are to be checked at commit time (as opposed to immediately).

2.7 The answer is yes to all three questions. For example, given the relation R(A,B,C), the rule that R must satisfy the MVD $A \to \to B|C$ can be expressed as follows:

```
RR : WHEN COMMITTING :
        ¬ EXISTS (X1->R WHERE
                EXISTS (X2->R WHERE
                        X1->A = X2->A AND
                        (¬ EXISTS (X3->R WHERE X3->B = X1->B
                                              AND X3->C = X2->C)
                        OR
                        ¬ EXISTS (X4->R WHERE X4->B = X2->B
                                              AND X4->C = X1->C))));
```

```
2.13 DSIR1   : WHEN COMMITTING :
               ¬ EXISTS (S WHERE STATUS <= 0) ;

     DPIR2   : WHEN COMMITTING :
               ¬ EXISTS (P WHERE P.CITY NOT IN
                             ('LONDON','PARIS','ROME')) ;
     DSPIR3  : WHEN COMMITTING :
               ¬ EXISTS (SP WHERE SP.QTYSHIP > SP.QTYORD) ;

     DIR6    : WHEN COMMITTING :
               ¬ EXISTS (SP WHERE
                     ¬ EXISTS (S WHERE S.S# = SP.S#)) ;

     DEIR7   : WHEN COMMITTING :
               ¬ EXISTS (E1->EMPLOYEE WHERE
                     ¬ EXISTS (E2->EMPLOYEE WHERE
                             E2->EMPLOYEE.EMP# =
                             E1->EMPLOYEE.MGR#)) ;

     DSPIR8  : WHEN COMMITTING :
               ¬ EXISTS (SPC3->SP WHERE SPC3->SP.QTY >
                             1.05 * SETAVG (SPC2->SP.QTY)) ;

     DSIR9   : WHEN COMMITTING :
               ¬ EXISTS (SC1->S WHERE IS_NULL (SC1->S.S#)
                     OR EXISTS (SC2->S WHERE SC2 ¬= SC1
                             AND SC2->S.S# = SC1->S.S#)) ;

     DSIR10  : WHEN COMMITTING :
               ¬ EXISTS (SC1->S WHERE
                     EXISTS (SC2->S WHERE SC2 ¬= SC1
                     AND SC2->S.SNAME = SC1->S.SNAME)) ;

     DIR11   : WHEN COMMITTING :
               ¬ EXISTS (X->SJT WHERE
                     EXISTS (Y->SJT WHERE
                             X->SJT.T  = Y->SJT.T AND
                             X->SJT.J ¬= Y->SJT.J)) ;
```

3
Concurrency

3.1 THE PROBLEM OF INTERFERENCE

In Chapter 2 we considered the question of ensuring that individual transactions are correct in themselves. Given a correct state of the database as input, an individually correct transaction will produce a correct state of the database as output *if executed in isolation*. (In the case of a read-only transaction, of course, the input and output states will be identical.) Even if all transactions are individually correct in this sense, however, it is still possible in a shared (multiuser) system for transactions that execute concurrently to interfere with one another in such a way as to produce an overall result that is *not* correct. Such interference can take many forms. The "lost update" problem (illustrated in Fig. 3.1) provides what is probably the best-known example. Other types of interference are discussed later in the chapter.

We explain Fig. 3.1 as follows. Transaction A is intended to add one to some field F in some record R; transaction B is intended to double the value of that same field. Thus, if the initial value of the field in question is 4, then running the two transactions one at a time (that is, without any concurrency) will produce a final value of 10 (if A is run before B) or 9 (if B is run before A). Either of these values may be considered a correct final result. However, the particular concurrent (interleaved) execution sequence shown in Fig. 3.1 produces a final result of 8. That particular execution sequence is therefore incorrect. We say that A's update is lost in this example because B overwrites it without even looking at it.

Note 1: We use "FIND R" as shorthand for a FIND that obtains addressability (by setting a cursor) to some specific record occurrence R, and "UPD R" as shorthand for an update operation on that same record via that same cursor.

Note 2: All examples in this chapter are deliberately simple, artificial, and rather "academic" in flavor. The reader should not conclude from this fact that concurrency problems are of only academic interest. We choose the examples we do be-

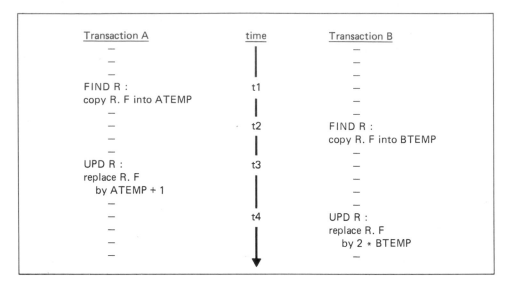

Fig. 3.1 A's update is lost at time t4.

cause realistic examples tend to obscure the underlying issues with many irrelevant details. But in an attempt to make the point that the problems *are* important in a real environment, we modify our lost update example as follows. Suppose record R is the seating record for a flight and field R.F gives the count of available seats on that flight. Let transactions A and B both be transactions that sell one seat on the flight and reduce that count by one. If A and B run interleaved as in Fig. 3.1, then the net effect will be that the count will be reduced by one instead of two.

It is clear, then, that in a multiuser environment some sort of *concurrency control mechanism* is needed in order to avoid problems such as that of Fig. 3.1. Let us consider that example in a little more detail. The essential problem is that A and B are both updating R.F on the basis of the *initial* value of that field—that is, neither one is seeing the output of the other. To prevent this situation there are basically three things a concurrency control mechanism might do:

a) It could prevent B's FIND at time t2, on the grounds that A already has addressability to R and may therefore be going to update it (for, if A does update it, then B should not be allowed to operate on the assumption that R still has its old value, but should somehow be forced to see that updated value instead).

b) It could prevent A's update at time t3, on the grounds that B already has addressability to R and has already seen the value before the update (and therefore can hardly be forced to see the updated value instead).

c) It could prevent B's update at time t4, on the grounds that A has already updated R and therefore B's update is based on a now obsolete value.

Cases (a) and (b) above can be handled by a concurrency control technique known as *locking,* and case (c) by a technique known as *timestamping.* (Case (b) can also be handled by timestamping.) Of these two techniques, locking is probably the more important. It is certainly the one more likely to be encountered in practice.[1] For this reason we devote most of this chapter to locking, but a brief description of timestamping is given in Section 3.14. In the next section we give an introduction to some of the basic concepts of locking, and show how locking can be used to solve the problem of Fig. 3.1 (actually by giving a "case (a)" solution).

We conclude this section with a warning that, once again, we are concerned with *principles* rather than with details of specific systems. In fact, the particular topic of concurrency, more than most, is characterized by a very great divergence of approaches to its support in implemented systems. In this chapter we attempt to impose a logical and systematic structure on this rather diffuse topic. The reader will realize, however, that the structure is largely a retrofit: Existing systems were (obviously) implemented before this particular structure was defined. Some discussion of the facilities provided in existing systems is given in Section 3.13. Also, in the body of the chapter we will make fairly extensive use of UDL [1.7] to illustrate the points under discussion. Please note, however, that our intent in such illustrations is merely to give some concreteness to the abstract ideas, not to describe the facilities of UDL per se.

3.2 EXCLUSIVE LOCKS

As indicated in the previous section, locking is a concurrency control technique—that is, a technique for regulating concurrent access to shared objects, such as records in a shared database. (*PLEASE NOTE:* In the particular case of a database we shall assume until further notice that records are the unit for locking purposes.) A transaction can *obtain a lock* on a record by issuing a request to a system component called the Lock Manager. The lock can be thought of as a control block that includes, among other things, the identification (ID) of the record with which it is associated—that is, the record that is locked—and the ID of the transaction holding the lock. If transaction T holds a lock on record R, then certain guarantees are made to T with respect to R; for example, T will almost certainly be guaranteed that no concurrent transaction will be able to update R until T releases its lock (which it does by means of another request to the Lock Manager). The precise nature of the guarantees depends on the lock *type.* In this section we introduce what is probably

---

1. At least in centralized systems. For distributed systems, where the tradeoffs are different, there is some feeling that techniques based on timestamping may be more appropriate [3.11, 3.12], and it is possible that such techniques will become more widely used in the future. Even if this should prove to be the case, locking techniques will continue to be important for centralized systems and also for individual sites within a distributed system. We defer specific discussion of distributed systems to Chapter 7.

the commonest type, the *exclusive* lock (or X lock). Additional lock types are discussed later in the chapter.

Exclusive locks can be defined as follows:

- If transaction T holds an exclusive lock on some object (say a database record), then no distinct transaction T' can acquire a lock of any type on that object until T releases its lock.

Exclusive or X locks provide us with a basis for solving the lost update problem. We introduce a *protocol* which we shall refer to as protocol PX:

- **Protocol PX.** Any transaction that intends to update a record R must first execute "XFIND R" to obtain addressability to that record *and to acquire an X lock on it.* If the lock cannot be acquired, the transaction goes into a wait state (the XFIND is accepted but not honored at this time); the transaction will resume processing when the record becomes available and the lock can be granted (the XFIND can now be honored).

Note 1: We use the notation "XFIND" as an explicit indication of the fact that the operation includes both the finding of the record and the acquisition of the lock. In practice the system will probably allow the normal FIND statement to be used, and will then issue the request for the X lock implicitly on the transaction's behalf as part of the normal execution of that FIND. In such a system protocol PX is enforced automatically—the application programmer need not be explicitly concerned with it at all. But for clarity we will always use "XFIND" when we wish to make it plain that the operation includes the acquisition of an X lock.

Note 2: The system must guarantee that a transaction that is forced to wait because of protocol PX *will* eventually come out of the wait state—that is, its XFIND will eventually be honored (unless the transaction is chosen as a deadlock victim, as discussed in Section 3.4, later). A simple technique for providing such a guarantee is to service all lock requests for a given object in first-come/first-served order. If the system does not provide such a guarantee, then it is possible for a transaction to wait forever for some lock. This condition is sometimes referred to as *livelock*.

The effect of applying protocol PX to the problem of Fig. 3.1 is shown in Fig. 3.2.

It can be seen that B is now made to wait at time t2, because its request for an X lock on R at that time conflicts with the X lock already held on R by A. Transaction B resumes after A releases its lock (which it does via the XRELEASE operator at time t4; see below for a discussion of this operator). The effect is thus to force B to see the value of R as updated by A. As indicated earlier, this corresponds to case (a) of the three possibilities outlined at the end of Section 3.1. If we assume again that the initial value of R.F is 4, then the overall effect of the interleaved execution of Fig. 3.2 is to produce a final value of 10, which, as we previously agreed, is one of the two possible correct outcomes.

Transaction A	time	Transaction B
—		—
—		—
—		—
XFIND R :	t1	—
copy R. F into ATEMP		—
—		—
—	t2	XFIND R :
—		wait
UPD R :	t3	wait
replace R. F		wait
by ATEMP + 1		wait
—		wait
[XRELEASE R]	t4	wait
	t5	(resume) XFIND R :
		copy R. F into BTEMP
		—
	t6	UPD R :
		replace R. F
		by 2 * BTEMP
		—
	t7	[XRELEASE R]

Fig. 3.2 B is forced to wait for A's update.

Note: The operation "XRELEASE R" is shown in square brackets in Fig. 3.2. The brackets are intended to act as a hint that exclusive locks are typically *not* released by a simple "XRELEASE" operator; in fact, data manipulation languages do not even provide such an operator. We shall discuss the question of exactly how locks *are* released in later sections of this chapter (Section 3.5 and onward).

We conclude this section with a note on DELETE and INSERT operations. As far as DELETE is concerned, it ought to be clear that the term "update" in protocol PX should be taken to include DELETE operations—that is, an attempt to execute "DELETE R" must be preceded by a successful "XFIND R." To see the need for this interpretation, consider the effect of replacing A's "UPD R" by "DELETE R" in Fig. 3.1. But what about INSERT? Here, of course, there is no question of finding and locking the record before "updating" it. Therefore, the operation "INSERT R" must itself be assumed to include the acquisition of an X lock on the newly inserted record R. (In practice the necessary lock request will normally be issued automatically as part of the execution of the ordinary INSERT statement.) Construction of an example showing the need for this lock is left as an exercise for the reader. Henceforth we shall, as usual, take the term "update" to include insertions and deletions as well.

3.3 SERIALIZABILITY

Our discussions in this chapter so far have rested on certain assumptions that bear closer examination. (The following argument was first developed (using different terminology) in a paper by Eswaran et al. [3.2].)

a) We started by assuming that all transactions are individually correct—that is, each transaction preserves the integrity of the database if executed in isolation.

b) It follows from (a) that, given any set of transactions, any *serial execution* of those transactions (that is, any execution of those transactions one at a time, in any order) also preserves the integrity of the database. Any serial execution is therefore correct.

c) Notice the word "any" in the preceding sentence. In the example of Fig. 3.1, we said that running A before B and running B before A could both be considered as producing a correct result, even though the results were different in the two cases. In other words, for concurrency-control purposes we do not recognize the possibility of one transaction having to run before another—or, to put it another way, we assume that transactions are all independent of one another. A practical consequence of this assumption is that, if transaction A does have to be run before transaction B, then the user cannot submit transaction B for execution until transaction A has completed.

d) The interleaved execution of Fig. 3.1 is incorrect because there is no serial execution of the transactions concerned that produces the same result. The interleaved execution of Fig. 3.2 is correct because it *does* produce the same result as some serial execution of those transactions. We say that an execution such as that of Fig. 3.2 is *serializable*. More precisely:

Definition. A given interleaved execution of some set of transactions is said to be serializable if and only if it produces the same result as some serial execution of those same transactions (that is, given an arbitrary initial database state as input, the interleaved execution produces the same output as some serial execution operating on the same initial database state).

The example of Fig. 3.2 shows how exclusive locking can be used to enforce serializability. It is important to understand that "serializable" does *not* necessarily mean "serialized"—transactions are still executing concurrently, but locking, or some other concurrency-control mechanism, is being used to synchronize them as necessary.

e) Finally, we adopt serializability as our *formal criterion for correctness* [3.2]. That is, a given interleaved execution sequence will be considered correct if and only if it is serializable. It follows that, if the system is such that the only execution sequences it supports are serializable sequences, then that system is guaranteed to be correct. In practice, however (as will be discussed later in the chapter), systems do not usually restrict themselves to serializable sequences only, since a given sequence may be nonserializable and yet may still be considered acceptable (*not* correct).

The notion of serializability is a great aid to clear thinking in this potentially confusing area. We therefore devote the remainder of this section to further discussion of the concept. First, let E be an (interleaved) execution of some set of transactions T1, T2, . . . , Tn. If E is serializable, then there exists some serial execution S of T1, T2, . . . , Tn, such that E is equivalent to S (produces the same result as S). S is said to be a *serialization* of E. Note that S need not be unique.

Now let Ti and Tj be any two transactions in the set T1, T2, . . . , Tn. Let us assume, without loss of generality, that transaction Ti precedes transaction Tj in the serialization S. Then, in the equivalent interleaved execution E, the *effect* must also be as if transaction Ti preceded transaction Tj. In other words, an informal but very helpful characterization of serializability is that, if A and B are any two transactions involved in some serializable execution, then either A logically precedes B or B logically precedes A in that execution; that is, *either B sees A's output or A sees B's.* (If A updates records R1, R2, . . . , Rm, and if B sees any of these records as input, then B sees them *either* all as updated by A *or* all as they were before being updated by A—not a mixture of the two.) Conversely, if the effect is *not* as if either A ran before B or B before A, then the execution is not serializable and not correct.

We note that if transactions A and B of the previous paragraph do not communicate with each other (that is, have no data requirements in common), then their relative order in the serialization S is immaterial. In other words, if S1 is a valid serialization of E, then the serial execution S2 obtained from S1 by interchanging A and B is another valid serialization of E.

We conclude this section with an example (Fig. 3.3) to stress the point once again that "serializable" is not the same as "serialized." Specifically, the example shows a serializable execution of three transactions A, B, and C, such that A logically precedes B, B logically precedes C, but C *actually* precedes A! The vertical bars in the figure are intended as explicit indications of transaction duration.

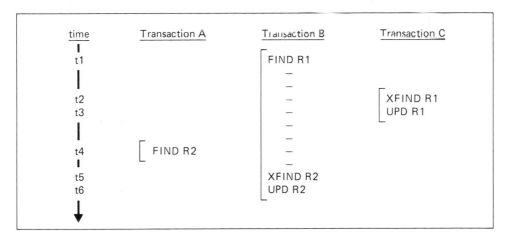

Fig. 3.3 A serializable execution of three transactions.

In this example, A logically precedes B because A sees R2 in its pre-B version, and B logically precedes C because B sees R1 in its pre-C version, yet C physically precedes A in actual execution sequence (C terminates before A starts). The execution is serializable because it is equivalent to the serial execution A-then-B-then-C (that is, A-then-B-then-C is a valid serialization). Note, however, that for this example to work we need to make some assumptions:

- If the "FIND R1" in B at time t1 acquires a lock on R1, then that lock must be released prior to time t2 in order for C to proceed. (Regardless of whether the "FIND R2" in A at time t4 acquires a lock on R2, B is able to proceed at time t5 because A has terminated by that time and so cannot be holding any locks at all.)

- R1 and R2 must be independent of each other; the "UPD R2" in B at time t6 must not depend in any way on the value of R1 at time t1. If this assumption is false, then B should have locked R1 at time t1 and should not have released its lock, contrary to the first assumption above. See Section 3.6, later.

To put it another way, if all transactions obey the *two-phase locking protocol* (to be discussed in Section 3.8), then the example does not work; that is, a serializable execution such as that in Fig. 3.3 cannot be produced if the two-phase locking protocol is enforced. The two-phase locking protocol would require B to obtain a lock on R1 at time t1 and to retain that lock until it terminates, with the result that the execution of C would be delayed until after the execution of B. It would thus no longer be true that C physically precedes A. In fact, if all transactions obey the two-phase locking protocol, and if in some serializable execution E transaction Ti physically terminates before transaction Tj, then it is always possible to find a serialization S of E such that Ti precedes Tj in that serialization. (This fact shows that the execution sequence in Fig. 3.3 cannot possibly be produced under the two-phase locking protocol.) We suggest that the reader study this example again after reading Section 3.8.

3.4 DEADLOCK

In Section 3.2 we showed how protocol PX (the exclusive locking protocol) can be used to solve the lost update problem. Unfortunately, that protocol can lead to problems of its own, in particular the problem of *deadlock*. Deadlock is a situation in which two or more transactions are in a simultaneous wait state, each waiting for one of the others to release a lock before it can proceed. Consider Fig. 3.4, which shows a deadlock involving two transactions. It is clear that, in theory at least, deadlocks involving three, four, or more transactions can also occur, though experience suggests that such cases are very uncommon in practice [3.6].

The problem of deadlock has been extensively studied in other contexts, such as that of operating systems, and various deadlock avoidance protocols have been defined [3.16]. For example, one common scheme is to impose a total ordering on

Transaction A	time	Transaction B
—		—
—		—
XFIND R1	t1	—
—		—
—	t2	XFIND R2
—		—
XFIND R2	t3	—
wait		—
wait	t4	XFIND R1
wait		wait
wait		wait
wait		wait

Fig. 3.4 Deadlock occurs at time t4.

all lockable objects, and then to refuse a lock request for an object Y if the requesting transaction already holds a lock for any object Z that appears later than Y in that ordering. Suppose, for instance, that such an ordering is defined for the records in the database, and suppose that R1 precedes R2 with respect to that ordering. Then B's request for a lock on R1 at time t4 would be rejected, and the deadlock would not occur.

Unfortunately, however, such deadlock-avoidance protocols are generally inapplicable in a database environment. For example, referring again to Fig. 3.4, transaction B may be unable to identify record R1, and hence unable to lock it, until it has locked and examined R2 (the identity of R1 may depend on values stored in R2). The fact is, the database environment is qualitatively different from other environments so far as locking problems are concerned. Among the reasons for this state of affairs are the following:

■ The set of lockable objects is not only very large (consisting possibly of millions of records), it also changes very dynamically (new records, possibly even new files, are constantly being created and existing ones destroyed).

■ Lockable objects (records) are typically addressed not by name but by content, so that it cannot be determined until execution time whether or not two distinct requests are for the same object.

■ The precise locking scope (specific set of records required) for a given transaction is usually determined dynamically.

It follows that the system must be prepared for the possibility of deadlock, in general. That is, the system must be prepared to detect the occurrence of deadlocks and to resolve them, or "break" them, when they do occur (but see Section 3.9).

Detecting deadlock is basically a matter of detecting a cycle in the so-called Wait-For graph—that is, the graph of "who is waiting for whom" [3.1]. This graph is constructed as follows. The nodes represent executing transactions, the edges represent waits. The system draws an edge from node Ti to node Tj when transaction Ti requires a lock on an object that is held by Tj, and erases that edge when Tj releases its lock. (We are describing only a very unsophisticated form of the graph.) It should be clear that if there are edges from T1 to T2, T2 to T3, . . . , T(n − 1) to Tn, and Tn to T1, then transactions T1, T2, . . . , Tn are deadlocked (see Exercise 3.6).

Checking for deadlock can be done whenever a lock request causes a wait[2] or on some periodic basis. Checking on every wait allows deadlocks to be detected as soon as they occur, but may impose too much overhead, especially as most checks will result in "no deadlock found"; checking less frequently reduces the overhead but may mean that some deadlocks are detected late. Alternatively the system may use a time-out mechanism, and simply assume that a transaction is deadlocked if it has done no work in a given time period.

Breaking a deadlock consists of choosing a "victim"—that is, one of the deadlocked transactions—and rolling it back. The victim is not necessarily the transaction that actually caused the deadlock; it may, for example, be the one that was most recently started, or the one holding the fewest locks, or the one that has made the fewest updates.[3] The rollback process involves, not only terminating the transaction and undoing all its updates, but also *releasing all its locks,* so that the resources concerned can now be allocated to other transactions. Note that the victim may have locked other system resources in addition to objects in the database; deadlock is a system-wide problem, not just a database problem. The Lock Manager should serve the entire system, not just the DBMS.

The question is, what should happen to the victim after the rollback has occurred? Deadlock is not like (say) arithmetic overflow; it is not really the result of a program error; it therefore seems a little harsh just to terminate the program out of hand (although some systems do this). Thus we find that some systems (System R is an example) simply pass control back to the victim with a return code indicating that the rollback has occurred. This return code can occur on any operation that requests a lock. The application program remains executing and can, for example, initiate another transaction in an attempt to redo the undone updates. In other systems, for example IMS, a fresh copy of the program is automatically loaded and given the same input message as before so that it can try its processing again. Such automatic retry is particularly desirable in an online environment, since ideally the end-user should not even be aware that rollback has occurred. On the other hand, the System

---

2. Note that the only possible time at which a deadlock can occur is when a lock request is accepted but not granted, and therefore causes a wait.

3. Care must be taken to avoid the possibility of some transaction repeatedly getting into a deadlock and being chosen as the victim every time, so that it never terminates. One way to prevent such a situation is always to choose the "youngest" transaction as the victim.

R approach is preferable in a batch environment, in which a single program execution may represent a sequence of many transactions. (The problem of dealing with a deadlock return code in such a program has points of similarity with the problem that also arises in such programs of dealing with a restart situation. See the discussion of "long transactions" in Section 1.3.)

3.5   THE LOST UPDATE PROBLEM REVISITED

The possibility that a transaction may be rolled back before reaching a successful conclusion—either because it has been chosen as the victim in a deadlock situation or for a variety of other reasons (discussed in Chapters 1 and 2)—has various implications in the area of concurrency control. Consider Fig. 3.5, in which B has seen data (at time t4) that "never existed," since when the rollback occurs at time t5 record R will be restored to its pre-A value. (Remember from Chapter 1 that if a transaction is rolled back, that is, does not reach a successful conclusion, then it is made as if it had never started.) We say that B has become "dependent on an uncommitted update"—an uncommitted update, or uncommitted change (or, as it is sometimes known, "dirty data"), being an update that is subject to possible rollback. Note that the sequence of events in Fig. 3.5 is not serializable.

Transaction A	time	Transaction B
—		—
—		—
—		—
XFIND R	t1	—
—		—
UPD R	t2	—
—		—
[XRELEASE R]	t3	—
—		—
—	t4	FIND R
—		—
*** ROLLBACK ***	t5	—
		—

Fig. 3.5 B is dependent on A's uncommitted update (at time t4).

Now consider Fig. 3.6 (in which B is *updating* record R and therefore requests it via an XFIND instead of just a simple FIND). Here the situation is even worse: When the rollback occurs, B's update to R is lost, because it is overwritten by R's original (pre-A) value—another version of the lost update problem. Again we do not have serializability.

Transaction A	time	Transaction B
—		—
—		—
—		—
XFIND R	t1	—
—		—
UPD R	t2	—
—		—
[XRELEASE R]	t3	—
—		—
—	t4	XFIND R
—		—
—	t5	UPD R
—		—
*** ROLLBACK ***	t6	—
		—

Fig. 3.6 B's update is lost at time t6.

While the situation in Fig. 3.5 may be tolerable in some circumstances (see below), that in Fig. 3.6 is definitely not. Hence, in order to avoid the possibility of losing updates through rollback, no transaction must *ever* be allowed to update an uncommitted change. We can achieve this state of affairs by disallowing the "XRELEASE" operation in transaction A; for if transaction A cannot release the lock on its uncommitted update in the first place, then transaction B in turn cannot acquire a lock on it and thus cannot update it. The lock can be released only when a point is reached at which it can be guaranteed that the update is no longer subject to possible rollback. That point is of course end-of-transaction, as explained in Chapter 1. We therefore introduce a new protocol, *protocol PXC,* which we obtain from protocol PX by appending the additional rule:

■   Exclusive locks are retained until end-of-transaction (COMMIT or ROLL-BACK).[4]

We can now see why, as indicated in Section 3.2, exclusive locks are not released by a simple "XRELEASE" operator (and why no such operator is even provided). Instead, the semantics of COMMIT and ROLLBACK are extended to include the release of such locks. In general, these operators will release *all* locks

---

4. If a transaction acquires an X lock on a record R and then relinquishes its addressability to that record without updating it (typically by moving the cursor on to some other record), then that lock could be released prior to end-of-transaction—though, as we shall show in Section 3.8, the execution may then no longer be serializable. (Releasing locks "early" is not a good idea, in general.) Alternatively (and more safely), the X lock could be downgraded to "shared" or S level (see Section 3.6). For simplicity we shall generally ignore both these possibilities.

held by the terminating transaction—not just exclusive locks, but also any other locks still held by the transaction at that time (see Sections 3.6 and 3.7).[5] In the case of COMMIT, any updates made by the transaction are now said to be committed. A committed update is guaranteed never to be rolled back.

Protocol PXC is sufficient to prevent loss of updates because of rollback. In terms of Fig. 3.6, B would go into a wait state at time t4; it would not actually obtain addressability to R (and a lock on R) until after time t6, and thus there would be no question of its update being lost because of A's rollback. What about the situation in Fig. 3.5? As already suggested, there are cases where it may be acceptable to permit a transaction to see (but not change) an uncommitted update. (The "see" operation is basically a special form of FIND that does not request a lock on the found record. The FIND at time t4 in Fig. 3.5 must be understood to be of this form. We shall have more to say on this topic in Section 3.12.) An example of such a situation might be a transaction that (1) is performing some sort of statistical analysis, (2) is not interested in 100 percent accuracy, and (3) would prefer not to be held up waiting for data to be committed and locks to be released. But in general such a transaction should operate with considerable circumspection.

As an aside, we remark that protocol PXC is actually stronger than is strictly necessary, in the following sense. To avoid the possibility of losing updates because of rollback, it is sufficient to guarantee merely that no transaction be allowed to update an uncommitted change. We could provide such a guarantee by allowing updates to be "committed" (and locks released) one by one as the updates are made, instead of saving them all up to end-of-transaction. If a rollback occurs then only uncommitted updates would need to be undone. But then of course the transaction would no longer be atomic (all or nothing); also, special and possibly rather complex application logic would be needed for trying again after a rollback, since in general some updates would have been done and some not (and some of those that have been done may even have been subsequently overwritten by other transactions). In practice, therefore, updates *are* normally all unlocked and committed together as stipulated by protocol PXC.[6]

---

5.   Actually, some locks may not even be released by COMMIT or ROLLBACK. See Section 3.12. We note also that, though for expository reasons we have treated protocols PX and PXC separately, in practice a system that supports protocol PX will almost certainly enforce the stronger protocol PXC automatically. That is, no special action is required on the part of the application programmer in regard to protocol PXC over and above any that may already be required for protocol PX.

6.   At the end of Section 1.1 we mentioned the possibility that some data may not be recoverable. Updates to nonrecoverable data cannot be automatically rolled back. There *may* therefore be no need to defer the unlocking of such updates to end-of-transaction. In UDL [1.7] the *baseset* (set of all records of a given record type) is assumed to be the data unit for recoverability purposes; transactions can access a given baseset in either DEFERRED or IMMEDIATE mode (DEFERRED means that locks on uncommitted updates are retained until end-of-transaction, IMMEDIATE means they are released immediately). The mode is specified as a suboption of PROCLEVEL(CHANGE) (see Section 3.11); DEFERRED is the default, and is the only possibility for a recoverable baseset.

3.6 SHARED LOCKS

A transaction may need to keep data locked even if it is not updating. Consider Fig. 3.7, which shows two transactions operating on account (ACC) records: Transaction A is summing account balances, transaction B is transferring an amount 10 from account 3 to account 1. The result produced by A (110) is obviously incorrect; if A were to go on to write this result back into the database, it would actually leave the database in an inconsistent state. It is clear that what A ought to do is to lock each account record as it reaches it, and retain those locks at least until the summation is complete; this will prevent B from updating an account record after A has seen it.

The locks set by A need not be exclusive (X locks), however. X locks would serve the purpose, of course, but they would also reduce concurrency unnecessarily. All that is required is to prevent concurrent transactions from *changing* the data —there is no harm in allowing them just to see it. Accordingly we introduce a second type of lock, the shared or S lock, with definition as follows:

- If transaction T holds a shared lock on some object (say a database record), then a distinct transaction T' can also acquire a shared lock on that object, but no distinct transaction T' can acquire an exclusive lock on that object until all shared locks on it have been released.

(Note that uncommitted updates are still required to be locked exclusive, as discussed in previous sections.) By analogy with "XFIND," we shall use "SFIND" (in UDL, "FIND . . . KEEP") to denote a FIND that includes a request to acquire an S lock on the found record. (In practice, again, the system may provide this function as part of the normal FIND operation.) The operation "SFIND R" is defined as follows: If the S lock cannot be acquired, the transaction goes into a wait state (the SFIND is accepted but not honored at this time); the transaction will resume processing when the lock can be granted (the SFIND can now be honored).

We also introduce an "SRELEASE" operator to release an S lock; note that it is not necessary to keep S locks until COMMIT, since by definition the locked objects cannot be uncommitted changes, and therefore are not subject to rollback.[7] The shorthand form "SRELEASE ALL" is used to release all S locks held by the transaction. (Actually, SRELEASE ALL might not in fact release *all* such locks. See Section 3.12.) In contrast to XRELEASE, data manipulation languages typically do provide an explicit form of the SRELEASE operator.

To return to the example of Fig. 3.7: Transaction A in that example should use "SFIND" for each ACCOUNT record, and can then use "SRELEASE ALL" to release the S locks on those records after the summation is complete. The effect on the example is shown in Fig. 3.8.

---

7. As indicated in Footnote 4, it is generally not a good idea to release locks before end-of-transaction, even if the data has not been updated (because serializability can no longer be guaranteed). But the fact is that most systems do permit such early release, which is why we discuss the possibility here.

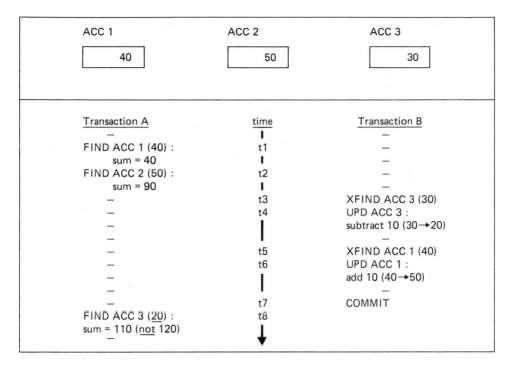

Fig. 3.7 Transaction A produces incorrect results.

ACC 1		ACC 2		ACC 3	
40		50		30	

Transaction A	time	Transaction B
—		—
SFIND ACC 1 (40) :	t1	—
sum = 40		—
SFIND ACC 2 (50) :	t2	—
sum = 90		—
—	t3	XFIND ACC 3 (30)
—	t4	UPD ACC 3 :
		subtract 10 (30→20)
—		—
—	t5	XFIND ACC 1 :
—		wait
SFIND ACC 3 :	t6	wait
wait		wait
wait		wait

Fig. 3.8 Deadlock occurs at time t6.

97

As can be seen, the result is that a deadlock occurs at time t6! A moment's reflection will show that this effect, undesirable as it may appear at first sight, is exactly what is wanted: The system's deadlock resolution mechanism will come into play, a victim will be selected and rolled back (giving the other transaction a chance to complete), and the victim can then try again.

The interaction between shared and exclusive locks can conveniently be expressed by means of a *compatibility matrix* (or compatibility table). See Fig. 3.9. The matrix is interpreted as follows. Consider some lockable object, say database record R; suppose that some transaction T currently has a lock on R as indicated by the entries in the column headings (X = exclusive lock, S = shared lock, dash = no lock); and suppose that some distinct transaction T' issues a request for a lock on R as indicated by the entries down the left-hand side (for completeness we again include the "no lock" case). An "N" indicates a conflict (the requesting transaction T' cannot acquire its lock), a "Y" indicates compatibility (the requesting transaction T' can acquire its lock). It follows from the definitions that the matrix must be symmetric.

	X	S	–
X	N	N	Y
S	N	Y	Y
–	Y	Y	Y

Fig. 3.9 Lock type compatibility matrix.

Note: Conflict usually means that the requesting transaction has to wait (as in our definitions of XFIND and SFIND). In some systems, however, control is given straight back to the requesting transaction with an indication that the data is locked, on the principle that there may be other useful work that can be done. UDL provides a NOWAIT option on FIND to request immediate return of control if the FIND encounters a lock in such a system. If a lock is encountered and NOWAIT has been specified in such a case, an interrupt occurs and control is passed to a special DENIAL procedure. Note that FIND . . . NOWAIT cannot possibly cause a deadlock.

A system that supports S locks in addition to X locks provides a basis for a slightly different approach to the lost update problem (original version, as described in Section 3.1). Basically, instead of requiring transactions to obtain an X lock on records at FIND time if those records are to be updated, we allow them to obtain an S lock instead, and "promote" that S lock to an X lock if and when the update actually occurs. The advantage of this approach, intuitively, is that fewer X locks are needed and hence concurrency is increased; the disadvantage, again intuitively, is that more deadlocks may occur. The approach thus involves replacing protocol PX by a revised protocol PS, as follows:

■ **Protocol PS.** Any transaction that intends to update a record R must first execute "SFIND R" to obtain addressability to that record and to acquire an S lock on it. After the transaction has acquired the lock, any subsequent attempt to update the record must be by means of an "UPDX R" operation, which not only updates the record but also promotes the S lock on that record to X level.

(As usual, "UPDX" is merely a notation. In practice the system will issue the necessary X lock request automatically as part of the normal update operation.)

We also replace protocol PXC by a revised protocol PSC accordingly. PSC is obtained from PS in exactly the same way as PXC was obtained from PX—namely, by appending the rule that X locks are retained until end-of-transaction.

The effect of applying protocol PS to the lost update problem of Fig. 3.1 is shown in Fig. 3.10.

It can be seen that protocol PS is a "case (b)" approach to the lost update problem (see the remarks on this subject in Section 3.1): Transaction A is made to wait at time t3. If transaction B were to go on to release its S lock on R, transaction A's update would subsequently be allowed. In the particular case at hand, however, transaction B attempts to promote its S lock to X level at time t4, at which point a deadlock occurs.

Transaction A	time	Transaction B
—		—
—		—
—		—
SFIND R :	t1	—
copy R. F into ATEMP		—
—		—
—	t2	SFIND R :
—		copy R. F into BTEMP
—		—
UPDX R :	t3	—
wait		—
wait		—
wait		—
wait	t4	UPDX R :
wait		wait
wait		wait
wait		wait

Fig. 3.10 Deadlock occurs at time t4.

The foregoing discussion of protocol PS (and protocol PSC) touches on the general topic of lock promotion. Our explanation of the compatibility matrix of Fig. 3.9 was in terms of *distinct* transactions T and T'. What if T and T' are not distinct? Suppose transaction T holds a lock of some type on some object and it requests another lock, of the same type or of a different type, on that same object. (This is exactly what happens when a successful "SFIND R" is followed by a request to "UPDX R.") Clearly, a transaction should not be allowed to lock *itself* out. Instead, the second request should be granted (unless it conflicts with a lock held by some distinct transaction, as in Fig. 3.10); and if the second request is for a lock type that is *stronger* than the type of the current lock, then the lock should be promoted to that stronger type. (So far we have discussed only two types of lock, X and S, but others will be introduced later in the chapter. See Section 3.11 for a general discussion of relative lock strengths.) Considerations of this nature suggest that a lock is a rather more complex object than the simple model presented at the beginning of Section 3.2, which consisted just of a pair:

```
< locked-object-ID, transaction-ID >
```

This is not the place for a comprehensive discussion of the internal structure of a lock, but it should be clear that the following information must be included in addition to the pair of items just mentioned:

- For each lock type (X, S, etc.),

  1. count of the number of times the transaction has explicitly requested the lock under this type;

  2. count of the number of times the system has implicitly requested the lock under this type on the transaction's behalf (for example, because the system automatically treats a FIND as an SFIND).

- Strongest lock type under which the lock is currently acquired.

A given object is considered to be locked if a corresponding lock exists in which any of the counts is nonzero. The semantics of operators such as XFIND, SFIND, SRELEASE, etc. must be defined appropriately in terms of those counts. For example, "SFIND R" could be defined to add one to the applicable count (among other things), and "SRELEASE R" to reduce that count by one (again, among other things).

Aside: In the case of lock type X, a count is not really necessary—all that is needed is a simple yes/no indicator (for we assume that, once an object is locked exclusive, that lock will not be released until end-of-transaction; as already indicated, there is no "XRELEASE" operator, other than COMMIT or ROLLBACK, to reduce such a count to zero). But for symmetry and to simplify our explanations we will assume throughout this chapter that there is indeed a count for each lock type, even for type X.

3.7   UPDATE LOCKS

As pointed out in the previous section, protocol PS suffers from a tendency to produce an increased number of deadlocks. In fact, experiments have shown [3.6] that, in a system supporting protocol PS, lock promotion requests such as those in Fig. 3.10 are the major source of deadlock (not the only source). Protocol PX, on the other hand, offers a lower degree of concurrency. Some systems therefore employ a slightly different protocol, which we will call protocol PU. Protocol PU involves a new type of lock, the *update lock* or U lock. Informally, a U lock represents an indication that the transaction *may* be going to update the record; it is compatible with S locks but not with other U locks, and of course not with X locks (see Fig. 3.11).

- **Protocol PU.** Any transaction that intends to update a record R must first execute "UFIND R" (in UDL, "FIND R . . . HOLD") to obtain addressability to that record and to acquire a U lock on it. After the transaction has acquired the lock, any subsequent update of the record (which must be via "UPDX R") will promote that lock to X level.

We also replace protocol PSC by a correspondingly revised protocol PUC, stipulating as usual that X locks are retained until end-of-transaction.

Referring again to Fig. 3.10, it should be clear that replacing the two SFINDs by UFINDs will prevent the deadlock. (It will also reduce concurrency to the level of that in Fig. 3.2, in this particular example; but, in general, protocol PU does permit slightly more concurrency than protocol PX.) Note that once a transaction has acquired a U lock on a record, that transaction is *guaranteed* to be able to update that record eventually (barring rollback, of course, and assuming that all transactions are following at least a protocol that requires them to obtain an X lock on an updated record at the time they update it, if not sooner).

If a transaction acquires a U lock on a record and then does not update that record after all, then the U lock can be released. (As usual, however, we do not recommend releasing locks early.) Alternatively (and more safely), the U lock could be downgraded to S level. For simplicity we shall generally ignore both these possibilities.

	X	U	S	—
X	N	N	N	Y
U	N	N	Y	Y
S	N	Y	Y	Y
—	Y	Y	Y	Y

Fig. 3.11 Lock type compatibility matrix (U locks included).

By now the reader may be somewhat confused by the number of different protocols introduced in this chapter so far. A brief review may be helpful (more protocols are still to come). We have discussed three protocols, protocols PSC, PUC, and PXC, any of which can be used to avoid the lost update problem. (We have also discussed protocols PS, PU, and PX, but in practice these three exist only as constituents of the three stronger protocols already mentioned.) A given system might enforce exactly one of the three (PSC, PUC, or PXC)—for example, System R enforces PSC, IMS enforces PUC—in which case all transactions operate in accordance with the same set of rules, and the application programmer probably need not be aware of those rules. Alternatively, the system might allow some transactions to follow one protocol and others another—for example, DBTG allows transactions to use either PSC or PXC. In this latter case programmers *must* be aware of the rules, since they are responsible for indicating which particular protocol they wish to follow.

3.8 TWO-PHASE LOCKING

So far we have said that locks on uncommitted updates must be held until end-of-transaction but that other locks *may* be released sooner. However, *any transaction that releases a lock and then goes on to acquire another lock always runs the risk of producing incorrect results.* That is, it is always possible to define a second transaction that could execute concurrently with the first in such a way that the interleaved execution is not serializable and therefore not correct. Putting matters more positively, we have the following *theorem* [3.2]:

Theorem. *If* all transactions obey the following rules:

a) before operating on any object the transaction first acquires a lock on that object; and

b) after releasing a lock the transaction never acquires any more locks;

then all interleaved executions of those transactions are serializable.

Anything less represents a trade-off (releasing locks earlier than allowed by the theorem may give more concurrency but may also produce the wrong answer). The trade-off may or may not be safe, as we shall see.

Note: The term "lock" in the theorem means any kind of lock (an S lock or stronger). As usual, of course, updates are assumed to be locked exclusive.

Let us examine what is going on here in a little more detail. First, a transaction that obeys rules (a) and (b) of the theorem is said to be *two-phase,* or equivalently to satisfy *the two-phase locking protocol* (2PL)[8]; the two phases are a *growing* phase,

---

8. Nothing to do with two-phase commit, incidentally.

during which locks are acquired, and a *shrinking* phase, during which they are released.[9] The theorem, which is accordingly called the two-phase locking theorem, may thus be restated:

If all transactions are two-phase, then all executions are serializable.

Note carefully, however, that the theorem does not state that all transactions *must* be two-phase for a given interleaved execution to be serializable. That is, the condition that all transactions be two-phase is *sufficient* but not *necessary* to guarantee serializability. An example will help to clarify this point. Let F, G, H be fields in the database (for simplicity we express the example directly in terms of fields rather than in terms of their containing records), and let transactions A and B be defined as follows:

```
(A)    H := F + 1 ;
(B)    F := G + 1 ;
```

Now consider Fig. 3.12. Given an initial state of the database in which $F = G = H = 0$, the possible correct results are those that would be produced by the two possible serial executions A-then-B and B-then-A:

```
Initially  :   F = 0,   G = 0,   H = 0
A-then-B   :   F = 1,   G = 0,   H = 1
B-then-A   :   F = 1,   G = 0,   H = 2
```

The interleaved execution of Fig. 3.12 produces

$$F = 1, \quad G = 0, \quad H = 1$$

(same as A-then-B). In fact, the execution of Fig. 3.12 is equivalent to the serial execution A-then-B, *regardless* of the actual data values involved for F, G, and H. That execution is thus serializable and so correct. However, the 2PL protocol would prohibit A's "XFIND H" at time t7; in other words, a system that enforced two-phase locking would fail transaction A at that time. Such a system could therefore not support this particular interleaved execution, even though it is correct.

Suppose, however, that the system does allow (shared) locks to be released early (that is, transactions are allowed to be non-two-phase), which is the case with all systems that this writer is aware of; and consider the person responsible for the design of application A. Under what circumstances can that designer safely decide to release the lock on F early? The answer is that such a decision is safe *if* the designer knows that transaction A will be executed in parallel only with transactions such as transaction B that do not interfere with it. The problem is that, while this condition

---

9. In the case of locks on uncommitted updates (that is, loosely speaking, in the case of *exclusive* locks), we already have the stronger requirement that this shrinking phase be compressed into a single operation (COMMIT or ROLLBACK) at end-of-transaction.

```
        Transaction A              time         Transaction B
        ( H := F + 1 )              |           ( F := G + 1 )
            —                       |               —
        SFIND F :                   t1              —
        copy F into ATEMP           |               —
            —                       |               —
        SRELEASE F                  t2              —
            —                       |               —
            —                       t3          SFIND G :
            —                       |           copy G into BTEMP
            —                       |               —
            —                       t4          XFIND F
            —                       |               —
            —                       t5          UPD F :
            —                       |           replace F
            —                       |               by BTEMP + 1
            —                       |               —
            —                       t6          COMMIT
            —                       |
        XFIND H                     t7
        (violates 2PL)              |
            —                       |
        UPD H :                     t8
        replace H
            by ATEMP + 1            |
            —                       |
        COMMIT                      t9
                                    ↓
```

Fig. 3.12 Interleaved execution of A and B is serializable, yet A is not two-phase.

may be satisfied at the time transaction A is designed, there is no guarantee that it will *always* be satisfied. Suppose we were to introduce a new transaction C, with definition

        (C)   F := H + 1 ;

Note that transactions A and C are interdependent, in the sense that each updates a field that is used as input by the other. Transactions A and B, by contrast, are such that only one of the pair, namely B, updates a field that is used as input by the other.

Now consider Fig. 3.13, which is derived from Fig. 3.12 by replacing transaction B by transaction C. With initial conditions as before, the possible correct results are as indicated below:

        Initially :   F = 0,   G = 0,   H = 0
        A-then-C :   F = 2,   G = 0,   H = 1
        C-then-A :   F = 1,   G = 0,   H = 2

```
         Transaction A              time        Transaction C
         ( H := F + 1 )              |          ( F := H + 1 )
            —                        |             —
         SFIND F :                  t1             —
         copy F into ATEMP           |             —
            —                        |             —
         SRELEASE F                 t2             —
            —                        |             —
            —                       t3          SFIND H :
            —                        |          copy H into CTEMP
            —                        |             —
            —                       t4          XFIND F
            —                        |             —
            —                       t5          UPD F :
            —                        |          replace F
            —                        |             by CTEMP + 1
            —                        |             —
            —                       t6          COMMIT
            —                        |
            —                        |
         XFIND H                    t7
            (violates 2 PL)          |
            —                        |
         UPD H :                    t8
         replace H                   |
            by ATEMP + 1             |
            —                        |
         COMMIT                     t9
                                     ↓
```

Fig. 3.13 Interleaved execution of A and C is not serializable.

The interleaved execution of Fig. 3.13 produces

$$F = 1, \quad G = 0, \quad H = 1$$

That execution is thus not serializable and not correct. (Again, the 2PL protocol would prohibit A's "XFIND H" at time t7, thus avoiding the incorrect execution.) In effect, therefore, the decision to release A's lock on F early amounts to an act of faith that A will never run in parallel with a transaction such as transaction C. Only if this act of faith can somehow be justified is such a decision totally safe.

The 2PL theorem therefore provides guidelines for the safe design of transactions. Unfortunately, our original statement of that theorem is a little misleading. The rules (a) and (b) are accurate as stated, but it must be clearly understood that sometimes it is the *nonexistence* of some data that is the "object" to be locked! The following example illustrates this point. Again, let F, G, H be fields in the database (for simplicity we again express the example in terms of fields, but note that we therefore have to assume that it is possible to create and destroy individual fields), and let transactions A and B be defined as follows:

```
(A)    if F exists
       then G := 1 ;
       else G := 0 ;

(B)    if F does not exist
       then
           do ;
               create F ;
               G := 1 ;
           end ;
```

Suppose that initially F does not exist, and consider the interleaved execution of Fig. 3.14. In this example there is in fact only one possible correct result:

```
A-then-B   :   F exists,   G = 1
B-then-A   :   F exists,   G = 1
```

The interleaved execution of Fig. 3.14 produces

```
F exists,   G = 0
```

and is thus not serializable and not correct. To force serializability, we need to be able to prevent B from creating F so long as A thinks that F does not exist. F is an example of what is called a *phantom* (as far as A is concerned). To prevent the creation of the phantom, A needs to be able to apply a lock to the *nonexistence* of F at time t1. Such a lock will cause transaction B to go into the wait state at time t3 (the time of the INSERT), because the INSERT will attempt to update that "nonexistence."

We will discuss the question of locking phantoms in Section 3.12. However, the following may be helpful if the reader is having difficulty in understanding the concept at this stage. Instead of thinking in terms of fields being created and destroyed, imagine instead that all fields "physically" exist all the time but that they all have a special associated indicator field to show whether they "logically" exist or not. Creating and destroying a field thus becomes a matter of updating the corresponding indicator field, and an existence test becomes a test on the value of this indicator field. The two "FIND F" statements in Fig. 3.14 wil have to be changed to "SFIND F" statements. Transaction A's SFIND at time t1 will then be successful, and F can be locked, regardless of whether the indicator field is set or not. Transaction B's SFIND will cause B to wait at time t3.

We conclude this section by reminding the reader that the example of Fig. 3.3 (Section 3.3) also shows a serializable execution in which at least one of the transactions (which?) is not two-phase. As indicated in Section 3.3, that execution is thus also one that could not be supported in a system that enforced the 2PL protocol.

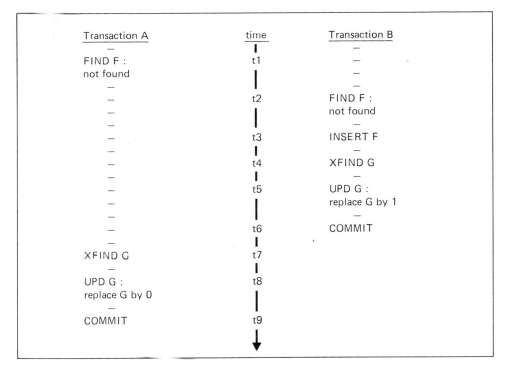

Fig. 3.14 Interleaved execution of A and B is not serializable.

3.9 DEADLOCK AVOIDANCE

We have already suggested, in Section 3.4, that systems generally allow deadlocks to occur rather than trying to avoid them. This statement is certainly true for most centralized systems, where avoiding deadlock is generally more costly than it is worth (the situation is different in a distributed system, where, as indicated earlier, the trade-offs are different). However, there do exist avoidance techniques that can be used in a database environment, and for completeness we include in this section a brief discussion of four of them: transaction scheduling, request rejection, transaction retry, and timestamping.

Transaction Scheduling

This approach involves scheduling transactions for execution in such a way that two transactions will simply not be run concurrently if their data requirements conflict. It obviously requires that each transaction's data requirements be known prior to execution time, which involves either explicit declaration of those requirements or some automatic analysis of the program at, for example, compile time. As pointed out in Section 3.4, however, the *precise* data requirements of a given transaction typically cannot be known until run time; as a result, the scheduling approach tends to be unnecessarily pessimistic. Consider the TRANSFER transaction of Chapter 1, for example. That transaction updates two ACCOUNT records. However, exactly which ones they are is not known until run time; the only safe assumption that can be made is that *any* ACCOUNT record may be updated, and hence the data requirements of TRANSFER must be assumed to span the entire set of ACCOUNTs. No other transaction that accesses any ACCOUNT records at all can be allowed to execute concurrently with TRANSFER. It is clear that this approach will tend to produce a rather low level of concurrency. (It is interesting to note that the earliest versions of IMS supported the scheduling approach but that later versions introduced record-level locking techniques along the lines discussed in this chapter.)

We remark that the scheduling approach is really a locking scheme in which (a) the lockable unit is an entire set of records instead of one individual record, and (b) locks are applied (tested and set) at program initiation time instead of during execution.

Request Rejection

A second way to prevent deadlock is simply to reject any lock request that if accepted would immediately cause it, returning a "request denied" indication to the transaction. (Note that accepting a lock request causes a deadlock if and only if the lock cannot be granted immediately—that is, the transaction goes into a wait state—*and* adding the appropriate edge to the Wait-For graph closes a cycle in that graph.) This solution is a little more flexible than the automatic resolution technique discussed in Section 3.4 (that is, choosing a victim and rolling that victim back); the transaction whose request is denied may be able to wait for a short timeout and then try its request again; even if it has no option but to issue an explicit ROLLBACK itself, at least it does have the chance to generate an appropriate output message or to tidy up other data files or variables before doing so.

Transaction Retry

The technique of this subsection was proposed by Rosenkrantz et al. [3.19] in the context of a distributed system, but it could also be used in a centralized system in principle. The technique comes in two versions, "Wait-Die" and "Wound-Wait." The basic idea in both is, again, to avoid the creation of a cycle in the Wait-For graph, but such avoidance is achieved, not by inspection of the graph, but by introduction of a suitable protocol that makes such cycles impossible. (Because of this fact, it is not actually necessary to maintain the graph at all; it is only necessary to be able to tell whether a given record is locked and, if so, by which transaction.) The protocol works as follows.

■ Every transaction is timestamped with its start-time. The system must guarantee
that no two transactions can start simultaneously and thus that timestamps are
unique.

■ When a transaction A requests a lock on a record that is already locked by
another transaction B, then one of two things happens:

a) In Wait-Die, A waits if it is older than B, otherwise it "dies"—that is, it is
rolled back and automatically retried;

b) In Wound-Wait, A waits if it is younger than B, otherwise it "wounds"
B—that is, B is rolled back and automatically retried. Note that the first
component of the name in each case (Wait- or Wound-) indicates what happens when A is *older* than B.

■ A transaction retains its original timestamp even if it is rolled back and retried.

Note, incidentally, that this *is* a locking technique, not a timestamping technique in
the sense of Section 3.14, even though timestamps are involved. Wait-Die guarantees that all waits consist of older transactions waiting for younger ones, Wound-
Wait guarantees that all waits consist of younger transactions waiting for older ones.
Whichever version is in effect, it is clear that it is impossible to find a sequence of
transactions T1, T2, T3, . . . , Tn such that T1 is waiting for T2, T2 is waiting for
T3, . . . , and Tn is waiting for T1; thus deadlock cannot occur.

The technique is illustrated in Figs. 3.15 and 3.16. We assume in both of these
figures that transaction A is older than (starts before) transaction B.

Transaction A (older)	time	Transaction B (younger)
—		—
—		—
XFIND R1	t1	—
—		—
—	t2	XFIND R2
—		—
XFIND R2	t3	—
wait		—
wait		—
wait	t4	XFIND R1 :
wait		*** ROLLBACK ***
wait		*** & RETRY ***
(resume) XFIND R2		
—		

Fig. 3.15 Wait-Die (example).

Transaction A (older)	time	Transaction B (younger)
—		—
—		—
XFIND R1	t1	—
—		—
—	t2	XFIND R2
—		—
XFIND R2	t3	*** ROLLBACK ***
—		*** & RETRY ***
—		

Fig. 3.16 Wound-Wait (example).

Rosenkrantz et al. [3.19] compare the performance of the two techniques and give a number of improvements on the basic algorithms as sketched above. They also prove that every transaction is guaranteed to terminate; that is, livelock cannot occur, and transactions can only be rolled back and retried a finite number of times.

We conclude this subsection by noting that timestamps per se are not actually essential to the foregoing schemes, as [3.19] points out. All that is needed is a means of assigning arbitrary unique identifiers to transactions. It is not even necessary to assign the identifiers in ascending sequence. (Terms such as "older" and "younger" will of course then have to be modified accordingly.) In fact, using timestamps as such may not be a very good idea, if accesses to the system clock are expensive; a simple system-maintained counter or pseudorandom-number generator may serve the purpose better.

Timestamping

Timestamping techniques are discussed in Section 3.14; we mention them here only for completeness. Briefly, one of the major advantages of such techniques is precisely that they are *not* locking techniques—no data is ever locked, and thus deadlock is impossible.

3.10 LOCKING GRANULARITY

So far we have generally assumed that the unit of locking is the individual record. However, locks can also be applied to larger or smaller units of data: for example, to an entire database, or to a file (a baseset in UDL terms—that is, the set of all records of a given type); or, going to the opposite extreme, to a specific field within an individual record. We speak of *locking granularity* [3.3, 3.4]. As usual, there is a trade-off: the finer the granularity, the greater the concurrency; the coarser, the fewer locks to be set and tested and the lower the overhead. For example, if a transaction has an X lock on an entire baseset, then there is no need to set X locks on individual records within that baseset, which obviously reduces the total number of locks; on the other hand, of course, no concurrent transaction will be able to access the baseset at all.

By way of example, we mention the fact that the *logical* concept of locking individual records is frequently implemented by *physically* locking pages or blocks (containing multiple records). This fact does not affect the model of locking we are presenting. But it does illustrate a general principle, which we shall call Implementation Principle No. 1: *The system can safely lock more than the minimum requested.* "Safely" here means that integrity is not compromised, though of course concurrency may suffer and there may be an increased chance of deadlock. (Also there is some danger that programs may come to rely on the fact that the implementation is doing more than is strictly necessary, and this could lead to problems in moving programs between systems.)

In passing we note another fairly obvious general principle, namely, Implementation Principle No. 2: *The system can safely retain locks longer than requested.*

We defer to the next section the question of how baseset locks are actually acquired. Here we content ourselves with noting that once acquired, such locks are normally released only when the program completes, not at COMMIT. A system that does release baseset locks at COMMIT (or on rollback, if control is returned to the transaction) must provide a means—possibly implicit—for the program to reacquire those locks before continuing. Moreover, the program may have to wait a very long time to reacquire a baseset lock if some other transaction has seized that baseset in the interim, which is a good argument against releasing such locks.

We also remark that update locks (U locks) really make sense only at the finest granularity. For example, in a system supporting record locking and baseset locking, U locks are applicable at the record level but not at the baseset level. This is because, by definition, acquiring a U lock on an object means that the transaction may subsequently attempt to promote that lock to X level, and dynamically promoting baseset-level locks in this way is likely to lead to unacceptable delays.

We conclude this section with a brief note concerning *fansets*. A database that includes fansets has two fundamentally distinct ways of representing information, via records and via parent-child links. The operators CONNECT, DISCONNECT, and RECONNECT provide for the creation, destruction, and modification of such links. For completeness it might be desirable to consider fansets and links, as well as basesets and records, as lockable resources. (A conscious decision *not* to take this approach was made in the design of UDL, to reduce complexity. Instead, CONNECT, DISCONNECT, and RECONNECT are considered as update operations against the corresponding parent and child records, and a transaction using them must acquire the necessary locks on those records or on their containing basesets.)

3.11 INTENT LOCKING

Suppose that a given transaction T wishes to process some baseset B, and suppose also that T requires B to be *stable*—that is, the logic of T is such that it cannot tolerate any changes occurring in B as a result of updates by concurrent transactions. Suppose also that T itself does not wish to make any changes in B either. T can achieve the desired stability by obtaining a shared lock (S lock) on B. On receipt of T's S lock request, the system must be able to tell whether any other transaction is already making changes to B, or, more generally, whether any other transaction already has an X lock on any record in B; if so, then T's request cannot be granted at this time. How can the system detect such a conflict?

It is obviously undesirable to have to examine every record in B to see whether any one of them is X-locked by any transaction, or to have to examine all existing X locks to see whether any one of them is for a record in B. Instead, we introduce yet another protocol, the *intent locking protocol*. We discuss this protocol in terms of basesets and records first, then extend it later to the general case. In the case of basesets and records, the protocol requires that transactions obtain an appropriate level of access to the baseset before they are allowed to operate on any records in that baseset. As we shall see, "obtaining an appropriate level of access" is equivalent to "acquiring a lock" (probably an *intent* lock). For definiteness we base the following discussion on UDL, but the concepts are generally applicable.

In UDL, the level of access required for a given baseset is expressed in the declaration of that baseset as the combination of a *processing level* (PROCLEVEL) and a *sharing level* (SHARELEVEL):

```
PROCLEVEL  ( REFERENCE or CHANGE )
SHARELEVEL ( NONE or REFERENCE or CHANGE )
```

(defaults underlined). Intuitively, PROCLEVEL specifies the type of processing this transaction intends to perform on the baseset in question, and SHARELEVEL specifies the transaction's stability requirements with respect to that baseset (that is, the type of processing the transaction can tolerate on this baseset on the part of concurrent transactions). For PROCLEVEL the possibilities are REFERENCE (default), meaning reference-type operations only, and CHANGE, meaning update-type operations (CHANGE subsumes REFERENCE). For SHARELEVEL the possibilities are NONE, REFERENCE, and CHANGE (default).

Aside: In UDL, PROCLEVEL and SHARELEVEL are specified declaratively, as already indicated. Dynamic specification could be supported in addition by introducing OPEN BASESET and CLOSE BASESET statements, if desired. Also, it would be possible to extend both PROCLEVEL and SHARELEVEL to allow explicit specification of, for example, "delete" intent, "update" intent against particular fields, and so on. But such extensions do not seem to offer any possibilities of increased concurrency (though they could be useful for authorization purposes).

We can now rephrase the question from the beginning of this section. Instead of explicitly requesting an S lock on baseset B, transaction T will instead specify SHARELEVEL (REFERENCE) for B, meaning that T has no objection to concurrent transactions *referencing* B but cannot tolerate them *changing* it. T will presumably also specify PROCLEVEL (REFERENCE) for B, since T itself does not intend to make any changes to B. The question is, then: On receiving T's request, how can the system tell whether any concurrent transaction is already using B in such a way as to conflict with T's requirements? The answer is, of course, that (a) the system is aware of all transactions currently using B, (b) for each such transaction it knows the applicable PROCLEVEL and SHARELEVEL, and finally (c) PROCLEVELs and SHARELEVELs interact with each other in a clearly defined manner. We can conveniently define those interactions by means of another compatibility matrix (Fig. 3.17). The row and column headings in that matrix show PROCLEVEL first, SHARELEVEL second (except for the "no access" entry, of course).

The matrix is interpreted as follows. Consider some baseset B; suppose that some transaction T currently has access to B as indicated by the entries in the column headings; and suppose that some distinct transaction T' requests access to B as indicated by the entries down the left-hand side (for completeness we include the "no access" case). An "N" indicates a conflict (transaction T' cannot have its request granted at this time), a "Y" indicates compatibility (transaction T' can have its request granted). The matrix is symmetric.

	(*) NONE	REFERENCE REFERENCE	REFERENCE CHANGE	CHANGE REFERENCE	CHANGE CHANGE	no access
(*) NONE	N	N	N	N	N	Y
REFERENCE REFERENCE	N	Y	Y	N	N	Y
REFERENCE CHANGE	N	Y	Y	Y	Y	Y
CHANGE REFERENCE	N	N	Y	N	N	Y
CHANGE CHANGE	N	N	Y	N	Y	Y
no access	Y	Y	Y	Y	Y	Y

(*) PROCLEVEL is irrelevant so far as conflicts are concerned if SHARELEVEL (NONE) is specified

Fig. 3.17 PROCLEVEL/SHARELEVEL compatibility matrix.

We have already indicated that the combination PROCLEVEL (REFERENCE) plus SHARELEVEL (REFERENCE) can be implemented by an S lock on the base-set. What about the other combinations? SHARELEVEL (NONE) clearly corresponds to an X lock, regardless of PROCLEVEL (though in fact if PROCLEVEL is specified as REFERENCE, SHARELEVEL (NONE) could safely be treated as SHARELEVEL (REFERENCE)—that is, an S lock would be adequate; such an implementation would provide increased concurrency at no cost in integrity). So we have the situation shown in Fig. 3.18.

X and S locks are inadequate to handle the remaining cases: An X lock would not allow SHARELEVEL (REFERENCE) or SHARELEVEL (CHANGE), an S lock would not allow SHARELEVEL (CHANGE) or PROCLEVEL (CHANGE), and hence neither one can appear in any of the "?" positions. (We are ignoring U locks since, as pointed out in the previous section, U locks do not really make sense at the baseset level.) What we do, therefore, is introduce three new *intent* lock types—IS (intent shared), IX (intent exclusive), and SIX (shared, intent exclusive)—which we may define very informally as follows. We suppose that transaction T is requesting a lock of the indicated type on baseset B. For completeness we include informal definitions of lock types S and X at the baseset level. We remark that, just as lock type U applies only at the record level, so the intent lock types apply only at the baseset level.

- IS

  T intends to set S locks on individual records in B, in order to guarantee the stability of those records while they are being processed.

- IX

  Same as IS, *plus* T may update individual records in B and will therefore set X locks on those records.

- S

  T can tolerate concurrent readers, but not concurrent updaters, in B. T itself will not update any records in B.

SHARE ⟶ PROC ↓	NONE	REFERENCE	CHANGE
REFERENCE	X or S	S	?
CHANGE	X	?	?

Fig. 3.18 PROCLEVEL/SHARELEVEL implementation in terms of baseset locks (preliminary version).

- **S I X**

  Combines S and IX: that is, T can tolerate concurrent readers, but not concurrent updaters, in B, *plus* T may update individual records in B and will therefore set X locks on those records.

- **X**

  T cannot tolerate any concurrent access to B at all; T itself may update individual records in B.

The formal definitions of these five lock types are given by another compatibility matrix (Fig. 3.19). In fact, Fig. 3.19 is an expanded version of the lock type compatibility matrix already given in Fig. 3.9 for lock types S and X only. (We are ignoring lock type U.)

The matrices in Figs. 3.17 and 3.19 are clearly identical, apart from their row and column headings. It follows that we now have an implementation for all combinations of PROCLEVEL and SHARELEVEL. The completed version of Fig. 3.18 is thus as shown in Fig. 3.20.

	X	S	IS	SIX	IX	−
X	N	N	N	N	N	Y
S	N	Y	Y	N	N	Y
IS	N	Y	Y	Y	Y	Y
SIX	N	N	Y	N	N	Y
IX	N	N	Y	N	Y	Y
−	Y	Y	Y	Y	Y	Y

Fig. 3.19 Lock type compatibility matrix (baseset-level locking).

SHARE ⟶	NONE	REFERENCE	CHANGE
PROC ↓			
REFERENCE	X or S	S	IS
CHANGE	X	SIX	IX

Fig. 3.20 PROCLEVEL/SHARELEVEL implementation in terms of baseset locks (final version).

If an X or S lock is applied at the baseset level, no record locking is necessary. If one of the intent locks is applied at the baseset level, the system must automatically apply record locking as follows.

■   IS

Each FIND must set an S lock on the record found. (Most systems will then automatically release the lock when the transaction gives up its addressability to the record—typically, when the transaction issues another FIND to move the cursor on to the next record. Once again, however, we remind the reader that we do not recommend releasing locks early. Explicit SFIND operations can be used, if available, to acquire the necessary S locks and *not* to release them automatically.)

■   IX

Each FIND must set a lock on the record found. The lock can be an S, U, or X lock. If the transaction updates the record, an S or U lock must be promoted to X level. If the transaction does not update the record, then the system will typically release the lock as for IS (see the comments above).

■   SIX

FIND need not set any locks (S locks are not needed at the record level). However, updated records must be locked exclusive.

To repeat: The foregoing remarks apply to the ordinary FIND statement. The transaction may additionally use explicit "SFIND," "UFIND," and "XFIND" operations, if available, to acquire locks over and above the implicit locks guaranteed as above and/or to retain locks longer than the duration guaranteed above. ("UFIND" and "XFIND" do not apply in the case of IS, of course.) In UDL, for example, as already mentioned, explicit "SFIND" and "UFIND" operations are specified by means of a KEEP option and a HOLD option, respectively, on the normal FIND statement. There is no direct UDL equivalent to "XFIND."

We are now in a position to state the intent locking protocol in a more general form.

■   Before a given transaction can acquire a lock of a given type on a given object, it must first acquire an appropriate intent lock (IS, IX, or SIX)—or stronger lock, see below—at the next coarser granularity. For example, to acquire an X lock on a record, the transaction must first acquire at least an IX or SIX lock on the baseset containing that record. (Acquiring the baseset lock may be done at program initiation time, as in UDL, or more dynamically—possibly not until the time the record lock itself is requested. See the discussion of System R in Section 3.13.)

Note clearly, however, that if a transaction has acquired an X or S lock at a given granularity, then no locks are needed at all at any finer granularity. If the transaction has acquired an SIX lock at a given granularity, then X locks are still necessary at finer granularities but S (and U) locks are not.

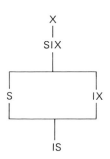

Fig. 3.21 Lock type precedence graph (baseset-level locking).

The notion of "stronger lock" (mentioned in the intent locking protocol) requires some explanation. Intuitively, it is clear that (for example) an X lock is "stronger" than an S lock. In fact, we may arrange the various lock types into a *precedence graph* (Fig. 3.21), which shows the relative strengths of all of them. This graph is interpreted as follows: Lock type L1 is *weaker* (lower in the graph) than lock type L2 if and only if, whenever there is an "N" (conflict) in L1's column in the compatibility matrix at a given position, there is also an "N" in L2's column at that same position (see Fig. 3.19). This definition of relative strength implies that a lock request that fails for a given lock type will certainly fail for a stronger lock type. (It also implies that lock types S and IX cannot be compared—that is, neither one is stronger than the other.) The concept of lock type precedence leads to Implementation Principle No. 3: *The system can safely treat a request for a given lock type as a request for any stronger type.* For example, a system that does not support S locks can interpret all requests for such locks as requests for X locks instead.

For completeness we give in Fig. 3.22 the precedence graph for record-level locks.

The intent locking protocol as stated earlier in this section is actually somewhat oversimplified, in that it assumes that the lockable object types—fields, records, basesets, etc.—form a strict hierarchy. In practice the presence of indexes, pointer chains, and other implementation structures means that it would be more accurate to consider the lockable object types as forming a *directed acyclic graph* [3.3, 3.4]. A hierarchy is merely a special case. For an example, consider Fig. 3.23. We interpret that figure as follows. In order to be able to locate an individual object of the type indicated by any given node, it is necessary first to have located at least one parent of

X
|
U
|
S

Fig. 3.22 Lock type precedence graph (record-level locking).

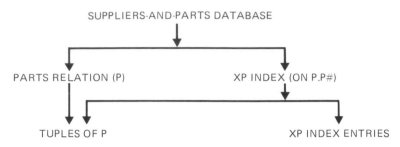

Fig. 3.23 Graph of lockable object types (example).

that object (along one edge of the graph). For example, to locate a particular P tuple, we must already have located the suppliers-and-parts database and either the containing relation (which we assume to give a sequential-scan access path to the tuples) or the index on that relation's primary key (which we assume for the sake of the example to be the only other access path for that relation).

We can now state the intent locking protocol in its most general form.

- Acquiring an X lock on a given object implicitly acquires an X lock on all children of that object.

- Acquiring an S or SIX lock on a given object implicitly acquires an S lock on all children of that object.

- Before a transaction can acquire an S or IS lock on a given object, it must first acquire an IS (or stronger) lock on at least one parent of that object.

- Before a transaction can acquire an IX, SIX, or X lock (or U lock) on a given object, it must first acquire an IX (or stronger) lock on all parents of that object.

- Before a transaction can release a lock on a given object, it must first release all locks it holds on all children of that object.

Thus, to execute the UDL statement

```
FIND NEXT (P WHERE P.COLOR = 'RED') ;
```

using a sequential scan of the P relation (see Fig. 3.23), the transaction must

a) Acquire either an IS or an IX lock on the suppliers-and-parts database. This lock can be acquired implicitly on the transaction's behalf at program initiation time. It will be an IX lock if the transaction has specified PROCLEVEL (CHANGE) for any baseset in the database, an IS lock otherwise.

b) Acquire at least an IS lock on the P relation. This lock can also be acquired at program initiation time. The precise type of lock acquired will depend on the PROCLEVEL and SHARELEVEL specified for P, as explained earlier (Fig. 3.20).

c) If the lock on the P relation is of type IX, SIX, or X, then acquire at least an IX lock on index XP. This lock can also be acquired at program initiation time, and will be of the same type as that acquired for relation P.

d) Unless the lock on the relation P is of type S, X, or SIX, acquire an S, U, or X lock on the specific P record found.

For more details of the intent locking protocol, the reader is referred to [3.3–3.5].

We conclude this section by giving yet another informal characterization of lock types X, S, SIX, IX, and IS, since this topic is the most important of those introduced in this section. (Again we ignore lock type U.) For simplicity we again talk in terms of a transaction T that is requesting a lock of the indicated type on a baseset B. An S, X, or SIX lock on B means that no concurrent transaction can make any changes in B at all. X and SIX both allow T to make changes in B, S does not. The advantage of an X lock over an SIX lock at the baseset level is that there is no need to set X locks on individual records, which may be significant if T will update many records in B. (Setting many locks implies overhead in both space and time, and could lead to abnormal termination if the Lock Manager runs out of space for its lock lists.) Reorganization and similar utilities, in particular, commonly use X locking at a very coarse granularity—sometimes even at the level of an entire database. Last, an IS or IX lock on B means that T is prepared to allow concurrent transactions to make changes in B. IX allows T itself to make changes in B, IS does not. As stated earlier, the three intent lock types (IS, IX, SIX) have no meaning at the record level (more accurately, at the finest granularity, whatever that happens to be).

3.12 LEVELS OF ISOLATION

Suppose that SHARELEVEL (CHANGE) has been specified for a baseset B. To what extent does the transaction have to be aware of the possibility of concurrent change in B? The answer to this question depends on the *level of isolation* specified for B (for the transaction). The concept of isolation level (under the name "degree of consistency") was introduced in [3.4], though there it was applied to an entire transaction rather than to the transaction's use of an individual baseset. In UDL isolation level is specified as a suboption of SHARELEVEL (CHANGE) (since it is irrelevant for other SHARELEVELs):

```
SHARELEVEL ( CHANGE [ ( isolation ) ] )
```

"Isolation" defines the degree of interference this transaction can tolerate with respect to this baseset; the higher the level, the lower the interference (and the lower the concurrency). Many levels can be defined; the following are some of the possibilities (expressed very informally).

Level 1: Don't let this transaction update any uncommitted changes in this baseset.

Level 2: Don't let this transaction see any uncommitted changes in this baseset.

Level 3: Don't let any other transaction change any record in this baseset to which this transaction currently has addressability.

Level 4: Don't let any other transaction change any record this transaction has seen in this baseset.

Level 5: Don't let this transaction be aware of any other transaction's existence at all, so far as this baseset is concerned.

Each level subsumes all preceding levels. This rule is actually slightly arbitrary—to be specific, level 3 does not actually imply level 2—but seems desirable for reasons of intellectual manageability. It leads to Implementation Principle No. 4: *The system can safely treat a request for a given level as a request for any higher level.* The default level in UDL is 5 (in practice keywords should be used rather than integers, for readability and also because it simplifies subsequent interpolation of intermediate levels).

The various levels merit some further discussion. Note first that *no* level allows the update of an uncommitted change. Level 1 does allow the transaction to see uncommitted changes, however. Not until we reach level 3 do we have "cursor stability"—that is, a guarantee that no record will be changed by any other transaction so long as this transaction has a cursor pointing to the record in question (and therefore has addressability to that record). At levels 1 and 2 an operation against a record may fail in various ways even though the transaction does have addressability to it; for an example, see Fig. 3.24. These two levels may seem undesirable from the programmer's point of view, but in fact are exactly the levels supported, for various pragmatic reasons, in certain implemented systems. At these levels the system does not automatically enforce any of the protocols PS, PU, or PX. However, the programmer can use explicit "SFIND," "UFIND," and "XFIND" operations, if available, to prevent surprises such as that of Fig. 3.24.

Transaction A	time	Transaction B
—		—
—		—
FIND R	t1	—
—	t2	—
—		FIND R
—	t3	—
—		DELETE R
—	t4	—
—		COMMIT
—	t5	
UPD R :		
fails because		
R not found !		
—		

Fig. 3.24 A has isolation level less than 3 for R baseset.

Level 3 isolation means that records to which the transaction currently has addressability do not change unpredictably, but others may. This level does not guarantee that the transaction will see the same value for a given record every time it accesses it—it is perfectly possible for a concurrent transaction to change the record (and commit the change) between two such accesses.

In level 4 the effect is as if every FIND were treated as an SFIND (or, in UDL terms, included a KEEP option); if transaction A of Fig. 3.7 had been using level 4, the problem illustrated there would not have arisen. Level 4 thus does guarantee that the transaction will see the same value every time it accesses a given record. But it does not handle the "phantom" problem [3.2], which we may illustrate as follows. Suppose that transaction T, operating at level 4 on the employee baseset, selects all employees with a salary of $20000. None of these records can now be changed by a concurrent transaction until T reaches a commit point. However, there is nothing to stop a concurrent transaction from creating a new employee with a salary of $20000, or updating an existing one so that the salary becomes $20000. If T now selects "employees with a salary of $20000" again it will discover a *phantom*—that is, a record it did not see on the previous occasion.

Level 5 does handle the "phantom" problem. Level 5 means, loosely, that the transaction is not aware of the existence of any concurrent transactions at all, at least so far as this baseset is concerned. (It differs from an X lock at the baseset level in that it does not preclude other transactions from accessing portions of the baseset that this transaction has not touched.) The intent of level 5 is that the transaction should see no changes at all, except of course for changes made by the transaction itself. Thus a request for employees with a salary of $20000 will select the same records every time it is executed—even in the special case where there are no such employees. The implication is that the *access path* used by the DBMS in selecting those records must be locked; for example, if an index on salaries is used, the index entry for $20000 must be locked.[10] This lock will prevent the creation of phantoms, because such creation would require the access path (the index entry, in our example) to be updated. In effect, then, avoiding phantoms requires the ability to lock the *nonexistence* of certain data (as suggested earlier in Section 3.8). See reference [3.24] for a detailed discussion of this problem.

Note: This discussion of level 5 touches on a point which is worth spelling out explicitly, namely that all the locking protocols described in this chapter apply not only to records explicitly requested by the transaction, but also to all records (and other objects) examined by the DBMS in responding to such explicit requests. For example, a search for the next employee record with salary = $20000 may have to wait on some prior employee record in sequence, even if that record does not have salary = $20000, simply because that prior record is locked by some other transaction.

---

10. If the access path is a sequential scan of the baseset, the whole baseset will have to be locked.

The record locking implications for the five isolation levels (in outline) are as follows. Note that the baseset lock must be IS or IX (because SHARELEVEL is CHANGE).

Level 1

"UPD R" implies: If R is locked by some other transaction, *conflict;* otherwise acquire an X lock on R. Release X locks at end of transaction.

Level 2

(Level 1, plus) "FIND R" implies: If R is X-locked by some other transaction, *conflict.*

Level 3

(Level 2, plus) "FIND R" implies: Acquire an S lock on R; release that lock when the cursor is set to a new value.

Level 4

(Level 3, but) retain the S locks until end of transaction.

Level 5

(Level 4, plus) "FIND R" implies: Acquire an S lock on the access path to R; retain that lock until end of transaction.

As already indicated in Sections 3.6 and 3.11, a transaction operating at level 3 or less on some baseset may need to use explicit locking operators (such as KEEP in UDL) in order to acquire locks over and above those guaranteed by that level, and thus to obtain an additional degree of integrity.[11] Note that the corresponding explicit release operators (RELEASE in UDL) can also be used, but that they will not release locks acquired on behalf of the transaction by implicit action of the system; that is, they cannot be used to *undermine* the guaranteed isolation level.

As an aside, we note that some systems (IMS is an example) provide a refinement on KEEP/RELEASE that we may call "keep classes." The basic idea is that KEEP can specify a "class identifier": The record concerned is then not only "kept" (S-locked), but is logically appended to the indicated *class.* (A class is simply a list of addresses of kept records.) It may even be possible to keep the same record simultaneously in multiple classes and/or multiple times in the same class, though these options are not available in IMS. An alternative form of RELEASE is then used to release all records in a specified class. Some examples of the use of "keep classes" in DBTG (the DBTG term is "keep lists") can be found in Volume I.

---

11. It follows from Section 3.8 that a transaction using isolation level less than 5 on some baseset always runs the risk of producing incorrect results (serializability is not guaranteed). Although there is no doubt that lower levels of isolation do have their uses, it is not easy to say exactly what the result of using a given lower level will be in any given situation, nor is it easy to provide the transaction designer with guidance as to what level to use (if the system permits any choice).

Finally, we remark that, in some systems, the implicit locks that are set to guarantee "cursor stability" for level 3 and above are retained across COMMIT (other systems release those locks and therefore set all cursors to null at COMMIT). Retention guarantees that cursor positioning is not lost at a commit point. Such locks can then be released when the cursor is set to a new value, as usual (isolation level 3 only); or the system may guarantee that the locks are retained even if a rollback occurs, in which case they cannot be released until the next commit point. The locks on "kept" records might also be treated in this fashion. In UDL a RETAIN option on COMMIT allows the transaction to indicate that it relies on the retention of such locks.

3.13   DATA MANIPULATION LANGUAGE LOCKING OPERATIONS

In this section we sketch very briefly the locking operations provided in various DMLs, namely UDL, SQL, DL/I, and DBTG. The section is intended primarily as a reference summary rather than as a detailed description of the various language facilities. In particular we are more concerned with concepts than with implementation details. When we say in our discussion of IMS, for example, that each "get" request is a request for at least two locks, we are ignoring the fact that the implementation may already have acquired at least one of those locks as part of a previous operation.

We begin with UDL, since we have already touched on many of the locking aspects of UDL in preceding sections, and drawing the material together now will provide a review of the underlying concepts. Also, UDL is intended to be suitable for implementation on a variety of distinct systems, and therefore includes a very comprehensive set of locking features (of course, a specific implementation would typically support only some subset of this total set). The UDL constructs may therefore help the reader to see how the facilities provided in various specific systems compare and relate to each other.

UDL

1. Declarative features

For each baseset the user specifies a processing level (PROCLEVEL) and a sharing level (SHARELEVEL). The possibilities are as follows:

```
PROCLEVEL   ( REFERENCE or CHANGE [ (mode) ] )
SHARELEVEL ( NONE or REFERENCE or CHANGE [ (isolation) ] )
```

(underlining indicates defaults). The interpretation of PROCLEVEL and SHARE-LEVEL in terms of lock types was given in Fig. 3.20. (Baseset locks in UDL are acquired at program initiation time and are held throughout execution. COMMIT and ROLLBACK operations do not release such locks.) "Mode" is DEFERRED or IMMEDIATE (default DEFERRED), and specifies whether locks on updated records in this baseset are to be released at end-of-transaction or immediately;

DEFERRED is the only possibility if the baseset is recoverable. "Isolation" identifies the isolation level required for this baseset (default level 5).

2. Manipulative features

Manipulative statements have locking implications only if record-level locking is in effect—that is, only if the PROCLEVEL/SHARELEVEL specification for the baseset in question is one of the following:

```
REFERENCE / CHANGE
CHANGE / REFERENCE
CHANGE / CHANGE
```

For other PROCLEVEL/SHARELEVEL combinations the locking aspects of manipulative statements are simply ignored. Assume therefore that one of the foregoing combinations has been specified. For brevity let us ignore IMMEDIATE mode (applicable only if PROCLEVEL is CHANGE—see Footnote 6, p. 95); let us similarly ignore isolation levels 1 and 2 (applicable only if SHARELEVEL is CHANGE—see Section 3.12). The major statements having locking implications are

- FIND
- updating operations
- KEEP and RELEASE
- COMMIT and ROLLBACK

We explain the effects of these operations in terms of the "counter" model of a lock (see Section 3.6); that is, we assume that each lock includes a set of counts, one for each lock type (X, S, etc.) under which the lock is currently held by the transaction. For simplicity we assume that these counts are all independent of each other, though in practice various optimizations are possible (for example, if the X-lock count is nonzero, the other counts are largely irrelevant). We assume that the first request for a lock on a given record causes a lock to be created, with all counts initially zero, and that a lock can be destroyed when the counts are all zero again. Our descriptions of the various DML statements do not include any explicit discussion of lock creation and destruction.

We give a brief summary of the operations first, before getting into details. For SHARELEVEL (CHANGE), FIND sets an S lock (or, if HOLD is specified, a U lock) on the record that is found; that lock can be released when the cursor is set to a new value (unless the isolation level is 4 or 5 or the FIND includes a KEEP option). FIND does not set any locks for other SHARELEVELs. Any updating operation sets an X lock on the affected record; that lock is retained until end-of-transaction. KEEP (not necessary if the isolation level is 4 or 5) sets a shared lock on a designated record; that lock is retained until RELEASE. (For clarity we will refer to locks that are set via KEEP as K locks rather than S locks.) COMMIT and ROLLBACK release all record locks, except possibly those guaranteeing cursor positions (COMMIT only).

Now for the details. (The following explanations may be skipped on a first reading.)

■   FIND

The general format of the FIND statement is

```
FIND record-reference SET ( cursor ) [ NOWAIT ] [ KEEP ] [ HOLD ] ;
```

(As indicated earlier, FIND has locking implications only if SHARELEVEL is CHANGE, so let us assume that this is the case. KEEP and HOLD are simply ignored otherwise. HOLD is also ignored if PROCLEVEL is REFERENCE.) Let the record to be found (that is, the record designated by the record-reference) be R, and let the cursor to be set be C. Suppose also that, prior to the FIND, cursor C points to record R′.

If R is not available and NOWAIT is specified, no record is found, C remains unchanged, and the DENIAL ON-condition is raised. We assume for the rest of this discussion that R *is* available. Let L(R) and L(R′) denote the locks on R and R′, respectively.

- If KEEP is specified, add one to the K-lock count in L(R).
- If HOLD is specified (and PROCLEVEL is SHARE), add one to the U-lock count in L(R); if HOLD is not specified (or PROCLEVEL is REFERENCE), add one to the S-lock count in L(R).
- If the isolation level is not 4 or 5, then: (a) If the FIND that previously set C to point to R′ added one to the U-lock count in L(R′), subtract one from the U-lock count in L(R′); (b) otherwise subtract one from the S lock count in L(R′).
- If the isolation level is 4 or 5 and if the FIND that previously set C to point to R′ added one to the U-lock count in L(R′), subtract one from the U-lock count in L(R′) and add one to the S-lock count in L(R′).

■   Updating operations

- Add one to the X-lock count in L(R).

Note: We have assumed throughout this chapter that in order to update a record it is first necessary to obtain addressability to that record (except for INSERT, of course), and protocols PX, PS, etc., were defined on the basis of that assumption. In fact, however, UDL allows "out of the blue" updates also—that is, updates in which the target record is designated by a general record-reference instead of by means of a cursor. For example:

```
ASSIGN NEW_SAL TO UNIQUE (EMP.SAL WHERE EMP.EMP# = '642332') ;
```

(ASSIGN is the update statement in the PL/I version of UDL.) For locking purposes, such operations are regarded as equivalent to a sequence of operations that (a) set a (system-supplied) cursor to the target record, (b) perform the update using

that system-supplied cursor to identify the record, and then (c) set the system-supplied cursor to null. For example, the ASSIGN statement above is equivalent to the
sequence

```
FIND UNIQUE (EMP WHERE EMP.EMP# = '642332') SET (SYS1) HOLD ;
ASSIGN NEW_SAL TO SYS1->EMP.SAL ;
ASSIGN NULL TO SYS1 ;
```

where SYS1 is a system-supplied cursor. Notice that the FIND statement includes a
HOLD option.

■   KEEP

The general format of KEEP is

```
KEEP record-reference ;
```

(KEEP is ignored if SHARELEVEL is REFERENCE.) Let the record designated by
the record-reference be R.

   – Add one to the K-lock count in L(R).

UDL does *not* provide "keep classes" (see Section 3.12). However, similar function
is provided by the ability to CONNECT records into (possibly local) *sequences* [1.7].

■   RELEASE

The general format of RELEASE is

```
RELEASE record-reference ;
```
or
```
RELEASE ALL ;
```

(RELEASE has no effect on basesets for which SHARELEVEL is REFERENCE.)
Let the record designated by the record-reference in the first format be R.

   – Set the K-lock count in L(R) to zero.

RELEASE ALL sets the K-lock count to zero in all record locks held by the transaction.

■   COMMIT

The general format is

```
COMMIT [ RETAIN ] ;
```

Regardless of whether RETAIN is specified:

   – Set all X-lock counts to zero.
   – Set all K-lock counts to zero.

If RETAIN is not specified, then also:

- Set all U-lock counts to zero.

- Set all S-lock counts to zero.

- Set all cursors to null.

■　ROLLBACK

Same as COMMIT without RETAIN.

■　Exceptions

For a brief note on the general approach to exception-handling in UDL, see Section 1.3. Two specific ON-conditions are provided for dealing with locking exceptions, DENIAL and ROLLBACK. The DENIAL condition is raised by a FIND that includes a NOWAIT option when the desired record is unavailable, as explained earlier. The ROLLBACK condition is raised if the transaction is rolled back but control is returned to the program (that is, the program is not terminated). Further details of these ON-conditions are beyond the scope of this text.

SQL (System R)

1. Declarative features

The System R Lock Manager (part of the Research Storage System—see Volume I) supports lock types X, S, SIX, IX, and IS. However, the SQL language has no declarative locking features as such. Instead, the implementation (the RSS) automatically acquires appropriate intent locks dynamically as necessary. For example, a SQL INSERT statement automatically causes an appropriate lock to be acquired on the table and segment containing the new record, assuming that the transaction does not already hold such locks (which it might do because of some previous SQL operation), and assuming also that the segment in question is a public segment. (In the case of a private segment locks are set at the segment level only, and the only relevant lock types are S and X. Control is returned to the user with a "request denied" indication if the lock cannot be acquired. This is the only situation in System R in which a locking conflict does not cause the requesting transaction to wait.)

Note: From the user's point of view the unit of locking for public data is always the individual record. However, the unit that is physically locked may be a record or a page or an entire segment, depending on the LOCKSIZE attribute of the segment in question (specified when the segment is "acquired" from the system; PAGE is the default). Also, the RSS may sometimes trade a group of locks at one granularity for a single lock at the next coarser granularity. See [3.6].

2. Manipulative features

System R supports protocol PSC (for data in public segments). As already indicated, no explicit locking operations are required on the part of the user, although an explicit LOCK statement is available (see below). Suppose, for example, that a transaction is using FETCH and UPDATE WHERE CURRENT to process a set of records. Conceptually, then, each FETCH will automatically acquire an S lock on the target record, each UPDATE WHERE CURRENT will automatically promote that lock to X level. (However, if the transaction has used the explicit LOCK statement to lock the entire table or segment, then no record locking will be necessary.) Appropriate intent locks will also be acquired as necessary. For example, if the page is the physical unit of locking, then the first FETCH on a given page will acquire an intent lock on that page; subsequent FETCHes against that page will not need to acquire the intent lock again.

Deadlock is resolved by rolling back one of the transactions involved (the victim is not restarted but is simply given a deadlock return code).

An explicit LOCK statement is provided to allow the user to request a single lock on an entire segment or table instead of having to acquire individual locks on the records in that segment or table:

$$
\text{LOCK} \left\{ \begin{array}{l} \text{TABLE table-name} \\ \text{SEGMENT segment-name} \end{array} \right\} \text{IN} \left\{ \begin{array}{l} \text{SHARE} \\ \text{EXCLUSIVE} \end{array} \right\} \text{MODE}
$$

(Vertical stacking of options within braces is intended to show that the options concerned are alternatives.) A SHARE (S) lock will be automatically promoted to X level if an update is made to the segment or table. Any locks acquired via the LOCK statement are retained until the next COMMIT AND RELEASE LOCKS, END TRANSACTION, or RESTORE TRANSACTION (see below).

System R also supports two isolation levels, known for historical reasons as 2 and 3 (default) but corresponding to levels 3 and 5 as we have defined them. The isolation level is defined in the BEGIN TRANSACTION statement and thus applies to all data accessed by the transaction, not to an individual segment or table.

END TRANSACTION and RESTORE TRANSACTION (SQL equivalent of ROLLBACK) release all locks held by the transaction. As explained in Section 1.7, SQL also provides a COMMIT operation, which is used to divide a long transaction into "subtransactions." The format of COMMIT is

```
COMMIT [ AND RELEASE LOCKS ]
```

All updates are committed. If "AND RELEASE LOCKS" is specified, all locks are released (except those guaranteeing cursor positions); otherwise, no locks are released, but all X locks are downgraded to S level.

DL/I (IMS)

This subsection describes the intent specification (PROCOPT) and "Program Isolation" features of IMS. It is an outline description only; for further details the reader is referred to [3.18]. Also, we do not discuss the Fast Path feature; the concurrency control aspects of Fast Path are rather different from those of the rest of IMS, at least in the case of Main Storage databases, and are discussed in Volume I.

1. Declarative features

Intent locks are specified in IMS by means of the PROCOPT (processing option) entry in the PCB. Let T be a given segment type, and let T-set be the set of all occurrences of T. Then (ignoring certain minor details):

- A PROCOPT entry of E (exclusive) for T is a request for an X lock on T-set.
- A PROCOPT entry of I, R, or D (insert, replace, or delete) for T is a request for an IX lock on T-set, with isolation level 3 ("cursor stability": the "cursor" is the PCB itself, which serves as a database position holder at run time).
- PROCOPT entry of G (get) or K (key sensitivity) for T is a request for an IS lock on T-set, again with isolation level 3.
- A PROCOPT entry of GO (express read) for T is a request for *no* lock on T-set and an isolation level of 1.

Notice that different PROCOPTs may be specified for the same segment type in different PCBs (for the same transaction). The actual type of lock that IMS applies to a given segment type must be at least as strong as the strongest PROCOPT specified for that segment type. In practice it may be even stronger. Partly this is because it is necessary to consider the *propagation* of intents through the hierarchical structure; for example, a PROCOPT of D for a given segment type automatically propagates to all physical descendant segment types, regardless of what is explicitly specified for those descendants. Several other considerations, such as the pointer combinations in effect, are also involved. For a fuller discussion of intent propagation, see [3.18].

2. Manipulative features

Individual segment locking is provided in IMS by the *Program Isolation* feature. The general approach is along the lines of protocol PUC; the details are a little different, however, as we now explain. (Note: "U lock" is not an IMS term.)

- A "get" request (regardless of whether "hold" is specified) for any individual segment[12] is a request for at least two and possibly three locks:

---

12. This includes the case of the implied get unique for the parent-to-be in an insert operation.

- a U lock on the root of the physical database record containing the segment;
- a U lock on the root of the logical database record containing the segment, if the segment is a logical child;
- a lock on the segment itself. This lock is a U lock if the "get" is a "get hold" or if it includes a Q command code (see below), an S lock otherwise.

Note that, as a consequence of the foregoing, no two transactions can be simultaneously positioned within the same "database record" (a database record in IMS consists of a root segment and all its descendants, to all levels).

■ Inserting a segment acquires an X lock on that segment.

■ Deleting or replacing a segment upgrades the existing U lock on that segment to X level.

■ Relinquishing addressability to a segment releases the U lock(s) on the corresponding root segment(s), and also the lock on the segment itself if that lock is an S lock or if it is a U lock and the "get" that acquired it did not include a Q command code.

The Q command code mentioned above is the IMS analogue of the KEEP option in UDL, except that the lock acquired is a U lock, not an S lock. For example, the DL/I operation

        GN   ACCOUNT *QB

will apply a U lock to the ACCOUNT segment found. The 'B' following the *Q is the lock *class* (see the discussion of keep classes in Section 3.12). The ACCOUNT segment can subsequently be released by the DL/I "dequeue" operation

        DEQ   B

which will release all segments (in all databases) locked in class B, except of course for any that have been updated and hence are locked exclusive. (There is a limit, specified via the MAXQ parameter in the PSB, on the number of segments the transaction can have locked under *Q at any one time. Also, if the ACCOUNT segment above is already " * Q-locked" in class A, say, the effect of the GN will be to move the segment out of class A and into class B.)

All segment locks are released at a synchronization point.

DBTG

1. Declarative features

Like System R, DBTG has no declarative locking features as such. Unlike System R, however, DBTG requires the transaction to READY the "realms" it intends to use, and for each such realm to specify an appropriate USAGE-MODE:

```
READY [ WITH NO WAIT ] realm-name
                USAGE-MODE IS share-level proc-level
```

where "share-level" and "proc-level" are as follows (by way of explanation we show the UDL equivalents in each case).

DBTG share-level	UDL SHARELEVEL
EXCLUSIVE PROTECTED SHARED	NONE REFERENCE CHANGE

DBTG proc-level	UDL PROCLEVEL
RETRIEVAL UPDATE	REFERENCE CHANGE

If the required realm is not available and WITH NO WAIT is specified, control is returned to the user with a suitable DB-STATUS value. Otherwise, conflicts cause the requesting user to wait. Details of how deadlock is to be handled are left to the implementor (this remark applies to all deadlocks, not just those that may occur on READY).

Realm locks are released by means of the FINISH statement:

```
FINISH realm-name
```

2. Manipulative features

DBTG basically supports protocol PSC, with the additional feature that the user can *optionally* acquire an X lock (not a U lock) on a record at FIND time, by specifying a FOR UPDATE clause in the FIND statement in question. Also, the user always holds at least an S lock on all records that are designated by at least one currency indicator or by at least one entry in at least one keep list (see below). S locks are released when the record concerned is no longer designated by any currency indicator, nor by any keep list entry; thus DBTG effectively supports isolation level 3, but the effect of level 4 can be achieved by means of keep lists. COMMIT and ROLLBACK release all record locks (thus setting all currency indicators to null and all keep lists to empty).

Keep lists are the DBTG analogue of keep classes. The address (database key value) of a given record is appended to the end of a specified keep list by means of the KEEP statement; similarly, the address of a given record is removed from a specified keep list by means of the FREE statement. For completeness we give the formats of these two statements here. The general format of KEEP is

```
KEEP [ database-key-identifier ] USING keep-list-name
```

where the possible formats for "database key identifier" are

$$
\text{CURRENT [record-name] [WITHIN } \left\{ \begin{array}{l} \text{set-name} \\ \text{realm-name} \end{array} \right\} \text{]}
$$

and

$$\begin{Bmatrix} \text{FIRST} \\ \text{LAST} \end{Bmatrix} \quad \text{WITHIN keep-list-name}$$

The general format of FREE is

```
FREE database-key-identifier
```

or

```
FREE ALL [ FROM keep-list-name ]
```

Note that a given record can be simultaneously designated by any number of distinct entries in any number of keep lists.

3.14   TIMESTAMP TECHNIQUES

We conclude this rather lengthy chapter with a brief introduction to timestamping techniques. As mentioned in Section 3.1, there is some possibility that such techniques will become more widespread as experience is gained with distributed database systems. Many variations on the basic idea can be defined [3.12]; however, they all rely on the fact that transactions can be assigned a unique identifier (the timestamp), which can be thought of as the transaction's start-time. In this section we content ourselves with a short description of the basic idea only. (As noted under "Transaction Retry" in Section 3.9, transaction identifiers need not actually be timestamps, but for simplicity we assume throughout this section that they are.)

A fundamental distinction between timestamping and locking techniques in general is that, whereas locking synchronizes the interleaved execution of a set of transactions in such a way that it is equivalent to *some* serial execution of those transactions, timestamping synchronizes that interleaved execution in such a way that it is equivalent to a *specific* serial execution—namely, that execution defined by the chronological order of the timestamps. (As we shall see, conflicts are resolved by restarting transactions. If a transaction is restarted, then it is assigned a new timestamp. The specific serial execution referred to above is that defined by the timestamps of *successfully completed* transactions.)

Since, by definition, there are no locks available to prevent a transaction from seeing uncommitted changes, it is necessary to defer all physical updates to COMMIT time (so that uncommitted changes as such are in fact never created). For a given transaction, if any physical update cannot be performed for any reason, then none of that transaction's physical updates is performed (the transaction is assigned a new timestamp and restarted).

A conflict occurs if a transaction asks to see a record that has already been updated by a younger transaction, or if a transaction asks to update a record that has already been seen or updated by a younger transaction. Conflicts are resolved by restarting the requesting transaction. Since physical updates are never written prior to COMMIT, transaction restart never requires any physical rollback.

Consider, then, a database record R. The system must maintain two synchronization values for R: FMAX (the timestamp of the youngest transaction that has successfully executed a "FIND R" operation) and UMAX (the timestamp of the youngest transaction that has successfully executed an "UPD R" operation; note that "UPD R" is not considered to be successfully executed until the transaction has completed its COMMIT). Let T be a transaction that attempts both "FIND R" and "UPD R" operations, and let t be the timestamp for T. Then (as suggested above) the basic timestamp concurrency control technique can be defined by the following rules.

- ```
  FIND  R:
  if  t  >=  UMAX
  then  /*  OK  -  accept  the  operation  */
      FMAX  :=  MAX  (t,FMAX)  ;
  else  /*  CONFLICT  */
      restart  T  ;
  ```
- ```
  UPD  R  /*  actually  COMMIT  -  see  text  */  :
  if  t  >=  FMAX  &  t  >=  UMAX
  then  /*  OK  -  accept  the  operation  */
      UMAX  :=  t  ;
  else  /*  CONFLICT  */
      restart  T  ;
  ```

Consider Fig. 3.1 once again. Suppose that transaction A is younger than transaction B, that is, timestamp(A) > timestamp(B). If the basic timestamp technique is in force (in which case each of the two "UPD R" operations must be considered part of the appropriate COMMIT), the result will be that B's update will fail and B will be restarted at time t4—as indicated in Section 3.1, a "case (c)" solution to the lost update problem. If transaction A had been older than transaction B instead of younger, transaction A would have been restarted at time t3 (a "case (b)" solution). The reader is invited to consider the effect of the rules given above on other possible interleaved executions of A and B. It is also instructive to consider the situation in which transaction B is replaced by a read-only transaction B', obtained from B by replacing the operation "UPD R" by an operation to "FIND R" a second time.

From the foregoing discussion it should be clear that, if timestamping is in force:

- Protocols PX, PXC, etc., do not apply.
- The locking implications of DML statements can simply be ignored.
- Livelock cannot occur.
- Deadlock cannot occur.
- Repeated restart *can* occur and must be guarded against somehow.
- PROCLEVEL and SHARELEVEL are still useful concepts, because they can be used to control transaction scheduling. That is, a form of locking, at a rather coarse granularity, is still in operation, but it takes effect at program initiation time rather than during transaction execution.

- The concept of isolation level does not apply.
- The COMMIT process itself must be atomic. Synchronization mechanisms (internal locks or latches [3.5]) will be needed to guarantee that this is so.

For a fuller discussion of timestamping techniques in general, including implementation issues, the reader is referred to [3.12].

EXERCISES

3.1 Why do data manipulation languages typically provide an SRELEASE operator but not an XRELEASE operator?

3.2 Define the term serializability.

3.3 State (a) the two-phase locking protocol, (b) the two-phase locking theorem.

3.4 Let transactions T1, T2, and T3 be as follows:

(T1)   A := A + 1 ;

(T2)   A := A * 3 ;

(T3)   A := A ** 2 ;

a) Suppose that these transactions are allowed to run concurrently. If A has initial value zero, how many possible correct results are there? Enumerate them.

b) Suppose the internal structure of T1, T2, T3 is as indicated below:

T1	T2	T3
F1: FIND A (copy into t1)	F2: FIND A (copy into t2)	F3: FIND A (copy into t3)
t1 := t1 + 1	t2 := 3 * t2	t3 := t3 ** 2
U1: UPD A (replace by t1)	U2: UPD A (replace by t2)	U3: UPD A (replace by t3)

If the transactions execute *without* any locking or other concurrency control mechanisms, how many possible interleaved executions are there? Assume that FIND and UPD are each atomic operations.

c) With the given initial value for A (zero), are there any interleaved executions of T1, T2, T3 that in fact produce a "correct" result and yet are not serializable?

d) Are there any interleaved executions of T1, T2, T3 that are in fact serializable but could not be produced if all three transactions obeyed the two-phase locking protocol?

3.5 Give the compatibility matrix for lock types X, S, SIX, IX, IS.

3.6 Define lock type U. Why are U locks generally not applicable other than at the finest granularity? Conversely, why are intent locks generally applicable only at levels above the finest granularity?

3.7 The following list represents the sequence of events in an interleaved execution of a set of transactions T1, T2, T3, . . . :

```
time t0         . . . . . . . . .
time t1     (T1)  :  FIND  A
time t2     (T2)  :  FIND  B
   -        (T1)  :  FIND  C
   -        (T3)  :  FIND  D
   -        (T4)  :  FIND  B
   -        (T5)  :  FIND  A
   -        (T2)  :  FIND  E
   -        (T2)  :  UPD   E
   -        (T3)  :  FIND  F
   -        (T2)  :  FIND  F
   -        (T5)  :  FIND  A
   -        (T5)  :  UPD   A
   -        (T1)  :  COMMIT
   -        (T6)  :  FIND  A
   -        (T5)  :  ROLLBACK
   -        (T6)  :  FIND  C
   -        (T6)  :  UPD   C
   -        (T7)  :  FIND  G
   -        (T8)  :  FIND  H
   -        (T9)  :  FIND  G
   -        (T9)  :  UPD   G
   -        (T8)  :  FIND  E
   -        (T7)  :  COMMIT
   -        (T9)  :  FIND  H
   -        (T3)  :  FIND  G
   -        (T10) :  FIND  A
   -        (T6)  :  FIND  C
   -        (T6)  :  COMMIT
   -        (T11) :  FIND  C
   -        (T12) :  FIND  A
   -        (T13) :  FIND  C
   -        (T11) :  UPD   C
   -        (T13) :  FIND  A
   -        (T10) :  UPD   A
time tn         . . . . . . . . .
```

Assuming that odd-numbered transactions obey protocol PSC and even-numbered transactions protocol PXC, and assuming also that no locks are released prior to end-of-transaction, draw a diagram showing the state of the Wait-For graph at time *tn*. Are there any deadlocks?

3.8 The following diagram (Fig. 3.25) represents a hypothetical interleaved execution of two transactions A and B—hypothetical in that it assumes that no concurrency control mechanism is in effect. What would happen under: (a) protocol PSC (with two-phase locking); (b) protocol PXC; (c) the Wait-Die protocol; (d) the Wound-Wait protocol; (e) the timestamping protocol described in Section 3.14?

Transaction A	time	Transaction B
(begin)	t1	
—		
—	t2	(begin)
—		—
FIND R1	t3	—
—		—
—	t4	FIND R2
—		—
FIND R2	t5	—
—		—
—	t6	FIND R1
—		—
UPD R2	t7	—
—		—
—	t8	UPD R1
—		—

Fig. 3.25 An interleaved execution.

3.9 State the intent locking protocol in its most general form. Assuming the structure given in Fig. 3.23 (graph of lockable object types), list the locks that must be acquired in order to execute the UDL statement

        FIND UNIQUE (P WHERE P.P#= 'P3') ;

Assume that PROCLEVEL and SHARELEVEL are both specified as CHANGE for all base-sets in the database and that protocol PSC is in effect for the transaction in question.

3.10 Define the five isolation levels as discussed in Section 3.12.

REFERENCES AND BIBLIOGRAPHY

3.1 P. F. King and A. J. Collmeyer. "Database Sharing—An Efficient Mechanism for Supporting Concurrent Processes." *Proc. NCC* (1973).

3.2 K. P. Eswaran, J. N. Gray, R. A. Lorie, and I. L. Traiger. "The Notions of Consistency and Predicate Locks in a Data Base System." *CACM* **19**, No. 11 (November 1976).

A classic paper. Introduces the notion of serializability (though not under that name), and gives a proof of the 2PL theorem. The second part of the paper addresses the problem of phantoms, shows that "predicate locks" (locks on the set of records satisfying some arbitrary predicate) can be used to solve this problem, and proposes that, for reasons of implementability, predicates be restricted to a particular (reasonable) simple form.

3.3 J. N. Gray, R. A. Lorie, and G. R. Putzolu. "Granularity of Locks in a Large Shared Data Base." *Proc 1st International Conference on Very Large Data Bases* (September 1975).

3.4 J. N. Gray, R. A. Lorie, G. R. Putzolu, and I. L. Traiger. "Granularity of Locks and Degrees of Consistency in a Shared Data Base." *Proc. IFIP TC-2 Working Conference on Modelling in Data Base Management Systems* (ed. G. M. Nijssen) (January 1976). North-Holland (1976).

These two papers [3.3, 3.4] overlap somewhat. Reference [3.3] introduces the basic ideas of intent locking and discusses some implementation issues; it also makes the case for supporting multiple lock granularities within a single system. Reference [3.4] introduces the concept of isolation levels (under the name "degrees of consistency"), and briefly discusses the intent locking and isolation level aspects of IMS and DMS 1100.

3.5 J. N. Gray. "Notes on Data Base Operating Systems." IBM Research Report RJ2188 (February 1978). Also published in R. Bayer, R. M. Graham, and G. Seegmuller (eds.), "Operating Systems: An Advanced Course." Springer-Verlag (1978).

Consolidates and amplifies much of the material of [3.2–3.4]. Also includes a section on "lock management pragmatics" (implementation considerations), which points out among other things that the connection between lock names and lockable objects is purely a matter of convention and is not understood by the Lock Manager, and gives a brief description of *latches* (a cheap, high-performance type of lock used internally by the Lock Manager itself to guarantee the atomicity of operations such as inserting a new element into a list; such locks typically make use of special machine instructions such as the IBM System/370 "compare and swap").

3.6 J. N. Gray. "Experience with the System R Lock Manager." IBM San Jose Research Laboratory: internal memo (Spring 1980).

This reference consists of a set of notes rather than a finished paper. But it contains some interesting claims, among them the following.

- Locking imposes about 10 percent processing overhead on on-line transactions, about 1 percent on batch transactions.

- Multiple lock granularities are desirable in practice (as suggested in [3.3]).

- Automatic "escalation" works well. (The System R Lock Manager attempts to balance the conflicting requirements of high concurrency and low lock management overhead by automatically replacing groups of fine-granularity locks by single coarse-granularity locks—for example, by trading a set of record locks for a single table lock.)

- Deadlocks are very rare in practice and never involve more than two transactions. Almost all deadlocks (97 percent) could be avoided by the introduction of U locks and protocol PUC (System R supports protocol PSC).

- "Level 5" isolation is more efficient, as well as safer, than "level 3" (these levels are referred to as levels 3 and 2, respectively, in System R).

3.7 J. N. Gray. "A Transaction Model." IBM Research Report RJ2895 (August 1980).

A concise summary of several theoretical results in concurrency control and transaction recovery. Includes a discussion of issues in distributed systems.

3.8 M. W. Blasgen, J. N. Gray, M. Mitoma, and T. G. Price. "The Convoy Phenomenon." IBM Research Report RJ2516 (May 1977; revised January 1979).

The "convoy phenomenon" refers to the problem encountered with high-traffic locks, such as the lock needed to write a record to the log, in systems with preemptive scheduling. If a transaction T is holding a high-traffic lock and is preempted by the system scheduler (that is, is forced into a wait state, for example because its time slice has expired), then a *convoy* of transactions will form, all waiting for their turn at the high-traffic lock. When T comes out of its wait state, it will soon release the lock, but (precisely because the lock is high-traffic) T itself will probably rejoin the convoy before the next transaction has finished with the resource, will therefore not be able to continue processing, and so will go into a wait state again. The problem is that the scheduler is usually part of the underlying operating system, not the DBMS, and is therefore designed to different performance parameters. As the authors observe, a convoy, once established, tends to be stable; the system is in a state of "lock thrashing," most of the CPU is dedicated to task switching, and not much useful work is being done. A suggested solution—barring the possibility of replacing the scheduler—is to grant the lock not on a first-come/first-served basis but rather in random order.

3.9 J. S. Nauman. "Observations on Sharing in Data Base Systems." *Proc. IFIP TC-2 Working Conference on Data Base Architecture* (eds. G. Bracchi and G. M. Nijssen) (January 1979). North-Holland (1979).

A discussion from the implementor's viewpoint.

3.10 P. P. Macri. "Deadlock Detection and Resolution in a CODASYL-Based Data Management System." *Proc. 1976 ACM SIGMOD International Conference on Management of Data* (June 1976).

Analyzes the deadlock handling provided in DMS 1100 and describes an improved technique.

3.11 P. A. Bernstein and N. Goodman. "Approaches to Concurrency Control in Distributed Database Systems." Tech. Report TR-26-78, Aiken Computation Laboratory, Harvard University (1978).

Though primarily concerned with distributed systems, this paper provides a useful summary of locking and timestamping techniques in general.

3.12 P. A. Bernstein and N. Goodman. "Timestamp-Based Algorithms for Concurrency Control in Distributed Database Systems." *Proc. 6th International Conference on Very Large Data Bases* (October 1980).

Describes more than 50 distinct concurrency control algorithms based on timestamping.

3.13 R. Munz and G. Krenz. "Concurrency in Database Systems—A Simulation Study." *Proc. 1977 ACM SIGMOD International Conference on Management of Data* (August 1977).

Suggests that savepoints [1.4] are not a good idea from a concurrency standpoint (though they may be desirable for other reasons).

3.14 D. R. Ries and M. R. Stonebraker. "Effects of Locking Granularity in a Database Management System." *ACM TODS* **2**, No. 3 (September 1977).

An early version of portions of [3.15]. Suggests that coarse-granularity locking is often entirely adequate.

3.15 D. R. Ries. "Effects of Concurrency Control on Database Management System Performance." Memo No. UCB/ERL M79/20 (April 1979), Electronics Research Laboratory, College of Engineering, University of California, Berkeley, CA 94720.

As a result of simulation studies of both centralized and distributed systems, this paper concludes that multiple locking granularities are needed, but that very often coarse granularities and predeclaration of intents give the best results.

3.16 E. G. Coffman, Jr., M. J. Elphick, and A. Shoshani. "System Deadlocks." *ACM Comp. Surv.* **3**, No. 2 (June 1971).

3.17 H. T. Kung and C. H. Papadimitriou. "An Optimality Theory of Concurrency Control for Databases." *Proc. 1979 ACM SIGMOD International Conference on Management of Data* (May 1979).

3.18 IBM Corporation. IMS/VS System/Application Design Guide. IBM Form No. SH20-9025.

3.19 D. J. Rosenkrantz, R. E. Stearns, and P. M. Lewis II. "System Level Concurrency Control for Distributed Database Systems." *ACM TODS* **3**, No. 2 (June 1978).

3.20 Z. Kedem and A. Silberschatz. "Non-Two-Phase Locking Protocols with Shared and Exclusive Locks." *Proc. 6th International Conference on Very Large Data Bases* (October 1980).

3.21 C. J. Date. "Locking and Recovery in a Shared Database System: An Application Programming Tutorial." *Proc. 5th International Conference on Very Large Data Bases* (October 1979).

An early and much abridged version of the present chapter.

3.22 H. T. Kung and J. T. Robinson. "On Optimistic Methods for Concurrency Control." *ACM TODS* **6**, No. 2 (June 1981).

Locking is a *pessimistic* concurrency control, in the sense that it assumes maximum contention among concurrent transactions. In practice it may be quite unlikely that a given data object is required simultaneously by more than one transaction. For example, if the database contains n pages, and each transaction accesses just one page (with all pages equally likely), then the chance of two concurrent transactions actually conflicting is only $1/n$. This paper proposes two *optimistic* concurrency controls that do not perform any locking at all (and are incidentally therefore deadlock-free). The methods work by allowing updates to occur *on a private copy* of the data concerned, and then checking (effectively at end-of-transaction) to see whether there are in fact any conflicts. If not, the updates are installed in the database (via a shadow mechanism similar to that of System R, so the updates are not actually written twice); otherwise the transaction is rolled back and restarted. It is suggested that such a scheme may be superior to locking in many situations—in particular, in systems that are dominated by queries (read-only transactions).

We note that the VERIFY/CHANGE mechanism of IMS Fast Path Main Storage Databases is an example of an optimistic concurrency control. See Volume I.

3.23 J. N. Gray, P. Homan, H. Korth, and R. Obermarck. "A Straw Man Analysis of the Probability of Waiting and Deadlock." IBM Research Report RJ3066 (February 1981).

Presents a very intuitive argument to support the following observed facts:

- Deadlocks and waits are rare.
- Deadlocks almost always involve precisely two transactions.
- The probability of a transaction waiting is proportional to the number of concurrent transactions.
- The probability of a transaction deadlocking is proportional to the number of concurrent transactions.

The analysis also suggests the following conclusions, which have *not* been observed:

- The number of waits is proportional to the square of the average number of requests per transaction.
- The number of deadlocks is proportional to the fourth power of the average number of requests per transaction.

3.24 P. A. Bernstein, N. Goodman, and M.-Y.Lai. "Laying Phantoms to Rest (By Understanding the Interactions Between Schedulers and Translators in a Database System)." Aiken Comp. Lab., Harvard Univ.: Tech. Report TR-03-81 (1981).

A phantom is a record or other object that is seen by one part of a transaction and not by another (loosely speaking; see Section 3.12). The phantom problem arises because of incompatibilities between user-level operations, on the one hand, and the system-level operations used to implement them, on the other. For example, a straightforward (sequential scan) implementation of the user-level operation "Find employees with salary = $20000" may indeed lock all records encountered during the scan, as required by two-phase locking, but those locks are not sufficient in themselves to prevent a concurrent transaction from inserting a *new* record that satisfies the predicate. Instead, it is necessary to have some additional object—Bernstein et al. suggest the end-of-file marker in the case at hand—that must be locked shared by a retrieve-only transaction and exclusive by an updating transaction. Yet the fact that such an object and the corresponding locks are required is not immediately obvious from the two-phase locking theorem, which deals only with user-level objects and operations and not with their system-level implementation. Thus, it is necessary to extend concurrency control theory to incorporate considerations arising from the translation from user- to system-level. This paper develops such an extended theory, and thus provides a basis for practical implementations (as opposed to theoretical models) that are provably correct.

ANSWERS TO SELECTED EXERCISES

3.4 (a) There are six possible correct results, corresponding to the six possible serializations of the three transactions (see below). With the given initial value of A, namely zero, it happens that the six results are not all distinct; but if the initial value had been one, say, then all six would have been different. (Exercise: Check this statement.)

Initially	: A = 0
T1-T2-T3	: A = 9
T1-T3-T2	: A = 3
T2-T1-T3	: A = 1
T2-T3-T1	: A = 1
T3-T1-T2	: A = 3
T3-T2-T1	: A = 1

b)   There are 90 distinct possible interleaved executions. We may represent the possibilities as follows. (Fi, Fj, Fk stand for the FIND operations F1, F2, F3, not necessarily in that order; similarly, Up, Uq, Ur stand for the UPD operations U1, U2, U3, again not necessarily in that order.)

Fi-Fj-Fk-Up-Uq-Ur	:	$3 * 2 * 1 * 3 * 2 * 1$	=	36 possibilities
Fi-Fj-Up-Fk-Uq-Ur	:	$3 * 2 * 2 * 1 * 2 * 1$	=	24 possibilities
Fi-Fj-Up-Uq-Fk-Ur	:	$3 * 2 * 2 * 1 * 1 * 1$	=	12 possibilities
Fi-Up-Fj-Fk-Uq-Ur	:	$3 * 1 * 2 * 1 * 2 * 1$	=	12 possibilities
Fi-Up-Fj-Uq-Fk-Ur	:	$3 * 1 * 2 * 1 * 1 * 1$	=	6 possibilities
		TOTAL	=	90 combinations

c)   Yes. For example, the interleaved execution F2-F3-U2-U3-F1-U1 produces the same result (one) as three of the six possible serializations of T1, T2, T3 (exercise: check this statement), and thus happens to be "correct" for the given input value of zero. But it must be clearly understood that this "correctness" is a mere fluke, and results purely from the fact that the initial data value happened to be zero and not something else. As a counterexample, consider what would happen if the initial value of A were one instead of zero. Would the result of the interleaved execution shown above still be the same as one of the genuinely correct results? (What *are* the genuinely correct results in this case?) If not, then the execution F2-F3-U2-U3-F1-U1 is not serializable.

d)   Yes. For example, the interleaved execution F1-F3-U1-U3-F1-U2 is serializable (it is equivalent to the serialization T1-T3-T2), but it cannot be produced if T1, T2, and T3 all obey the two-phase locking protocol. For suppose that T1, T2, and T3 do all obey that protocol, in conjunction with (say) protocol PSC (in other words, a transaction acquires an S lock on an object when it finds it, upgrades that lock to X level if the object is updated, does not release X locks until end-of-transaction, and never requests any more locks once any locks have been released). Then operation F3 will acquire an S lock on A on behalf of transaction T3; operation U1 in transaction T1 will thus not be able to proceed until that lock has been released, and that will not happen until transaction T3 terminates (in fact, T3's lock will be upgraded to X level first).

This exercise illustrates very clearly the following important point. Given a set of transactions and a set of initial values for the input parameters to those transactions: (1) Let ALL be the set of all possible interleaved executions of those transactions; (2) let "CORRECT" be the set of all interleaved executions of those transactions that either are guaranteed to produce a correct answer or at least happen to produce a correct answer for the given input; (3) let SERIALIZABLE be the set of all serializable executions of those transactions; and (4) let PRODUCIBLE be the set of all executions producible via the two-phase locking protocol. Then, in general,

PRODUCIBLE ⊂ SERIALIZABLE ⊂ ''CORRECT'' ⊂ ALL

where "⊂" represents the operation of (proper) set inclusion.

3.7 At time t*n* the graph looks like this:

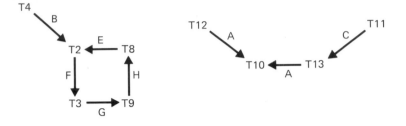

(For clarity we have labeled the edges with the name of the required resource.) There is one deadlock, involving transactions T2, T3, T9, and T8.

3.8 (a) Deadlock occurs at time t8.

    b) Deadlock occurs at time t6.

    c) Transaction B dies at time t6.

    d) Transaction B dies at time t5.

    e) Transaction A restarts at time t7.

3.9 The following locks must be acquired:

      an IX lock on the database,

      an IX lock on the P relation,

      an IX lock on index XP,

      an S lock on the P record for part number P3.

4
Security

4.1 INTRODUCTION

The term "security" is used in a database context to mean the protection of the database against unauthorized disclosure, alteration, or destruction. There are numerous aspects to the security problem, among them the following.

- Legal, social, and ethical aspects (for example, does the person making the request, say for a customer's credit, have a legal right to the requested information?);

- Physical controls (for example, should the computer room or terminal room be locked or otherwise guarded?);

- Policy questions (for example, how does the enterprise decide who should be allowed access to what data?);

- Operational problems (for example, if a password scheme is used, how are the passwords themselves kept secret?);

- Hardware controls (for example, does the central processor provide any security features, such as storage protection keys or a privileged operation mode?);

- Operating system security (for example, does the underlying operating system erase the contents of storage and data files when they are finished with?);

and finally

- Issues that are the specific concern of the database system itself (for example, can a user simultaneously be given access to field A and denied access to field B, if A and B are both part of the same database record?).

In this chapter we limit ourselves for the most part to consideration of issues in this last category. More general discussions, covering some or all of the other aspects indicated above, can be found in many places; see, for example, the books by Fernandez, Summers, and Wood [4.1], Martin [4.2], Martin and Norman [4.3], and Hoffman [4.4, 4.5]—also the survey papers by Hoffman [4.7], Hsiao et al. [4.10], and Denning and Denning [4.12].

We start with one example (based on one given by Conway, Maxwell, and Morgan [4.14]) that illustrates to some extent the nature of the problem. Suppose that the database includes a relation

```
EMPLOYEE ( EMP#, NAME, ADDRESS, DEPT#, SALARY, ASSESSMENT )
```

(where ASSESSMENT is the manager's evaluation of the employee's performance). Then each of the following statements indicates a level of access to this relation that might reasonably be granted to some particular category of user.[1]

1. The user has unconstrained access to the entire relation for all types of operation.

2. The user has no access to any part of the relation for any type of operation.

3. The user may see any part of the relation, but may not change it.

4. The user may see exactly one record in the relation (that user's "own" record), but may not change it.

5. The user may see exactly one record in the relation (the user's own), and within that record may alter the NAME and ADDRESS values but nothing else.

6. The user may see only the EMP#, NAME, ADDRESS, and DEPT# fields, and within any one record may alter only the NAME, ADDRESS, and DEPT# values.

7. The user may see the EMP# and SALARY fields, and within any one record may alter the SALARY value, but only between the hours of 9 A.M. and 5 P.M. and only from a terminal located in the payroll office.

8. The user may see the EMP# and SALARY fields, and within any one record may alter the SALARY value, if and only if the current SALARY value is less than 25,000 dollars.

9. The user may apply statistical operators to the SALARY field (for example, to obtain average salary per department), but may not see or alter individual values.

10. The user may see the EMP# and ASSESSMENT fields, and within any one record may alter the ASSESSMENT value, if and only if that user is the manager of the department identified by the DEPT# value.

---

1. By "user" here we mean either an application programmer or an end-user at a terminal—that is, someone who is trying to access the database *via the system* (the DBMS). The case of a user who attempts to bypass the system is considered separately in Section 4.7. (For convenience we generally retain the term "user" even for a would-be infiltrator, though it is perhaps somewhat inappropriate for someone who is trying to breach the system.)

The foregoing list, which is by no means exhaustive, should begin to give some idea of the range and flexibility required of a general-purpose security enforcement scheme. In the remainder of this chapter we consider some of the technical safeguards and countermeasures that can be used in the implementation of such a scheme. The general structure of the chapter is as follows. First we discuss (in Section 4.2) the question of user identification. Then we examine in the next two sections techniques for formulating and enforcing security constraints. Section 4.5 considers data classification schemes. Section 4.6 introduces the special problems of so-called statistical databases; and, finally, Section 4.7 discusses techniques for scrambling or *encrypting* data to guard against wiretapping and similar threats.

4.2   IDENTIFICATION AND AUTHENTICATION

From the definition of security given at the start of the chapter, it follows that the system must not allow any operation to be performed on the database unless the user is *authorized* for the operation concerned. For each user, therefore, the system must maintain a record—usually called the *user profile*—specifying the data objects the user is authorized to access and the operations the user is authorized to perform on those objects. (Alternatively the system might maintain a record for each *object*—an "object profile"—specifying the users that are allowed to access that object. For example, the Multics file system [4.35] operates in this fashion. The two approaches are functionally equivalent, however; for definiteness, therefore, we continue to talk in terms of *user* profiles.)

Before accessing the database, then, users will have to *identify* themselves (that is, say who they are—for example, by entering an operator number at a terminal). This step will direct the system to the appropriate user profile. Normally, users will then go on to *authenticate* their identification (that is, prove they are who they say they are—for example, by supplying a password supposedly known only to the system and to legitimate users of the operator number given in the identification step). In general, the identification/authentication procedure can be repeated as many times as desired. In the case of an on-line user, for example, it will normally form part of the process of signing on to the system, and thus be performed once per terminal session; but it might be repeated as frequently as once per individual operation if the database contained particularly sensitive information.

The process of *identification* may involve supplying an operator number, as in the example above, or using machine-readable identity cards or badges. Many terminals now available have special features to assist in this process, such as the ability to suppress the display of data being entered to preserve its secrecy, the ability to read specially designed cards or badges, and the ability to furnish a unique terminal identification to the computer (this latter can help by informing the system *where*, as well as who, the user is). Special terminals that allow identification by voiceprint or fingerprints have also been suggested (in such cases authentication as a separate step would not be necessary).

The process of *authentication* involves supplying information known only to the person the user has claimed to be in the identification procedure. This may be done by giving a password, as in the example above, or by answering some question from the system. It is possible to devise quite simple authentication procedures that are almost impossible to crack. One such procedure, due to Earnest, is described by Hoffman [4.7] somewhat as follows. First the system supplies the user with a pseudorandom number x. The user then performs some simple mental transformation T on x and sends the result $y = T(x)$ back to the system. The system then performs the same transformation on x and verifies that the result is indeed y. Any would-be infiltrator would see at most the values x and y, from which it should be almost impossible to work out exactly what the transformation is—even for a fairly simple T, such as the following:

$$T(x) = (\text{sum of 1st, 3rd, 5th, . . . digits of } x)^2 + (\text{hour of the day})$$

Petersen and Turn [4.8] discuss a number of other authentication techniques, including "one-time-use" passwords and "hang-up and call-back" procedures. Some others are discussed by Hoffman [4.7].

We do not consider the question of user identification any further here. Instead, we shall simply assume (just as the DBMS must assume) that an access request that purports to come from some given user U does in fact come from that user. In the next section we consider the problem of ensuring that the DBMS will honor the request only if user U is authorized to perform the operations that the request implies.

4.3 AUTHORIZATION RULES

The topic of security has certain similarities with that of integrity (Chapter 2). The system must allow *authorization rules* (analogous to integrity rules) to be expressed in some high-level language such as SQL or QUEL.[2] In System R, for instance, the SQL GRANT statement performs this function; for example, the statement

```
GRANT SELECT ON S TO JONES
```

specifies that user Jones is authorized to perform SELECT operations on relation S. This information will be recorded in the user profile for Jones. (Incidentally, GRANT is a dynamically executable statement, like all other SQL statements, and can therefore be issued at any time.)

Like integrity rules, authorization rules will be compiled and stored in the system dictionary, and, once entered into the system, will be enforced from that time on. The authorization rules compiler and the corresponding enforcement mechanism (to be discussed later) together make up the *security subsystem*.

---

2. It should also allow such rules to be deleted and modified.

It is convenient to consider the set of all user profiles as a matrix A (the *authorization matrix*), in which rows correspond to users and columns correspond to data objects. The entry A[*i,j*] represents the set of authorization rules that apply to user *i* with respect to data object *j*. (Row *i* thus constitutes the user profile for the *i*th user.) A simple example is shown in Fig. 4.1.

The granularity of the objects for which columns may exist in the authorization matrix is one measure of the sophistication of the system concerned. For example, some systems will support authorization only at the level of whole relations, others will permit authorization at the level of individual fields. (Most recent systems typically do support field-level control.) However, a more significant measure is given by the range of entries permitted within the body of the matrix. The simple example of Fig. 4.1 illustrates what may be called *value-independent control*, since authorization is based purely on the *names* of objects and not on their value. Note that the system can enforce value-independent controls without having to access the data objects themselves.

To provide value-*dependent* control, we can extend the entries in the matrix to incorporate an optional *access predicate*. For example, the entry

```
SELECT  *
FROM    S
WHERE   STATUS < 50
```

might be used to allow SELECT access to some suppliers and not others. (We deliberately use a SQL-like syntax in our examples, for tutorial reasons. But the reader should not infer that authorization rules are actually expressed in this way in System R. See Section 4.4 for details of how System R does express such rules, and also for a discussion of other implemented systems.)

	Data object 1 (relation S)	Data object 2 (relation P)	Data object 3 (relation SP)
User 1 (Smith)	NONE	SELECT	ALL
User 2 (Jones)	SELECT	UPDATE	SELECT DELETE UPDATE
User 3 (Blake)	NONE	NONE	SELECT
User 4 (Clark)	NONE	NONE	NONE
User 5 (Adams)	ALL	ALL	ALL

Fig. 4.1 Example of an authorization matrix.

To return to the authorization matrix: We can provide *statistical* control by allowing entries to include statistical operators, such as AVERAGE, in addition to the usual SELECT, INSERT, etc. (Statistical controls can be provided in conjunction with both value-dependent and value-independent controls.) Moreover, the access predicate might be allowed to include references to system variables such as time-of-day or terminal addresses, thus providing the basis for *context-dependent* controls—see numbers (7) and (10) in the list of statements in Section 4.1. For example, number (10) might be handled by means of the two authorization rules

```
SELECT  EMP#, ASSESSMENT        UPDATE  EMPLOYEE
FROM    EMPLOYEE                SET     ASSESSMENT = parameter
WHERE   DEPT# =                 WHERE   DEPT# =
        (SELECT DEPT#                   (SELECT DEPT#
         FROM    DEPARTMENT              FROM    DEPARTMENT
         WHERE   MGR# = user)           WHERE   MGR# = user)
```

where *user* denotes a system variable (kept with the user profile) representing the user attempting the access, and *parameter* denotes an arbitrary new ASSESSMENT value. (We are assuming that the database contains another relation DEPART-MENT, with primary key DEPT# and with a field MGR# identifying the manager of the department in question.)

Authorization rules can also specify that certain field *combinations* are prohibited, even though the individual fields within the combination may be accessible. For example, a given user might be allowed to see employee names and employee salaries, but not in combination:

```
SELECT  NAME         plus    SELECT  SALARY
FROM    EMPLOYEE             FROM    EMPLOYEE
```

but *not*

```
SELECT  NAME, SALARY
FROM    EMPLOYEE
```

It is also necessary to control access to *programs*. That is, the authorization matrix should include a column corresponding to each program that accesses the database; the only possible entries in such a column would be RUN (authority to execute the program) and NONE (no access allowed). Authority to modify the program can be handled by considering the program text as a *data* object, just like any other data object.

Finally, it is obviously important to control access to the authorization matrix itself (particularly update access, of course). Such control can be provided by considering the matrix itself as yet another data object in the system, like program text above.

The Arbiter

Now let us briefly consider the process of enforcing the rules given in the authorization matrix. In general, an access predicate may refer to any data whatsoever in the entire database. We assume, therefore, that there exists a highly privileged and protected program, the security enforcer or *arbiter*, which has unconstrained access to the entire database and whose function is to check each access request and to grant or deny permission, as appropriate. Consider a request R[i,j] for some type of access from user i to object j. The arbiter will inspect the authorization matrix entry A[i,j] and go through a sequence of tests to determine whether to grant or deny the request. Figure 4.2 shows a possible test sequence (the figure is a simplified version of a proposal originally due to Codd [4.15], and is expressed in terms of the relational model). The figure is arranged such that the tests are in order of increasing complexity, so that the arbiter may reach its final decision as quickly as possible. "Accessible" and "prohibited" in the figure should be interpreted as accessible or prohibited according to the user profile for user i (that is, the ith row of the matrix).[3] Note that each test after the first is performed only if the preceding test gives the result NO; the arbiter's final decision is reached as soon as a test gives a result of YES. If all tests given the answer NO, the arbiter should inform the user that the request is denied because of lack of information in the system (as opposed to being explicitly forbidden).

Test number	Action if YES
1. Are all *relations* mentioned in R[i,j] unconditionally accessible?	Grant
2. Is there a *relation* mentioned in R[i,j] that is unconditionally prohibited?	Deny
3. Are all *attributes* mentioned in R[i,j] unconditionally accessible?	Grant
4. Is there an *attribute* mentioned in R[i,j] that is unconditionally prohibited?	Deny
5. Are all *attribute combinations* mentioned in R[i,j] unconditionally accessible?	Grant
6. Is there an *attribute combination* mentioned in R[i,j] that is unconditionally prohibited?	Deny
7. For each sensitive attribute combination mentioned in R[i,j], is there a *predicate* in R[i,j] that constrains values of the participating attributes to lie within accessible ranges?	Grant
8. Is there a sensitive attribute combination mentioned in R[i,j] that has a subcombination whose values are permitted by the *predicate* in R[i,j] to lie within a prohibited range?	Deny

Fig. 4.2 Security interrogation sequence.

3. In evaluating an access predicate from entry A[i,j], the arbiter may have to inspect some other entry A[i,k] in the same row. For example, a request for suppliers who supply a specified part requires SELECT authority for relation SP as well as for relation S.

Note that tests 1–6 are value-independent and can therefore be done at compile time. Tests 7 and 8 are value-dependent. Of course, even if a check can be done at compile time, it is still necessary to check at execution time that the authorization rules have not changed in the interim.

If a request R[i,j] has to be denied, what action should the arbiter take? The answer to this question will clearly depend on many factors, including the nature of the attempted violation, the sensitivity of the data, whether the request came from an on-line user or a batch program, and so on. In particularly sensitive situations it may be necessary to terminate the program or to lock the terminal keyboard; in less critical cases it may be sufficient merely to return an appropriate exception code to the user. It may also be desirable to record attempted breaches of security in the log ("threat monitoring"), to permit subsequent analysis of such attempts and also to serve in itself as a deterrent against illegal infiltration. In general, required violation responses will be specified as yet another component of the authorization rule entries in the authorization matrix (cf. the violation-response component of integrity rules, described in Chapter 2).

We conclude this section by noting three "security axioms" [4.15] that place some restrictions on the authorization rules that can sensibly be specified, and thus indicate some economies that can be made within those specifications as they actually appear within the system dictionary. Note: The second and third of the axioms rest on the assumption that if users are allowed to update an object, then they should also be allowed to see it.

- If user i has conditional SELECT access to attribute combination A subject to predicate P, then user i also has conditional SELECT access to every sub-combination of A, and no predicate for any subcombination can be stronger (more restrictive) than P.

- If user i has conditional UPDATE access to attribute combination A subject to predicate P, then user i also has conditional SELECT access to A, and the predicate concerned cannot be stronger than P.

- If user i does not have SELECT access to attribute combination A, then user i does not have UPDATE access to A either.

4.4 SOME EXISTING SYSTEMS

We illustrate the concepts introduced in the previous section by briefly examining the security aspects of System R, INGRES, Query By Example, IMS, DBTG, and UDL.

System R

Two more or less independent features of the system are involved in the provision of security in System R: (1) the view mechanism, which can be used to hide sensitive data from unauthorized users; and (2) the authorization subsystem itself, which allows users having specific access rights selectively and dynamically to grant those rights to others (and subsequently to revoke those rights, if desired). We examine each of these features in turn.

1. The view mechanism

Consider the EMPLOYEE relation of Section 4.1 once again. The following examples represent some views that might be defined on that relation.

a) For a user allowed access to employee records but not to the SALARY and ASSESSMENT fields:

```
DEFINE VIEW    BASICINFO
    AS SELECT EMP#, NAME, ADDRESS, DEPT#
       FROM    EMPLOYEE
```

b) For a user allowed access to employee records for employees in department D3 only:

```
DEFINE VIEW    D3EMPS
    AS SELECT EMP#, NAME, ADDRESS, SALARY, ASSESSMENT
       FROM    EMPLOYEE
       WHERE   DEPT# = 'D3'
```

c) For a user allowed access to the EMP# and SALARY fields but only where the current salary is less than 25,000 dollars:

```
DEFINE VIEW    JUNIOREMPS
    AS SELECT EMP#, SALARY
       FROM    EMPLOYEE
       WHERE   SALARY < 25000
```

d) For a user allowed access to employee records only for employees belonging to the department for which the user is the manager:

```
DEFINE VIEW    MYEMPS
    AS SELECT *
       FROM    EMPLOYEE
       WHERE   DEPT# =
              (SELECT DEPT#
               FROM    DEPARTMENT
               WHERE   MGR# = USER)
```

USER is a SQL reserved word that denotes the current user (cf. the similar example in Section 4.3).

e) For a user allowed access only to average salary per department, not to individual salaries:

```
DEFINE VIEW    AVGSALS
    AS SELECT DEPT#, AVG(SAL)
       FROM    EMPLOYEE
       GROUP   BY DEPT#
```

(Note: The definer of the foregoing views must have at least SELECT authority on the underlying EMPLOYEE table. See the discussion of GRANT and REVOKE, later.)

As the examples illustrate, a given user can easily be restricted to a vertical subset [example (a)], a horizontal subset [examples (b), (c), and (d)], or a statistical summary [example (e)] of a given relation. The table below relates these examples to the various categories of authorization control (value-independent, etc.) introduced in the previous section.

Category of control	Examples
value-independent	(a), (e)
value-dependent	(b), (c), (d)
statistical	(e)
context-dependent	(d)

Operations on views in System R are converted at compile time into corresponding operations on the underlying base table(s). Hence even value-dependent controls can be enforced at compile time instead of at execution time; for example, to check that a given program does not see employees with a salary of 25,000 dollars or more, it is sufficient to check at compile time that the program accesses the JUNIOREMPS view and not the EMPLOYEE base table. Note, however, that we are not saying that *all* value-dependent controls can be enforced at compile time in this way. For example, some systems will reject a query if the cardinality of the result set is less than some predefined lower bound (see Section 4.6). Such a check will normally have to be performed at execution time.

The view mechanism thus provides an important measure of security "for free" in System R. However, this approach to security does suffer from certain drawbacks, some of which are discussed below.

■   It can be cumbersome in the case where the user is to be granted different levels of access (SELECT, UPDATE, etc.) to different subsets of the same table. Suppose, for example, that the user is to be allowed to see all employee salaries but is to be allowed to update them only if the employee concerned belongs to department D3. Then two views will be needed:

```
DEFINE VIEW    ALLSALS              DEFINE VIEW    D3SALS
    AS SELECT EMP#, SALARY              AS SELECT EMP#, SALARY
       FROM    EMPLOYEE                    FROM    EMPLOYEE
                                           WHERE   DEPT# = 'D3'
```

SELECT operations can be directed at ALLSALS but UPDATE operations must be directed at D3SALS instead. This fact can lead to somewhat obscure programs. Consider, for example, the structure of a program that scans and prints all employee salaries and also updates some of them (those for department D3) as it goes.

■   When a record is inserted or updated through a view, System R does not require that the new or updated record satisfy the predicate in the view definition. (If it does not, then it will vanish from the view, as explained in Volume I, but it will still appear in the underlying base table.) Thus, for example, view JUNIOREMPS can prevent the user from seeing salaries of 25,000 dollars or more, but it cannot prevent the user from creating such a salary (assuming that the user has INSERT or UP-DATE authority on JUNIOREMPS, of course). For example, the statement

```
INSERT INTO JUNIOREMPS (EMP#, SALARY): <'E5', 100000>
```

will have such an effect (assuming that employee E5 does not already exist in the underlying EMPLOYEE base table). In other words, it is not possible to give a user the ability to insert records into some subset of a table while at the same time preventing that user from inserting records into the rest of the table.

■   When a record is inserted through a view, any fields of the underlying base table that do not appear in the view are set to null in the new record. Thus, for example, if a record is inserted via view D3EMPS, that new record will have a DEPT# value of null, not D3, and so will not appear in the view. (This is arguably a problem of integrity rather than security.) Thus, to give some user the ability to create new employee records for department D3 (only) and not have those records "vanish," we need a view similar to D3EMPS but extended to include the DEPT# field—even though that field will have the same known value D3 in every record in the view. In fact, as pointed out in the previous paragraph, even this will not prevent the user from creating employee records with some other DEPT# value. What is needed to overcome these difficulties is (a) a means of specifying default values for omitted fields on a view-by-view basis, plus (b) a requirement that new and updated records submitted via a view, after incorporation of such default values if applicable, do in fact satisfy the view-defining predicate.

2. GRANT and REVOKE

The view mechanism just discussed allows the database to be subsetted in various ways so that sensitive information can be hidden from unauthorized users. However, it does not allow for the specification of the operations that *authorized* users may execute against such subsets. This function is performed by the SQL statements GRANT and REVOKE, which we now discuss.

In order to be able to perform any operation at all in System R, the user must hold the appropriate *access privilege* for that operation (otherwise the operation is rejected with an exception code). The following is a complete list of the access privileges recognized by System R.

■   For tables (base tables or views):

```
SELECT
UPDATE                 (can apply to any subset of the fields in the table)
INSERT
DELETE
INDEX                  (authority to create an index on the table)
EXPAND                 (authority to add a field to the table)
ALL PRIVILEGES         (all of the above)
```

INDEX and EXPAND apply only to base tables, not to views. Note that there are no "CREATE" and "DROP" privileges (see the discussion of special privileges below).

- For programs:

  RUN

- Special privileges:

  RESOURCE
  DBA

When System R is initially installed, at least one user must be identified to the system as having the special privilege "database administrator authority" (DBA authority). DBA authority allows the holder to perform any valid operation in the system, including in particular the operation of granting privileges (possibly including DBA authority itself) to other users. The initial holder of DBA authority can thus choose whether to retain the greatest possible control over the system or to delegate some portions of that control (in a controlled manner) to others.

"Resource authority" (RESOURCE) is required to create a new base table. The creator of a new base table is automatically given all table privileges for that table, and, moreover, holds "the GRANT option" (see later) for all those privileges, which means that the creator can grant those privileges to other users. However, only the creator (or a holder of DBA authority) can DROP the table.

As mentioned earlier, the definer of a view must have at least SELECT authority over all tables referenced in the view definition. The definer is automatically given full table privileges on the view, subject to (a) the privileges held on the tables referenced in the definition, (b) the applicability of such privileges (INDEX and EXPAND never apply to views), and (c) the constraints on the updatability of views. For example, if the view is a join, then the definer will not receive UPDATE authority for it, even if UPDATE authority is held on all underlying tables. (Joins are not updatable in System R, as explained in Volume I.)

No particular privilege is required to create (precompile) a new System R program. The creator of a program is automatically given RUN authority for that program. If the creator also has all privileges required by all SQL statements in the program *and*, where applicable, holds the GRANT option for all those privileges, then that user is also given the GRANT option for the RUN privilege on the program.

In order for user A to be able to grant some privilege P to some other user B, user A must hold the GRANT option for that privilege P. User A will hold the GRANT option for a given privilege P if A is the creator of the object concerned, as explained above, or if A has been granted privilege P "with the GRANT option." Privileges are granted by means of the GRANT statement:

```
GRANT privileges [ ON object ] TO users [ WITH GRANT OPTION ]
```

Some examples:

```
GRANT SELECT, DELETE, UPDATE ON SP TO JONES

GRANT SELECT ON SP TO BLAKE WITH GRANT OPTION

GRANT UPDATE (STATUS, CITY) ON S TO CLARK

GRANT ALL PRIVILEGES ON SP TO SMITH WITH GRANT OPTION

GRANT DBA TO CLARK

GRANT DELETE ON SP TO BLAKE, ADAMS

GRANT SELECT ON SP TO PUBLIC
```

PUBLIC is shorthand for a list of all users (that is, any user who can sign on to the system can exercise the specified privilege). Notice the field-specific UPDATE privilege in the third example above.

If user A has granted privilege P to user B, then user A may subsequently *revoke* privilege P from user B by means of the REVOKE statement:

```
REVOKE privileges [ ON object ] FROM users
```

Some examples:

```
REVOKE DELETE ON SP FROM JONES, BLAKE

REVOKE UPDATE ON S FROM CLARK

REVOKE DBA FROM CLARK
```

Revocation cascades; that is, if A grants P to B, B in turn grants P to C, and then A revokes P from B, then P is automatically revoked from C also (unless C has also been granted P by some other independent user). The details of this process are not straightforward; the interested reader is referred to references [4.17, 4.18] for a thorough discussion of the problem.

There is no field-specific form of the REVOKE statement. Note also that it is not possible to revoke the GRANT option on a privilege without at the same time revoking the privilege itself.

User privileges are recorded in certain tables in the System R dictionary (the table-, field-, program-, and user-authorization tables). These tables thus constitute the System R authorization matrix (or set of user profiles). They can be queried using normal SQL SELECT statements, like other tables in the dictionary.

INGRES

Authorization constraints in INGRES are handled analogously to integrity constraints (see Chapter 2); that is, access requests are dynamically modified prior to execution by appending an appropriate authorization constraint predicate. The following example illustrates this process.

Example. Suppose that user U is allowed to access employee records, but only for employees in department D3. This authorization constraint can be expressed in QUEL, the INGRES data sublanguage, as follows:

```
RANGE OF EX IS EMPLOYEE
DEFINE PERMIT RETRIEVE ON EX TO U
                WHERE EX.DEPT# = 'D3'
```

Now suppose that user U issues the following QUEL request (an attempt to retrieve employee number and salary for all employees earning more than 25,000 dollars a year):

```
RANGE OF EY IS EMPLOYEE
RETRIEVE (EY.EMP#, EY.SALARY) WHERE EY.SALARY > 25000
```

INGRES will convert the request into the following form:

```
RANGE OF EY IS EMPLOYEE
RETRIEVE (EY.EMP#, EY.SALARY) WHERE EY.SALARY > 25000
                              AND (EY.DEPT# = 'D3')
```

The result of executing this modified RETRIEVE will be to return the information the user wants, but only for employees in department D3.

The technique of dynamically modifying requests before execution resembles the view-based approach of System R, at least in principle, inasmuch as it allows value-dependent controls to be enforced at compile time (thought in fact INGRES is an interpretive system and so does not take advantage of this possibility). The technique also overcomes the first of the disadvantages mentioned earlier for the view-based approach (see the discussion of System R). To be specific, in INGRES the user can express all operations directly in terms of the EMPLOYEE relation, instead of having to use different views for different operations, because different operations on the same relation can be dynamically modified by different authorization predicates. However, the other problems mentioned in the discussion of System R apply to INGRES also.

The general format of the QUEL "DEFINE PERMIT" statement is as follows:

```
DEFINE PERMIT operations ON relation [ (attributes) ]
                         TO user
                       [ AT terminal ]
                       [ FROM time1 TO time2 ]
                       [ ON day1 TO day2 ]
                       [ WHERE predicate ]
```

It is thus possible, not only to limit a given user's access to a given relation to some specific set of operations on some specific row-and-column subset of that relation, but also to insist that all such access be made from a specific terminal and/or at some specific time.

For further details of the INGRES query modification scheme, the reader is referred to [4.19].

Query By Example

The IBM implementation of Query By Example [4.20] supports certain forms of authorization constraint. Other possible forms are discussed in [4.21]. As with all QBE definitions, authorization constraints are specified by filling in entries in blank tables; that is, the user enters "authorization" rows (specified by "I.AUTH", with a specification of the operation concerned ["P.", "I.", "D.", or "U."] and the identification of the user being authorized), making use of constant elements and example elements in the normal QBE fashion. We give a single example in Fig. 4.3 (corresponding to statement number (8) in Section 4.1); "uid" in that figure represents the user identification for the user being authorized. Authorization constraints can be queried (printed), updated, and deleted in a similar manner.

EMPLOYEE	EMP #	SALARY
I AUTH (P., U.). uid	EX	SX < 25000

Fig. 4.3 Example of a QBE authorization constraint.

The remarks made earlier comparing the approaches of INGRES and System R apply also to QBE versus System R, *mutatis mutandis.* For more information on the QBE approach, see [4.20] and [4.21].

IMS

The security aspects of IMS fall into two broad categories: those concerned with end-user access to transactions, and those concerned with transaction access to data. The first of these applies only if the Data Communications feature is installed, the second applies even in a pure batch environment. We therefore consider the latter case first.

In the case of access from a transaction to a database, IMS provides *value-independent* control only (the concepts of value-dependent, context-dependent, and statistical control are not supported). All such access is in terms of an appropriate program communication block, or PCB. The PCB specifies the segments and fields to which the transaction is "sensitive" and thus, by exclusion, prevents access to all "nonsensitive" data (except that deletion of a parent segment will cause deletion of all descendants of that segment, regardless of whether the transaction is "sensitive" to them or not, as explained in Volume I). In addition, the transaction is constrained to those operations defined by the PROCOPT entries in the PCB. A PCB may therefore be seen, *very* approximately, as the IMS analogue of a System R view, together with certain explicit access privileges on that view. Note, however, that the controls are enforced at execution time, not compile time, because IMS (like INGRES) is an interpretive system.

We turn now to the question of authorizing end-user access to transactions. IMS provides a wide range of facilities in this area, including the following:

- *sign-on verification*, to identify the end-user concerned;
- *authorization checking,* to ensure that the end-user is authorized to invoke the transaction being requested;
- *terminal security,* to ensure that specific transactions (and/or specific system commands) are invoked only from specific terminals;

and

- *password checking,* to ensure that specific transactions (and/or specific system commands) are executed only if appropriate passwords are supplied.

Attempted security violations are recorded on the IMS log and optionally cause a message to bc sent to the IMS operator (threat monitoring).

For further details of security in IMS, see reference [4.22].

DBTG

The only security feature provided by DBTG is the *subschema* (analogous to a PCB in IMS, but without the processing intents). A given transaction is not able to access any data not explicitly included in the applicable subschema (except that, as in IMS, "cascade erase" can affect hidden data; so also can STORE and MODIFY under certain circumstances). For more details see [4.36].

Note: The original DBTG proposals included an additional security mechanism based on "access control locks" and "access control keys." However, this mechanism suffered from a number of deficiencies and was subsequently deleted from the specifications [2.12, 4.36].

UDL

UDL is a *programming language,* not a system, and thus generally assumes that security is provided by some extralingual mechanism. However, the PROCLEVEL specification within a baseset declaration (see Chapter 3) permits some limited value-independent checks to be applied at compile time.

4.5 DATA CLASSIFICATION

The authorization-matrix approach discussed in Section 4.3 (and illustrated in Section 4.4) is very general; it allows the specification of any combination of privileges on any combination of data objects for any combination of users. Some systems employ a more rigid, but much simpler, scheme based on *data classification*. Each data object (file, etc.) is assigned a *classification level*. Typical levels might be

- top secret,
- secret,
- confidential,
- unclassified.

Each level is more restrictive than those that follow it; that is, we can define a total ordering among the levels (top secret > secret > confidential > unclassified). Users, in turn, are assigned a *clearance level* (top secret, secret, etc.), and the simple rules are imposed that

a) User *i* can see object *j* only if the clearance level of *i* is greater than or equal to the classification level of *j*;

b) User *i* can modify object *j* only if the clearance level of *i* is equal to that of *j*.

This scheme represents a particularly simple form of value-independent control. One advantage of the approach is that the system can enforce certain *flow controls*. A problem with schemes based on the general authorization matrix of Section 4.3 is that they permit a user who is authorized to see confidential data to copy that data into a nonconfidential file, thus making it available to unauthorized users. Under the classification scheme sketched above, however, rules (a) and (b) together guarantee that such an illegal information flow cannot occur.

We do not consider classification schemes any further in this book. They tend to be most useful, not so much in general-purpose database systems, but rather in special-purpose systems in which the data has a rather static and rigid structure, as is the case in (for example) military environments, or in operating systems (as opposed to database systems). For more information on such schemes the reader is referred to [4.11] and [4.12] and to the references contained therein.

4.6 STATISTICAL DATABASES

A *statistical database* is a database, such as a census database, that (a) contains a large number of individually sensitive records, but (b) is intended to supply only statistical summary information to its users, not information referring to some specific individual [4.24]. In other words, the only permissible queries are those that apply some statistical function such as COUNT, SUM, or AVERAGE to some subset of the records in the database. The difficulty is that, as reference [4.12] puts it, ". . . summaries contain vestiges of the original information; a snooper might be able to (re)construct this information by processing enough summaries. This is called *deduction of confidential information by inference*."

Example. Suppose the database, which for simplicity we assume consists of a single relation (STATS), is as shown in Fig. 4.4. Suppose some (authorized) user U is intent on discovering Able's salary and tax payment. Suppose also that U knows from outside sources that Able is a programmer and is male; and consider queries Q1 and Q2 below.

```
Q1  : SELECT  COUNT(*)
        FROM    STATS
        WHERE   SEX = 'M'
        AND     OCCUPATION = 'PROGRAMMER'    Response: 1
```

NAME	SEX	DEPENDENTS	OCCUPATION	SALARY	TAX	AUDITS
Able	M	3	programmer	25K	5K	3
Baker	F	2	physician	65K	5K	0
Clark	F	0	programmer	28K	9K	1
Downs	F	2	builder	30K	6K	1
East	M	2	clerk	22K	2K	0
Ford	F	1	homemaker	15K	0K	0
Green	M	0	lawyer	95K	0K	0
Hall	M	3	homemaker	22K	1K	0
Ives	F	4	programmer	32K	5K	1
Jones	F	1	programmer	30K	10K	1

Fig. 4.4 The STATS database.

```
Q2   : SELECT  SUM(SALARY), SUM(TAX)
       FROM    STATS
       WHERE   SEX = 'M'
       AND     OCCUPATION = 'PROGRAMMER'     Response: 25K, 5K
```

The security of the database has clearly been compromised, even though U has issued only legitimate statistical queries. As the example illustrates, if the user can find a predicate P that identifies a unique record in the database, then that record can no longer be considered secure. This fact suggests that the system should refuse to respond to a query for which the cardinality of the identified subset of records in the database is less than some lower bound b.[4] It likewise suggests that the system should also refuse to respond if the cardinality is greater than $n-b$ (where n is the total number of records in the database); for the compromise above could equally well be obtained from the sequence of queries Q3–Q6 below:

```
Q3   : SELECT  COUNT(*)
       FROM    STATS                         Response: 10

Q4   : SELECT  COUNT(*)
       FROM    STATS
       WHERE   NOT
               (SEX = 'M' AND
               OCCUPATION = 'PROGRAMMER')     Response:   9
                                              Subtract
                                              (Q3 - Q4): 1

Q5   : SELECT  SUM(SALARY), SUM(TAX)
       FROM    STATS                         Response: 364K, 43K
```

---

4. It should obviously refuse to respond to any query for which the predicate is a simple equality condition on the primary key.

```
Q6   : SELECT  SUM(SALARY),  SUM(TAX)
       FROM    STATS
       WHERE   NOT
               (SEX = 'M' AND
               OCCUPATION = 'PROGRAMMER')    Response:   339K,  38K
                                             Subtract
                                             (Q5 - Q6):   25K,   5K
```

(Q3 and Q4 show that the predicate SEX = 'M' AND OCCUPATION = 'PRO-GRAMMER' uniquely identifies Able. Q5 and Q6 therefore allow Able's salary and tax to be easily deduced.)

Unfortunately, it is easy to show that simply restricting the set of queries to those with result set cardinality c in the range $b \leq c \leq n-b$ is inadequate to avoid compromise, in general. Consider Fig. 4.4 again, and suppose that $b = 2$; queries will be answered only if their result set cardinality c is in the range $2 \leq c \leq 8$. The predicate

```
       SEX = 'M' AND OCCUPATION = 'PROGRAMMER'
```

is thus not admissible. But consider the following sequence (Q7–Q10):

```
Q7   : SELECT  COUNT(*)
       FROM    STATS
       WHERE   SEX = 'M'                     Response: 4

Q8   : SELECT  COUNT(*)
       FROM    STATS
       WHERE   SEX = 'M'
       AND     NOT
               (OCCUPATION = 'PROGRAMMER')   Response: 3
```

From Q7 and Q8, the user can deduce that there exists exactly one male programmer, who must therefore be Able (since the user already knows that this description fits Able). Able's salary and tax are thus given by deduction from Q9 and Q10:

```
Q9   : SELECT  SUM(SALARY),  SUM(TAX)
       FROM    STATS
       WHERE   SEX = 'M'                     Response:   164K,  8K

Q10  : SELECT  SUM(SALARY),  SUM(TAX)
       FROM    STATS
       WHERE   SEX = 'M'
       AND     NOT
               (OCCUPATION = 'PROGRAMMER')   Response:   139K,  3K
                                             Subtract
                                             (Q9 - Q10):  25K,   5K
```

The predicate

```
       SEX = 'M' AND NOT (OCCUPATION = 'PROGRAMMER')
```

is called an *individual tracker* for Able [4.23], because it enables the user to track down information concerning Able. In general, if the user knows a predicate P that identifies some specific record R, and if P can be expressed in the form P1 AND P2, then the predicate P1 AND NOT P2 is a tracker for R (provided that predicates P1 and (P1 AND NOT P2) are both admissible, that is, both identify result sets with cardinality in the range b to $n-b$). This is because the set of records identified by predicate P is identical to the difference between the set identified by predicate P1 and the set identified by predicate (P1 AND NOT P2). See Fig. 4.5.

Total set of records (entire database)

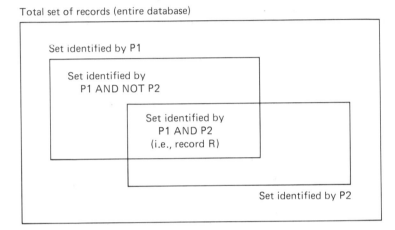

Fig. 4.5 The individual tracker P1 AND NOT P2:

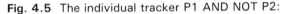

Reference [4.23] generalizes the foregoing ideas and shows that, for *almost any* statistical database, a "general tracker" (as opposed to a set of individual trackers) can always be found. A general tracker is a predicate that can be used to find the answer to *any* inadmissible query—that is, any query involving an inadmissible predicate. (By contrast, an individual tracker works only for queries involving some *specific* inadmissible predicate.) In fact, any predicate with result set cardinality c in the range $2b \leq c \leq n-2b$ is a general tracker[5] (b must be less than $n/4$, which it typically will be in any realistic situation). Once such a predicate is found, a query involving an inadmissible predicate P can be answered as illustrated by the following example. (For definiteness we take the case where the result set cardinality corresponding to P is less than b. The case where the cardinality is instead greater than $n-b$ is handled similarly.)

---

5. It follows from the definition that the predicate T is a general tracker if and only if the predicate NOT T is also a general tracker.

Example. Assume again that $b = 2$; then a general tracker is any predicate with result set cardinality c in the range $4 \leq c \leq 6$. Suppose again that user U knows from outside sources that Able is a male programmer—that is, predicate P is

```
SEX = 'M' AND OCCUPATION = 'PROGRAMMER'
```

(as before)—and suppose that U wishes to discover Able's salary. We will use a general tracker twice, first to ascertain that predicate P is in fact a unique identifier for Able (Steps 2–4 below), and then to determine Able's salary (Steps 5–7).

Step 1: Make a guess at a predicate T that will serve as a general tracker. As our guess we choose T to be the predicate

```
AUDITS = 0
```

Step 2: Find total number of individuals in the database, using the predicates T and NOT T.

```
Q11 : SELECT COUNT(*)
      FROM   STATS
      WHERE  AUDITS = 0                    Response:      5

Q12 : SELECT COUNT(*)
      FROM   STATS
      WHERE  NOT
             (AUDITS = 0)                  Response:      5
                                           Add
                                           (Q11 + Q12): 10
```

In this particular example it can easily be seen at this point that predicate T is in fact a general tracker.

Step 3: Find sum (total number of individuals in database) plus (total number satisfying predicate P), using the predicates P OR T and P OR NOT T.

```
Q13 : SELECT COUNT(*)
      FROM   STATS
      WHERE  (SEX = 'M' AND
             OCCUPATION = 'PROGRAMMER')
      OR     AUDITS = 0                    Response:      6

Q14 : SELECT COUNT(*)
      FROM   STATS
      WHERE  (SEX = 'M' AND
             OCCUPATION = 'PROGRAMMER')
      OR     NOT
             (AUDITS = 0)                  Response:      5
                                           Add
                                           (Q13 + Q14): 11
```

Step 4: From the results so far we have that the number of individuals satisfying predicate P is one (result of Step 3 minus result of Step 2); that is, P designates Able uniquely.

Now we repeat (Steps 5 and 6) the queries of Steps 2 and 3, but using SUM instead of COUNT.

Step 5: Find total salary, using the predicates T and NOT T.

```
Q15 :  SELECT  SUM(SALARY)
         FROM    STATS
         WHERE   AUDITS = 0                    Response:       219K
```

```
Q16 :  SELECT  SUM(SALARY)
         FROM    STATS
         WHERE   NOT
                 (AUDITS = 0)                  Response:       145K
                                               Add
                                               (Q15 + Q16): 364K
```

Step 6: Find sum of Able's salary and total salary, using the predicates P OR T and P OR NOT T.

```
Q17 :  SELECT  SUM(SALARY)
         FROM    STATS
         WHERE   (SEX = 'M' AND
                 OCCUPATION = 'PROGRAMMER')
         OR      AUDITS = 0                     Response:       244K
```

```
Q18 :  SELECT  SUM(SALARY)
         FROM    STATS
         WHERE   (SEX = 'M' AND
                 OCCUPATION = 'PROGRAMMER')
         OR      NOT
                 (AUDITS = 0)                   Response:       145K
                                               Add
                                               (Q17 + Q18): 389K
```

Step 7: Find Able's salary by subtracting total salary from result of previous step.

```
                                               Response:       25K
```

Figure 4.6 illustrates the general tracker.

If the initial guess was wrong and predicate T turns out not to be a general tracker, then one or other of the predicates (P OR T) and (P OR NOT T) may be inadmissible. For example, if the result set cardinalities for P and T are p and t, respectively, where $p < b$ and $b \le t \le 2b$, then it is possible that the result set cardinality for (P OR T), which cannot exceed $(p + t)$, is less than $2b$. In such a situation it is necessary to make another guess at a tracker T and try again. Reference [4.23] suggests that the process of finding a general tracker is not difficult in

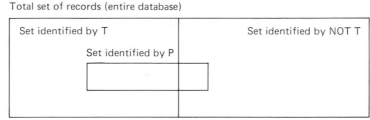

Fig. 4.6 The general tracker T:

$$SET(P) = SET(P\ OR\ T) + SET(P\ OR\ NOT\ T) - SET(T\ OR\ NOT\ T)$$

practice. In our particular example, the initial guess *is* a general tracker (its result set cardinality is 5), and Q13 and Q14 are both admissible queries.[6]

To summarize this section so far: A general tracker "almost always" exists, and is usually both easy to find and easy to use. In fact, it is often possible to find a tracker quickly by simply guessing [4.23]. Even in those cases where a general tracker does not exist, reference [4.23] shows that specific trackers can usually be found for specific queries. We conclude that security in a statistical database is a real problem. What can be done about it? Several suggestions have appeared in the literature, but none seems totally satisfactory at the present time [4.23]. For example, one possibility is "data swapping"—that is, interchanging field values among records in such a way that overall statistical accuracy is preserved, so that even if a specific value is identified there is no way of knowing which particular individual that value belongs to. The difficulty with this approach lies in finding sets of records whose values can be exchanged in such a fashion. Similar limitations apply to most other suggested solutions, though the proposals of [4.25] and [4.26] look promising. For the present it seems that we must agree with Denning's conclusions [4.23]: "Compromise is straightforward and cheap. The requirement of complete secrecy of confidential information is not consistent with the requirement of producing exact statistical measures for arbitrary subsets of the population. At least one of these requirements must be relaxed before assurances of security can be believed."

4.7 DATA ENCRYPTION

We have assumed so far in this chapter that any would-be infiltrator will be using the normal system facilities for accessing the database. We now turn our attention to the case of a "user" who attempts to bypass the system—for example, by physically removing part of the database (stealing a disk pack), or by tapping into a

---

6. By definition a general tracker works for an *arbitrary* inadmissible predicate P. For some specific P a tracker T that is not a *general* tracker (because its result set cardinality is not in the range $2b$ to $n-2b$) may still be sufficient, without actually being a specific "individual" tracker (that is, without being of the form P1 AND NOT P2).

communications line,[7] or by running a program that breaks through the defenses of the underlying operating system—often not difficult—and masquerades as the DBMS itself. The most effective countermeasure against all such threats is *data encryption*—that is, storing and transmitting all data, messages, passwords, etc., in an encrypted form.

In order to discuss some of the concepts of data encryption, we introduce the following terms. The original data is called the *plaintext*. The plaintext is *encrypted* (or *enciphered* or *scrambled* or simply *transformed*) by subjecting it to an *encryption algorithm*, whose inputs are the plaintext and an *encryption key*; the output from this algorithm, the encrypted form of the plaintext, is called the *ciphertext*. The details of the encryption algorithm are made public, or at least are not specially concealed, but the encryption key is kept secret. The ciphertext, which should be unintelligible to anyone not holding the encryption key, is what is stored in the database or transmitted down the communication line.

Example.   Let the plaintext be the string

    AS KINGFISHERS CATCH FIRE

(For simplicity we assume that the only data characters we have to deal with are upper-case letters and blanks.) Let the encryption key be the string ELIOT; and let the encryption algorithm be as follows.

Step 1:   Divide the plaintext into blocks of length equal to that of the encryption key:

    A S b K I   N G F I S   H E R S b   C A T C H   b F I R E

(we now show blank characters explicitly as b).

Step 2:   Replace each character of the plaintext by an integer in the range 0–26, using b = 00, A = 01, . . ., Z = 26:

    0119001109 1407060919 0805181900 0301200308 0006091805

Step 3:   Repeat Step 2 for the encryption key:

    0512091520

---

7. As Petersen and Turn point out in [4.8], the communication lines are actually the most vulnerable part of the system. Using only comparatively inexpensive equipment, an infiltrator could monitor all communication between a genuine user and the database, discover passwords (for example), and thus be able to masquerade as that user on a subsequent occasion. By tapping a special terminal into the line, an infiltrator could (a) cancel a genuine user's sign-off signal in order to continue operating in that user's name; (b) perform "between lines" entry to the system when a genuine user is holding the line but is inactive; or (c) perform "piggy-back" entry to the system by selectively intercepting messages and then releasing them with modifications.

Step 4: For each block of the plaintext, replace each character by the sum, modulo 27, of its integer encoding and the integer encoding of the corresponding character of the encryption key:

```
0119001109  1407060919  0805181900  0301200308  0006091805
0512091520  0512091520  0512091520  0512091520  0512091520
----------  ----------  ----------  ----------  ----------
0604092602  1919152412  1317000720  0813021801  0518180625
```

Step 5: Replace each integer encoding in the result of Step 4 by its character equivalent:

F D I Z B   S S O X L   M Q b G T   H M B R A   E R R F Y

The decryption procedure for this example is straightforward, *given the key.* (*Exercise:* Decrypt the ciphertext shown above.) The question is, how difficult is it for a would-be infiltrator to determine the key without prior knowledge (given matching plaintexts and ciphertexts)? In our simple example the answer is, fairly obviously, "not very"; but, equally obviously, much more sophisticated schemes can easily be devised. Ideally the scheme employed should be such that the "work factor" involved in breaking it far outweighs any potential advantage to be gained in doing so [4.7]. The accepted ultimate objective for such schemes is that the *inventor* of the scheme, holding matching plaintext and ciphertext, should be unable to determine the key, and hence unable to decipher another piece of ciphertext. In any case, keys need not be static; they can be changed at mutually agreed intervals; and it would seem prudent to arrange matters such that the interval between changing them is less than the time it would take to discover the existing key.[8]

We conclude this introductory discussion by pointing out that, even in a system that supports encryption, data must be processed in its plaintext form at the central processing unit (for example, for comparisons to operate correctly), and that therefore there is still a risk of the data being accessible to concurrently executing programs or appearing in a storage dump. Also, as reference [4.16] points out, there are severe technical problems in providing indexes over encrypted data and in maintaining encrypted information in the system log.

The Data Encryption Standard

The encryption example discussed earlier made use of a *substitution* procedure: An encryption key was used to determine, for each character of the plaintext, a ciphertext character to be substituted for that character. Substitution is one of the two

---

8. It has been suggested that the weakness of encryption schemes in practice is not so much the danger that keys might be *deduced*, using recognized cryptanalysis techniques, but rather the difficulty of keeping the keys secret in the first place—the *key management* problem [4.12].

basic approaches to encryption as traditionally practiced; the other is *permutation*, in which plaintext characters are simply rearranged into some different sequence. Neither of these approaches is particularly secure in itself, but algorithms that combine the two can provide quite a high degree of security. In 1977 such a hybrid scheme, designed and developed by IBM, was adopted by the National Bureau of Standards [4.27] as the official Data Encryption Standard (DES), to be used by federal agencies[9] and anyone else who wishes to do so. The algorithm is suitable for implementation on an LSI chip, which means that devices that incorporate it can operate at a high data rate. A number of IBM devices support the DES.

To use the DES, plaintext is divided into 64-bit blocks and each block is encrypted using a 64-bit key (actually the key consists of 56 bits plus 8 parity bits, so there are not 2^{64} but only 2^{56} possible distinct keys). A block is encrypted by applying an initial permutation to it, then subjecting the permuted block to a sequence of 16 complex substitution steps, and finally applying another permutation, the inverse of the initial permutation, to the result of the last of those steps. The substitution at the ith step is not controlled directly by the encryption key K but by a key Ki that is computed from the values K and i. For details see [4.27].

The DES has the property that the decryption algorithm is identical to the encryption algorithm, except that the Ki's are applied in reverse order.

The Data Encryption Standard is not without its critics. Many experts feel that 56-bit keys are inadequate and that the key size should be increased to 128 bits. It has been claimed that it would be possible, using a powerful enough but conventional computer, to locate a given 56-bit key with an exhaustive search in less than 24 hours. On the other hand, supporters of the DES point out that double application of the DES algorithm (that is, applying it twice in series) simulates the effect of doubling the key size, and that in any case (as mentioned in Footnote 8) the encryption algorithm itself is unlikely to be the weak point in the overall security system.

Public-Key Encryption

Much interest has been generated recently by the possibility of "public-key" encryption schemes. In such schemes, both the encryption algorithm *and the encryption key* are made freely available; thus anyone can convert plaintext into ciphertext. But the corresponding *decryption key* is kept secret (public-key schemes involve *two* keys, one for encryption and one for decryption). The decryption key cannot feasibly be deduced from the encryption key; thus even the person performing the original encryption cannot perform the corresponding decryption if not authorized to do so.

The original idea of public-key encryption is due to Diffie and Hellman [4.31]. We describe a specific scheme, proposed by Rivest, Shamir, and Adleman [4.32], to

---

9. Except for data that is classified under the National Security Act (1947) or Atomic Energy Act (1954).

show how such a system might work. This scheme is based on the following two facts:

1. There is a known fast algorithm for determining whether a given (large) number is prime[10];
2. There is no known fast algorithm for determining the prime factors of a given (large) nonprime number.

By way of illustration, reference [4.33] (quoting Rivest) states that testing whether a given 130-digit number is prime would take about 7 minutes of computer time on a given machine, whereas finding the two prime factors of a number obtained by multiplying together two 63-digit primes would take about 40 quadrillion years on the same machine (one quadrillion = 1,000,000,000,000,000).

The scheme of [4.32] works as follows.

■   Choose, randomly, two distinct large primes p and q, of say about 100 digits each, and compute the product $r = p * q$.

■   Choose, randomly, a large integer e that is relatively prime to $(p-1) * (q-1)$; that is, the greatest common divisor of e and $(p-1) * (q-1)$ is 1. The integer e is the encryption key. (Note: Choosing e is straightforward. For example, any prime greater than both p and q will do.)

■   Take the decryption key, d, corresponding to e to be the unique "multiplicative inverse" of e, modulo $(p-1) * (q-1)$; that is,

$$d * e = 1, \text{ modulo } (p-1) * (q-1) .$$

The algorithm for computing d is straightforward and is given in [4.32].

■   Publish the integers r and e but not d. (The scheme thus reduces the key management problems mentioned earlier, since the only key to be kept secret is d, and only people doing the decrypting need that key.)

■   To encrypt a piece of plaintext P (which we assume for simplicity to be an integer less than r), replace it by the ciphertext C, computed as follows:

$$C = P^e \text{ modulo } r .$$

Efficient techniques for computing C from P, e, and r (and P from C, d, and r—see next paragraph) are given in [4.32].

---

10. The algorithm is based on Fermat's theorem that if p is prime and if $n < p$, then

$$n^{p-1} = 1 \text{ (modulo } p) .$$

Thus, to test whether a given number q is prime, we choose a number n ($n < q$) at random, raise it to the power $(q-1)$, and divide the result by q. If the remainder is not 1, then q is not prime. If the remainder is 1, then we choose a different n and try again. If the remainder is 1 for every one of a small set of randomly chosen n's, then q is almost certainly prime. See [4.32] for more details.

■ To decrypt a piece of ciphertext C, replace it by the plaintext P, computed as follows:

$$P = C^d \text{ modulo } r \ .$$

Reference [4.32] proves that this scheme works—i.e., that decryption of C using d does in fact recover the original P as it was prior to encryption using e. However, computation of d knowing only r and e (and not p or q) is infeasible, as we claimed earlier. Thus anyone can encrypt plaintext, but only authorized users (holding d) can decrypt ciphertext.

We give a trivial example to illustrate the procedure. For obvious reasons we restrict ourselves to very small numbers throughout.

Example. Let $p = 3$, $q = 5$; then $r = 15$, and the product $(p-1) * (q-1) = 8$. Let $e = 11$ (a prime greater than both p and q). To compute d, we have

$$d * 11 = 1, \text{ modulo } 8,$$

whence $d = 3$.

Now let the plaintext P consist of the integer 13. Then the ciphertext C is given by

$$
\begin{aligned}
C &= P^e \text{ modulo } r \\
&= 13^{11} \text{ modulo } 15 \\
&= 1792160394037 \text{ modulo } 15 \\
&= 7 \ .
\end{aligned}
$$

Now the original plaintext P is given by

$$
\begin{aligned}
P &= C^d \text{ modulo } r \\
&= 7^3 \text{ modulo } 15 \\
&= 343 \text{ modulo } 15 \\
&= 13 \ .
\end{aligned}
$$

The encryption and decryption algorithms used in the prime-number scheme outlined above are examples of what Diffie and Hellman call *trap-door one-way functions* [4.31]. A trap-door one-way function e is a function with the following properties:

1. For all positive integers x, $e(x)$ exists, is positive, and is unique;
2. There exists an inverse function d such that, for all positive integers x, $d(e(x)) = x$;
3. Efficient algorithms exist for computing $e(x)$ and $d(x)$, given x;
4. It is computationally infeasible to discover d given e.

Any function satisfying these four conditions will be suitable as the basis for a public-key encryption scheme.

Because functions *e* and *d* are inverses of each other, public-key encryption schemes also permit encrypted messages to be "signed" in such a way that the recipient can be certain that the message originated with the person it purports to have done (that is, "signatures" cannot be forged). Suppose that A and B are two users who wish to communicate with each other using a public-key encryption scheme. Then A and B will each publish an encryption algorithm (including in each case the encryption key to be used), but of course will keep the corresponding decryption algorithm and key secret, even from each other. Let the encryption algorithms be ENCRYPT_FOR_A and ENCRYPT_FOR_B (for encrypting messages to be sent to A and B, respectively), and let the corresponding decryption algorithms be DECRYPT_FOR_A and DECRYPT_FOR_B, respectively. ENCRYPT_FOR_A and DECRYPT_FOR_A are inverses of each other, as are ENCRYPT_FOR_B and DECRYPT_FOR_B.

Now suppose that A wishes to send a piece of plaintext P to B. Instead of simply computing ENCRYPT_FOR_B(P) and transmitting the result, A first applies the *decryption* algorithm DECRYPT_FOR_A to P, then encrypts the result and transmits that as the ciphertext C:

```
ENCRYPT_FOR_B ( DECRYPT_FOR_A ( P ) ) = C
```

On receipt of C, user B applies the decryption algorithm DECRYPT_FOR_B, and then the *encryption* algorithm for A, producing the final result P:

```
  ENCRYPT_FOR_A ( DECRYPT_FOR_B ( C ) )
= ENCRYPT_FOR_A ( DECRYPT_FOR_B ( ENCRYPT_FOR_B
                                ( DECRYPT_FOR_A ( P ) ) ) )
= ENCRYPT_FOR_A ( DECRYPT_FOR_A ( P ) )
= P
```

Now B knows that the message did indeed come from A, because ENCRYPT_FOR_A will only produce P if the algorithm DECRYPT_FOR_A was used in the encryption process, and that algorithm is known only to A. No one, *not even B*, can forge A's signature.

EXERCISES

4.1 Suppose Fig. 4.4 (STATS) represents a System R base table. Write SQL statements to give:

    a) User Ford SELECT privileges over the entire table;

    b) User Smith INSERT and DELETE privileges over the entire table;

    c) Each user SELECT privileges over that user's own record (only);

    d) User Nash SELECT privileges over the entire table and UPDATE privileges over the SALARY and TAX fields (only);

    e) User Todd SELECT privileges over the NAME, SALARY, and TAX fields (only);

    f) User Ward SELECT privileges as for Todd and UPDATE privileges over the SALARY and TAX fields (only);

    g) User Pope full privileges (SELECT, UPDATE, INSERT, DELETE) over records for programmers (only);

    h) User Jones SELECT privileges as for Todd and UPDATE privileges over the TAX and AUDITS fields (only);

    i) User King SELECT privileges for maximum and minimum salaries per occupation class (but no other privileges);

    j) User Clark DROP privileges on the table.

4.2 For each of parts (a) through (j) under Exercise 4.1, write SQL statements to remove the indicated privileges from the user concerned.

4.3 Design an implementation scheme for the SQL statements GRANT and REVOKE that takes into account the cascade effect of REVOKE.

4.4 Consider Fig. 4.4 once again. Suppose we know from outside sources that Hall is a homemaker with at least two dependents. Write a sequence of statistical queries in SQL that will reveal Hall's TAX and AUDITS figures, using an individual tracker. Assume as in Section 4.6 that the system will not respond to queries with a result set cardinality less than 2 or greater than 8.

4.5 Repeat Exercise 4.4, but using a general tracker instead of an individual tracker.

4.6 Decrypt the following ciphertext (which was produced in a manner similar to that used in the "AS KINGFISHERS CATCH FIRE" example in Section 4.7, but using a different encryption key):

    FNWAL   JPVJC   FPEXE   ABWNE   AYEIP   SUSVD

[*Hint:* The encryption key is five characters long.]

4.7 Write a program to test whether an arbitrary integer N is prime.

4.8 Show that it is necessary in the public-key encryption scheme of [4.32] for the primes p and q to be distinct. [*Hint:* Suppose they are not. Choose $p = q = 5$, say, and consider what happens in encrypting the plaintext integer 10.]

4.9 (Taken with permission from "Mathematical Games: A New Kind of Cipher That Would Take Millions of Years to Break," by Martin Gardner [4.33]. Copyright 1977 by Scientific American, Inc. All rights reserved.) The following ciphertext was computed by Rivest and his colleagues from an English sentence plaintext by (a) converting the plaintext to an integer by setting blank = 00, A = 01, etc., and then (b) using the prime-number encryption scheme, taking e as 9007 and r as

11438162575788886766923577997614661201021829672124236256256184293
57069352457338978305971235639587050589890751475992900268795435 41

(which is the product of a 64-digit prime p and a 65-digit prime q).

Ciphertext:

```
9686 9613 7546 2206
1477 1409 2225 4355
8829 0575 9991 1245
7431 9874 6951 2093
0816 2982 2514 5708
3569 3147 6622 8839
8962 8013 3919 9055
1829 9451 5781 5154
```

Rivest and his colleagues are offering a prize of $100 to the first person who successfully deciphers this message.

REFERENCES AND BIBLIOGRAPHY

4.1 E. B. Fernandez, R. C. Summers, and C. Wood. *Database Security and Integrity.* Reading, Mass.: Addison-Wesley (1981).

4.2 J. Martin. *Security, Accuracy, and Privacy in Computer Systems.* Englewood Cliffs, N.J.: Prentice-Hall (1973).

4.3 J. Martin and A. R. D. Norman. *The Computerized Society.* Englewood Cliffs, N.J.: Prentice-Hall (1970); Pelican Books (1973).

An extensive set of predictions concerning the impact of computers on society. The book is divided into three parts: "Euphoria," in which the advantages are imaginatively described; "Alarm," in which the nature of the threat to privacy (among other problems) is spelled out in detail; and "Protective Action," in which possible safeguards (technical and legislative) are examined and various recommendations made. Chapters 14–15 and 24–27 are specifically concerned with privacy.

4.4 L. J. Hoffman (ed.). *Security and Privacy in Computer Systems.* Los Angeles, Calif.: Melville Publishing Company (1973).

A good collection of "readings" (technical papers and other articles) on the topic of security, classified under the headings

- Civil Liberties Threats
- A Cram Course in Threats and Countermeasures
- Privacy Transformations
- Models for Secure Systems
- Statistical Data Banks
- Is There Hope in Hardware?
- Security in Existing Systems

The last section includes a discussion of IBM's Resource Access Control Facility (RACF).

4.5 L. J. Hoffman. *Modern Methods for Computer Security and Privacy.* Englewood Cliffs, N.J.: Prentice-Hall (1977).

4.6 R. A. DeMillo, D. P. Dobkin, A. K. Jones, and R. J. Lipton (eds.). *Foundations of Secure Computation.* New York: Academic Press (1978).

The proceedings of a workshop, classified under the following general headings:

- Data Base Security
- Encryption as a Security Mechanism
- Design-Oriented Models of Operating System Security
- Theoretical Models of Operating System Security

4.7 L. J. Hoffman. "Computers and Privacy: A Survey." *ACM Comp. Surv.* **1,** No. 2 (June 1969).

This early paper is divided into four sections: (a) "The privacy problem," a discussion of the potential dangers inherent in "the databank society"; (b) "Legal and administrative safeguards," a review of the then legal position; (c) "Technical methods proposed to date" (the longest section); and (d) "Promising research problems." An annotated bibliography is included.

4.8 H. E. Petersen and R. Turn. "System Implications of Information Privacy." *Proc. SJCC* **30** (1967). Also published in [4.4].

A classic paper in the field.

4.9 J. G. Bergart, M. Denicoff, and D. K. Hsiao. "An Annotated and Cross-Referenced Bibliography on Computer Security and Access Control in Computer Systems." Technical Report OSU-CISRC-TR-72-12, Computer and Information Science Research Center, Ohio State University, Columbus, Ohio 43210 (November 1972).

A useful survey of published material in the field prior to 1973.

4.10 D. K. Hsiao, D. S. Kerr, and S. E. Madnick. "Privacy and Security of Data Communications and Data Bases." In *Issues in Data Base Management* (eds. H. Weber and A. I. Wasserman): *Proc. 4th International Conference on Very Large Data Bases* (September 1978). North-Holland (1978).

4.11 C. Wood, E. B. Fernandez, and R. C. Summers. "Data Base Security: Requirements, Policies, and Models." *IBM Sys. J.* **19,** No. 2 (1980).

Discusses the authorization matrix model of access control in some depth, and also gives an introduction to data classification schemes.

4.12 D. E. Denning and P. J. Denning. "Data Security." *ACM Comp. Surv.* **11,** No. 3 (September 1979).

A tutorial, covering "access control" (that is, authorization constraints and the authorization matrix), flow controls, "inference control" (the statistical database problem), and cryptographic controls.

4.13 I. S. Herschberg. "Case Studies in Breaking the Security of Time-Sharing Systems." In *Proc. IBM Data Security Symposium* (April 1973). IBM Form No. G520-2838.

An entertaining description of how security was deliberately breached in a number of (unspecified!) systems. In all cases it proved possible to breach the system while acting as a legitimate user, using only publicly available information, and leaving absolutely no trace of the intrusion. The writer concludes that suppliers' claims with respect to the security of their systems should not be taken at face value, but that a community of sophisticated users intent on finding possible breaches and informing suppliers of them may eventually be a major force behind the provision of truly secure systems.

4.14 R. W. Conway, W. L. Maxwell, and H. L. Morgan. "On the Implementation of Security Measures in Information Systems." *CACM* **15,** No. 4 (April 1972). Also published in [4.4].

The paper that introduced the authorization matrix model. Discusses several implemented systems in terms of this model, in particular a system called ASAP that was implemented by the authors. Emphasizes the advantages of making as many access control decisions as possible at compile time rather than at execution time.

4.15 E. F. Codd. "Access Control Principles for Security and Privacy in Integrated Data Banks." IBM internal memo (July 1970).

4.16 D. D. Chamberlin et al. "Data Base System Authorization." In [4.6].

A good general discussion that provides some of the rationale behind the System R security mechanism [4.17, 4.18]. Includes a brief summary of the (rather unsophisticated) approach to security found in most database installations today, with some comments on why the situation is likely to change.

4.17 P. P. Griffiths and B. W. Wade. "An Authorization Mechanism for a Relational Data Base System." *ACM TODS* **1,** No. 3 (September 1976).

Describes the authorization mechanism originally proposed for System R (the implemented scheme differs from this proposal on a number of points of detail). See also [4.18].

4.18 R. Fagin. "On an Authorization Mechanism." *ACM TODS* **3,** No. 3 (September 1978).

An extended corrigendum to [4.17]. Under certain circumstances the mechanism of [4.17] would revoke a privilege that ought not to be revoked. This is because, under the original scheme, if one user grants a particular privilege multiple times to another user, then all but the first of these grants are ignored. Suppose, for example, that the following sequence of operations occurs (all grants assumed to include the GRANT option):

Time t1: A grants P to B

Time t2: B grants P to C

Time t3: C grants P to D

Time t4: A grants P to C

Time t5: C grants P to D [ignored]

Time t6: B revokes P from C

At time t6, P is revoked from D, even though it ought not to be (since the grant at t5 can be seen as passing on to D the privilege that C obtained from A at t4, and that privilege has not been revoked). Fagin's paper corrects this flaw.

4.19 M. R. Stonebraker and E. Wong. "Access Control in a Relational Data Base Management System by Query Modification." *Proc. ACM National Conference 1974.*

4.20 IBM Corporation. Query-by-Example Terminal User's Guide. IBM Form No. SH20-2078.

4.21 M. M. Zloof. "Security and Integrity within the Query-by-Example Data Base Management Language." IBM Research Report RC6982 (February 1978).

4.22 IBM Corporation. IMS/VS System/Application Design Guide. IBM Form No. SH20-9025.

4.23 D. E. Denning, P. J. Denning, and M. D. Schwartz. "The Tracker: A Threat to Statistical Database Security." *ACM TODS* **4**, No. 1 (March 1979).

4.24 D. E. Denning. "A Review of Research on Statistical Data Base Security." In [4.6].

4.25 L. L. Beck. "A Security Mechanism for Statistical Databases." *ACM TODS* **5**, No. 3 (September 1980).

> Shows that any database that gives statistically accurate responses is vulnerable to compromise regardless of the techniques used to protect it, but that the number of queries needed to effect such compromise can be made arbitrarily large if moderate variations can be permitted in query responses. The method works by introducing controlled random perturbations of the data in responding to a query. In computing a sum, for example, each field value to be included in the summation is modified by $(x * d + y)$, where d is the difference between the field value and the mean of such values, and x and y are independent random variables generated for each such field in accordance with specific rules.

4.26 D. E. Denning. "Secure Statistical Databases with Random Sample Queries." *ACM TODS* **5**, No. 3 (September 1980).

> Suggests a new inference control [4.12] called *random sample queries*. The method works as follows. As the system locates a record R satisfying a given selection predicate P, it applies a function $f(P,R)$ to determine whether or not to include R in the result set. The function f is defined in terms of subordinate functions that map P and R into random sequences of bits and then compare the results. Any given query is guaranteed to give the same answer every time it is executed (contrast the proposal of [4.25]). The paper shows that (a) this technique can provide accurate statistics at low overhead, (b) compromise is still possible unless the system refuses to respond to queries with result set cardinality too low or too high, but that (c) compromise is no longer possible using the general tracker technique of [4.23].

4.27 U.S. Department of Commerce/National Bureau of Standards. Data Encryption Standard. Federal Information Processing Standards Publication 46 (1977 January 15).

4.28 W. F. Ehrsam, S. M. Matyas, C. H. Meyer, and W. L. Tuchman. "A Cryptographic Key Management Scheme for Implementing the Data Encryption Standard." *IBM Sys. J.* **17**, No. 2 (1978).

> As pointed out earlier in this chapter, key management is likely to be a significant problem in any scheme based on encryption, such as the DES scheme (less so in the public-key schemes). This paper proposes a set of protocols (for both database and data communications) that use a "master key" to encrypt all other keys, thus reducing the problem to one of protecting a single key. Other keys are changed very frequently, for example, once per terminal session in the case of a data communication key. The master key and encryption/decryption algorithm are kept in nonvolatile, protected storage (the *cryptographic facility*). The algorithm also operates within this facility, so that intermediate results are also hidden.

4.29 S. M. Matyas and C. H. Meyer. "Generation, Distribution, and Installation of Cryptographic Keys." *IBM Sys. J.* **17**, No. 2 (1978).

> Discusses techniques for managing the multitude of keys required by the protocols of the previous paper [4.28].

4.30 R. E. Lennon. "Cryptography Architecture for Information Security." *IBM Sys. J.* **17**, No. 2 (1978).

Discusses the impact of DES considerations on IBM's Systems Network Architecture (SNA).

4.31 W. Diffie and M. E. Hellman. "New Directions in Cryptography." *IEEE Transactions on Information Theory IT-22* (November 1976).

The paper that introduced the concept of public-key encryption.

4.32 R. L. Rivest, A. Shamir, and L. Adleman. "A Method for Obtaining Digital Signatures and Public-Key Cryptosystems." *CACM* **21**, No. 2 (February 1978).

4.33 M. Gardner. "A New Kind of Cipher That Would Take Millions of Years to Break." *Scientific American* **237**, 2 (August 1977).

A good informal introduction to the work on public-key encryption. The title may be an overclaim (see annotation to [4.34]).

4.34 A. Lempel. "Cryptology in Transition." *ACM Comp. Surv.* **11**, No. 4: Special Issue on Cryptology (December 1979).

An excellent survey. The article discusses classical techniques, current implementations (including the DES), a variety of public-key schemes, and the question of complexity (for example, can formal measures be obtained of the security or "breakability" of a given encryption scheme?). To quote: "One of the major shortcomings of currently practiced cryptography—the DES as well as the new public schemes—is the lack of *proof* that any of these schemes are indeed as hard to break as they are deemed (or claimed) to be . . . [Proponents of DES] cite as evidence of its strength the many man/computer years spent on futile attempts to break it . . . [Proponents of the public-key schemes] invoke the intractability of the computational task facing a cryptanalyst armed with the best *publicly* known algorithms for factorization [and the like] . . . [But] if some organization with a motive for secrecy were to have a feasible algorithm for, say, factoring 200-digit integers, it would have little inclination to publicize the fact [let alone the algorithm]."

4.35 R. C. Daley and P. G. Neumann. "A General Purpose File System for Secondary Storage." *Proc. FJCC* **27** (1965).

A description of the Multics file system, including detailed consideration of the access control facilities. The database is viewed as a file hierarchy, in which the terminal nodes are data files and all other nodes are directory files. Access control is handled by associating a list (a "file profile") with each node specifying all permitted users of the file corresponding to that node and each user's permitted "modes" (write, read only, etc.) on that file. The hierarchical structure allows factoring to be applied to the file pro files (an entry common to all nodes subordinate to some given node can be factored out and placed at the given node).

4.36 CODASYL COBOL Committee. COBOL Journal of Development (1978).

ANSWERS TO SELECTED EXERCISES

4.1 a) GRANT SELECT ON STATS TO FORD

b) GRANT INSERT, DELETE ON STATS TO SMITH

c) DEFINE VIEW MYREC AS
    SELECT * FROM STATS WHERE NAME = USER

GRANT SELECT ON MYREC TO PUBLIC

d) GRANT SELECT, UPDATE (SALARY, TAX) ON STATS TO NASH

e) DEFINE VIEW NST AS
    SELECT NAME, SALARY, TAX FROM STATS

GRANT SELECT ON NST TO TODD

f) DEFINE VIEW NST AS
    SELECT NAME, SALARY, TAX FROM STATS

GRANT SELECT, UPDATE (SALARY, TAX) ON NST TO WARD

g) DEFINE VIEW PROGRAMMERS AS
    SELECT * FROM STATS WHERE OCCUPATION = 'PROGRAMMER'

GRANT ALL PRIVILEGES ON PROGRAMMERS TO POPE

"ALL PRIVILEGES" includes INDEX and EXPAND, in general, but these operations do not apply to a view.

h) DEFINE VIEW NST AS
    SELECT NAME, SALARY, TAX FROM STATS
DEFINE VIEW NTA AS
    SELECT NAME, TAX, AUDITS FROM STATS

GRANT SELECT ON NST TO JONES
GRANT UPDATE (TAX, AUDITS) ON NTA TO JONES

i) DEFINE VIEW SALBOUNDS AS
    SELECT OCCUPATION, MAX(SALARY), MIN(SALARY)
    FROM   STATS
    GROUP   BY OCCUPATION

GRANT SELECT ON SALBOUNDS TO KING

j) GRANT DBA ON STATS TO CLARK

4.2 a) REVOKE SELECT ON STATS FROM FORD

b) REVOKE INSERT, DELETE ON STATS FROM SMITH

c) REVOKE SELECT ON MYREC FROM PUBLIC

or perhaps simply

DROP VIEW MYREC

For answers (d) through (j) below we generally ignore the possibility of simply dropping the view (if applicable).

d) `REVOKE SELECT, UPDATE ON STATS FROM NASH`

e) `REVOKE SELECT ON NST FROM TODD`

f) `REVOKE SELECT, UPDATE ON NST FROM WARD`

g) `REVOKE ALL PRIVILEGES ON PROGRAMMERS FROM POPE`

h) `REVOKE SELECT ON NST FROM JONES`
   `REVOKE UPDATE ON NTA FROM JONES`

i) `REVOKE SELECT ON SALBOUNDS FROM KING`

j) `REVOKE DBA ON STATS FROM CLARK`

4.4 Individual tracker for Hall:

```
DEPENDENTS > 1 AND NOT (OCCUPATION = 'HOMEMAKER')
```

```
SELECT  COUNT(*)
FROM    STATS
WHERE   DEPENDENTS > 1              Response: 6
```

```
SELECT  COUNT(*)
FROM    STATS
WHERE   DEPENDENTS > 1
AND     NOT
        (OCCUPATION = 'HOMEMAKER')  Response: 5
```

Hence the predicate

```
DEPENDENTS > 1 AND OCCUPATION = 'PROGRAMMER'
```

uniquely identifies Hall.

```
SELECT  SUM(TAX), SUM(AUDITS)
FROM    STATS
WHERE   DEPENDENTS > 1              Response: 24K, 5
```

```
SELECT  SUM(TAX), SUM(AUDITS)
FROM    STATS
WHERE   DEPENDENTS > 1
AND     NOT
        (OCCUPATION = 'HOMEMAKER')  Response: 23K, 5
```

Hence Hall's tax and audits figures are 1K and zero, respectively. Note that all result set cardinalities are within bounds.

4.5 General tracker: SEX = 'F'

```
SELECT  SUM(TAX), SUM(AUDITS)
FROM    STATS
WHERE   SEX = 'F'                   Response: 35K, 4
```

```
SELECT  SUM(TAX), SUM(AUDITS)
FROM    STATS
WHERE   NOT
        (SEX = 'F')                 Response: 8K, 3
```

Hence total tax and total number of audits are 43K and 7, respectively.

```
SELECT   SUM(TAX), SUM(AUDITS)
FROM     STATS
WHERE    (DEPENDENTS > 1 AND
          OCCUPATION = 'HOMEMAKER')
OR        SEX = 'F'                      Response: 36K, 4

SELECT   SUM(TAX), SUM(AUDITS)
FROM     STATS
WHERE    (DEPENDENTS > 1 AND
          OCCUPATION = 'HOMEMAKER')
OR        NOT
          (SEX = 'F')                    Response: 8K, 3
```

Adding these responses and subtracting the totals previously calculated, we have again that Hall's tax and number of audits are 1K and zero, respectively.

4.6 The encryption key is APRIL.

5
Data Models

5.1 INTRODUCTION

This chapter and the next are devoted to the topic of *data models:* that is, to the problem of how information can be represented and manipulated within the formal framework of a database system. So far in this book we have generally assumed that readers are broadly familiar with at least the relational model, and probably with the hierarchical and network models as well (a tutorial treatment of this material can be found in Volume I). Now we take a deeper look at the overall problem. First we examine the concept of "data model" itself. Then we present a formal definition of the basic (*n*-ary) relational model, in order to pave the way for our discussions of the extended relational model in the next chapter. We also discuss some additional basic models: the binary relational, irreducible relational, and functional data models, which for convenience we group together under the general heading of irreducible models. We then go on to consider a rather specific question, namely the question of *null values,* which is concerned with the handling of missing information. Finally, we examine some extended or "semantic" models—that is, models that attempt to incorporate more meaning or semantics than do the basic models. (Note, however, that the distinction between "basic" and "extended" models is far from clearcut.) That examination, which forms the last section of the present chapter, sets the scene for the next chapter, which consists of a detailed presentation of one particular extended model, namely Codd's extended relational model RM/T.

5.2 WHAT IS A DATA MODEL?

We define a *data model* to consist of three components:

- a collection of object types;
- a collection of operators;
- a collection of general integrity rules.

For example, in the relational model, the objects are relations and domains, the operators are those of the relational algebra, and the integrity rules (simplifying somewhat) are as follows: (1) No component of a primary key value can be null; (2) every nonnull foreign key value must match some existing primary key value somewhere.

The *object types* are the basic building blocks of the data model. That is, the logical structure of any database that conforms to the model is built out of objects of those types, and only those types. As an example, a relational database is built out of domains and relations; it does *not* contain any interrelational links or access paths, because such links are not one of the object types of the relational model.

The *operators* provide a means for manipulating a database that is composed of valid instances of the object types. The effect of applying one of these operators (or, more generally, some valid combination of these operators) to a given database will be to identify some subset of the total data content of that database. That subset can then serve as the basis for a variety of operations, including the following (among others):

- retrieval (that is, defining a set of data that is the result of a query);
- update (that is, defining a set of data to be modified or deleted);
- defining the set of data to be accessible through a view;
- defining access rights (that is, defining a set of data to which authorization can be granted);
- defining stability requirements (that is, defining the scope of a locking operation);
- defining some specific integrity constraint (over and above the general constraints that are built into the data model itself).

The *integrity rules* constrain the set of valid states of databases that conform to the model. Note, however, that the rules are *general* and will need to be complemented by a set of more specific rules in any specific situation, as indicated above. These more specific rules will constrain the set of valid states still further (see Chapter 2).

Aside: The foregoing definition of data model is based on one given by Codd [5.9]. In fact, the entire concept of data model was first formulated by Codd (in the context of the relational model) in his original 1970 paper [5.8]. Hierarchical and network *implementations* existed prior to that time, but hierarchical and network *models* were not defined until later (by a process of abstraction from those implementations), when it became desirable to compare the different approaches on a common level of abstraction. By contrast, relational implementations did not appear until after the definition of the relational model, and were founded on that definition.

The primary purpose of any data model, relational or otherwise, is of course to provide a formal means of representing information and a formal means of manipulating such a representation. For a particular model to be useful for a particular application, there must clearly exist some simple correspondence between the components of that model and the elements of that application; that is, the process of mapping elements of the application into constructs of the model must be reasonably straightforward. To put it another way, a data model should possess some generally accepted *interpretation*. For example, in the case of the relational model, we might say, loosely, that the intended interpretation of a primary key is as the unique identifier of some entity. However, any such interpretation is necessarily intuitive, and hence outside the *formal* scope of the model per se. In this chapter we are primarily concerned with data models in their formal aspect.

In many ways a data model can be regarded as simply a rather abstract *programming language*. After all, programming languages also consist of a collection of object types, a collection of operators, and a collection of integrity rules (an example of such a rule is that which states that the value of the pointer in a PL/I pointer-qualified reference must not be null). There are some differences, of course. For one thing, data models obviously concentrate on those constructs (objects, operators, integrity rules) that are relevant to *database* programming, as opposed to more conventional programming (we are using the term "programming" here in a very general sense to encompass all formal interactions with a computer system). By contrast, conventional programming languages concentrate on such matters as arithmetic operations, input/output, flow of control, etc. A more significant difference is that a data model, unlike a programming language, does not prescribe any specific syntax for its objects and operators. Instead, it merely specifies, in rather abstract terms, those objects and operators that should have *some counterpart* in any concrete realization of that data model. A particular data model may thus be capable of realization in a variety of different concrete styles. In the case of the relational model, for instance, SQL and QBE provide two quite distinct examples of such concrete styles.

To repeat, therefore: A data model can be thought of as a programming language, albeit one that is at a much higher level of abstraction than that of most such languages. The analogy, like all analogies, should not be taken too far; nevertheless, it is valuable as an aid to understanding, and it can lead to helpful insights into the nature of various problems, and indeed into some of the basic concepts, in the database management field. By way of illustration, we list below some familiar database concepts and give in each case a programming language interpretation.

- A database is simply a (large, structured) *variable*. The *database schema* (or *database intension*) defines the *type* of that variable. Similarly, a relation is also a variable, and the corresponding *relation schema* (relation intension) gives the type of that variable; and so on.

- A *database instance* (or *database state* or *database extension*) is a value of the variable defined by the database schema. Similarly, a relation instance (state, extension) is a value of the variable defined by some relation schema, and so on. (The value of a variable changes with time, whereas the type does not.)

■   The term "relation" in the previous two paragraphs was tacitly being used to mean a *real* relation (a "base table"). *Virtual* relations ("views") are a little different. In fact, we can distinguish two kinds of view—basically, those that are updatable and those that are not. An updatable view may be thought of as a simple *reference* to one or more underlying real relations (or portions thereof). In effect, the view simply introduces a new name for existing data, and the user can use that name to access and manipulate that data. There are analogies between such a view and an overlay-defined variable in conventional programming. A nonupdatable view, by contrast, represents a *totally separate variable*—that is, a new object, with a value and a name of its own. The value of the new variable is obtained by evaluating an *operational expression* (such as X UNION Y), rather than a simple reference (such as X). Such a view is analogous to the system-generated *temporary* variables created in a programming language system for arithmetic expressions (such as X + Y).

Some examples may help to explain these analogies. Given the PL/I declarations

```
DCL ALPHA CHARACTER (10) ;
DCL BETA  CHARACTER (3)
          DEFINED ALPHA POSITION (5) ;
```

the variable BETA is a reference to a substring (character positions 5–7) of the variable ALPHA. BETA is updatable, and an update to BETA is in fact an update to the underlying variable ALPHA. By contrast, given

```
DCL GAMMA FIXED BINARY (31) ;
DCL DELTA FIXED BINARY (31) ;
```

it is not possible to update the expression GAMMA + DELTA (say). Such an expression corresponds to a system-generated temporary variable, and there is no direct way to refer to that variable; and even if there were, updating that variable would have no effect on the variables GAMMA and DELTA themselves.[1]

Another way of looking at this question is to think of a view as a *function*. A reference to the view is an invocation of the function. For updatable views, the function simply returns (the appropriate portions of) the underlying variable itself (or variables themselves); for nonupdatable views, it returns a new variable, distinct from the underlying variable(s) from which that new variable is derived. Again the distinction between the two cases is clear.

---

1. We do not mean to imply that a view that is defined via an "operational expression" can never be updatable. It depends basically on whether there is any well-defined way of getting back to the underlying base data from the view. In the case of GAMMA + DELTA there is no such way. But if GAMMA and DELTA were character strings instead of numbers, and if the "operational expression" were GAMMA||DELTA (where || stands for concatenation), then it might be argued that the concatenated string *could* be updated and that updates to either portion of it could be unambiguously mapped back to GAMMA or DELTA, as appropriate. Thus in the relational model, for example, it *may* be possible to update a view whose definition involves a join, under certain circumstances. In fact we shall rely on such a possibility in the next chapter. See [5.29].

■   A *data definition language* (DDL) provides a specific syntax for declaring data-base variables, relation variables, etc. In other words, the DDL provides a concrete realization of the declarative operators of the data model. Similarly, a *data manipulation language* (DML) provides a concrete realization of the manipulative operators of the data model.

■   A *database management system* (DBMS) is an implementation of some specific DDL and DML. Just as a programming language implementation typically involves both compiler and interpreter (run-time library) aspects, so also will a DBMS. For example, in System R, most SQL statements are compiled before execution, but certain statements, such as those dealing with authorization, are handled interpretively. It is true, however, that most present-day database management systems are rather inflexible in this regard, treating declarative and manipulative operations quite separately (typically, declarative operations are always compiled and manipulative operations always interpreted; note that this is the opposite of what is done in System R).

It is also possible to give programming language interpretations to such notions as reorganization, recovery, and so on, but the foregoing list is sufficient to give the general idea. However, we use the analogy once more to make one further point. Just as every implementation of, for example, PL/I is slightly different from every other—that is, supports a slightly different dialect of the PL/I language—so every implementation of, for example, the relational model will also be somewhat different from every other. But it is reasonable to speak of a "family" of relational implementations, as distinct from, say, network implementations, just as it is reasonable to speak of a family of PL/I implementations as distinct from COBOL implementations. There is a difference, however, as pointed out earlier. Since the relational model (for example) can be implemented in a variety of different concrete styles, the family of relational implementations must be considered as being divided into various "subfamilies"—a QBE subfamily, a SQL subfamily, and so on. The remarks made earlier about every implementation having its own idiosyncrasies then apply within each such subfamily.

Aside: In view of the remarks made in the foregoing paragraph, it is worth digressing for a moment to consider exactly what it is that constitutes a "relational system." The relational model as formally defined in Section 5.3 can be seen as an *ideal* against which specific implementations can be measured. To this writer's knowledge, no single implementation currently supports every single feature of that ideal; particular features may be omitted from particular implementations for a variety of pragmatic reasons. What is more, different features may be omitted from different implementations. Such omissions do not necessarily mean that the system concerned is "not relational." But there must be some *minimum subset* of the ideal (the complete relational model) that a system must support in order to qualify as relational. Codd in his 1981 Turing Lecture [5.44] proposes the following as that minimum:

1. the tabular data structure (without any user-visible navigational links between tables);

2. the relational algebra operators SELECT, PROJECT, and JOIN (either natural join or equijoin).[2] Support for these operators must not require predefinition of any physical access paths.

Systems that support (1) but not (2) may be called *tabular* or *semirelational* (see Volume I).

We should not leave this topic (the analogy with programming languages) without pointing out that there is another major area in which data models differ from conventional programming languages: namely, data models include, at least implicitly, the notion of *transaction*. The requirement for this notion arises from a combination of two things: (1) The fact that the set of valid database states is constrained by the existence of certain integrity rules, as explained earlier; (2) the fact that, in general, it may not be possible for the database to go from one valid state to another without passing through some invalid state on the way. These considerations lead to the need for the concept of a *unit of integrity* (that is, a transaction), and in particular to the requirement for a "commit" operator to trigger integrity checking. (They also, of course, lead to the requirement for the associated concept of *rollback*.) See Chapters 1 and 2 for an extended discussion of these ideas.

Transactions are also the unit of sharing in a concurrent-user system. While perhaps not usually considered part of the data model per se, the concept of dynamically sharing variables and the operators needed to control such sharing (see Chapter 3) have been given much more attention—and are probably much better understood—in the context of data models than in that of traditional programming languages.

We conclude this section by considering the question "What are data models for?" As stated earlier, the general objective is to provide a formal system for the representation and manipulation of information. A list of more specific objectives (some of which have already been discussed) is given below:

- To serve as a focus for database system architecture.
- To serve as a tool for checking the correctness of specific database system implementations.
- To provide a basis for the development of database design techniques.
- To provide a basis for the design of specific data definition languages and data manipulation languages (DDLs and DMLs).
- To allow functional requirements and performance requirements to be separately addressed (physical data independence).
- To allow individual requirements and community requirements to be separately addressed (logical data independence).
- To provide a yardstick for the evaluation and comparison of specific database systems.
- To serve as an educational vehicle.

---

2. These operators are chosen because they are easily the most important ones in practice.

■ To serve as a vehicle for research into various aspects of database management, such as the problem of distributed databases. (The data model per se does not solve such problems, but it does provide a precise framework for their formulation that is independent of any specific implementation. Proper formulation of any problem is a prerequisite to solving that problem.)

In regard to the first point above, we can relate the idea of a data model to the well-known three-level architecture of ANSI/SPARC [5.6, 5.7]. The data model concept has a reasonable interpretation at each of the three levels; that is, we can sensibly speak of an external (or user) data model, a conceptual data model, and an internal (or storage) data model.[3] Present-day systems tend not to permit much variation between the external and conceptual levels, although they do support significant variation between those two levels and the internal level. One of the goals of the extended models, to be discussed later, is to provide for greater variability between the first two levels. Note that, as a consequence of these interpretations, we view the operators supported at each level as being of equal importance with the objects or data structures supported at that level.

5.3 THE RELATIONAL MODEL

In this section we present a simplified formal definition of the concepts of the basic relational model. Our definitions cover the following concepts, among others:

Relational database

■ domain
■ relation
      (i.e., relation variable)
■ · real relation
      (base relation)
■ virtual relation
      (view)
■ degree
■ attribute
■ tuple
■ candidate key
■ primary key
■ alternate key

Relational operations

■ union
■ difference
■ product
      (i.e., extended Cartesian product)
■ theta-selection
■ projection
■ theta-join
■ equijoin
■ natural join
■ relational-assignment

Relational rules

■ entity integrity
■ referential integrity

---

3. Reference [5.6] uses these terms (external model, etc.) to refer to the data structures alone. In fact, many writers (among them the present author in the 1st and 2nd editions of Volume I) use "data model" to mean just a data structure, and ignore the operator and integrity rule aspects. This usage does not do justice to the data model concept.

As stated above, we are concerned in this section with *formal* definitions of these concepts; we will not generally be discussing their intended interpretation (the reader is assumed to be familiar with such informal aspects already). Our purpose in defining the concepts formally here is to provide a convenient source of reference for the material and to lay the groundwork for our subsequent presentation of the extended relational model. However, it is certainly not essential to absorb all the detail of this section in order to be able to understand the topics that follow. In fact, we strongly recommend that the reader skim over this section very lightly on a first or second reading, and possibly on subsequent readings too. We do not pretend that formal definitions are easy to read. Also, it should be stressed at the outset that the precise scope of "the relational model" as defined herein reflects to some extent a personal choice on the part of the writer. Other definitions are possible, and may either include additional concepts or exclude some concepts that are included here. See, for example, reference [5.10].

We begin with the notion of *relational-system*. (Note: For the purposes of this section we shall use certain typographical conventions whenever we wish to be formal. First, all terms to be formally defined will be hyphenated, if necessary, to exclude any intervening blanks. Second, terms defined by means of the production rules of Figs. 5.1 and 5.2, such as ⟨relational-database⟩, will additionally be enclosed in angle brackets.) A relational-system is a database system constructed in accordance with the relational model. More formally, a relational-system consists of three components: a ⟨relational-database⟩, a collection of ⟨relational-operation⟩s, and two ⟨relational-rule⟩s. We examine each of these components in turn.

Relational Database

As already indicated, it is convenient to summarize the structure of a ⟨relational-database⟩ by means of a set of production rules (Fig. 5.1). Please note that Fig. 5.1 is *not* a proposal for a concrete syntax for relational database declarations; rather, it is an *abstract* syntax, whose function is merely to indicate the abstract structure of the various objects being defined. Observe in particular that the syntax does not include any mention of the parentheses or other separators that would be needed in practice to avoid ambiguity.

In presenting the syntax we make use of the following convenient shorthand. Let ⟨xyz⟩ be an arbitrary syntactic category. Then the expression ⟨xyz-set⟩ is also a syntactic category, representing an unordered, possibly empty set of objects of type ⟨xyz⟩.

Now we discuss the constructs of Fig. 5.1 in detail. The following paragraphs are numbered to correspond to the production rules of the figure.

1. A ⟨relational-database⟩ consists of a set of ⟨domain⟩s and a set of ⟨relation⟩s. Two points arise immediately. First, note that we are using the term ⟨relational-database⟩ to mean, specifically, a *variable,* in the sense of Section 5.2; the value of this variable is assumed to change with time. Similar remarks apply to ⟨relation⟩ (but not to ⟨domain⟩; a ⟨domain⟩ is *not* a variable, and its value does not change

```
 1.  ⟨relational-database⟩
       ::=   ⟨domain-set⟩ ⟨relation-set⟩
 2.  ⟨domain⟩
       ::=   ⟨domain-name⟩ ⟨domain-value-set⟩
             ⟨ordering-indicator⟩
 3.  ⟨domain-name⟩
       ::=   ⟨name⟩
 4.  ⟨domain-value⟩
       ::=   ⟨atom⟩
 5.  ⟨ordering-indicator⟩
       ::=   YES | NO
 6.  ⟨relation⟩
       ::=   ⟨named-relation⟩ | ⟨unnamed-relation⟩
 7.  ⟨named-relation⟩
       ::=   ⟨real-relation⟩ | ⟨virtual-relation⟩
 8.  ⟨real-relation⟩
       ::=   ⟨relation-name⟩ ⟨attribute-set⟩
             ⟨primary-key⟩ ⟨alternate-key-set⟩ ⟨tuple-set⟩
 9.  ⟨relation-name⟩
       ::=   ⟨name⟩
10.  ⟨attribute⟩
       ::=   ⟨attribute-name⟩ ⟨domain-name⟩
11.  ⟨attribute-name⟩
       ::=   ⟨name⟩
12.  ⟨primary-key⟩
       ::=   ⟨candidate-key⟩
13.  ⟨candidate-key⟩
       ::=   ⟨attribute-name-set⟩
14.  ⟨alternate-key⟩
       ::=   ⟨candidate-key⟩
15.  ⟨tuple⟩
       ::=   ⟨attribute-value-set⟩
16.  ⟨attribute-value⟩
       ::=   ⟨attribute-name⟩ ⟨domain-value⟩
17.  ⟨virtual-relation⟩
       ::=   ⟨relation-name⟩ ⟨relational-expression⟩
18.  ⟨unnamed-relation⟩
       ::=   ⟨relational-expression⟩
```

Fig. 5.1 The structure of a relational-system (Part 1 of 3): the ⟨relational-database⟩.

with time). Second, our definition of relational-system is still rather static, the previous point notwithstanding; that is, the ⟨relational-operation⟩s (defined in Fig. 5.2, later) make no provision for adding new ⟨named-relation⟩s to the database, nor for destroying existing ⟨named-relation⟩s, nor for any other changes to the database declaration. Extension of the definitions to handle these aspects is beyond the scope of this chapter.

2. A ⟨domain⟩ consists of a ⟨domain-name⟩, a (fixed, nonempty) set of ⟨domain-value⟩s, and an ⟨ordering-indicator⟩.

3. A ⟨domain-name⟩ is simply a ⟨name⟩, representing the name of the ⟨domain⟩ concerned. (We do not define ⟨name⟩s any further in this syntax.) Every ⟨domain⟩ in a given ⟨relational-database⟩ must have a unique ⟨domain-name⟩.

4. A ⟨domain-value⟩ is an ⟨atom⟩—that is, a value that is nondecomposable so far as the relational-system is concerned. All ⟨domain-value⟩s for a given ⟨domain⟩ are of the same data-type. We choose not to formalize the notion of "data-type" in this presentation.

Note: We assume for the present that ⟨domain⟩s may include null values—that is, that the null value is a legal ⟨atom⟩. However, we do not consider null values in any real depth until Section 5.5. In particular, we do not consider prior to that section the special treatment required by null values in the definition of ⟨relational-operation⟩s such as ⟨union⟩.

5. The ⟨ordering-indicator⟩ indicates whether the ⟨domain⟩ concerned is ordered—that is, whether the operator "is greater than" is applicable between pairs of ⟨atom⟩s from the ⟨domain⟩.

6. A ⟨relation⟩ is either a ⟨named-relation⟩ or an ⟨unnamed-relation⟩.

7. A ⟨named-relation⟩ is either a ⟨real-relation⟩ or a ⟨virtual-relation⟩.

8. A ⟨real-relation⟩ consists of a ⟨relation-name⟩, a nonempty set of ⟨attribute⟩s, a ⟨primary-key⟩, a set of ⟨alternate-key⟩s, and a (time-varying) set of ⟨tuple⟩s.

9. A ⟨relation-name⟩ is a ⟨name⟩ (it is the name of the ⟨named-relation⟩ concerned). Every ⟨named-relation⟩ in a given ⟨relational-database⟩ must have a unique ⟨relation-name⟩.

10. An ⟨attribute⟩ consists of an ⟨attribute-name⟩ and a ⟨domain-name⟩. The ⟨domain⟩ identified by ⟨domain-name⟩ is said to *correspond to* the ⟨attribute⟩ identified by ⟨attribute-name⟩ (see paragraph 11); equivalently, the ⟨attribute⟩ identified by ⟨attribute-name⟩ is said to be *defined on* the ⟨domain⟩ identified by ⟨domain-name⟩. The number of ⟨attribute⟩s in the ⟨attribute-set⟩ of a given ⟨relation⟩ is the *degree* of the ⟨relation⟩ concerned.

Note: As we shall see later, *all* ⟨relation⟩s (⟨real-relation⟩s, ⟨virtual-relation⟩s, and ⟨unnamed-relation⟩s) possess an ⟨attribute-set⟩. For reasons to be explained, however, our formalism shows ⟨attribute-set⟩ as an explicit component of ⟨real-relation⟩s only. Similar remarks apply to ⟨primary-key⟩, ⟨alternate-key-set⟩, and ⟨tuple-set⟩; see paragraphs 12–16.

11. An ⟨attribute-name⟩ is a ⟨name⟩ (it is the name of the ⟨attribute⟩ concerned). No two ⟨attribute⟩s of a given ⟨relation⟩ can have the same ⟨attribute-name⟩.

12. A ⟨primary-key⟩ is a ⟨candidate-key⟩ (see paragraph 13). Every ⟨relation⟩ has exactly one ⟨primary-key⟩.

13. A ⟨candidate-key⟩ is a nonempty set of ⟨attribute-name⟩s. Every ⟨attribute-name⟩ appearing in a given ⟨candidate-key⟩ must be the ⟨attribute-name⟩ for some ⟨attribute⟩ of the ⟨relation⟩ concerned. Every ⟨candidate-key⟩ of a ⟨relation⟩ R satisfies the following two properties:

■ Uniqueness property

   At any given time, no two ⟨tuple⟩s of the current ⟨tuple-set⟩ of R have the same combination of ⟨attribute-value⟩s for the set of ⟨attribute⟩s designated by the specified ⟨attribute-name-set⟩ (see paragraphs 15 and 16).

■ Minimality property

   No ⟨attribute-name⟩ can be discarded from the specified ⟨attribute-name set⟩ without destroying the uniqueness property.

Conversely, any ⟨attribute-name-set⟩ possessing these two properties is a ⟨candidate-key⟩.

For a given ⟨relation⟩, exactly one ⟨candidate-key⟩ is (arbitrarily) designated as the ⟨primary-key⟩, and all other ⟨candidate-key⟩s are designated as ⟨alternate-key⟩s (for that ⟨relation⟩). Note: The distinction between ⟨primary-key⟩ and ⟨alternate-key⟩ is significant in practice only for ⟨real-relation⟩s, not for ⟨virtual-relation⟩s and not for ⟨unnamed-relation⟩s.

14. An ⟨alternate-key⟩ is a ⟨candidate-key⟩. Every ⟨relation⟩ has zero or more ⟨alternate-key⟩s. See paragraph 13.

15. A ⟨tuple⟩ is a set of ⟨attribute-value⟩s. The ⟨tuple-set⟩ of a given ⟨relation⟩ represents, informally, the *value* of that ⟨relation⟩. Let R be a ⟨relation⟩ and let T be the ⟨tuple-set⟩ within R at some particular time. Then every ⟨tuple⟩ of T *conforms to* the ⟨attribute-set⟩ of R; that is, it contains exactly one ⟨attribute-value⟩ for each distinct ⟨attribute⟩ of R, and the ⟨attribute-name⟩ within that ⟨attribute-value⟩ is the name of that ⟨attribute⟩ (see paragraph 16).

16. An ⟨attribute-value⟩ consists of an ⟨attribute-name⟩ and a ⟨domain-value⟩. The ⟨domain-value⟩ is a value from the (unique) ⟨domain⟩ corresponding to the ⟨attribute⟩ identified by ⟨attribute-name⟩. (Informally, we often consider the ⟨domain-value⟩ alone as the "attribute-value," and ignore the ⟨attribute-name⟩ component.)

17. A ⟨virtual-relation⟩ consists of a ⟨relation-name⟩ and a ⟨relational-expression⟩. The ⟨relational-expression⟩ is an expression of the relational algebra, whose function is to specify the definition of the ⟨virtual-relation⟩ in terms of other ⟨named-relation⟩s in the ⟨relational-database⟩ (see Fig. 5.2). The ⟨virtual-relation⟩, like a ⟨real-relation⟩, possesses both ⟨attribute⟩s and a ⟨tuple-set⟩; however, the ⟨attribute⟩s and ⟨tuple-set⟩ of a ⟨virtual-relation⟩ are derived, in a manner to be explained later, from the ⟨relational-expression⟩, and are therefore not shown as separate syntactic components. We also omit any mention of ⟨candidate-key⟩ (and ⟨primary-key⟩ and ⟨alternate-key⟩); while these concepts do apply to ⟨virtual-relation⟩s, they are not particularly significant in this context, and we exclude them from our formalism accordingly.

18. An ⟨unnamed-relation⟩ consists of a ⟨relational-expression⟩. Informally, the ⟨unnamed-relation⟩ represents the result of evaluating that ⟨relational-expression⟩. The remarks in paragraph 17 concerning ⟨attribute⟩s, ⟨tuple-set⟩, and ⟨candidate-key⟩s (and ⟨primary-key⟩ and ⟨alternate-key⟩s) apply to ⟨unnamed-relation⟩s also, *mutatis mutandis*.

Relational Operations

The operations of the relational algebra are an integral component of the relational model. A particular relational implementation may support the operators of the algebra directly, or it may provide some alternative set of constructs, such as those of the relational calculus (tuple version or domain version). Here we consider just the algebraic operators, since they are in a sense the most fundamental. Again we present our definitions in terms of a set of production rules (Fig. 5.2); again this syntax should not be construed as a proposal for a concrete language.

We also define a ⟨relational-assignment⟩ operator (not part of the relational algebra per se). The function of this operator is to assign the result of evaluating some specified ⟨relational-expression⟩ to some specified ⟨real-relation⟩.

Before explaining Fig. 5.2 in detail, we introduce a convenient simplifying notation, which we define as follows.

■ The expression $R(A1:D1, \ldots, An:Dn)$ denotes a ⟨relation⟩ called R, of degree n, with ⟨attribute-set⟩ $(A1:D1, \ldots, An:Dn)$—that is, with ⟨attribute⟩s A1, ..., An, defined on ⟨domain⟩s D1, ..., Dn, respectively. When the ⟨domain⟩s are irrelevant to the purpose at hand, we shall abbreviate the expression to just $R(A1, \ldots, An)$. If the ⟨attribute⟩s are also irrelevant, we shall abbreviate the expression still further to simply R.

```
19. ⟨relational-operation⟩
      ::=   ⟨relational-algebra-operation⟩
            | ⟨relational-assignment⟩      •

20. ⟨relational-algebra-operation⟩
      ::=   ⟨union⟩
            | ⟨difference⟩
            | ⟨product⟩
            | ⟨theta-selection⟩
            | ⟨projection⟩

21. ⟨union⟩
      ::=   UNION ⟨relation-name⟩ ⟨relation-name⟩
                                  ⟨correspondence⟩

22. ⟨correspondence⟩
      ::=   ⟨attribute-name-pair-set⟩

23. ⟨attribute-name-pair⟩
      ::=   ⟨attribute-name⟩ ⟨attribute-name⟩

24. ⟨difference⟩
      ::=   DIFFERENCE ⟨relation-name⟩ ⟨relation-name⟩
                                       ⟨correspondence⟩

25. ⟨product⟩
      ::=   PRODUCT ⟨relation-name⟩ ⟨relation-name⟩

26. ⟨theta-selection⟩
      ::=   THETA_SELECT ⟨relation-name⟩ ⟨theta-comparison⟩

27. ⟨theta-comparison⟩
      ::=   ⟨attribute-name⟩ ⟨theta⟩ ⟨comparand⟩

28. ⟨theta⟩
      ::=   = | ¬= | < | <= | > | >=

29. ⟨comparand⟩
      ::=   ⟨atom⟩ | ⟨attribute-name⟩

30. ⟨projection⟩
      ::=   PROJECT ⟨relation-name⟩ ⟨attribute-name-set⟩

31. ⟨relational-assignment⟩
      ::=   ASSIGN ⟨relation-name⟩
                   ⟨relational-expression⟩ ⟨correspondence⟩

32. ⟨relational-expression⟩
      ::=   ⟨relation-name⟩
            | ⟨relational-algebra-operation⟩
            | ⟨relation-literal⟩

33. ⟨relation-literal⟩
      ::=   ⟨attribute-set⟩ ⟨tuple-set⟩
```

Fig. 5.2   The structure of a relational-system (Part 2 of 3): the ⟨relational-operation⟩s.

■   Similarly, we shall use (A1:a1, . . . ,An:an) to denote a ⟨tuple⟩ of R(A1, . . . ,An). Here a1, . . . ,an are values of ⟨attribute⟩s A1, . . . ,An, respectively (and are therefore drawn from ⟨domain⟩s D1, . . . ,Dn, respectively).

We shall also need the notion of *union-compatibility.*

■   Two ⟨relation⟩s of degree *n*, say R(A1, . . . ,An) and S(B1, . . . ,Bn), are said to be *union-compatible with respect to a correspondence C,* if and only if C is a set of exactly *n* ordered pairs of ⟨attribute-name⟩s (Ai, Bj) (i,j = 1, . . . ,n), and the following three conditions hold:

a) each ⟨attribute-name⟩ for R is some Ai (i = 1, . . . ,n);

b) each ⟨attribute-name⟩ for S is some Bj (j = 1, . . . ,n);

c) within each pair (Ai,Bj) of the set, the ⟨attribute⟩s designated by Ai and Bj have the same corresponding ⟨domain⟩.

Note that, for given R and S, there may exist more than one such C—that is, more than one correspondence satisfying conditions (a), (b), and (c).

We now continue with our detailed explanations.

19. A ⟨relational-operation⟩ is either a ⟨relational-algebra-operation⟩ or a ⟨relational-assignment⟩.

20. A ⟨relational-algebra-operation⟩ is a ⟨union⟩, a ⟨difference⟩, a ⟨product⟩, a ⟨theta-selection⟩, or a ⟨projection⟩. The result of evaluating a ⟨relational-algebra-operation⟩ is to generate an ⟨unnamed-relation⟩. As explained earlier (paragraph 18), that ⟨unnamed-relation⟩ possesses both an ⟨attribute-set⟩ and a ⟨tuple-set⟩; moreover, each ⟨tuple⟩ in that ⟨tuple-set⟩ conforms to that ⟨attribute-set⟩, in the sense of paragraph 15. The rules for generating the ⟨attribute-set⟩ and ⟨tuple-set⟩ are explained in paragraphs 21–30 below.

21. The ⟨union⟩ operator is defined as follows. Let R(A1:D1, . . . ,An:Dn) and S(B1:D1, . . . ,Bn:Dn) be two ⟨named-relation⟩s that are union-compatible with respect to the correspondence C = ((A1,B1), . . . ,(An,Bn)). The ⟨union⟩ of R and S over this particular correspondence, denoted UNION(R,S,C), is an ⟨unnamed-relation⟩ in which

a) the ⟨attribute-set⟩ is (U1:D1, . . . ,Un:Dn), where each Ui is (arbitrarily) that one of the pair (Ai,Bi) that precedes the other in lexicographic ordering;

b) the ⟨tuple-set⟩ is defined as follows. The ⟨tuple⟩ (U1:u1, . . . ,Un:un) appears in the ⟨tuple-set⟩ if and only if the ⟨tuple⟩ (A1:u1, . . . ,An:un) appears in R or the ⟨tuple⟩ (B1:u1, . . . ,Bn:un) appears in S (or both).

22. See the definition of union-compatibility, earlier.

23. See the definition of union-compatibility, earlier.

24. The ⟨difference⟩ operator is defined as follows. Let $R(A1:D1, \ldots, An:Dn)$ and $S(B1:D1, \ldots, Bn:Dn)$ be two ⟨named-relation⟩s that are union-compatible with respect to the correspondence $C = ((A1,B1), \ldots, (An,Bn))$. The ⟨difference⟩ of R and S over this particular correspondence, denoted DIFFERENCE(R,S,C), is an ⟨unnamed-relation⟩ in which

a) the ⟨attribute-set⟩ is $(A1:D1, \ldots, An:Dn)$;

b) the ⟨tuple-set⟩ is defined as follows. The ⟨tuple⟩ $(A1:a1, \ldots, An:an)$ appears in the ⟨tuple-set⟩ if and only if it appears in R and the ⟨tuple⟩ $(B1:a1, \ldots, Bn:an)$ does not appear in S. Note that the ⟨difference⟩ of S and R over C, DIFFERENCE(S,R,C), is also defined.

25. The ⟨product⟩ of two *differently named* ⟨named-relation⟩s $R(A1:D1, \ldots, Am:Dm)$ and $S(B1:E1, \ldots, Bn:En)$, denoted PRODUCT(R,S), is an ⟨unnamed-relation⟩ in which

a) the ⟨attribute-set⟩ is $(RA1:D1, \ldots, RAm:Dm, SB1:E1, \ldots, SBn:En)$—note the attribute renaming, which guarantees that ⟨attribute-name⟩s in the ⟨attribute-set⟩ of the ⟨product⟩ are unique;

b) the ⟨tuple-set⟩ is defined as follows. The ⟨tuple⟩ $(RA1:a1, \ldots, RAm:am, SB1:b1, \ldots, SBn:bn)$ appears in the ⟨tuple-set⟩ if and only if the ⟨tuple⟩ $(A1: a1, \ldots, Am:am)$ appears in R and the ⟨tuple⟩ $(B1:b1, \ldots, Bn:bn)$ appears in S.

Note 1: The ⟨product⟩ as defined above represents what is sometimes called the *extended Cartesian product*.

Note 2: We assume the existence of an aliasing operator, which permits the introduction of a new ⟨relation-name⟩ for a given ⟨named-relation⟩. Such an operator is discussed informally in Volume I. If it is necessary to form the ⟨product⟩ of some ⟨named-relation⟩ R with itself, the aliasing operator can be used to create an alias, S say, for R, so that the ⟨product⟩ can still be expressed in terms of two different ⟨relation-name⟩s.

26. The ⟨theta-selection⟩ operator is defined as follows. Let $R(A1:D1, \ldots, An:Dn)$ be a ⟨named-relation⟩. Let *theta* denote any one of the comparison operators $=, \neg =, <, <=, >$, and $>=$. Let *theta-comparison* denote any comparison of the form "Ai *theta* vi", where vi either is a ⟨domain-value⟩ from Di or is another ⟨attribute-name⟩ Aj of R also defined on Di $(i,j = 1, \ldots, n)$. (We assume that *theta* is applicable to Di.) The ⟨theta-selection⟩ of R with respect to this particular theta-comparison, THETA_SELECT(R, Ai *theta* vi), is an ⟨unnamed-relation⟩ in which

a) the ⟨attribute-set⟩ is $(A1:D1, \ldots, An:Dn)$;

b) the ⟨tuple-set⟩ is defined as follows. The ⟨tuple⟩ $(A1:a1, \ldots, An:an)$ appears in the ⟨tuple-set⟩ if and only if it appears in R and "Ai *theta* vi" evaluates to true for this ⟨tuple⟩.

27. See paragraph 26.

28. See paragraph 26.

29. See paragraph 26.

30. The ⟨projection⟩ operator is defined as follows. Let $R(A1, \ldots, An)$ be a ⟨named-relation⟩, and let $(Ai, \ldots, Aj)$ be a subset of the ⟨attribute-name⟩s specified in the ⟨attribute-set⟩ of R. The ⟨projection⟩ of R over this subset, denoted $PROJECT(R,(Ai, \ldots, Aj))$, is an ⟨unnamed-relation⟩ in which

  a) the ⟨attribute-set⟩ is $(Ai{:}Di, \ldots, Aj{:}Dj)$, where each Dk $(k = i, \ldots, j)$ is the Dk corresponding to Ak in the ⟨attribute-set⟩ of R;

  b) the ⟨tuple-set⟩ is defined as follows. The ⟨tuple⟩ $(Ai{:}ai, \ldots, Aj{:}aj)$ appears in the ⟨tuple-set⟩ if and only if a ⟨tuple⟩ exists in the ⟨tuple-set⟩ of R having ai as its Ai-value, $\ldots$, aj as its Aj-value.

31. The ⟨relational-assignment⟩ operator is defined as follows. The ⟨relation-name⟩ must be the ⟨name⟩ of a ⟨real-relation⟩, R say. Let R have ⟨attribute⟩s $A1, \ldots, An$. Let X be a ⟨relational-expression⟩ and let C be a ⟨correspondence⟩. The ⟨relational-assignment⟩ of X to R in accordance with C, denoted $ASSIGN(R,X,C)$, causes the existing ⟨tuple-set⟩ of R to be replaced by a new ⟨tuple-set⟩, as follows:

  a) X is evaluated (see paragraph 32), to yield an ⟨unnamed-relation⟩. Let us refer to this ⟨unnamed-relation⟩ as S, and let the ⟨attribute⟩s of S be $B1, \ldots, Bn$.

  b) R and S must be union-compatible with respect to C. Let corresponding ⟨attribute⟩s of R and S under C be $(A1,B1), \ldots, (An,Bn)$.

  c) The ⟨tuple⟩ $(A1{:}a1, \ldots, An{:}an)$ appears in the new ⟨tuple-set⟩ of R if and only if the ⟨tuple⟩ $(B1{:}a1, \ldots, Bn{:}an)$ appears in the ⟨tuple-set⟩ of S. We remark that a given ⟨relational-assignment⟩ will fail if the would-be new ⟨tuple-set⟩ of R violates any integrity constraints that are applicable to R.

32. A ⟨relational-expression⟩ is a ⟨relation-name⟩, a ⟨relational-algebra-operation⟩, or a ⟨relation-literal⟩. The result of evaluating a ⟨relational-expression⟩ is to generate an ⟨unnamed-relation⟩, as explained earlier. In the case of a ⟨relation-name⟩, the ⟨unnamed-relation⟩ has an ⟨attribute-set⟩ and a ⟨tuple-set⟩ identical to those of the designated ⟨named-relation⟩. In the case of a ⟨relational-algebra-operation⟩, the ⟨unnamed-relation⟩ has an ⟨attribute-set⟩ and a ⟨tuple-set⟩ that are derived in accordance with paragraphs 21–30 above. In the case of a ⟨relation-literal⟩, the ⟨unnamed-relation⟩ has an ⟨attribute-set⟩ and a ⟨tuple-set⟩ as specified by that ⟨relation-literal⟩ (see paragraph 33).

33. A ⟨relation-literal⟩ consists of an ⟨attribute-set⟩ and a set of ⟨tuple⟩s. Each ⟨tuple⟩ in the ⟨tuple-set⟩ must conform to the ⟨attribute-set⟩. Intuitively, ⟨relation-literal⟩s permit the insertion of new ⟨tuple⟩s into the ⟨relational-database⟩ (via a ⟨union⟩ operation), and the deletion of existing ⟨tuple⟩s from the ⟨relational-database⟩ (via a ⟨difference⟩ operation).

Relational Algebra: Additional Operators

Our formal definitions have deliberately restricted themselves to a very primitive (but relationally complete) set of operations. In practice, a relational *implementation* should provide various refinements on this primitive version, for both usability and efficiency. We consider some such refinements very briefly.

Intersection, join, division

The relational algebra as usually defined includes not only the operators defined above, but also the operators *intersection, join,* and *division* [5.10]. We excluded these latter operators from our formalism because they are not true primitives—each can be defined in terms of the other operators, as shown in Volume I. However, the *join* operator is so important in practice that we give a definition of it here, for purposes of reference. (Actually, as we shall see, the term "join" is used generically to refer to several related but distinct operators.) Let relations $R(A1, \ldots, Ai:D, \ldots, Am)$ and $S(B1, \ldots, Bj:D, \ldots, Bn)$ be such that attributes Ai and Bj are defined on the same domain D. Let *theta* be any one of the comparison operators $=$, $\neg =$, $<$, $< =$, $>$, and $> =$ that is applicable to domain D. The *theta-join* of R on Ai with S on Bj, THETA_JOIN $(R, S, Ai$ *theta* $Bj)$, is an unnamed-relation with attribute-set as for PRODUCT(R,S). The tuple-set in this relation consists of all tuples

```
(RA1:a1,...,RAi:ai,...,RAm:am,SB1:b1,...,SBj:bj,...,SBn:bn)
```

such that $(A1:a1, \ldots, Ai:ai, \ldots, Am:am)$ appears in the current tuple-set of R, $(B1:b1, \ldots, Bj:bj, \ldots, Bn:bn)$ appears in the current tuple-set of S, and "ai *theta* bj" evaluates to true. (The theta-join of R and S is thus obtained by taking the product of R and S and then applying a theta-selection to it.)

   If *theta* is equality, the theta-join is said to be an *equijoin*. In the case of the equijoin, the projections of the result on Ai and on Bj are necessarily identical. Let C be the set of all attributes of the equijoin *except* Ai (or except Bj). The projection of the equijoin on C is called the *natural join* of R and S (on Ai and Bj).

Extended and combined operations

It is desirable to provide shorthand equivalents for commonly occurring sequences of the primitive operations. We note some possible shorthands here.

- Allow the operands of the relational-algebra-operations to be specified as arbitrary relational-expressions, enclosed in parentheses if necessary to avoid ambiguity, instead of only as relation-names.

- Introduce an extended "selection" operator in which the second operand is an arbitrary Boolean combination of simple theta-comparisons.

- Introduce an analogously extended "join" operator.

- Allow the target for relational-assignment to be a virtual-relation as well as a real-relation (for "updatable" virtual-relations).

- Introduce explicit "insert," "delete," and "update" operations, instead of relying purely on relational-assignment and appropriate use of the union and difference operators.

Operators to handle null values

The relational algebra as defined by Codd in [5.10] includes certain additional operators for dealing with null values—for example, a "maybe" version of THETA_SELECT that selects tuples for which the theta-comparison evaluates to unknown, rather than to true. As indicated earlier, however, we defer detailed discussion of null values—and their effect on the relational algebra, in particular—to a later section (Section 5.5).

Relational Rules

As already indicated, the basic relational model includes two general integrity rules. (A specific relational-system will typically also include some specific "local" integrity rules.) We define the two general rules here (Fig. 5.3). Our definitions are in the spirit of reference [5.10]; regarding Rule 2 ("referential integrity"), however, it has been suggested that the formalism of [5.10] is not entirely satisfactory [5.40]. We have already pointed out in Chapter 2 that Rule 2 is not a complete control in itself on the referential integrity problem; loosely speaking, it is "necessary but not sufficient" (that is, a database could conform to the requirements of Rule 2 and yet still be in violation of some referential constraint). Reference [5.11] contains a detailed discussion of this topic and presents a more general proposal for expressing referential constraints—a proposal, incidentally, that (unlike Rule 2 as shown in Fig. 5.3) does not require the notion of "primary domain" at all. That proposal is discussed briefly in the answer to Exercise 2.3 (Chapter 2).

Note that the two rules refer to ⟨real-relations⟩s only, not to ⟨virtual-relation⟩s and not to ⟨unnamed-relation⟩s.

Some Consequences of the Definitions

We conclude this section by showing informally how the definitions given earlier lead to certain well-known and important relational properties.

- Within a given relation, no two tuples are identical (at any given time). This follows from the fact that the tuples within the relation at any given time are defined to constitute a *set*, and sets by definition do not contain duplicate elements.

- As a consequence of the previous point, the requirement that relations—in particular, real relations—always have a primary key is a reasonable (that is, consistent) one. This follows from the fact that at least the combination of *all* attri-

---

Integrity Rule 1 (Entity Integrity)
  Let ⟨attribute⟩ A of ⟨real-relation⟩ R be a component of the ⟨primary-key⟩
  of R. Then ⟨attribute⟩ A cannot accept null values. That is, no ⟨tuple⟩ of R
  can include an ⟨attribute-value⟩ in which the ⟨attribute-name⟩ is A and the
  ⟨domain-value⟩ is null.

Integrity Rule 2 (Referential Integrity)
  Let ⟨domain⟩ D be such that there exists a ⟨real-relation⟩ with (single-
  attribute) ⟨primary-key⟩ defined on D. Then D may optionally be
  designated as a *primary* ⟨domain⟩.

  Now let R(. . .,A:D, . . .) be a ⟨real-relation⟩ with ⟨attribute⟩ A defined
  on primary ⟨domain⟩ D. Then every ⟨tuple⟩ of R must satisfy the constraint
  that the ⟨domain-value⟩ corresponding to ⟨attribute⟩ A within that ⟨tuple⟩
  must be either (a) null, or (b) equal to k, say, where k is the ⟨domain-value⟩
  corresponding to the ⟨primary-key⟩ within some ⟨tuple⟩ of some ⟨real-rela-
  tion⟩ S with ⟨primary-key⟩ defined on D. R and S need not be distinct. The
  ⟨attribute⟩ A of R is said to be a *foreign key*.

Fig. 5.3   The structure of a relational-system (part 3 of 3): the ⟨relational-rule⟩s.

butes has the uniqueness property, and hence that at least one candidate key
(the set of all attributes, if necessary) always exists.

- Within a given relation (more accurately, within the tuple-set of a given relation), tuples are unordered. This also follows from the fact that a relation is a
  set—sets by definition have no ordering.

- Within a given relation, attributes are unordered. This follows from the fact
  that the collection of attributes of the relation is also defined as a set.

- All attribute-values are atomic; in other words, all relations are *normalized*.
  Equivalently, all relations are in *first normal form*. This level of normalization
  is required by the relational algebra. Higher levels, such as 4NF, are useful for
  database design purposes but are not an intrinsic part of the relational model
  per se.

5.4   IRREDUCIBLE MODELS

Many writers—see, for example, Kent [5.12]—have objected that the *n*-ary relational model is still somewhat too implementation-oriented (a tuple is too much like
a record, which is not a "natural" real-world construct), and that the purposes of a
data model are better served by a formalism in which "atomic facts" are separated

from one another. For example, considering the familiar suppliers-and-parts database, the information carried by the *n*-ary relation

    S(S#,SNAME,STATUS,CITY)

might be better expressed as the combination of the three binary relations

    SN(S#,SNAME)   ST(S#,STATUS)   SC(S#,CITY)

(domains omitted for brevity). In this latter version each relation represents a single "atomic fact"—that is, each relation represents the relationship between a specific entity (a supplier in the example) and one of its properties (name, status, or city in the example).

Out of such considerations three similar but distinct data models have evolved, which we will refer to as the binary relational, irreducible relational, and functional data model, respectively. Each of these in turn (like the *n*-ary relational model and, to a lesser extent, the network model) has led to developments in the general area of extended models. We therefore devote this section to a brief outline of these three approaches.

Note 1:   There is considerable overlap among these three models, and the literature in this area is not particularly clear, nor easy to read. In particular, several systems that are described as binary relational would more accurately be characterized as functional. Hence our assignment of a particular label, such as "functional," to a particular system, such as DIAM II [5.18, 5.19], may not be in agreement with existing descriptions of that system. However, all three approaches do involve a general notion of *irreducibility*, and we can therefore finesse the problem of classification somewhat by grouping all three under the general heading of "irreducible models."

Note 2:   In what follows we deliberately treat each of the three irreducible models as (essentially) a specialization of the *n*-ary relational model. It is our opinion that such a presentation, stressing the similarities and differences of these models vis-à-vis the relational model, is both valid and useful as an aid to understanding. However, we recognize that such an interpretation may give a slant or emphasis to the ideas that the original proponents did not intend—even that it may be claimed to miss the point in some way. In an attempt to redress the balance, therefore, we give a brief alternative characterization of the ideas—adapted with permission from Kent [5.40]—at the end of the section.

Binary Relational Models

The basic object type in binary relational models is, of course, the binary relation. As already indicated, each binary relation is intended to represent a single type of "atomic fact"—that is, the relationship between a single entity type and a single corresponding property type. Consider the suppliers-and-parts example again. We have already shown a set of relations corresponding to *suppliers:*

SN(S#,SNAME)   ST(S#,STATUS)   SC(S#,CITY)

Similarly, for *parts* we might have

PN(P#,PNAME)   PL(P#,COLOR)   PW(P#,WEIGHT)   PC(P#,CITY)

We make the following observations. (For brevity, all are expressed in terms of suppliers only, but of course analogous considerations apply to parts in every case.)

■   The concept of domain is still relevant.

■   The primary key (S#) must be repeated in every relation.

■   Every relation is necessarily in at least BCNF and almost certainly in 4NF and 5NF also (see Volume I), and is thus *in itself* free of the redundancies and anomalies that can occur in connection with relations that are not in BCNF. Note carefully, however, that this fact does not imply that the concepts of "further normalization" described in Volume I are no longer applicable. Suppose, for example, that suppliers satisfy the additional functional dependency CITY→STATUS (over and above the functional dependencies implied by the uniqueness of supplier numbers). To keep the example simple, let us also agree to ignore supplier names for the moment. Suppliers then *could* legally be represented (as above) by the combination

SC(S#,CITY)   and   ST(S#,STATUS)

—that is, this decomposition is nonloss—but such a representation is unwise, as explained in Volume I: Although it is true that SC and SS are (necessarily) each in BCNF, they are not *independent,* in the sense that they can be freely and independently updated. In fact, all updates to either one must be checked against the other to ensure that the functional dependency CITY→STATUS is not violated (inconsistencies can occur without such checking). A preferable decomposition is

SC(S#,CITY)   and   CT(CITY,STATUS)

These two relations *are* independent of each other and can be independently updated. Thus, the mere fact that all relations are binary does not automatically mean that the database design is a good one. For further discussion of the relevance of normalization concepts to binary relations, see Codd's discussion of the "binary decomposition trap" in [5.10].

■   If, say, the status for a particular supplier is null (unknown), we can represent that fact by simply excluding that supplier from relation ST; we do not need to include a tuple in ST showing that supplier with a null value for STATUS.

■ Certain interrelational constraints are required. Informally, we need to be able to express the fact that each of the three relations SN, ST, and SC refers to the same set of suppliers. However, we *cannot* say that the set of supplier numbers is the same in each relation, because of the previous point. In fact, any one of the three relations could include an S# value that does not appear in either of the others. It would be possible to impose the restriction that one of the relations, say SN, must contain *all* existing S# values (even those for which SNAME is unknown); we could then define referential constraints from ST.S# to SN.S# and from SC.S# to SN.S#. But this approach introduces a degree of arbitrariness and an unpleasant asymmetry into the structure. A better solution is to introduce a *unary* relation, S say, with sole attribute S#, whose function is precisely to list all known suppliers. There will then be three referential constraints, one from each of the binary relations to the unary relation S. "Binary relational model" may thus be a somewhat misleading term, since unary relations will typically also be supported.

■ More objects, and hence more names, are needed than with the *n*-ary approach. The *n*-ary version of suppliers, for example, involves

```
4 domains:     DS#, DSNAME, DSTATUS, DCITY (say)
1 relation:    S
4 attributes:  S.S#, S.SNAME, S.STATUS, S.CITY
```

By contrast, the binary version (if we agree to introduce a unary relation S for supplier numbers) involves

```
4 domains:     DS#, DSNAME, DSTATUS, DCITY
4 relations:   S, SN, ST, SC
7 attributes:  S.S#
               SN.S#, SN.SNAME
               ST.S#, ST.STATUS
               SC.S#, SC.CITY
```

One point in favor of the binary structure in this example is that each supplier property has its own corresponding relation name *and* its own corresponding attribute name, both of which could be exploited to mnemonic advantage.

■ Now consider the question of operators. Since binary relations (and unary relations) are just a special case of *n*-ary relations, it follows that the *n*-ary relational operators apply. However, the result of such an operation is not necessarily another binary (or unary) relation. Consider the query "Retrieve full details for all suppliers." The result of this query, obtained by joining relations S, SN, ST, and SC on S#, is a relation of degree 4.[4] Thus the "binary" model will probably have to be ready to deal with relations of arbitrary degree.

───────────

4. By join here we mean the natural join. We are assuming for the moment that every supplier is in fact represented in each of the relations. In Section 5.5 we shall discuss the "outer join" operator, which will allow us to deal with a supplier who does not appear in some relation (because the corresponding attribute-value is null for that supplier).

■   As the foregoing paragraph suggests, access operations tend to be more complex (that is, involve more joins) in the binary approach than in the *n*-ary approach.

■   One further point is that some decompositions into binary relations are questionable, to say the least. It is not clear, for example, that there is anything to be gained by spreading an employee's DATE_OF_HIRE across three separate relations, one each for YEAR, MONTH, and DAY.

We have not yet considered the question of representing *shipments* in the binary model. Recall that shipments are represented by a ternary relation

```
SP(S#,P#,QTY)
```

in the *n*-ary approach. This relation, though of degree 3, already corresponds to a single "atomic fact," namely, the relationship between a supplier/part combination and a quantity, and it cannot be nonloss-decomposed into a set of projections. There are however two "artificial" ways of reducing it to binary form.

■   The first involves what are sometimes called "nested binaries," and is recommended by both [5.13] and [5.14]. Intuitively, the technique involves converting the unnested ternary relation SP(S#,P#,QTY) into the nested binary relation

```
SPX(SPY(S#,P#),QTY)
```

For example the SP *triple* (S1,P1,300) would be represented as the *pair* (S1,P1) in the binary relation SPY, together with the *pair* (alpha,300) in the binary relation SPX—where "alpha" is a system-generated identifier that designates the SPY pair (S1,P1). In other words, the binary relations are

```
SPX(SPID,QTY)      and       SPY(S#,P#)
```

where attribute SPID represents identifiers for S#/P# pairs.

Disadvantages of this approach include the following:

a) Values of attribute SPID (such as "alpha" in the example) are in fact addresses or *pointers*. One of the advantages of the relational model is precisely that it does not include any pointers. In fact, there is no way *within the relational algebra* of accessing a given SPX tuple from the corresponding SPY tuple, or vice versa; it would be necessary to introduce some new operators, one to return the address of a specified tuple and one to return a tuple given its address.

b) The representation is asymmetric.

c) Because of point (b), manipulation is asymmetric also.

d) The nesting is not always obvious. On what basis does the database designer choose the structure ((S#,P#),QTY) over the other two possibilities, ((S#,QTY),P#) and ((P#,QTY),S#)? Even if the answer is "obvious" in this particular case, it is not always so. Consider, for example, the supplier-part-project relation (S#,P#,J#,QTY) from Volume I. Kent [5.12] discusses this question in some depth.

■ The second (preferred) reduction method is based on "anchored binaries" (see, for example, reference [5.12]). This technique requires the introduction of a single-attribute primary key for shipments, say SHIP# (there is thus a one-to-one correspondence between SHIP# values and S#/P# pairs). The degree-4 relation (SHIP#,S#,P#,QTY) can now be treated just like relations S and P: that is, it can be replaced by (say) the collection

```
H(SHIP#)    HS(SHIP#,S#)    HP(SHIP#,P#)    HQ(SHIP#,QTY)
```

plus appropriate constraints. (Exercise: What are they?)

The "anchored" reduction is preferable in that it does not involve either the pointers or the arbitrariness of the "nested" reduction. On the other hand, we have had to introduce an additional, and arguably artificial, attribute; and shipments now require a total of 15 names, as opposed to 10 in the nested reduction and 7 in the original ternary representation. (Exercise: Do you agree with these figures?)

Irreducible Relational Models

As pointed out in the previous subsection, the ternary relation SP(S#,P#,QTY) is *irreducible,* in the sense that it already corresponds to a single atomic fact and cannot be nonloss-decomposed into a set of projections. The irreducible relational model, introduced by Hall et al. [5.15] and also recommended by Falkenberg [5.16], is similar to the binary relational model, except that reduction is to irreducible relations only and not necessarily all the way to binary relations. An irreducible relation consists of (a) a primary key, possibly composite, together with (b) at most one other attribute, possibly composite. The "other attribute" will be composite if and only if it consists of a reference to some entity, and that entity is identified by a composite primary key.[5] For example, suppose that departments are identified by the combination (DIVISION#,DEPARTMENT#), and consider a relation connecting employees (identified by EMPLOYEE#) to their departments.

The model of Hall et al. [5.15] also included the concept of *surrogates.* Briefly, a surrogate is a system-generated entity identifier that is guaranteed never to change. We defer detailed discussion of this topic (which is independent of the irreducible relational model as such) to Chapter 6. However, we note here that a consequence of the surrogate notion is that an irreducible relation in the model of [5.15] never has a composite "other attribute."

Functional Models

To judge by the number of proposals (see, for example, Abrial [5.17], Senko [5.18], Bracchi [5.20], Sharman [5.21], Munz [5.22], Buneman and Frankel [5.23], and Shipman [5.24]), the functional model is the most popular of the irreducible

---

5. We observe that the objective of irreducibility would still suggest that DATE_OF_HIRE be spread across three relations (one each for YEAR, MONTH, and DAY), and that this example therefore does *not* provide another instance in which the "other attribute" would be composite.

approaches. The reason for this state of affairs seems to be the fact that it is possible to define access languages that have an immediate intuitive appeal, as we shall show. Most of the observations made earlier concerning binary relations still apply to the functional model.

The functional model involves "entities" and "functions." Entities are represented by unary relations. Functions are represented by *directed, many-to-one* binary relations (in fact, "directed binary relational model" might be a more descriptive name). For example, suppliers could be represented by a unary relation S of supplier identifiers (that is, surrogates), plus a collection of functions:

```
S#      :   S -> CHAR5
SNAME   :   S -> CHAR20
STATUS  :   S -> NUM3
SCITY   :   S -> CHAR15
```

The last of these, for example, is read as: "SCITY is a function from S to CHAR15." That is, given a value *s* from the unary relation S, there exists precisely one value corresponding to *s* under the function SCITY in the (system-supplied) unary relation called CHAR15 (which we assume consists of all character strings of length 15).[6] Notice that we use SCITY as the function-name rather than as an attribute-name; attributes as such are not part of the model.

Similarly, parts could be represented as a unary relation P of part identifiers, plus functions:

```
P#      :   P -> CHAR6
PNAME   :   P -> CHAR20
COLOR   :   P -> CHAR6
WEIGHT  :   P -> NUM4
PCITY   :   P -> CHAR15
```

and shipments by a unary relation SP of shipment identifiers, plus functions:

```
SP_S  :   SP -> S
SP_P  :   SP -> P
QTY   :   SP -> NUM5
```

The first of the three shipment functions, SP_S, can be read as "SP_S is a function from the unary relation SP of shipment identifiers to the unary relation S of supplier identifiers." That is, given a value *sp* from SP identifying a shipment, there exists precisely one value *s* in S identifying a supplier and corresponding to *sp* under the function S_SP (i.e., given a shipment, there exists precisely one corresponding supplier).

---

6. It would be more accurate to describe CHAR15 as a domain, rather than a unary relation—its value does not change with time, unlike (for example) the unary relation S. In fact, of course, CHAR15 is nothing more than one of the standard elementary data types. Such a data type can be regarded as a rather primitive kind of domain (primitive in that it has almost no semantic interpretation attached to it).

As already indicated, a function is actually a binary relation. The function SCITY, for example, consists of all ordered pairs ⟨s,scity⟩, where s is a supplier identifier and *scity* is the 15-character name of that supplier's city.

Given a function f: A→B, the value of B, b say, corresponding under f to a given value a of A is referred to as "f(a)" or "f OF a." Thus, for example, we can refer to the city for a given supplier s as SCITY(s) or SCITY OF s. If we wish to refer to the suppliers for a given city, we need the *inverse* of the SCITY function—that is, the set, CITYS say, of all ordered pairs ⟨scity,s-set⟩, where scity is the name of a supplier city and *s-set* is the set of all supplier identifiers for suppliers in that city. (Note that this inverse function is set-valued, and that it therefore corresponds to an *unnormalized* relation.) We might declare this inverse function explicitly:

```
CITYS   :   CHAR15 -> S
            INVERSE OF SCITY
```

Alternatively we might bundle the declaration of CITYS with that of SCITY:

```
SCITY   :   S -> CHAR15
            INVERSE CITYS
```

Another possibility is to use a convention for the automatic generation of names for inverse functions. For example, we might obtain such names by appending a star to the original function name; thus, for example, SCITY* would refer to the inverse of SCITY. We shall use this "star convention" for the remainder of this subsection.

Figure 5.4 is a diagrammatic representation of the suppliers-and-parts example. "Entities" (unary relations) are shown as ellipses, functions are shown as labeled directed arrows. Inverse functions are not shown. We remark that diagrams such as this one are similar to the "semantic nets" used in the artificial intelligence field [5.25].

We can now illustrate the claim made earlier that the functional model lends itself to the design of attractive access languages. The basic point is that the *composition* of two functions is itself another function; for example, given functions f1: A→B and f2: B→C, the composition of f1 and f2, written f1 OF f2 or f1·f2, is a function from A to C. Consider, for example, the query "Retrieve the names of parts supplied by suppliers located in London." We can express this query as

```
PNAME OF SP_P OF SP_S* OF SCITY* OF 'LONDON'
```

or

```
PNAME · SP_P · SP_S* · SCITY* ( 'LONDON' )
```

(whichever is preferred).

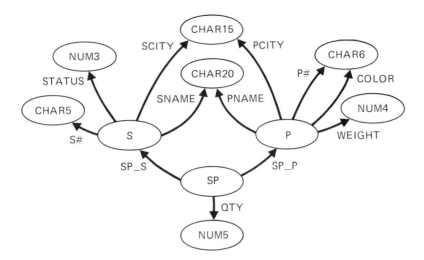

Fig. 5.4 A functional representation of suppliers and parts.

Another common convention is to allow the name of the *target* for a given function to serve by default as the name of that function. For example, we can refer to the (unique) function from SP to S by the name S, and to the (unique) function from SP to P by the name P. Similarly, we can refer to both SP_S* and SP_P* by the name SP. (The ambiguity can be resolved for any given appearance of the name by means of the function *argument:* "SP OF S" refers to SP_S* , "SP OF P" refers to SP_P* .) If we apply this convention to the query above, the expression becomes

```
PNAME OF P OF SP OF SCITY* OF 'LONDON'
```

or

```
PNAME · P · SP · SCITY* ( 'LONDON' )
```

In (pidgin) English: "Retrieve part-names of parts of shipments of suppliers where supplier-city is London." Note, however, that this simple form of query-expression is certainly not adequate to handle all types of query. Extensions are necessary to deal with (for example) the simultaneous retrieval of multiple attributes of an entity, or the simultaneous retrieval of attributes of multiple entities (a join-like operation). Such extensions require functions that can return tuple-valued results, instead of only single values. Similarly, it is desirable to introduce functions that can accept multiple arguments, in order to handle queries such as "Find the quantity of part Y shipped by supplier X." (It is difficult to represent functions like these in the simple diagrammatic form of Fig. 5.4.) A good example of a language that provides such features is DAPLEX [5.24]. See also FQL [5.23].

An Alternative View

As we mentioned at the beginning of this section, it is possible to view the irreducible models in a manner other than that in which we have presented them so far. To paraphrase Kent [5.40]:

It is possible to describe two schools of modeling, which might be called *record-like* and *graph-like*. [The relational model clearly falls into the record-like school; it is contended that the irreducible models should be seen as falling into the graph-like school.] The essential difference between the two schools might be characterized as *singular vs. replicated references:*

1. In the graph-like school, there exists literally one occurrence of any given atom. All relationships involving that atom are strung off that one occurrence, exactly like a set of edges connecting to the same node in a graph. Sets such as (x,y) and (x,z) do not denote two occurrences of x (as they would if they were tuples); they simply denote the involvement of x in two sets.

2. The record-like school involves replicated references. The expressions (x,y) and (x,z) really do denote multiple occurrences of x.

One consequence is an entirely different view of referential integrity. In a record-like approach, an insertion of (x,y) may require one to look around (this is the sense exposed to users of the model) to see if another occurrence of x exists in some appropriate place. In the graph-like approach the question simply does not arise; it is simply not possible to insert (x,y) unless x and y already exist; the insertion simply has the sense of drawing a line between things already in existence. (There are also corresponding differences in the two approaches concerning the manner in which x is inserted, that is, its existence announced.)

He goes on to say (again paraphrasing):

The irreducible models should not be defined on the same set of objects as the relational model. They are better expressed in terms of a different set of objects. Many of the comparisons and criticisms [in the three subsections above] are applicable only because the models have been described in relational terms.

Let us analyze these comments, concentrating for brevity on just the functional model. It is of course true that a database constructed in accordance with that model can be perceived as a graph rather than as a collection of records or tuples. (In fact, it is probably true that a similar statement can be made for *any* data model.) It is also true that there are differences in the way that referential integrity is perceived in the two approaches. But it is not clear that the distinctions are particularly significant. We may characterize those distinctions as follows:

1. In the relational case, the constraint that a reference from (say) a shipment entity to a supplier entity must designate a known, existing supplier must be *separately and explicitly stated.*

2. In the functional case, that constraint is *built into the data structure itself.*

The functional (graph-like) view may thus be seen as equivalent to a relational (record-like) view *plus* certain explicitly stated constraints. To put it another way, it would be possible in the relational case—in the *absence* of any such explicit statements—for a state of the database to exist in which the constraints are violated; in the functional case, by contrast, such a situation cannot occur. The functional (graph-like) view thus does offer an advantage over the relational (record-like) view, in that it is not necessary to state certain referential constraints explicitly. How significant is this advantage?

In considering this question, we make the point that the constraints themselves are not the whole story. Certain additional specifications are also needed to indicate what should happen on an attempt to violate those constraints (see Chapter 2, also reference [5.11]). It is not sufficient (for example) merely to insist that every shipment refers to an existing supplier; it is also necessary to specify (for example) the effect of attempting to delete a supplier if that supplier currently has any shipments (should the delete cascade, or should it be prohibited?). Thus *some* explicit statement is needed in both approaches.

We suggest, therefore, that a more fundamental question is the following: What is the *operational* distinction between the two perceptions? What operators are available to the user for manipulating a graph-like database? For example, what does the user have to do to insert a new object into the database, if that object must satisfy some referential constraint? Consider the question of creating a shipment for S1 and P1, using the functional representation shown in Fig. 5.4. In DAPLEX the user would have to write

```
for a new SP
    begin
        let S (SP) = the S such that S# (S) = 'S1'
        let P (SP) = the P such that P# (P) = 'P1'
        let QTY (SP) = 300
    end
```

If we choose to view the functions of Fig. 5.4 as "record-like" binary relations, the foregoing operation might instead be expressed

```
begin
    acquire a surrogate, say x, for the new SP
    insert (x,'S1') into SP_S
    insert (x,'P1') into SP_P
    insert (x,300) into QTY
end
```

Comparing these two formulations, it is apparent that the user has to specify exactly the same parameters ('S1', 'P1', and 300) in each case, and that exactly the same possible outcomes—in particular, the same failures—can occur in each case. Specifically, each one will fail if supplier S1 or part P1 does not already exist. Similar observations apply to other examples. It therefore seems debatable whether there is truly any fundamental distinction between the two styles of perception.

This concludes our short survey of irreducible models. We have now completed our discussion of "basic" data models, and are effectively ready to embark on an introduction to the "extended" models. However, there is one additional topic that needs to be discussed at some point, namely null values, and we choose to address this topic first before getting into details of semantic modeling as such.

5.5   NULL VALUES

In this section we consider the topic of null values in some depth. We begin by defining the term "null value" and by outlining the problems that null values are intended to solve. We go on to discuss the properties of null values in detail, and describe some extensions to the relational model for dealing with such values. We then discuss some of the difficulties that occur in connection with the null value concept. It is our opinion that the problem is generally not well understood, and that any attempt to incorporate support for null values into an implemented system should be considered premature at this time. We sketch an alternative approach based on the concept of *default* values.

First we assume that, barring explicit constraints to the contrary, every attribute of every relation may potentially accept a null value, which we denote by "?". The null value may be thought of as a placeholder for some "real" (nonnull) value in the domain of the attribute concerned. Its interpretation is thus "value at present unknown"; we note, however, that other types of null can be defined—for example, a null meaning "property inapplicable." We do not consider any of these other types of null here.

Why do we need the concept of a null value? The short answer is that real-world information is very frequently incomplete, and we need some way of handling such incompleteness in our formal systems. For example, historical records sometimes include such entries as "Date of birth unknown"; meeting agendas often show a speaker as "To be announced"; and police records frequently include the entry "Present whereabouts unknown." To put the matter into more specific database terms, null values facilitate the *automatic* support of situations such as the following (by "automatic support" we mean support that does not require any special action on the part of the user):

1. A new tuple is to be created, but the user is unable to supply values for certain attributes at this time. (The user may not even be aware of the existence of those attributes.) The system can supply null values for the new tuple in those attribute positions.

2. A new attribute is to be added to an existing real relation. The value of the new attribute can be set to null in all existing tuples.

3. An aggregate function, such as AVG, is to be applied to some attribute of some relation. In computing the function, it is desirable for the system to be able to recognize and ignore tuples for which no nonnull value has yet been supplied for the attribute in question. (But note carefully that it is also desirable for users to under-

stand what is going on in such a situation; otherwise they may be surprised to discover that, for example, the average is not equal to the sum divided by the count.)

4. An aggregate function such as AVG is to be applied to some attribute of some relation, and that relation happens to be currently empty. Raising an exception condition in such a situation can lead to awkwardness for the user—particularly if the function reference is embedded within a predicate (for example, take the query "Find departments for which the average employee salary is greater than $50000," and consider what the system should do if it encounters a department that currently has no employees). It seems preferable to define the function in such a way that it will return a null value if its argument set happens to be empty.

Let F be a field (attribute) that can accept null values. To represent a null value of F in the database, it is necessary to find a bit configuration that is different from all "legal" bit configurations for F (that is, those configurations representing all possible nonnull values of F). For example, if the data-type of F is packed decimal, then any bit configuration in which the sign code (rightmost 4 bits) is invalid could be used to represent a null value. If no such "illegal" bit configuration exists—that is, if all possible bit configurations represent some legal nonnull value—then it is necessary to introduce a *hidden field* for F. In this case, every instance of F in the database will have an associated instance of the hidden field—call it H—whose value indicates to the system whether the corresponding F-value is to be ignored or not (is null or not). Theoretically H need be no more than a single bit wide, though for pragmatic reasons it may be more convenient to let it occupy an entire byte.

A Scheme for Handling Nulls

As stated at the beginning of the section, it is our feeling that nulls should *not* be supported. To justify this position, however, we first have to indicate exactly what such support would consist of. We therefore present in this subsection a detailed scheme for dealing with null. The development that follows is similar but not identical to that of [5.10].

Let *theta* denote any one of $=$, $\neg =$, $<$, $\leq$, $>$, and $\geq$. What is the result of evaluating the comparison "x *theta* y", if x or y, or both, happen to be null? Since by definition null represents an unknown value, we define the result in every case to be unknown (null) also, rather than true or false.[7] To deal with null values properly, therefore, it is necessary to adopt a 3-valued logic, in place of the more usual 2-valued logic. This 3-valued logic is defined by the truth tables in Fig. 5.5. We remark that the unknown truth-value can intuitively be interpreted as "maybe."

---

7. As a consequence of this definition, the comparison "$x = y$" (taking *theta* as equality) evaluates to null if x or y *or both* happen to be null; that is, the value of "null = null" is *null,* not true. It follows that the comparison "$x = x$" does not necessarily yield the value true—it cannot be false, but it may be unknown. Intuitively speaking, it is this fact—that "null = null" does not evaluate to true—that is at the root of most of the problems that arise over null.

AND	T	?	F		OR	T	?	F		NOT	
T	T	?	F		T	T	T	T		T	F
?	?	?	F		?	T	?	?		?	?
F	F	F	F		F	T	?	F		F	T

Fig. 5.5 Truth tables for 3-valued logic.

Similarly, let *alpha* denote any one of the arithmetic operators $+$, $-$, $*$, $/$, and let x and y denote any two numeric values. Then the value of the arithmetic expression "x *alpha* y" is defined to be null if x is null or y is null or both. Unary (prefix) $+$ and $-$ are treated analogously: that is, if x is null, then $+x$ and $-x$ are also considered to be null.

Next, consider the question of whether sets are allowed to contain null values. Suppose, for example, that the collection C = (1,2,3,?) is to be permitted as a legal set. Then there are two possibilities:

a) the particular null value appearing in C is of course unknown, but is known to be distinct from 1 and 2 and 3;

b) the null value in C is *completely* unknown (that is, it may in fact stand for one of the values 1, 2, 3), in which case the cardinality of C in turn is unknown (it may be either 3 or 4).

Possibility (a) implies that we must be prepared to deal with a variety of distinct nulls—a null that is known not to be 1, a null that is known not to be 2, a null that is known not to be 1 or 2, and so on. Possibility (b) has effectively the same implication; for example, the best that a COUNT function applied to C can do is to return the value "unknown, but known to be either 3 or 4"—which is simply another example of a "distinguished null."

Since both these possibilities lead to difficulties, we propose the following approach. Sets per se are not allowed to contain any null values at all. Instead, we introduce a new construct which we will call an *n-set*. An *n*-set of cardinality r is a collection of r values, in which at most one value is null and no two nonnull values are equal to each other. A set is a special case of an *n*-set. We permit at most one null value in an *n*-set to avoid (again) the difficulties of "distinguished nulls"; our feeling is that it does not seem wise to tackle such refinements before the simpler problem is fully understood. (But see Lipski [5.26] for a proposal that does address the more general problem.)

Next, we assign an extended meaning to the term *duplicate*. A duplicate with respect to a given *n*-set N is defined to be a value v such that an element exists in N with value equal to v, or, if v happens to be null, an element exists in N with the null value. (Informally, an attempt to introduce a duplicate into N via INSERT or UPDATE will be rejected.)

We now define the existential and universal quantifiers, as follows. Let N be an *n*-set containing precisely the values v1, v2, . . . , vr (at most one of which can be null); let *x* be a variable that ranges over N (that is, a variable whose permitted values are precisely v1, v2, . . . , vr); and let *p(x)* be a predicate in *x*. The truth value of

```
∃x ( p(x) )
```

is defined to be the same as the truth value of

```
p(v1) OR p(v2) OR . . . OR p(vr)
```

The truth value of

```
∀x ( p(x) )
```

is defined to be the same as the truth value of

```
p(v1) AND p(v2) AND . . . AND p(vr)
```

Now let *x* be any value (possibly null). We define the membership condition

```
x memberof N
```

to be equivalent to the expression

```
x = v1 OR x = v2 OR . . . OR x = vr
```

In other words, if N contains a nonnull value *vi* such that "$x = vi$" is true, the membership condition is true; otherwise, if N contains a value *vi*, possibly null, such that "$x = vi$" is unknown, the membership condition is unknown; otherwise it is false. Some examples:

```
2 memberof (2,3,?)    :    true
4 memberof (2,3,?)    :    unknown
? memberof (2,3,?)    :    unknown
? memberof (2,3)      :    unknown
4 memberof (2,3)      :    false
```

Now let N1 and N2 be two *n*-sets. The subset condition

```
N1 subsetof N2
```

is defined to be equivalent to

```
COUNT(N1) <= COUNT(N2) AND ∀x ( ∃y ( x = y ) ) ,
```

where *x* and *y* range over N1 and N2 respectively, and where the function COUNT applied to an *n*-set of cardinality *r* is defined to return the value *r*. The requirement "COUNT(N1) $<=$ COUNT(N2)" is included to prevent, for example, the *n*-set (3,4,5) from being considered as a subset of the *n*-set (3,?). (The COUNTs of these two *n*-sets are 3 and 2, respectively.)

We can now proceed to develop a revised version of the relational model in which the fundamental domains are not sets but n-sets. We do not give the complete formal development here. However, we sketch the main points informally below.

■   The Cartesian product of a collection of domains (n-sets) D1, D2, . . . , Dn, written D1 × D2 × · · · × Dn, is defined as the set of all possible tuples (d1,d2, . . . ,dn) such that d1 is a duplicate of some value in D1, d2 is a duplicate of some value in D2, . . . , and dn is a duplicate of some value in Dn. Note carefully that we are using "duplicate" in the special sense of the term defined a few pages back (page 212). Note too that the Cartesian product is a *set,* not an n-set.

■   It follows from the definition that the Cartesian product D1 × D2 × · · · × Dn cannot contain two distinct tuples that are duplicates of each other—where, again, we are using "duplicate" in an extended sense:

Definition.   Two tuples (d1,d2, . . . ,dn) and (e1,e2, . . . ,en) are said to be duplicates of each other if and only if, for all i ($i = 1, . . . ,n$), either di and ei are both nonnull and di = ei, or di and ei are both null.

■   We define a relation on domains (n-sets) D1, D2, . . . , Dn to be a subset of the Cartesian product D1 × D2 × · · · × Dn. Of course, we are considering only the "tuple-set" component of the relation here, in the terminology of Section 5.3. Also, we assume for simplicity that the left-to-right ordering of domains (and hence attributes) is significant.

■   It thus follows that a relation also can never contain two distinct tuples that are duplicates of each other. In particular, a relation (like a Cartesian product) can contain at most one tuple consisting entirely of null values. (A *real* relation cannot contain such a tuple at all, by virtue of Integrity Rule 1.) We define the operators of the relational algebra carefully to ensure that these properties are preserved (see below).

■   Note that tuples in which some or all component values are null are still well-formed tuples (they are not themselves considered as null values). A tuple consisting entirely of null values is not itself the same thing as a "null tuple"—just as, for example, the set whose sole member is the empty set is not itself an empty set. We do not use the concept of a "null tuple" at all, in fact.

Effect on the Relational Algebra

The effect of the development in the preceding subsection on the operators of the relational algebra is as follows (in outline). Note: At first glance, the definitions below may appear to be equivalent to those given earlier for these operations (where null values were ignored). However, they are different. The differences stem from the extended meaning we have assigned to the term "duplicate tuple."

Union

The union of two union-compatible relations R and S is the relation consisting of all tuples t such that t is a duplicate of some tuple in R or of some tuple in S (or both). For example, if relations R and S are as follows,

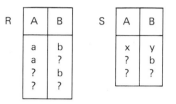

R	A	B
	a	b
	a	?
	?	b
	?	?

S	A	B
	x	y
	?	b
	?	?

then their union is

A	B
a	b
a	?
?	b
?	?
x	y

Difference

The difference of two union-compatible relations R and S (in that order) is the relation consisting of all tuples t such that t is a duplicate of some tuple in R and not of any tuple in S. For example, if R and S are as under "Union," their difference (R − S) is

A	B
a	b
a	?

Product

The product operation is unchanged.

Theta-selection

The theta-selection operation is unchanged, but we should stress that tuples appear in the result only when the theta-comparison evaluates to true, not to false and not to unknown.

Projection

The projection of a relation R over the attributes A*i*, . . . ,A*j* is the relation obtained from R by eliminating attributes from R that are not included in the set A*i*, . . . ,A*j* and then eliminating redundant duplicate tuples from what remains. For example, if R is as under "Union," the projection of R on attribute A is

Additional Operators

We now introduce some additional operators to assist in dealing with null values. First, it is necessary to define a truth-valued function IS_NULL, whose argument is an arbitrary (scalar) expression and whose value is true if the argument evaluates to null, false otherwise. Using this function, we can define two new algebraic operators, MAYBE_SELECT and MAYBE_JOIN. Basically, MAYBE_SELECT selects tuples for which the value of a specified attribute is null, and MAYBE_JOIN joins tuples for which the value of either of the joining attributes is null:

```
MAYBE_SELECT ( R, Ai )
    =  THETA_SELECT ( R, IS_NULL ( Ai ) )

MAYBE_JOIN ( R, S, Ai, Bj )
    =  THETA_SELECT ( PRODUCT ( R, S ),
                    ( IS_NULL ( RAi ) OR IS_NULL ( SBj ) ) )
```

(We are assuming here that THETA_SELECT has been extended to accept any relation-expression as its first argument and any truth-valued expression as its second argument. Our version of the "maybe operators" is not quite the same as that given in reference [5.10].)

We illustrate the need for MAYBE_SELECT by means of an example.

Example   Suppose that in the supplier relation S(S#,SNAME,STATUS,CITY), certain supplier cities are unknown. The two operations

```
THETA_SELECT ( S, CITY = 'LONDON' )
```

and

```
THETA_SELECT ( S, CITY ¬= 'LONDON' )
```

between them will then *not* select all S tuples. (As a matter of fact, neither will the single operation

```
THETA_SELECT ( S, CITY = CITY ) ,
```

as is suggested by Footnote 7, earlier.) To select the remaining S tuples, we need

```
MAYBE_SELECT ( S, CITY )
```

The justification for MAYBE_JOIN is similar.

It is also necessary to define some additional forms of join. In the normal theta-join, a given tuple of one relation simply does not participate in the result if there does not exist a tuple in the other relation such that the joining condition evaluates to true for those two tuples. Let us agree to call such nonparticipating tuples "unmatched tuples." The normal theta-join thus loses information for unmatched tuples. (So of course does the maybe-join.) We therefore define an "outer" theta-join [5.27–5.29], which preserves such information by appending certain additional tuples to the result of the normal theta-join. There is one such additional tuple for each unmatched tuple from each of the original relations; it consists of a copy of that unmatched tuple, extended with null values in the other attribute positions. Figure 5.6 shows an example of outer *equi*join (in practice one of the most useful of the various possible outer joins).

S

S#	CITY
S7	London
S8	Paris
S9	?

P

P#	CITY
P7	London
P8	Madrid
P9	?

Outer equijoin of S and P on
S. CITY and P. CITY

SS#	SCITY	PP#	PCITY
S7	London	P7	London
S8	Paris	?	?
S9	?	?	?
?	?	P8	Madrid
?	?	P9	?

Fig. 5.6 Example of outer equijoin.

We note that it is also possible to define a *left* outer join, which preserves unmatched tuples only for the first relation of the pair, and a *right* outer join, which preserves unmatched tuples only for the second. The *symmetric* outer join (that is, the outer join as described previously) is then the union of the left and right outer joins. See [5.29] for a detailed discussion of these operations.

It is also possible to define an outer *natural* join. The definition is deceptively similar to that of the outer theta-join, and goes as follows. The outer natural join of two relations is obtained by appending certain additional tuples to the result of the normal natural join of those relations. There is one such additional tuple for each unmatched tuple from each of the original relations; it consists of a copy of that unmatched tuple, extended with null values in the other attribute positions. Figure 5.7 shows the outer natural join of the relations S and P of Fig. 5.6. For simplicity we ignore the attribute renaming rules in the result.

It is a remarkable fact that the outer natural join is not a projection of the outer equijoin, in general (as Figs. 5.6 and 5.7 illustrate). However, the outer natural join can be obtained from the outer equijoin by "coalescing" the joining attributes of the outer equijoin into a single attribute, as follows:

1. Let the joining attributes be RA and SB, and let *t* be a tuple of the outer equijoin. Perform steps 2 and 3 for each such tuple *t*.

Fig. 5.7 Example of outer natural join.

2. Define the value $j(t)$ as follows:

If the RA-value of t and the SB-value of t are both nonnull, then they must be equal; in this case set $j(t)$ equal to their common value.

If the RA-value of t and the SB-value of t are both null, then set $j(t)$ equal to null.

If one of the two values (RA-value of t, SB-value of t) is null and the other is not, set $j(t)$ equal to the nonnull value of the pair.

3. Replace the RA-value of t by the value $j(t)$ and eliminate the SB-value.

Consequences of the Foregoing Treatment

It is this writer's opinion that the scheme presented in the previous subsection for the treatment of null values is as reasonable as any that has been given in the literature. However, it still suffers from a number of problems, which we now proceed to discuss. Note: All of the following problems, except apparently those concerned with functional dependencies, *can* be explained away; they are problems of intuition, rather than fundamental problems. But the cumulative effect of so many intuitive difficulties is to give an impression of inelegance, to say the least.

In what follows, all values should be considered as nonnull unless explicitly stated otherwise.

■   Let R(A,B,C) be a relation satisfying the functional dependency A→B. (Note: We do not assume that attribute A is a candidate key. Of course, if it is not, then R is not in BCNF.) Can attribute A accept null values?

1. Suppose the answer is yes. In this case, can R contain two tuples (?,b1,c1) and (?,b2,c2), where b1 and b2 are distinct? If so, then the two null values must be different (because of the dependency), which leads us into the problem of "distinguished nulls" once more. If not, then the second tuple (that is, whichever is submitted second) is presumably rejected on the grounds that it *may* violate the dependency, which leads to further difficulties. Consider, for example, the relation

EMP(SS#,JOB,EMP#), where EMP# is the primary key and SS# stands for social security number. (We deliberately order the attributes to suggest the correspondence A:SS#, B:JOB, C:EMP#.) The rule for social security numbers is that they are unique if nonnull—but they *may* be null. We cannot reasonably reject an EMP tuple having a null SS# value just because such a tuple already exists; thus we are forced into having to admit that we do not have a functional dependency of JOB on SS#. This is unfortunate, since JOB clearly *is* functionally dependent on SS# if we ignore the nulls.

Another, perhaps more serious objection to permitting attribute A to take on null values—regardless of whether tuples (?,b1,c1) and (?,b2,c2) are both allowed to exist—is that the normalization procedure breaks down. For example, a fundamental theorem that is used to support that procedure is the following: If relation R(A,B,C) satisfies the functional dependency A→B, then R can be nonloss-decomposed into its projections R1(A,B) and R2(A,C)—that is, R can be recovered by taking the natural join of R1 and R2 on A. It is easy to see that this theorem is no longer true if A can accept null values. For example, if R is as follows,

R	A	B	C
	a1	b1	c1
	?	b2	c2

then the projections R1 and R2 and the corresponding natural join are

R1	A	B
	a1	b1
	?	b2

R2	A	C
	a1	c1
	?	c2

A	B	C
a1	b1	c1

(For simplicity we again ignore the attribute renaming rules in the join.) Incidentally, the maybe join and the outer join are of no help with this problem.

2. Suppose then that the answer is no (that is, attribute A cannot accept null values). Then again we have to admit (in the EMP example) that JOB is not functionally dependent on SS#, since SS# can be null. Moreover, another consequence of this decision is that Integrity Rule 1 ("entity integrity") will now apply to all *candidate* keys, not just to the primary key.

3. We can avoid some of the foregoing problems by refining the definition of functional dependence, as follows: Attribute R.B is functionally dependent on attribute R.A if and only if each *nonnull* value of R.A. has associated with it exactly one value of R.B (at any one time). This revision would permit any number of tuples of the form (?,b,c), where b and c are arbitrary, to be inserted into R without violating

the dependency A→B. (*Updating* a null A-value to some nonnull value would be subject to the usual checks, of course.) But this solution does not address the objection mentioned under (1) above concerning the normalization procedure.

We note that if R.A is an alternate key (*not* the primary key), then at any given time *at most one* tuple of R can have a null A-value (this fact follows from our definition of duplicate values).

■   Again, let R(A,B,C) be a relation with the functional dependency A→B. Can attribute B accept null values?

If A is a candidate key the answer must be yes, for otherwise no nonkey attribute would ever be allowed to accept null values. What if A is not a candidate key? If the answer is yes in this case, R cannot contain two distinct tuples (a1,b1,c1) and (a1,?,c2), because of the dependency; the "?" would have to be equal to b1, contrary to the intuitive interpretation of null as unknown. The system could *set* the null to b1, of course; but then the tuple (a1,?,c2) would or would not be a duplicate of the tuple (a1,b1,c1)—and the INSERT thus would or would not fail—depending on whether c1 and c2 were duplicates. It seems preferable to prohibit null values for B if A is not a candidate key, though admittedly the argument is not very strong.

The reader is referred to [5.30] for a formal treatment of null values in functional dependencies.

■   Consider the following program fragments:

```
(1)  x := y ;              (2)  if y = y
     if x = y                   then executable-unit-1
     then executable-unit-1
```

In conventional programming, barring side-effects and the like, we can guarantee that "executable-unit-1" will be executed in both cases. If we introduce null values, however, and if *y* happens to have the null value, then executable-unit-1 will not be executed in either case—which seems an affront to intuition. To obtain the same guarantees as before in the face of the possibility that *y* might be null, the programmer must write

```
(1)  x := y ;              (2)  if IS_NULL ( y )
     if ( IS_NULL ( x ) and      or y = y
         IS_NULL ( y ) )          then executable-unit-1
     or x = y
     then executable-unit-1
```

■   The interpretation of nulls is not obvious. We have considered only the "unknown value" null in our treatment so far. However, consider the two binary relations ES(EMP#,SALARY) and EM(EMP#,MAIDEN_NAME). Let *e* denote some particular employee that is known to exist. The absence of a tuple for *e* from ES would typically be construed as "salary unknown," whereas the absence of a tuple for that same employee from EM would typically be taken to mean *property inapplicable*. Of course, there may be employees represented in ES but not EM, and vice versa. If we perform an outer natural join of ES and EM on EMP#, how should we interpret the null values that appear in the result? (Of course, this question is significant only if "value unknown" nulls and "property inapplicable" nulls behave differently under the operations of the relational algebra.)

■ We have already indicated that (for example) "suppliers in London" and "suppliers not in London" together do not in general account for *all* suppliers. Of course, we can justify this state of affairs: "Suppliers in London" really means "suppliers *known to the system* to be in London," and "suppliers not in London" really means "suppliers *known to the system* not to be in London" . . . but the distinction is subtle, and one that is liable to mystify the user.

■ We have assigned the unknown truth-value to all comparisons involving null and some other (null or nonnull) value. However, if we ask to see *all* tuples in a relation ordered by values of some attribute—say employees in salary order—the tuples having null values for that attribute must appear *somewhere* in that ordering, implying that in this context comparisons such as "null > *v*" (where *v* is a nonnull value) do have a known truth-value. (Moreover, those tuples will probably all appear together, implying also that in this context null values are all equal to each other.) Of course, it can be argued that (a) imposing a sequence on a set of tuples for the purpose of processing those tuples one by one, and (b) performing comparisons between pairs of tuples of that set to determine the relative values of some attribute, are two quite distinct operations; but again it is rather a nice distinction.

■ We need a number of additional operations, including in particular the outer equijoin (see [5.10] for details of other operators). Moreover, the outer equijoin suffers from the nonintuitive property that, unlike the normal equijoin, it does not generalize nicely to *n* relations where *n* > 2. Consider the following relations:

S	S#	SCITY
	S1	London
	S2	Paris

P	P#	PCITY
	P1	Paris
	P2	Oslo

J	J#	JCITY
	J1	Oslo
	J2	London

The outer equijoin of S and P on SCITY and PCITY is

S#	SCITY	P#	PCITY
S1	London	?	?
S2	Paris	P1	Paris
?	?	P2	Oslo

(again ignoring the attribute renaming rules in the join). Let us refer to this result as XSP. Then:

a) The outer equijoin of XSP and J on SCITY and JCITY is

S#	SCITY	P#	PCITY	J#	JCITY
S1	London	?	?	J2	London
S2	Paris	P1	Paris	?	?
?	?	P2	Oslo	?	?
?	?	?	?	J1	Oslo

b) The outer equijoin of XSP and J on PCITY and JCITY is

S#	SCITY	P#	PCITY	J#	JCITY
S1	London	?	?	?	?
S2	Paris	P1	Paris	?	?
?	?	P2	Oslo	J1	Oslo
?	?	?	?	J2	London

Note that these two results (a) and (b) are different. Thus it is not possible to refer unambiguously to "the outer equijoin of S, P, J on SCITY, PCITY, JCITY"; the value of the outer equijoin differs depending on whether the joining conditions are

```
SCITY = PCITY AND SCITY = JCITY
```

or

```
SCITY = PCITY AND PCITY = JCITY ,
```

or indeed

```
SCITY = JCITY AND PCITY = JCITY ,
```

the third possibility (exercise for the reader). This is unfortunate, since these three conditions are intuitively all equivalent to each other, and indeed would actually be so in the absence of null values. (We note, however, that the foregoing ambiguity does not arise with the outer *natural* join.)

■   The duplicate elimination rule is difficult to justify intuitively. Specifically, it appears that (again) "null = null" has to be regarded as true in this context, though it is unknown in others.

Implementation Anomalies

The problems outlined so far are all problems of *definition*—that is, conceptual difficulties arising from the very notion of null. Even if those problems can all be resolved satisfactorily, however, it is extremely likely that inconsistencies will occur in any specific implementation, precisely because of the subtle and counterintuitive nature of the definitions. By way of illustration, we describe below some aspects of the behavior of nulls in a specific system, namely System R, that could lead to user confusion.

■ Null values are implemented by hidden fields in the database. However, it is necessary to expose those fields in the interface to a host programming language such as PL/I, because PL/I has no notion of null.[8] Thus, for example, a PL/I programmer might write

```
$SELECT   STATUS
   INTO    $ST : STX
   FROM    S
   WHERE   S# = 'S4' ;
   IF STX < 0 THEN
   /* selected STATUS value is null */ . . .
```

The "indicator variable" STX corresponds to the hidden field for STATUS. Such variables must be declared and manipulated by the programmer (that is, tested on retrieval and set on update). It is not clear that the programmer is really being saved very much work, therefore; moreover, treating null values differently on different sides of the interface is potentially confusing.

As another example, if F and G are two fields in table T, the UPDATE statement to set F equal to G is

```
$UPDATE T
   SET     F = G . . .
```

but the UPDATE statement to set F equal to a host language variable H is (for instance)

```
$UPDATE T
   SET     F = $H : HX . . .
```

(assuming in both cases that the expression on the right-hand side of the SET clause may evaluate to null).

We remark in passing that the hidden field technique is wasteful of storage space in those cases where a special value of the real field (say −1 for an HOURS_WORKED field) could be set aside to serve as the "null" value for that field.

■ Indicator variables are not permitted in all contexts where host variables can appear (lack of orthogonality). For example, the following is illegal:

```
$UPDATE P
   SET     COLOR = 'PURPLE'
   WHERE   CITY = $CT : CTX ;
```

---

8. The PL/I "null string" and "null pointer" are nothing to do with null in our sense, of course—on the contrary, each represents a specific *known* value (the null string is really an *empty* string, the null pointer is an explicitly *invalid* pointer).

Instead, the programmer must write

```
IF CTX < 0
THEN $UPDATE P
        SET     COLOR = 'PURPLE'
        WHERE   CITY IS NULL ;
ELSE $UPDATE P
        SET     COLOR = 'PURPLE'
        WHERE   CITY = $CT ;
```

■   To test (in a WHERE clause) whether a field is null, SQL provides the special comparison "field IS NULL" (the SQL implementation of MAYBE_SELECT). It is not intuitively obvious why the user has to write "field IS NULL" and not "field = NULL"—especially as the format "field = NULL" *is* used in the SET clause of the UPDATE statement to assign the null value to a field. (In fact, the comparison "field = NULL" is illegal.)

■   Null values are considered as duplicates of each other for purposes of indexing and for duplicate elimination. Thus, for example, a UNIQUE index over a given field X will permit at most one null value for X, and "SELECT UNIQUE Y" will return at most one null value for Y (regardless of whether a unique index exists over field Y). Null values are also considered as duplicates of each other (and to be greater than all nonnull values) for ordering purposes. However, null values are *not* considered as duplicates of each other for grouping purposes. Thus, for example, "GROUP BY Z" will generate a distinct group for each null value occurring in field Z.

■   Null values are always eliminated from the argument to a built-in function such as SUM or AVG, regardless of whether UNIQUE is specified in the function reference—*except* for the case of COUNT(*), which counts all rows, including duplicates and including all-null rows. Thus, for example, given

```
SELECT AVG (STATUS) FROM S   -   Result: x
SELECT SUM (STATUS) FROM S   -   Result: y
SELECT COUNT (*)    FROM S   -   Result: z
```

there is no guarantee that $x = y/z$.

■   As explained earlier, expressions of the form "x alpha y" where x and y are numeric values, *alpha* is an arithmetic operator ($+$, $-$, etc.), and x or y or both happen to be null, are considered to evaluate to null. In particular, "$x - x$" is null, not zero, if x is null, just as "$x = x$" is unknown, not true, in the same situation. As a consequence, the function reference SUM(F) (for example) is *not* semantically equivalent to the expression

$$f1 + f2 + \cdots + fn$$

(where f1, f2, . . . , fn are the values appearing in field F at the time of evaluation).

Perhaps even more counterintuitively, the expression

```
SUM (F1 + F2)
```

is not equivalent to the expression

```
SUM (F1) + SUM (F2)
```

Default Values

The concept of default values leads to a less ambitious but more straightforward approach to the question of missing information: less ambitious, in that it requires more effort on the part of the user, but more straightforward in that it is simple and avoids all the difficulties of the null value scheme (except for very minor ones). In outline the approach works as follows.

■ Associated with the declaration of each domain is the designation of some value from that domain as the corresponding *default* value. For example,

```
DCL LOCATION DOMAIN CHARACTER(15) VARYING DEFAULT ( '???' ) ;
DCL WEIGHT   DOMAIN FIXED(5,1)                DEFAULT ( 0 ) ;
```

■ Associated with the declaration of each attribute of each real relation is an optional NODEFAULT specification. NODEFAULT is assumed for all attributes that participate in a primary key. (It is *not* assumed for attributes that participate only in an *alternate* key.) An attribute for which NODEFAULT applies does not have a default value. Other attributes inherit their default value from the corresponding domain.

■ When a new tuple is inserted into a real relation,

 a) the user must supply a value for every attribute that does not have a default value;

 b) for other attributes, the system will supply the applicable default value if the user does not supply a value.

■ The built in function DEFAULT(R.A), where R is a relation and A an attribute of that relation, returns the default value applicable to R.A. It is an error if no such default value exists.

■ Integrity Rules 1 and 2 are revised to refer to default values in place of null values. In other words (loosely speaking): (1) No component of a primary key can accept default values; (2) every nondefault value of a foreign key must match some existing primary key value somewhere.

■ In applying an aggregate function such as AVG to a particular attribute, the user must specify an explicit predicate to exclude default values, if that is what is desired: for example,

```
SELECT AVG (SP.QTY)
FROM   SP
WHERE  QTY ¬= DEFAULT (SP.QTY)
```

▪   Aggregate functions such as AVG are extended to include an optional additional argument, defining the value to be returned if the first argument evaluates to the empty set: for example,

```
SELECT DEPT#
FROM   DEPT
WHERE  50000 <
        (SELECT AVG(SALARY,0)
         FROM   EMP
         WHERE  EMP.DEPT# = DEPT.DEPT#)
```

If the second argument is omitted, the default value for the attribute specified by the first argument is assumed. It is an error if the first argument evaluates to the empty set and no default value exists in this case.

▪   The MAYBE_SELECT and MAYBE_JOIN operators are no longer needed. The outer join operations *are* needed, but are redefined to generate default values rather than nulls. (Unfortunately it is still the case that the outer equijoin does not generalize nicely to *n* relations for *n* > 2. It is also still the case that the outer natural join is not a projection of the outer equijoin, in general.)

▪   For some attributes it may be the case that every value of the underlying domain is a possible real (nondefault) value. Such cases must be handled by explicit, user-controlled fields (as with the host side of the interface in System R).

▪   Most of the functional dependency problems go away. In particular, the normalization procedure no longer breaks down. (However, we still have to admit in the social security number example that JOB is not functionally dependent on SS#. What is needed is a means of specifying that *nondefault* values of attribute SS# are unique—just as a means is needed of referring to nondefault values of a foreign key in connection with the revised version of Integrity Rule 2.)

To sum up: The whole point of the default-value approach is that a default value is a normal value and behaves in predictable ways. It is therefore intuitively more satisfactory than the null-value approach. It is true that it requires more explicit involvement on the part of the user; nevertheless, there seems little reason to be hopeful that further research on null values will lead to any significant breakthroughs, and this writer, at least, feels strongly that default values represent the preferred alternative.

5.6   SEMANTIC DATA MODELING

As we pointed out in Section 5.1, the distinction between "basic" and "extended" data models is not clearcut. Generally speaking, extended models attempt to reflect more of the structure of the real world—that is, they endeavor to incorporate more "semantic" features—than do the basic models. For example, a particular extended model might understand that one entity type (for example, the shipment entity type) really serves to associate together two others (for example, suppliers and parts), and might thus be able to enforce some appropriate integrity constraints. Observe, however, that the basic models are not totally devoid of semantic aspects; consider, for instance, the domain and primary key features of the basic relational model. Note too that the extended models are only "slightly more semantic" than the earlier models; to paraphrase [5.10], capturing the meaning of data is a never-ending task, and we can expect to see continuing developments in this area as our understanding continues to evolve. The term *semantic data model,* sometimes used to refer to one or other of the extended models, is thus not particularly apt. On the other hand, "semantic data modeling" *is* an appropriate label for the overall activity of attempting to represent meaning.[9] In this section we present a short introduction to some of the ideas underlying this activity.

We can characterize the general approach to the semantic modeling problem as follows.

1. First, we try to identify a set of *semantic* concepts that appear to be useful in talking informally about the real world. Examples of such concepts are *entity, property*, and *association*. Informally, we might agree that the real world consists of entities that possess properties, are linked together in associations, etc.

2. Next, we devise a set of corresponding *symbolic* (formal) constructs and rules to represent these semantic concepts. For example, the extended relational model RM/T provides *E-relations* to represent entities, *P-relations* to represent properties, and a rule that says that every entry in a P-relation must have a corresponding entry in an E-relation (to reflect the fact that every property must be a property of some entity).

3. We also develop a set of *operators* for manipulating those constructs. For example, RM/T provides the *repeated outer natural join,* which can be used to join together an E-relation and its corresponding P-relations, and thus to collect together all properties for a given entity.

The constructs, rules, and operators of paragraphs (2) and (3) above together constitute an extended data model ("extended," that is, if the constructs are a superset of those of some one of the basic models; but, as we have indicated several times already, there is not really a clear distinction between what is basic and what is extended in this context).

Figure 5.8 lists some useful semantic concepts and gives an informal definition and some examples in each case. The examples are deliberately chosen to illustrate the fact that a given object of the real world may well be regarded as an entity by some people, as a property by others, and as an association by still others. It is a goal of semantic modeling—not yet fully achieved—to allow such flexibility of interpretation.

---

9. Of course, the term also includes the application of any of the basic models as a special case.

Concept	Informal definition	Examples
ENTITY	A distinguishable object—we assume that entities can be categorized into entity *types*	Supplier, Part, Shipment Employee, Department Person Composition, Concerto
PROPERTY	A piece of information that describes an entity	Supplier number Shipment quantity Employee department Person height

ASSOCIATION	A relationship connecting entities	Shipment
		  (supplier-part)
		Assignment
		  (employee-department)
		Performance
		  (composition-
		  orchestra-conductor)

SUBTYPE	Entity type X is a subtype of entity type Y if and only if every X is necessarily also a Y	Employee is a subtype of Person Concerto is a subtype of Composition

Fig. 5.8 Some useful semantic concepts.

We now proceed to sketch some of the proposals in the semantic modeling field very briefly. The proposals we discuss all build on the basic relational model, though some also incorporate ideas from one or other of the irreducible models. For an approach that is based on the network model instead, see Bachman [5.36]. Some other proposals are described in [5.38] and [5.39].

The ''Basic Semantic Model''

Some of the earliest work in this field is that of Schmid and Swenson, who proposed a "basic semantic model" in [5.31]. In outline, their approach is as follows. The world is considered as consisting of *objects* (entities) and *associations*. An object can be either *independent* or *dependent*; the difference is that a dependent object must be "existence-dependent" on some independent object, whereas independent objects exist in their own right. For example, in a personnel database, EMPLOYEEs might be independent objects, whereas EMPLOYEE_CHILDREN might be dependent objects (an EMPLOYEE_CHILD can exist in the database only if the corresponding EMPLOYEE also exists in the database). Both dependent and independent objects can have properties (reference [5.31] uses the term "characteristics").

On the basis of the foregoing ideas, Schmid and Swenson go on to classify relations into five different categories, according to the type of information they represent. For example, a type 1 relation represents an independent object type, a type 5 relation represents an association type. The type of each relation is specified in the database schema (see Fig. 5.9, which illustrates types 1 and 5). Associated with this categorization is a set of integrity rules; for example, an association can be created only if all associated objects already exist (that is, a tuple can be inserted into a type 5 relation only if all appropriate type 1 tuples already exist). Conversely, an object cannot be deleted if it currently participates in any associations. These rules are understood and enforced by the system. Note that the rules are *more specific* than the two integrity rules of the basic relational model.

Schmid and Swenson did not propose any new operators as such; since the fundamental data construct is still the *n*-ary relation, the usual relational operators apply directly (but note that the integrity rules imply that some operators may be rejected and others may have (predictable) side-effects). They did however point out

```
INDEPENDENT OBJECTS
    SUPPLIER IDENTIFIED BY S#
             IN ASSOCIATION SP VIA S#
             DESCRIBED BY RELATION S
    PART     IDENTIFIED BY P#
             IN ASSOCIATION SP VIA P#
             DESCRIBED BY RELATION P

ASSOCIATIONS
    SHIPMENT IDENTIFIED BY (S#,P#)
             DESCRIBED BY RELATION SP

RELATIONS
    S (type 1) PRIMARY KEY (S#)
               ( S# ...,
                 SNAME ...,
                 ..... )
    P (type 1) PRIMARY KEY (P#)
               ( P# ...,
                 PNAME ...,
                 ..... )
    SP (type 5) PRIMARY KEY (S#,P#)
               ( S# ...,
                 P# ...,
                 QTY ... )
DOMAINS
    S# .....
    .....
```

Fig. 5.9 Suppliers-and-parts using the model of Schmid and Swenson (outline only, and somewhat simplified).

that their categorization of relations could serve as a basis for the provision of multiple views of a database at multiple levels of abstraction, thus foreshadowing the work of Smith and Smith on aggregation (to be discussed later in this section). One drawback to their proposal (recognized in [5.31]) is that associations and objects are distinct; that is, an association is not an object, and so cannot have properties and cannot participate in other associations. We ignored the first of these restrictions in Fig. 5.9.

The Entity-Relationship Approach

The term "entity-relationship approach" derives from a paper by Chen [5.32]. The proposals of that paper are not significantly different from those of Schmid and Swenson, however, except in terminology. Chen uses the terms *regular entity, weak entity,* and *relationship* in place of *independent object, dependent object,* and *association,* respectively. Relations are classified by type ("regular entity," etc.) in the schema. Like Schmid and Swenson, Chen defines a set of integrity rules; one difference of detail is that Chen proposes that deletion of an entity should cascade to cause deletion of corresponding relationships, instead of prohibiting the original deletion if any such relationships exist. Unlike Schmid and Swenson, Chen also proposes a set of operators; however, he does not define them precisely (they appear to be strictly less powerful than the relational algebra—for example, they do not include a join).

A shortcoming of the original proposal [5.32] is that (as in [5.31]) a relationship is not an entity, and so cannot itself participate in further relationships.

The entity-relationship approach has evolved somewhat since the publication of [5.32] and has generated considerable interest in recent years. A collection of papers devoted to various topics of related interest can be found in Chen [5.5].

Data Abstraction

Following Smith and Smith [5.33, 5.34], we introduce the concept of *data abstraction.* By an abstraction of a particular database, we mean a view of that database in which certain details are deliberately suppressed. For example, at one level it is possible to consider the suppliers-and-parts database as containing supplier and part entities and shipments that associate those entities, without paying any attention to the *properties* of those entities and associations. The purpose of an abstraction is to allow the user to concentrate on relevant details and to ignore irrelevant details (where the meaning of "relevant" depends on the user and the application in hand).

Smith and Smith define two kinds of abstraction, aggregation and generalization.

■   *Aggregation* is a form of abstraction in which a relationship among objects is regarded as a higher-level object, with lower-level details suppressed. Thus, for example, an entity can be regarded as a relationship between an identity and a set of properties (low level of abstraction), or as an object in its own right, with any or all properties ignored (higher level of abstraction). Similarly, an association can be regarded as a relationship among the participating entities or as an object in its own right (relation SP can be thought of as representing supplier-part associations or as shipments, whichever makes more sense for the application); and so on. Aggregation is handled in the basic relational model by the familiar virtual relation or "view" mechanism.

■   *Generalization* is a form of abstraction in which a set of similar objects is regarded as a higher-level object, with lower-level details suppressed. There are in turn two kinds of generalization:

1. We can generalize from a specific object to the set of all objects of that type. For example, we can generalize from an individual employee entity to the EMPLOYEE entity type. In performing such a generalization, we are ignoring differences of detail between individual employees. This kind of generalization is supported in the basic relational model by collecting tuples of a given format together into a single relation.

2. We can generalize from objects of different types to an object of a common, higher type. For example, we can generalize from "domestic trips" and "foreign trips" to "trips in general." In other words, the DOMESTIC_TRIP and FOREIGN_TRIP entity types are both *subtypes* of the TRIP entity type. A domestic trip and a foreign trip are both trips, and they have certain properties in common (for example, name of the employee making the trip); but perhaps domestic trips have properties that do not apply to foreign trips, or vice versa (for example, the property DOLLAR_EXCHANGE_RATE might apply only to foreign trips). Thus we might represent trips by a collection of three relations: TRIP, which gives all common properties, and DOMESTIC_TRIP and FOREIGN_TRIP, which give properties specific to those subtypes. Any individual trip will then be represented both in TRIP and in exactly one of DOMESTIC_TRIP and FOREIGN_TRIP.

The type/subtype generalization is not directly supported in the basic relational model. In the trips example, the user could design the database to include the three relations as suggested, but the system would not be aware of any connection among those relations and therefore could not automatically enforce any corresponding integrity constraints. The type/subtype notion *is* supported in various extended models such as RM/T. We therefore defer detailed discussion of it to the next chapter.

EXERCISES

5.1 The following diagram represents a ...ierarchical database (containing *two* hierarchies) that was used as the basis of several examples in Volume I.

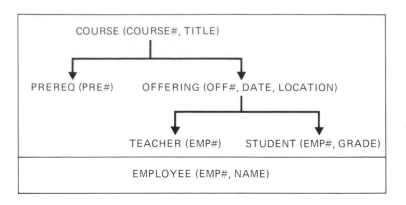

Give equivalent databases using

    a) the *n*-ary relational model;

    b) the binary relational model;

    c) the irreducible relational model;

    d) the functional model.

Give appropriate referential constraints in each case.

5.2 For each of your solutions to Exercise 5.1, write a retrieval expression to

    a) find date and location of all offerings of course C1;

    b) find all students of all offerings of course C1;

    c) find the grade obtained by employee E1 on course C1;

    d) find all teachers of all immediate prerequisites of course C1;

    e) find all teacher employee numbers and, for each teacher, the names of all locations of all offerings taught by that teacher.

5.3 Taking some suitable language (for example, SQL) as a base, define an appropriate syntax for the outer join operation.

5.4 Given the following relations:

S	S#	SCITY
	S1	Paris
	S2	Berne
	S3	Oslo
	S4	?
	S5	Paris

P	P#	PCITY
	P1	Paris
	P2	Berne
	P3	Rome
	P4	?
	P5	?

J	J#	JCITY
	J1	Paris
	J2	Rome
	J3	Oslo
	J4	?
	J5	Rome

show the result value for each of the following:

    a) the projection of S on SCITY;

    b) the union of result (a) and the projection of P on PCITY;

    c) the difference of result (a) and the projection of P on PCITY (in that order);

d) the intersection of result (c) and the projection of J on JCITY;

e) the product of P and J;

f) the maybe join of P and J on PCITY and JCITY;

g) the outer equijoin of P and J on PCITY and JCITY;

h) the outer equijoin of S and result (g) on SCITY and PCITY;

i) the outer equijoin of S and result (g) on SCITY and JCITY;

j) the outer equijoin of S and P on SCITY and PCITY;

k) the outer equijoin of result (j) and J on PCITY and JCITY;

l) the outer natural join of S, P, and J on SCITY, PCITY, and JCITY.

5.5 Develop a formal definition of the network model, along the lines of that given for the relational model in Section 5.3.

5.6 Extend the formalism of Section 5.3 to include such operations as creating a new named relation.

5.7 Consider the type/subtype notion introduced at the end of Section 5.6. For symmetry let us agree to refer to *super*type and subtype, instead of just type and subtype. Let S be a supertype and let S1 and S2 be two subtypes of S. Which of the following are reasonable statements concerning S, S1, S2? You may find it helpful to think in terms of the TRIP example of Section 5.6. (Note: The concepts involved in this exercise are discussed in depth in the next chapter. Thinking about them now will help prepare you for that chapter.)

a) S will have a property indicating, for each individual instance of S, whether that individual is an instance of S1 or of S2.

b) S1 and S2 "span" S—that is, every instance of S is either an instance of S1 or an instance of S2.

c) S may have further subtypes that are quite independent of S1 and S2.

d) An individual instance of S can never be an instance of both S1 and S2.

e) S may in turn be a subtype of some higher supertype.

f) S1 could be a subtype of some other supertype S′ as well as of S.

g) An individual instance of S1 might not be an instance of S at all.

h) An individual instance of S1 might dynamically become an instance of S2, with or without losing its S1 status.

REFERENCES AND BIBLIOGRAPHY

References [5.1–5.5] are conference proceedings, in which can be found many of the more specific references listed subsequently and also a variety of other more or less relevant material.

5.1 M. L. Brodie and S. N. Zilles (eds.). *Proc. Workshop on Data Abstraction, Databases and Conceptual Modelling.* ACM SIGART Newsletter No. 74 (January 1981); ACM SIGMOD Record 11, No. 2 (February 1981); ACM SIGPLAN Notices 16, No. 1 (January 1981).

5.2 J. W. Klimbie and K. L. Koffeman (eds.). "Data Base Management." North-Holland (1974).

5.3 B. C. M. Douqué and G. M. Nijssen (eds.). "Data Base Description." North-Holland (1975).

5.4 G. M. Nijssen (ed.). "Modelling in Data Base Management Systems." North-Holland (1976).

5.5 P. P. -S. Chen (ed.). "Entity-Relationship Approach to Systems Analysis and Design." North-Holland (1980).

5.6 ANSI/X3/SPARC Study Group on Data Base Management Systems. Interim Report. FDT (ACM SIGMOD bulletin) **7**, No. 2 (1975).

5.7 D. C. Tsichritzis and A. Klug (eds.). "The ANSI/X3/SPARC DBMS Framework: Report of the Study Group on Data Base Management Systems." *Information Systems* **3** (1978).

5.8 E. F. Codd. "A Relational Model of Data for Large Shared Data Banks." *CACM* **13**, No. 6 (June 1970).

5.9 E. F. Codd. "Data Models in Database Management." In [5.1].

5.10 E. F. Codd. "Extending the Database Relational Model to Capture More Meaning." *ACM TODS* **4**, No. 4 (December 1979).

5.11 C. J. Date. "Referential Integrity." *Proc. 7th International Conference on Very Large Data Bases* (September 1981).

The proposals of this paper are sketched in the answer to Exercise 2.3 (Chapter 2).

5.12 W. Kent. "Data and Reality." North-Holland (1978).

5.13 G. Bracchi, A. Fedeli, and P. Paolini. "A Multilevel Relational Model for Data Base Management Systems." In [5.2].

5.14 P. J. Titman. "An Experimental Data Base System Using Binary Relations." In [5.2].

5.15 P. Hall, J. Owlett, and S. J. P. Todd. "Relations and Entities." In [5.4].

5.16 E. Falkenberg. "Concepts for Modelling Information." In [5.4].

5.17 J. R. Abrial. "Data Semantics." In [5.2].

5.18 M. E. Senko. "DIAM II with FORAL." In [5.3].

5.19 M. E. Senko. "DIAM as a Detailed Example of the ANSI/SPARC Architecture." In [5.4].

5.20 G. Bracchi, P. Paolini, and G. Pelagatti. "Binary Logical Associations in Data Modelling." In [5.4].

5.21 G. C. H. Sharman. "Update-by-Dialogue: An Interactive Approach to Database Modification." *Proc. 1977 ACM SIGMOD International Conference on Management of Data.*

5.22 R. Munz. "Design of the WELL System." In [5.5].

5.23 O. P. Buneman and R. E. Frankel. "FQL—A Functional Query Language." *Proc. 1979 ACM SIGMOD International Conference on Management of Data.*

5.24 D. Shipman. "The Functional Data Model and the Data Language DAPLEX." *ACM TODS* **6**, No. 1 (March 1981).

5.25 J. Mylopoulos. "An Overview of Knowledge Representation." In [5.1].

5.26 W. Lipski, Jr. "On Semantic Issues Connected with Incomplete Information Databases." *ACM TODS* **4,** No. 3 (September 1979).

5.27 I. J. Heath. Private communication (April 1971).

5.28 M. Lacroix and A. Pirotte. "Generalized Joins." ACM SIGMOD Record **8,** No. 3 (September 1976).

5.29 C. J. Date. "The Outer Join." Submitted to *8th International Conference on Very Large Data Bases* (September 1982).

> A detailed analysis of the outer join operation. Includes a concrete proposal for supporting outer joins in a relational data sublanguage such as SQL.

5.30 Y. Vassiliou. "Functional Dependencies and Incomplete Information." *Proc. 6th International Conference on Very Large Data Bases* (October 1980).

5.31 H. A. Schmid and J. R. Swenson. "On the Semantics of the Relational Data Model." *Proc. 1975 ACM SIGMOD International Conference on Management of Data.*

5.32 P. P. -S. Chen. "The Entity Relationship Model Toward a Unified View of Data." *ACM TODS* **1,** No. 1 (March 1976).

5.33 J. M. Smith and D. C. P. Smith. "Database Abstractions: Aggregation." *CACM* **20,** No. 6 (June 1977).

5.34 J. M. Smith and D. C. P. Smith. "Database Abstractions: Aggregation and Generalization." *ACM TODS* **2,** No. 2 (June 1977).

5.35 A. Pirotte. "The Entity-Property-Association Model." MBLE Report R343, available from Manufacture Belge de Lampes et de Matériel Electronique, Brussels, Belgium (March 1977).

5.36 C. W. Bachman. "The Role Concept in Data Models." *Proc. 3rd International Conference on Very Large Data Bases* (1978).

5.37 L. Kerschberg, A. Klug, and D. C. Tsichritzis. "A Taxonomy of Data Models." Technical Report, Computer Systems Research Group (CSRG), University of Toronto (1976).

5.38 M. M. Hammer and D. J. McLeod. "The Semantic Data Model: A Modelling Mechanism for Database Applications." *Proc. 1978 ACM SIGMOD International Conference on Management of Data.*

5.39 B. Sundgren. "The Infological Approach to Data Bases." In [5.2].

5.40 W. Kent. Private communication (May 1981).

5.41 E. F. Codd. "Understanding Relations" (Installment No. 4). *FDT* (bulletin of ACM SIGMOD) **6,** No. 3 (1974).

> Includes some comments on the relative merits of n-ary relations and functions as the basis for a data model.

5.42 C. J. Date. "A Formal Definition of the Relational Model." ACM SIGMOD Record (to appear 1982).

> This paper is adapted from Section 5.3 of the present chapter.

5.43 C. J. Date. "Null Values in Database Management." *Proc. 2nd British National Conference on Databases* (BNCOD-2), Bristol, England (July 1982).

This paper is adapted from Section 5.5 of the present chapter.

5.44 E. F. Codd. "Relational Database: A Practical Foundation for Productivity." *CACM* **25**, No. 2 (February 1982).

This is the paper Codd presented on the occasion of his receiving the 1981 Turing Award. It discusses the well-known "application backlog" problem: The demand for computer applications is growing fast—so fast that data-processing departments, whose responsibility it is to provide those applications, are lagging further and further behind in their ability to meet that demand. There are two complementary ways of attacking this problem: (1) Provide DP professionals with new tools to increase their productivity; (2) Allow end-users to interact directly with the database, thus bypassing the DP professional entirely. Both approaches are needed, and in this paper Codd suggests that the necessary foundation for both is provided by relational technology. In support of this position, Codd quotes the experience gained with the IBM product SQL/DS and with System R (its prototype predecessor), as well as with other relational systems such as INGRES.

The paper also proposes a classification scheme for relational systems (touched on in Section 5.2). A system is *relational* if it supports tabular data structures and the relational algebra operators SELECT, PROJECT, and (equi- or natural) JOIN; these three operators together constitute the *relational processing capability*. It is *semirelational* (or simply *tabular*) if it supports tabular structures but does not have the relational processing capability. It is *relationally complete* if it supports the full relational algebra. And it is *fully relational* if it supports the full relational model, as defined in, for example, Section 5.3. Furthermore, a system has the *uniform relational property* if it supports relational processing (SELECT, PROJECT, and JOIN) in a uniform manner through both an interactive interface and a programming interface. System R and INGRES are examples of systems having this property. (They are also both "relationally complete," but not "fully relational.")

The paper also discusses the performance of relational systems, and concludes with some comments on needed and likely future developments in the relational technology field.

ANSWERS TO SELECTED EXERCISES

5.1 We give a solution to part (a) only (to serve as a better basis for conversion into the other representations).

```
COURSE     (COURSE#,TITLE)
           PRIMARY KEY (COURSE#)

PREREQ     (COURSE#,PRE#)
           PRIMARY KEY (COURSE#,PRE#)

OFFERING (COURSE#,OFF#,DATE,LOCATION)
           PRIMARY KEY (COURSE#,OFF#)
```

```
TEACHER    (COURSE#,OFF#,EMP#)
           PRIMARY KEY (COURSE#,OFF#,EMP#)

STUDENT    (COURSE#,OFF#,EMP#,GRADE)
           PRIMARY KEY (COURSE#,OFF#,EMP#)

EMPLOYEE   (EMP#,NAME)
           PRIMARY KEY (EMP#)
```

Referential constraints:

We use the syntax of [5.11] to express an appropriate set of constraints. For brevity we omit the delete and update rules, and simply assume that DELETING CASCADES and UPDATING CASCADES apply in every case.

```
PREREQ.COURSE# ->> COURSE.COURSE#

PREREQ.PRE# ->> COURSE.COURSE#

OFFERING.COURSE# ->> COURSE.COURSE#

TEACHER.(COURSE#,OFF#) ->> OFFERING.(COURSE#,OFF#)

TEACHER.EMP# ->> EMPLOYEE.EMP#

STUDENT.(COURSE#,OFF#) ->> OFFERING.(COURSE#,OFF#)

STUDENT.EMP# ->> EMPLOYEE.EMP#
```

5.2 We give solutions corresponding to 5.1(a) only. Our solutions are expressed in SQL; equivalent expressions in some other formalism, such as the relational algebra, are of course essentially identical.

```
a) SELECT  DATE, LOCATION
   FROM    OFFERING
   WHERE   COURSE# = 'C1'

b) SELECT  EMP#
   FROM    STUDENT
   WHERE   COURSE# = 'C1'

c) SELECT  GRADE
   FROM    STUDENT
   WHERE   COURSE# = 'C1'
   AND     EMP# = 'E1'

d) SELECT  EMP#
   FROM    TEACHER, PREREQ
   WHERE   TEACHER.COURSE# = PREREQ.PRE#
   AND     PREREQ.COURSE# = 'C1'

e) SELECT  EMP#, LOCATION
   FROM    TEACHER, OFFERING
   WHERE   TEACHER.COURSE# = OFFERING.COURSE#
   AND     TEACHER.OFF# = OFFERING.OFF#
```

5.3 See reference [5.29].

5.4 For simplicity we ignore any necessary attribute renaming in the following answers.

a)

SCITY
Paris
Berne
Oslo
?

b)

CITY
Paris
Berne
Oslo
?
Rome

c)

CITY
Oslo

d)

CITY
Oslo

e) The result is a relation of degree 4, with attributes P#, PCITY, J#, JCITY, and with a tuple-set containing 25 tuples (all possible combinations of a tuple of P and a tuple of J).

f)

P#	PCITY	J#	JCITY
P4	?	J1	Paris
P4	?	J2	Rome
P4	?	J3	Oslo
P4	?	J4	?
P4	?	J5	Rome
P5	?	J1	Paris
P5	?	J2	Rome
P5	?	J3	Oslo
P5	?	J4	?
P5	?	J5	Rome
P1	Paris	J4	?
P2	Berne	J4	?
P3	Rome	J4	?

g)

P#	PCITY	J#	JCITY
P1	Paris	J1	Paris
P2	Berne	?	?
P3	Rome	J2	Rome
P3	Rome	J5	Rome
P4	?	?	?
P5	?	?	?
?	?	J3	Oslo
?	?	J4	?

h)

S#	SCITY	P#	PCITY	J#	JCITY
S1	Paris	P1	Paris	J1	Paris
S2	Berne	P2	Berne	?	?
S3	Oslo	?	?	?	?
S4	?	?	?	?	?
S5	Paris	P1	Paris	J1	Paris
?	?	P3	Rome	J2	Rome
?	?	P3	Rome	J5	Rome
?	?	P4	?	?	?
?	?	P5	?	?	?
?	?	?	?	J3	Oslo
?	?	?	?	J4	?

i)

S#	SCITY	P#	PCITY	J#	JCITY
S1	Paris	P1	Paris	J1	Paris
S2	Berne	?	?	?	?
S3	Oslo	?	?	J3	Oslo
S4	?	?	?	?	?
S5	Paris	P1	Paris	J1	Paris
?	?	P2	Berne	?	?
?	?	P3	Rome	J2	Rome
?	?	P3	Rome	J5	Rome
?	?	P4	?	?	?
?	?	P5	?	?	?
?	?	?	?	J4	?

j)

S#	SCITY	P#	PCITY
S1	Paris	P1	Paris
S2	Berne	P2	Berne
S3	Oslo	?	?
S4	?	?	?
S5	Paris	P1	Paris
?	?	P3	Rome
?	?	P4	?
?	?	P5	?

k) Same as (h) [necessarily].

l)

S#	P#	J#	CITY
S1	P1	J1	Paris
S5	P1	J1	Paris
S2	P2	?	Berne
S3	?	J3	Oslo
?	P3	J2	Rome
?	P3	J5	Rome
S4	?	?	?
?	P4	?	?
?	P5	?	?
?	?	J4	?

5.7 For this exercise to make sense, it is necessary to assume for the most part that S1 and S2 are subtypes of S "per the same category." Two subtypes T1 and T2 are in *different* subtype categories if the procedure for deciding whether a given entity is or is not an instance of T1 is quite independent of the procedure for deciding whether that entity is or is not an instance of T2. DOMESTIC_TRIP and FOREIGN_TRIP, for example, are subtypes of TRIP per the same category; but if TRIP also had two further subtypes TRIP_BY_MANAGER and TRIP_BY_NON_MANAGER, then (say) FOREIGN_TRIP and TRIP_BY_MANAGER would be independent subtypes—the question of whether a given trip was overseas and the question of whether it was made by a manager would be quite independent of each other (in theory). For additional discussion of these ideas, see Chapter 6.

a) If S1 and S2 "span" S [see (b)], then probably not. Otherwise yes.

b) Possibly but not necessarily.

c) Yes.

d) If S1 and S2 are subtypes within the same category, then probably true; otherwise false.

e) Yes.

f) Yes.

g) Possible but perhaps unlikely (see "alternative generalization" in Section 6.10).

h) True. If S1 and S2 are subtypes within the same category, then the S1 status will probably be lost; otherwise it need not be.

6
The
Extended
Relational
Model RM/T

6.1 INTRODUCTION

This chapter consists of a detailed presentation of Codd's extended relational model RM/T. It is of course based on reference [6.1], but incorporates a number of improvements and refinements developed by Codd and the present author since the original publication of [6.1] in 1979. It also goes beyond reference [6.1] in that it makes use of an illustrative syntax to show how RM/T might actually be perceived by the user, an aspect not addressed in any depth in the original paper. Furthermore, we have made several improvements of a purely cosmetic nature in order to simplify the overall presentation; for example, we have used less abstract names for several of the RM/T catalog objects discussed in Section 6.11. (For similar reasons we have chosen an illustrative syntax that is deliberately rather wordy, in the hope that examples in that syntax will therefore be easy to understand. A practical implementation would certainly wish to refine and simplify that syntax in a variety of ways.)

The basic assumption underlying RM/T is that the real world can be modeled in terms of *entities*. Entities are represented by *E-relations* and *P-relations,* both of which are specialized forms of the general *n*-ary relation; E-relations are used to record the fact that certain entities exist, and P-relations are used to record certain properties of those entities. A variety of relationships can exist among entities—for example, two or more entities may be linked together in an *association,* or a given entity type T1 may be a *subtype* of some other type T2 (in the sense of Chapter 5—that is, every entity of type T1 is necessarily also an entity of type T2). RM/T includes a formal *catalog* structure by which such relationships can be made known to the system; the system is therefore capable of enforcing a variety of *integrity constraints* that are implied by the existence of such relationships (for example, it can enforce the constraint that the entities participating in an association must exist before the association itself is allowed to exist). Finally, a number of high-level *operators* are provided to facilitate the manipulation of the various RM/T objects (E-relations, P-relations, catalog entries, and so on).

The plan of the chapter is as follows. Section 6.2 discusses the entity concept in a little more depth, and amplifies the notion of entity *type* and introduces the notion of entity *classification*. Sections 6.3–6.5 are concerned with the representation of entities in RM/T: Section 6.3 discusses *surrogates* (entity identifiers), Section 6.4 discusses E-relations, and Section 6.5 discusses P-relations. *Entity referencing*—a concept present in the basic relational model but considerably elaborated in the extended model—is the topic of Section 6.6. Sections 6.7 and 6.8 then go on to consider *characteristic entities* and *associative entities,* respectively. (Entities are classified into kernel, characteristic, and associative entities; a characteristic entity is one that describes some other entity, an associative entity is one that links two or more other entities, and a kernel entity is one that is neither characteristic nor associative.) Section 6.9 considers *designative* entities (a designative entity is one that refers to or "designates" some other related entity, as an employee, for example, might designate a department, or a book might designate a publisher). Section 6.10 is concerned with entity *subtypes* and *supertypes*. The new integrity rules, Rules 3–8, are introduced at appropriate points in Sections 6.3–6.10. Finally, Section 6.11 describes the RM/T catalog; Section 6.12 considers the new RM/T operators; and Section 6.13 then summarizes the main points of the entire chapter.

6.2   ENTITIES

As indicated in the introduction, the whole of RM/T is built around the concept of "entity." More precisely, RM/T formalizes certain aspects of the entity notion (and related notions), using the constructs of the basic relational model as a foundation. Formally, of course, the entity notion itself is undefined, and must remain so;[1] what RM/T does is to provide a set of formally defined objects that behave in ways that mimic some aspects of the behavior of entities in the real world. *Informally*, we may say that an entity is *any distinguishable object*—where the "object" in question may be as concrete or as abstract as we please. The fundamental assumptions of RM/T, then, are that the real world may be perceived in terms of entities, and that the database will contain a model or representation of that perception.

It is also assumed that entities can be categorized into entity *types*. For example, every employee is considered to be an instance of the EMPLOYEE entity type. The advantage of such categorization is that it enables us to impose a simple regular

---

1. We have already pointed out in Chapter 5 that the notion of entity is *relative*, in the sense that a given object of the real world may be regarded as an entity by some people but as something else, say a property, by others. As we shall see, RM/T goes a considerable way toward supporting such a relativistic view of the world.

structure on the database: Entities of the same type have certain properties in common (for example, all employees have an employee number, a name, a salary, a department, and so on), and hence we can factor out that commonality and achieve some (fairly obvious) economies of representation.

Entity Classification

It is also possible—and, for similar reasons, desirable—to introduce an (informal) classification scheme for entities and entity types, as follows. We define three kinds or *classes* of entity:

Characteristic A characteristic entity is an entity whose sole function is to qualify or describe some other entity; for example, an individual order line might be a characteristic entity that describes a purchase order entity.

Associative An associative entity is an entity whose function is to represent a many-to-many (or many-to-many-to many, etc.) relationship between two or more other entities; for example, a shipment represents an association between a supplier and a part.

Kernel A kernel entity is an entity that is neither characteristic nor associative; for example, purchase orders, suppliers, and parts might all be kernel entities. The kernel entities in a given database are what that database is "really all about."

In addition, any entity may have one or more properties whose function is to identify or *designate* some other related entity or entities; for example, each employee entity will typically designate some corresponding department entity and/or some corresponding manager entity. Entities such as employees in this example are said to be *designative*. Kernel, characteristic, and associative entities may all be designative in addition.

Entity Subtypes and Supertypes

Finally, it is also possible that a given entity type X may have one or more *subtypes* Y, Z, ... Entity type Y is a subtype of entity type X (and entity type X is a *supertype* of entity type Y) if and only if every entity of type Y is necessarily also an entity of type X. For example, the MANAGER entity type is a subtype of the EMPLOYEE entity type (every manager must necessarily also be an employee). Characteristic, associative, and kernel entity types can all have subtypes; a subtype of a characteristic entity type is also characteristic, a subtype of an associative entity type is also associative, and a subtype of a kernel entity type is also kernel. Moreover, a subtype of a designative entity type is also designative. We give an example of this last case only (the other cases are similar). If employees designate departments, and if managers are a subtype of employees, then managers are also designative because (of course) they necessarily also designate departments.

6.3 SURROGATES

Consider a database, say the suppliers-and-parts database, that is constructed in accordance with the *basic* relational model. By definition, that database contains representatives of certain real-world entities; for example, entities of type *supplier* are represented by tuples in relation S. Since entities are distinguishable in the real world, their representatives in the database must also be distinguishable. In the basic relational model, this *entity identification* function—more accurately, entity *representative* identification function—is performed by user-defined, user-controlled primary keys. For example, "supplier representatives" (tuples in relation S) are identified by values of the S# attribute; and those S# values are assigned and controlled by the human user. Those S# values are then used elsewhere in the database (for example, in shipment tuples) to serve as *references* to the entities in question.

However, such user-defined, user-controlled primary keys ("user keys") suffer from certain shortcomings, which we now briefly discuss.

1. They are subject to change.

    As an example, take a database of botanical information that identifies plants by their scientific names. Those names change from time to time as botanical researchers learn more about plant classification, interspecies relationships, and so on. For a more prosaic example, consider what happens to department numbers (a common example of a user key) when a company reorganizes. Changes such as these can have major repercussions in a database system, because of the existence in the database of entity references that use the old identifiers.

2. Different user keys may be used to identify the same entity.

    For example, "William Shakespeare," "Will Shakespeare," "Shakespeare, W.," "Shakespeare, Wm."—etc., etc., etc.—may all refer to the same entity. (We have all suffered at one time or another from some system's inability to eliminate duplicates from a mailing list.) The different user keys need not even be drawn from the same domain; for example, suppliers might be identified by supplier numbers in some references and supplier names in others. Each of these possibilities has the consequence that a join on user keys might not be the same as an "entity join" (see [6.2] for an extensive discussion of this topic).

3. It may be necessary to record information concerning an entity—perhaps just the *existence* of the entity—that does not have a user key.

    Examples are an employee who has left the company but is entitled to certain benefits on reaching retiring age and so must still be kept on the records, or a house that is still under construction and has not yet been assigned a street address.

Surrogates are intended to address these problems. As indicated in Chapter 5, a surrogate is a *system-generated entity identifier*. The basic idea is as follows. First, the user language must include a CREATE ENTITY operator of some kind ("CREATE ENTITY *REPRESENTATIVE*" would be more accurate, of course, but it is (regrettably) common to ignore such refinements). Executing a CREATE ENTITY operation will cause the system to generate a new surrogate value that is unique with respect to all surrogates that exist *or ever have existed* within this particular database. The generated surrogate value is guaranteed never to change—it is *permanently* associated with the entity in question,[2] even if that entity is removed from the database entirely (which happens as the result of a DESTROY ENTITY operation, of course). The reason for not reusing surrogate values is to avoid difficulties if it should ever become necessary to reinstate old information from archive storage.

It follows from the foregoing that users can cause the system to create surrogates. However, users are not allowed to *see* those surrogates, nor do they have any control over their actual value (they might not even be aware of their existence, in some cases). The reason for these restrictions is to prevent users from creating entity references within the database that the system is unaware of, and that are thus beyond the system's control. (Entity references are discussed in Section 6.6.)

Surrogates do not make user keys obsolete, as we shall see in our examples later in this chapter; on the contrary, user keys will still frequently be required to identify entities outside the database environment (think of account numbers, license plate numbers, social security numbers, and so on). But *within the database* all entity identification and entity referencing is performed via surrogates; that is, primary and foreign key values in the database are now all surrogates, and user keys are considered merely as properties of the entities concerned, just like all other properties. And users are no longer compelled to invent an artificial user key in those situations where no "natural" user key exists (see Section 6.7 for an example).

6.4   THE E-DOMAIN, E-ATTRIBUTES, AND E-RELATIONS

We come now to the first of the formal constructs of RM/T, namely the *E-domain* (E for entity). The E-domain is *the domain of all possible surrogate values*. Any attribute defined on this domain we shall refer to as an *E-attribute*. We use the symbol "¢" as the name of the E-domain; we also impose the rule that the same symbol must appear as the final character of the name of every E-attribute (for example, we shall use "S¢" as the name of an E-attribute that contains surrogates for suppliers). Certain of the new RM/T operators discussed in Section 6.12 will rely on this naming rule.

---

2. Actually this statement is a slight simplification. In fact, surrogates might sometimes have to change under the covers (for example, if two distinct databases are merged), but such changes must always be concealed from the user.

Next we introduce *E-relations*. The database contains one E-relation for each entity type. The E-relation for a given entity type is a unary relation that lists the surrogates of all entities of that type currently existing in the database. The primary purpose of an E-relation is thus to record the existence of the entities in question, and hence to serve as a central reference point for all other entries in the database that concern those entities in any way. By convention,

a) the E-relation for a given entity type is given the same name as that entity type;

b) its single attribute (which is of course an E-attribute) is given a name that is obtained by appending a trailing "¢" to the relation-name.

Let us make these ideas a little more concrete by considering an example.

Example   Suppose we wish to construct an RM/T version of the suppliers-and-parts database. First we will need to establish the existence of three entity types:

```
CREATE  E_RELATION  S ;
CREATE  E_RELATION  P ;
CREATE  E_RELATION  SP
        ASSOCIATING ( S ... , P ... ) ;
```

("CREATE E_RELATION" is part of the hypothetical syntax mentioned in the introduction to this chapter. The ASSOCIATING specification will be explained later, in Section 6.8.) The effect of these three statements is to create three (empty) E-relations called S, P, and SP, with attributes S¢, P¢, and SP¢ respectively (each of these is an E-attribute and is defined on the E-domain). The CREATE ENTITY operator mentioned in Section 6.3 can now be used to cause entries (surrogates) to be made in these E-relations for specific suppliers, parts, and shipments. This operator is considered in more detail in Section 6.5.

As indicated in Chapter 5 (and in earlier sections of the present chapter), some entities can be of multiple types. The example we used in Chapter 5 concerned trips: DOMESTIC_TRIP and FOREIGN_TRIP were both subtypes of the supertype TRIP. In RM/T terms we would have three E-relations for these three entity types:

```
CREATE  E_RELATION  TRIP ;
CREATE  E_RELATION  DOMESTIC_TRIP
                    SUBTYPE OF TRIP ... ;
CREATE  E_RELATION  FOREIGN_TRIP
                    SUBTYPE OF TRIP ... ;
```

The attributes (E-attributes) of these three relations are TRIP¢, DOMESTIC_TRIP¢, and FOREIGN_TRIP¢, respectively. Every surrogate appearing in the DOMESTIC_TRIP or FOREIGN_TRIP E-relation will also appear in the TRIP E-relation. Creating an entity of type DOMESTIC_TRIP or FOREIGN_TRIP will cause the system to assign a new surrogate and to enter that surrogate into the DOMESTIC_TRIP or FOREIGN_TRIP E-relation (as applicable) *and* into the TRIP E-relation. We shall consider this topic further in Section 6.10.

We conclude this section by introducing the first of the new integrity rules ("entity integrity in RM/T"). We refer to this rule as Integrity Rule 3, since Rules 1 and 2 of the basic relational model still apply (though, as we shall see, Rule 2 is almost totally superseded by a set of more specific rules, to be discussed in subsequent sections). Rule 3 is a consequence of the fact that surrogates are intended to be *permanent* entity identifiers.

Integrity Rule 3 (Entity Integrity in RM/T)

E-relations accept insertions and deletions but not updates.

Also (in accordance with Integrity Rule 1), E-relations do not accept null values. Note: RM/T as defined in reference [6.1] includes a scheme for handling null values similar to that sketched in Chapter 5. In particular, it assumes the existence of a null *surrogate* value, referred to as "E-null." Our own preference, as indicated in Chapter 5, is for a scheme based on *default* values, but for the purposes of the present chapter it makes little difference which approach is adopted.

6.5   PROPERTIES AND P-RELATIONS

We use the unqualified term "property" to mean an *immediate, single-valued* piece of information that describes an entity in some way. For example, supplier number, supplier name, status, and city are all properties of suppliers (note that the user key—supplier number—is considered as a property just like the other attributes). By "immediate" we mean that the property concerned is genuinely a property of the entity in question and not of some related (e.g., characteristic) entity. We shall consider multivalued properties in Section 6.7. We shall also consider "nonimmediate" properties in that same section.

The property types for a given entity type are represented by a set of *P-relations*. In the case of suppliers, for example, we might have the three P-relations shown below:

```
SKN   ( S¢, S#, SNAME )
ST    ( S¢, STATUS )
SC    ( S¢, CITY )
```

(we ignore domains for the moment). The precise manner in which properties are grouped into P-relations is left to the discretion of the database designer; at one extreme all properties may be bundled together into a single P-relation, at the other extreme each property may have a (binary) P-relation of its own. By convention, the set of P-relations for a particular entity type satisfies the following two conditions:

a) the primary key of every P-relation in the set is an E-attribute with the same name as the single attribute of the corresponding E-relation;

b) no two P-relations in the set have any attribute-names in common except as specified under (a).

Observe that the three P-relations SKN, ST, and SC shown earlier do satisfy these two requirements. Those three P-relations might be defined as follows:

```
CREATE P_RELATION SKN FOR E_RELATION S
       PROPERTIES ( S#       DOMAIN ( S# ) ,
                    SNAME   DOMAIN ( SNAME ) ) ;

CREATE P_RELATION ST FOR E_RELATION S
       PROPERTIES ( STATUS DOMAIN ( STATUS ) ) ;

CREATE P_RELATION SC FOR E_RELATION S
       PROPERTIES ( CITY    DOMAIN ( LOCATION ) ) ;
```

(We assume that the domains S#, SNAME, STATUS, and LOCATION have already been defined; also we assume in our hypothetical syntax that the specification "FOR E_RELATION S" is adequate to define the primary key S¢, and do not give any further specification for that attribute.) If it is desirable for the system to continue to enforce the constraint that every supplier has a unique, nonnull supplier number—which presumably it is—then we might specify (say)

```
USER KEY ( S# )
```

in the definition of the E-relation S; and similarly for SNAME, if desired.

To enter supplier S1 into the database (for example), a user might now write

```
CREATE ENTITY OF TYPE S ( S#      := 'S1',
                          SNAME   := 'SMITH',
                          STATUS := 20,
                          CITY    := 'LONDON' ) ;
```

The effect of this operation is

a) to generate a new surrogate, say *alpha*, and to insert it into the E-relation called S;

b) to insert the tuple

    (S¢:alpha, S#:'S1', SNAME:'SMITH')

into the P-relation SKN;

c) to insert the tuple

    (S¢:alpha, STATUS:20)

into the P-relation ST;

d) to insert the tuple

    (S¢:alpha, CITY:'LONDON')

into the P-relation SC.

The relevant part of the database now looks like this:

E-relation:

S

S¢
alpha

P-relations:

SKN

S¢	S#	SNAME
alpha	S1	Smith

ST

S¢	STATUS
alpha	20

SC

S¢	CITY
alpha	London

To the user, however, the CREATE ENTITY operation looks very much like a normal INSERT TUPLE operation. In the example, the user can think of suppliers as being represented by a single degree-4 relation called S, with attributes S#, SNAME, STATUS, and CITY:

S

S#	SNAME	STATUS	CITY
S1	Smith	20	London

The user may or may not also be aware of the fact that suppliers are actually identified by surrogates, depending on the application in hand and the sophistication of the user. This is therefore a good place to point out that RM/T is primarily of interest to the database *designer*; the additional objects, operators, etc. are of little concern to the ordinary user, who can for the most part continue to view the database in a straightforward and familiar manner. In other words, RM/T provides a basis for designing the *conceptual* level of the system (that is, the conceptual schema); it also provides a set of operators to convert that conceptual design into a variety of more "user-friendly" external schemas.

Let us digress for a moment to consider the "more user-friendly" external schema of the example (the degree-4 relation S) in slightly more detail. The degree-4 relation S is obtained by taking the *repeated outer natural join* of the E-relation S and the P-relations SKN, ST, and SC over the S¢ attribute, and then eliminating the S¢ attribute from the result (see Example 6.12.1). Repeated outer natural join is one of the RM/T operators referred to above. The reason we have to perform an *outer* join is that an entity that is represented in a given E-relation does not necessarily have to be represented in every corresponding P-relation. For example, a given supplier might not have an entry in the P-relation SC. Such an omission would normally be taken to mean that the CITY for the supplier concerned is null—that is, unknown, or not applicable.

Note that if the user is to be allowed to operate wholly in terms of the degree-4 relation S—in particular, if the user is to be allowed to update that relation, as we implied with our CREATE ENTITY example above—then the system must be ready to support update operations on certain kinds of derived relation. Further work is needed here to pin down the requirements more precisely.

It follows from the foregoing remarks that CREATE ENTITY is an *external* (or user-level) operation, rather than a conceptual-level operation. The following more primitive operations are required within the system in order to support such a user-level operation:

■   an operation to acquire a new surrogate (ACQUIRE SURROGATE);

■   an operation to enter a surrogate into an E-relation (INSERT INTO E_RELATION);

■   an operation to enter a surrogate and one or more associated property values into a P-relation (INSERT INTO P_RELATION).

We repeat that this more primitive level of the system should *not* expose the surrogate values to users at higher levels.

Turning now to the part entity type, we can create P-relations PKN, PL, PW, and PC (say), as follows:

```
CREATE P_RELATION PKN FOR E_RELATION P
         PROPERTIES ( P#      DOMAIN ( P# ) ,
                      PNAME   DOMAIN ( PNAME ) ) ;

CREATE P_RELATION PL FOR E_RELATION P
         PROPERTIES ( COLOR   DOMAIN ( COLOR ) ) ;

CREATE P_RELATION PW FOR E_RELATION P
         PROPERTIES ( WEIGHT DOMAIN ( WEIGHT ) ) ;

CREATE P_RELATION PC FOR E_RELATION P
         PROPERTIES ( CITY    DOMAIN ( LOCATION ) ) ;
```

We remark that parts provide a good example of an entity type for which user keys are definitely needed (those keys will appear on customer order forms, in sales catalogs, in instruction manuals, and so on).

Now what about shipments? We propose the following design.

```
CREATE P_RELATION SPSP FOR E_RELATION SP
         PROPERTIES ( S¢ SURROGATE FOR S ,
                      P¢ SURROGATE FOR P ) ;

CREATE P_RELATION SPQ FOR E_RELATION SP
         PROPERTIES ( QTY DOMAIN ( QTY ) ) ;
```

In other words, each shipment is represented by a surrogate (in the E-relation SP) together with three property values: a supplier surrogate S¢ and a part surrogate P¢ (both in the P-relation SPSP), and a quantity value QTY (in the P-relation SPQ). Note that we explicitly define attribute S¢ of relation SPSP as SURROGATE FOR S (and similarly for attribute P¢), instead of simply specifying DOMAIN(¢). Note too that the user keys S# and P# do *not* appear. As a result of this latter point, if (for example) the user key "S1" changes to "S51", say, it is not necessary to cascade the change to all shipments for that supplier. Of course, it would be possible to include S# and P# as properties of shipments, but the effect would be to undermine the advantage of using surrogates in the first place.[3]

To create the shipment for supplier S1 and part P1, with quantity 300, a user can now write

```
CREATE ENTITY OF TYPE SP
     ( S¢   := ( SKN.S¢ WHERE SKN.S# = 'S1' ) ,
       P¢   := ( PKN.P¢ WHERE PKN.P# = 'P1' ) ,
       QTY := 300 ) ;
```

We are assuming now that the user *is* aware of the fact that suppliers and parts are designated by surrogates (within the context of shipments); notice that the user is able to make use of those surrogates without having to know their actual values. Alternatively, the user could be given an external view of shipments as the familiar degree-3 relation SP; the view definition would involve

a) forming the outer natural join of the E-relation SP and the P-relations SPSP and SPQ over SP¢;

b) forming the regular natural join—*not* the outer join (why not?)—of the result of step (a) and the P-relation SKN over S¢;

c) forming the regular natural join of the result of step (b) and the P-relation PKN over P¢;

d) eliminating attributes S¢, P¢, SP¢, SNAME, and PNAME from the result of step (c) by projection.

(As an aside, we remark that the regular join could be used in step (a), as well as in steps (b) and (c), if we could rely on every shipment appearing in relation SPQ.) With this view, the "CREATE ENTITY" operation shown above can be simplified to

```
CREATE ENTITY OF TYPE SP
               ( S#   :=   'S1',
                 P#   :=   'P1',
                 QTY :=   300 ) ;
```

---

3. On the other hand, if S# and P# are not included as properties of shipments, then it will not be possible to specify "USER KEY (S#,P#)" in the shipment E-relation. If each shipment is still to have a unique, nonnull (S#,P#) value combination, then that constraint will have to be explicitly stated elsewhere.

The system would have to map this operation into the appropriate set of operations on the underlying conceptual-level relations. (Exercise: What are those operations? Assume that a shipment cannot be created if the specified supplier and part do not already exist, and that each shipment is required to have a unique (S#,P#) value combination.)

It is important to understand that *every* E-relation has a corresponding set (possibly empty) of P-relations. If a given entity is of multiple types (that is, is represented in multiple E-relations), then it will have properties corresponding to each of those types, in general. For example, a given FOREIGN_TRIP will have some properties (such as DOLLAR_EXCHANGE_RATE) that apply to foreign trips only, plus other properties (such as TOTAL_EXPENSE) that apply to every trip. Thus the attribute DOLLAR_EXCHANGE_RATE will appear in a P-relation for FOREIGN_TRIPs, the attribute TOTAL_EXPENSE will appear in a P-relation for TRIPs. By convention, the P-relations for a given entity type do not have any attribute-names in common with the P-relations for any supertype, at any level, of that entity type. (This rule allows supertype properties to be automatically "inherited" by subtypes of that supertype, without any risk of ambiguity. See Section 6.10.)

We come now to the second of the new integrity rules ("property integrity"). This rule is a consequence of the fact that every property value in the database must describe some entity that is also represented in the database.

Integrity Rule 4 (Property Integrity)

> If a tuple t appears in a P-relation P, then the (surrogate) primary key value of t must appear in the E-relation corresponding to P.

Rule 4 affects the operations INSERT INTO P_RELATION and DELETE FROM E_RELATION: INSERT INTO P_RELATION will be accepted only if the relevant surrogate exists in the corresponding E-relation, DELETE FROM E_RELATION will cause all relevant tuples to be deleted from the corresponding P-relations.[4] Of course, Rule 4 per se will not be directly visible to a user who is operating at the external or "CREATE ENTITY" level rather than at the RM/T level, since there is no way for such a user to create a property value that is not tied directly to its corresponding entity.

---

4. For reasons of space we do not discuss UPDATE operations explicitly in this chapter. Also, we discuss the integrity rules (not just Rule 4, but also the other rules introduced later in the chapter) as if all checks were applied immediately, that is, at the time of issuing the operation concerned. In practice it may be preferable in some situations to defer the checks to end-of-transaction.

6.6 ENTITY REFERENCES

The integrity rule introduced at the end of the previous section (property integrity) is actually a special case of a referential integrity rule. As explained earlier in this book (Chapter 2), such rules define various *referential constraints.* Loosely speaking, a referential constraint arises whenever some relation R1 includes an attribute, called a foreign key, whose values are required to match the values of the primary key of some other relation R2. The foreign key values in R1 are *references* to entities identified by the primary key values in R2. The purpose of referential constraints is of course to ensure that every such entity reference in the database really does correspond to some known entity in the database.

The topic of referential integrity is discussed in the context of the basic relational model in Chapter 2 and in reference [6.5]. However, the extended model RM/T provides a much tighter set of controls on the problem than does the basic model. In the first place, foreign key values are required to match, not just a primary key value appearing in *some* relation, but very specifically a primary key value appearing in an *E-relation.* (We have already pointed out in Section 6.4 that all primary keys, and hence all foreign keys, are E-attributes in RM/T.)[5] Thus the notion that every foreign key value must identify some *entity* (rather than just some tuple in some relation) is captured more explicitly than in the basic model.

In the second place, entity references are categorized in RM/T into several disjoint classes, as follows:

a)   property references;

b)   characteristic references;

c)   association references;

d)   designation references;

e)   subtype references.

Each class is characterized by its own specific set of rules and its own specific effect on insertions and deletions (and updates). *Property references,* class (a), have already been discussed in Section 6.5; a property reference is a reference from a P-relation (via its E-attribute primary key) to the corresponding E-relation, and is governed by Integrity Rule 4. The other types of reference, classes (b) through (e), are discussed in Sections 6.7, 6.8, 6.9, and 6.10, respectively. Note: Reference [6.1] includes no mention of class (d), the designation references.

---

5. We remark in passing that primary keys and foreign keys therefore always consist of a single attribute in RM/T, never a combination of attributes (except as indicated in Footnote 11, page 259). The basic model, by contrast, does permit multiattribute primary keys, and this fact considerably complicates the treatment of referential constraints (witness [6.5]).

6.7   CHARACTERISTIC ENTITIES

We use the term "characteristic entity" to mean an entity whose sole function (within the universe of discourse in which we happen to be interested) is to qualify or describe some other "superior" entity. The characteristic entity is subordinate to, *and existence-dependent on,* that superior entity. For example, the individual line items on a purchase order could be considered as characteristic entities that qualify that purchase order (and the purchase order would then be the corresponding superior entity for those line items).

   The need for characteristic entities arises from the possibility that a given entity may have *multivalued* properties (we are using "property" here in its ordinary English sense, rather than in the special sense of Section 6.5). Thus, characteristics represent the RM/T approach to the well-known phenomenon of *repeating fields* and *repeating groups* in classical data processing. Let us consider the purchase order example in more detail. In the basic relational model, we would represent this situation by the two relations (say)

```
ORDER    ( ORDER#, CUSTOMER, DATE, TOTAL_AMOUNT )
         PRIMARY KEY ( ORDER# )

ORDLINE ( ORDER#, LINE#, ITEM, QTY, PRICE, AMOUNT )
         PRIMARY KEY ( ORDER#, LINE# )
```

The immediate, single-valued properties of an order are the order number, the customer, the date, and the total amount. For any given order, the order line information represents a set of *multivalued* properties for that order; the immediate, single-valued properties of a given order line can be regarded as *nonimmediate* (second-level) properties of the original order. Note the referential constraint that a given order line can exist only if the corresponding order exists.

   In RM/T we would handle this example as follows. Orders are considered as superior entities and are supported by an E-relation (ORDER) and a set of P-relations for the properties ORDER#, CUSTOMER, DATE, and TOTAL_AMOUNT. For simplicity, let us group all these properties together into a single P-relation ORDER_PROPERTIES:

```
CREATE E_RELATION ORDER ;

CREATE P_RELATION ORDER_PROPERTIES
                  FOR E_RELATION ORDER
         PROPERTIES ( ORDER#        DOMAIN ( . . . ) ,
                      CUSTOMER      DOMAIN ( . . . ) ,
                      DATE          DOMAIN ( . . . ) ,
                      TOTAL_AMOUNT DOMAIN ( . . . ) ) ;
```

   Order lines are considered as characteristic entities qualifying orders. Since they are entities, they are supported by an E-relation and a set of P-relations, like all entities, but it is *required* that exactly one of the attributes in those P-relations be an E-attribute whose values identify entities of the superior type. The name of that attribute must be the same as that of the sole attribute of the E-relation corresponding to the superior type. For example (again assuming just one P-relation for simplicity):

```
CREATE E_RELATION ORDLINE
                    CHARACTERISTIC OF ORDER ;
```

The specification CHARACTERISTIC OF ORDER indicates that this is a *characteristic E-relation,* and that the superior E-relation is ORDER.

```
CREATE P_RELATION ORDLINE_PROPERTIES
                    FOR E_RELATION ORDLINE
        PROPERTIES ( SURROGATE FOR ORDER ,
                     ITEM    DOMAIN ( . . . ) ,
                     QTY     DOMAIN ( . . . ) ,
                     PRICE   DOMAIN ( . . . ) ,
                     AMOUNT  DOMAIN ( . . . ) ) ;
```

The entry SURROGATE FOR ORDER defines an E-attribute within the P-relation ORDLINE_PROPERTIES called (by convention) ORDER¢. ORDLINE_PROPERTIES is an example of a *characteristic P-relation.* The attribute ORDLINE_PROPERTIES.ORDER¢ represents a *characteristic reference* from ORDLINE to ORDER. The database structure is as indicated below (with some sample surrogates shown):

E-relations:

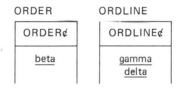

ORDER	ORDLINE
ORDER¢	ORDLINE¢
beta	gamma
	delta

P-relations:

ORDER_PROPERTIES

ORDER¢	ORDER#	CUSTOMER	DATE	TOTAL_AMOUNT
beta	. . . .	. . . .	. .	. . . . .

ORDLINE_PROPERTIES

ORDLINE¢	ORDER¢	ITEM	QTY	PRICE	AMOUNT
gamma	beta	. .	. . .	. . .	. .
delta	beta	. .	. . .	. . .	. .

Note that a characteristic entity *is* an entity and can therefore have lower-level characteristic entities that describe it. We might extend our previous example to make orders a characteristic entity type subordinate to customers; order lines would then be a second-level characteristic of customers (and so on, to any number of levels). By convention, no property of a characteristic entity type can have the same attribute-name as any property of any superior entity type, at any level. (This rule allows characteristic properties to be "promoted" to the superior level without any risk of ambiguity. See Example 6.12.2.)

Note also in our example that we have chosen *not* to include LINE# as a property of an order line (though there would be nothing wrong in doing so). It is at least arguable that LINE# is an "artificial" attribute, introduced into the basic model representation purely because otherwise there would be no guarantee that individual lines of a given order are always distinguishable from each other in that representation. In the RM/T representation, the necessary distinguishability is provided by the E-attribute ORDLINE¢. But it should be clearly understood that a consequence of our choice to drop line numbers is that the user *must* now be aware of surrogates (of their existence, that is, not of their actual values). In other words, it is no longer possible to define an external view of order lines as a degree-6 relation

```
    ORDLINE ( ORDER#, LINE#, ITEM, QTY, PRICE, AMOUNT )
```

—the best we can do is to define a view

```
    ORDLINE ( ORDER#, ORDLINE¢, ITEM, QTY, PRICE, AMOUNT ) ,
```

in which the user is aware of the existence and purpose of the attribute ORDLINE¢ but cannot see the specific values of that attribute. This example may be regarded as typical, in that it illustrates the considerations that will apply whenever an entity has no obvious user key in the real world. (The definition of the ORDLINE view above will involve (a) forming the outer natural join of the E-relation ORDER and the P-relation ORDER_PROPERTIES over ORDER¢; (b) forming the outer natural join of the E-relation ORDLINE and the P-relation ORDLINE_PROPERTIES over ORDLINE¢; (c) forming the outer natural join of the results of (a) and (b) over ORDER¢; (d) eliminating all unneeded attributes from the result of (c) by projection.)

Characteristic entities are constrained by another new integrity rule.

Integrity Rule 5 (Characteristic Integrity)

A characteristic entity cannot exist in the database unless the entity it most immediately describes is also in the database.

Rule 5 has consequences for several operations: for example, INSERT INTO E_RELATION (for a characteristic E-relation) requires an accompanying INSERT INTO P_RELATION for the P-relation that includes the characteristic reference attribute. Of course, this rule, like Rule 4, will not be directly visible to a user who operates at the "CREATE ENTITY" level. Instead, such a user will perceive a familiar foreign-key/primary-key relationship between an *n*-ary relation representing the characteristic entity type and an *n*-ary relation representing the superior entity type. That foreign key will not be allowed to take on null values. Deleting an instance of the superior entity type, or updating the primary key of such an instance, will automatically cascade to all corresponding characteristic entities.

We conclude this section by stressing once again that the whole point of characteristic entities is that they are existence-dependent on their superior entity. If it were possible, for example, for an order line to exist *without* a corresponding order existing, then order lines should not be considered characteristics of purchase orders. Let us examine this point in a little more depth.

1. Assume that we have two entity types, X and Y, such that for every instance of X there are multiple corresponding instances of Y (X-to-Y is one-to-many).[6] Under what circumstances can Y be considered a characteristic entity type for X?

2. There are two cases to consider:

Case (a). The correspondence between X and Y *partitions* Y, in the sense that every instance of Y corresponds to precisely one instance of X (Y-to-X is one-to-one).[7]

Case (b). The correspondence does not partition Y—that is, a given instance of Y may correspond to any number of instances of X, including zero (Y-to-X is one-to-many).[8]

3. As an example of Case (a), let X be departments and Y employees, under the constraint that every employee belongs to precisely one department. Despite that constraint, it is unreasonable to consider employees as *existence-dependent* on departments, and thus, for example, to cascade deletes of departments down to corresponding employees. Rather, we would probably want to introduce a rule prohibiting the deletion of any department having a nonempty set of employees. The notion of characteristics is thus not applicable here (instead, we would treat employees as an independent entity type, having a property whose values *designate*

---

6. Read: "For one instance of X, there are many instances of Y." This is a *directed* correspondence.

7. Read: "For one instance of Y, there is one instance of X" (also a directed correspondence).

8. Read: "For one instance of Y, there are many instances of X" (also a directed correspondence).

departments; see Section 6.9). The point is, the fact that the correspondence X-to-Y is one-to-many does not automatically imply that Y is a characteristic of X, even if the inverse correspondence Y-to-X is one-to-one.

 4. As an example of Case (b), let X be projects and Y employees, under the constraint that employees may be assigned to any number of projects (possibly zero) at any given time. Projects and employees are then best considered as independent (kernel) entity types, and the employee-project relationship can then be seen to be an *association* between those two kernels[9] (see Section 6.8). The notion of characteristics does not apply at all in this case.

   To summarize: Entity type Y can be considered as a characteristic entity type for entity type X only if (a) X-to-Y is one-to-many and Y-to-X is one-to-one, *and* (b) each instance of Y is existence-dependent on the corresponding instance of X. There certainly are real-world situations in which (a) and (b) both apply; in fact, RM/T itself provides several examples—for instance, the P-relations corresponding to a given E-relation are certainly existence-dependent on that E-relation, and each P-relation corresponds to precisely one E-relation. But it would be possible to apply RM/T without making any use of characteristics at all (though it would then be necessary to specify the applicable delete rules, etc., explicitly).[10] Moreover, if characteristics *are* used, then there is always the possibility that an entity type that was previously classified as characteristic becomes a kernel instead, with consequent disruptive changes to the database design.

6.8   ASSOCIATIVE ENTITIES

We define an *association* to be a many-to-many (or many-to-many-to-many, etc.) relationship involving two or more otherwise independent entities (not necessarily distinct or of distinct types). By "independent" here we mean that none of the entities concerned is existence-dependent on any of the others. Shipments provide an example, in which the entities being associated are of course suppliers and parts. Associations are normally regarded as entities in their own right, and are thus represented by an E-relation and a set of P-relations; in Section 6.5, for example, shipments were represented by the E-relation SP(SP¢) and the two P-relations SPSP

---

9. X-to-Y and Y-to-X are both one-to-many correspondences in this case. If the correspondence is one-to-many in both directions, as in this example, then it is usual to describe the *undirected* correspondence X:Y as "many-to-many."

10. This fact should not be construed as a drawback, since such rules must be specified explicitly anyway in the case of associations and designations (see, for example, the discussion of Integrity Rule 6 in Section 6.8). The CHARACTERISTIC OF (etc.) syntax can be regarded as merely a shorthand notation for the specification of a particular combination of such rules.

(SP¢,S¢,P¢) and SPQ(SP¢,QTY). Since an association is an entity, it may have lower-level (characteristic) entities describing it, and it may participate in higher-level associations.[11]

The definitions of the E-relation and a possible set of P-relations for the entity type "shipment" were given in outline in Sections 6.4 and 6.5. We now show them in full detail:

```
CREATE  E_RELATION  SP
           ASSOCIATING ( S VIA S¢ , P VIA P¢ ) ;

CREATE  P_RELATION  SPSP  FOR  E_RELATION  SP
           PROPERTIES ( S¢ SURROGATE FOR S ,
                        P¢ SURROGATE FOR P ) ;

CREATE  P_RELATION  SPQ FOR E_RELATION SP
           PROPERTIES ( QTY DOMAIN ( QTY ) ) ;
```

The specification

```
ASSOCIATING ( S VIA S¢ , P VIA P¢ )
```

for the E-relation SP means that, within the set of P-relations for SP, there must be exactly one property called S¢ and defined as SURROGATE FOR S, and exactly one called P¢ and defined as SURROGATE FOR P. These properties represent the *association references* (see Section 6.6). The names S¢ and P¢ for these properties are arbitrary (except that they must terminate in "¢"). We might agree in the case at hand that it is unnecessary to specify any names, and then simply take the names S¢ and P¢ as the obvious defaults; but in general it must be possible to provide explicit names, because of the possibility that the entity types being associated might not be

---

11. Reference [6.1] also allows "nonentity associations" (pun intended). A nonentity association is represented by a single *n*-ary relation, with an E-attribute for each of the entity types involved in the association and zero or more additional attributes for immediate properties of the association. Those E-attributes together constitute the primary key for that *n*-ary relation (this is the only situation in the formalism of [6.1] in which a primary key is not a simple surrogate). Shipments, for example, could be represented by the degree-3 relation SP(S¢,P¢,QTY), with primary key the combination (S¢,P¢). Nonentity associations are not considered as entities in their own right; they have no surrogates of their own and no E-relation (and no P-relations or characteristic relations). There is thus no system-controlled way to refer to such an association from elsewhere in the database. In particular, a nonentity association cannot possess any multivalued properties (characteristics), nor can it participate in another association.

The primary reason for including nonentity associations in [6.1] was an expository one—namely, to illustrate the weakness of the concept, in contrast with the notion of regarding associations as entities in their own right. RM/T can, and preferably should, be applied without involving the concept at all. For the most part, therefore, we will exclude consideration of nonentity associations from our discussions in this chapter.

distinct. The familiar bill-of-materials structure, for example, would typically be represented in RM/T as follows:

```
CREATE  E_RELATION  P ;

CREATE  P_RELATION  P_PROPERTIES  FOR  E_RELATION  P . . . ;

CREATE  E_RELATION  PP
        ASSOCIATING  ( P  VIA  MAJOR_P¢ ,
                       P  VIA  MINOR_P¢ ) ;

CREATE  P_RELATION  PP_PROPERTIES  FOR  E_RELATION  PP
        PROPERTIES  ( MAJOR_P¢  SURROGATE  FOR  P ,
                      MINOR_P¢  SURROGATE  FOR  P ,
                                      . . . . . ) ;
```

Again the property names (MAJOR_P¢ and MINOR_P¢) are arbitrary, except for the trailing "¢".

Let us agree to refer to the entity types that are associated via a given associative entity type as *participants* in that association. The association then *references* those participants (as suggested in Section 6.6), and is therefore subject to a certain integrity rule, as follows.

Integrity Rule 6 (Association Integrity)[12]

Let A be an associative entity type, and let E be the set of E-attributes whose function is to identify the participants in A. Then a given instance of A can exist in the database only if, for that instance, each E-attribute in E either (a) has the value E-null, or (b) identifies an existing entity of the appropriate type.

For example, assuming that "nulls not allowed" applies to attributes S¢ and P¢ of the P-relation SPSP, a shipment can exist in the database only if the corresponding supplier and part also exist in the database. Conversely, if (say) attribute SPSP.S¢ can accept null values, then it is possible for a shipment to exist in the database for which the supplier is unknown. (Note that attribute SPSP.S¢ is not a component of the primary key of SPSP, so that such a situation would not be in violation of Integrity Rule 1.) For the purposes of this chapter, however, we shall assume that nulls are *not* allowed for an E-attribute unless "nulls allowed" is explicitly stated for that E-attribute in the definition of the relevant P-relation.

Rule 6, like Rule 2 in the basic model (but unlike Rules 4 and 5), is deliberately not very specific. Consider the shipment example once again. The rule clearly prohibits the creation of a shipment that refers to a nonexistent supplier or nonexistent part. However, it does not specify what should happen on an attempt to delete a supplier or part for which there currently exist one or more shipments. Should the

---

12. *Nonentity associations* are governed by Integrity Rule 2 of the basic relational model. In fact, nonentity associations provide the sole justification for retaining that rule in RM/T (in all other cases Rule 2 can be replaced by one of the more specific rules discussed in this chapter). Note that the E-domain is the only "primary domain" in RM/T (see Chapter 5).

delete be rejected, or should it cascade to those shipments? The answer to such a question clearly depends on the application in hand, in general: In some situations an attempt to delete a participant in an association should be rejected, whereas in other cases the delete should cascade. Thus Rule 6 will need to be extended in any specific situation to include an appropriate set of additional, explicit specifications indicating what should be done in the face of an attempt to violate the rule. Details of possible specifications are left as an exercise for the reader.

6.9 DESIGNATIVE ENTITIES

We define a *designation* to be a many-to-one relationship involving two otherwise independent entities (not necessarily distinct or of distinct types).

To provide an example, let us extend the suppliers-and-parts database to include cities as an independent entity type:

```
CREATE E_RELATION CITY ;

CREATE P_RELATION CITY_PROPERTIES
                  FOR E_RELATION CITY . . . ;
```

We therefore accordingly replace the P-relations SC and PC (giving supplier city and part city respectively) by the following:

```
CREATE P_RELATION SC FOR E_RELATION S
          PROPERTIES ( CITY¢ SURROGATE FOR CITY ) ;

CREATE P_RELATION PC FOR E_RELATION P
          PROPERTIES ( CITY¢ SURROGATE FOR CITY ) ;
```

We also extend the definitions of E-relations S and P appropriately:

```
CREATE E_RELATION S
          DESIGNATING ( CITY VIA CITY¢ ) ;

CREATE E_RELATION P
          DESIGNATING ( CITY VIA CITY¢ ) ;
```

Attribute SC.CITY¢ represents a *designation reference* to entity type CITY from entity type S (and similarly for PC.CITY¢ and P). S and P are *designative* entity types. A designation reference is thus an entity reference that is none of the following:

a) a reference from a P-relation to the E-relation for the entity type described by that P-relation (a property reference);

b) a reference from a characteristic P-relation to the E-relation for the immediately superior entity type (a characteristic reference);

c) a reference from a P-relation for an associative entity type to the E-relation for a participant in that association (an association reference);

d) a reference from an E-relation for an entity subtype to the E-relation for an immediate supertype of that subtype (a subtype reference—see Section 6.10).

We use the term "designative entity type" to mean any entity type that possesses a property that represents a designation. Kernel, associative, and characteristic entity types can all be designative in addition. Note that, in general, it is necessary to provide an explicit name for the referencing attribute in a designation (that is, an attribute such as attribute SC.CITY¢ in the example), just as it is necessary to provide explicit names for the referencing attributes in an association, and for the same reason.

Designative entities are subject to the following rule.

Integrity Rule 7 (Designative Integrity)

Let D be a designative entity type, and let E be the set of E-attributes representing designations by D. Then a given instance of D can exist in the database only if, for that instance, each E-attribute in E either (a) has the value E-null, or (b) identifies an existing entity of the appropriate type.

For example, assuming that "nulls not allowed" applies to attribute CITY¢ of the P-relation SC, a supplier can exist in the database only if the corresponding city also exists in the database. (Rule 7, like Rule 6, will need to be extended in any specific situation to include an appropriate set of explicit specifications indicating what should be done if the rule is violated. We do not discuss this aspect further here.)

It is clear that Integrity Rules 6 and 7 are rather similar, and that the notions of association and designation have a lot in common. In fact, an associative entity can be thought of as a designative entity that involves at least two designations. (This is only another way of expressing the well-known fact that a many-to-many relationship can be represented as a combination of two many-to-one relationships.) For example, we can regard a shipment either as an entity that *associates* a supplier and a part, or as an entity that *designates* a supplier and *designates* a part. The only distinction is that an associative entity *must* involve at least two references to other entities, whereas a designative entity need only involve one. Thus "designation" is actually the more primitive notion, and "association" could be *defined* as a designative entity that involves at least two designations—with the further restriction that *no two instances of the associative entity type in question designate exactly the same combination of participants* (at any given time). Thus, for example, shipments can reasonably be regarded as an *association* between suppliers and parts, because no two individual shipments have the same combination of values for the property pair (SPSP.S¢, SPSP.P¢). By contrast, if employees belong to departments and are assigned to projects, then they *cannot* reasonably be regarded just as associations between departments and projects, even though again two designations are involved, because two distinct employees might simultaneously have the same department and the same project (in any case, it is intuitively more appealing to think of employees as existing in their own right and simply designating those other entities). We conclude that both concepts, association and designation, should be supported in the RM/T formalism.

6.10 ENTITY TYPES

The notion of entity subtypes and supertypes has been discussed briefly in several sections of the present chapter. We now examine it in detail.

Any given entity is of at least one entity type; for example, any given employee is an instance of the EMPLOYEE entity type. An entity may be of several types simultaneously. For example, a given employee may simultaneously be

a) an EMPLOYEE;

b) a MANAGER (where MANAGER is an immediate *subtype* of EMPLOYEE, or, equivalently, EMPLOYEE is an immediate *supertype* of MANAGER);

c) an ENGINEER (where ENGINEER is another immediate subtype of EM-PLOYEE);

d) an ELECTRONICS_ENGINEER (where ELECTRONICS_ENGINEER is an immediate subtype of ENGINEER, and consequently a second-level subtype of EMPLOYEE);

e) a STOCKHOLDER (an independent entity type, that is, an entity type that is neither a subtype nor a supertype of EMPLOYEE);

f) a CUSTOMER (another independent entity type);

and so on. When a new entity is first entered into the database, the user must specify at least one type for that entity. The system will assign a surrogate value to the new entity and will enter it into the E-relation for the specified entity type, and also into all applicable supertype E-relations (for example, creating an instance of ELEC-TRONICS_ENGINEER will cause the new surrogate to be entered into the ELEC-TRONICS_ENGINEER, ENGINEER, and EMPLOYEE E-relations). Note that a given entity may acquire or lose types dynamically (for example, an employee may become a stockholder).

Type Hierarchies

A given entity type and its immediate subtypes, their immediate subtypes, and so on, together constitute the *type hierarchy*—also called the *generalization hierarchy*—for the entity type in question. See Fig. 6.1 for an example. The term "generalization" derives from the fact that, for example, ENGINEER is a generalization of both ELECTRONICS_ENGINEER and MECHANICAL_ENGINEER; equivalently, ELECTRONICS_ENGINEER and MECHANICAL_ENGINEER are both *specializations* of ENGINEER, in the sense that all the properties (and characteristics and associations and designations) that apply to an engineer also apply to both electronics engineers and mechanical engineers (an instance of the *property inheritance rule*). The converse is not true, of course; there will be properties (etc.) that apply, for example, to electronics engineers in particular but not to engineers in general.

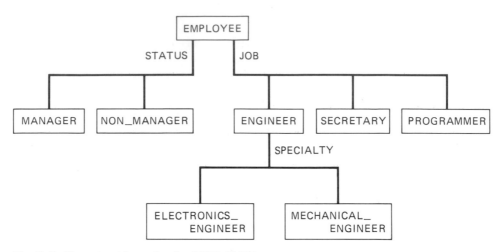

Fig. 6.1 The type hierarchy for EMPLOYEE.

The example of Fig. 6.1 also illustrates the fact that a given supertype may be divided into several distinct *categories* of subtypes: in the example, MANAGER and NON_MANAGER form one such category (for supertype EMPLOYEE); ENGINEER, SECRETARY, and PROGRAMMER form another (again for supertype EMPLOYEE); and ELECTRONICS_ENGINEER and MECHANICAL_ENGINEER form another (for supertype ENGINEER). The categories are indicated by the labels on the edges in the type hierarchy (STATUS, JOB, and SPECIALTY). We assume that a given instance of the supertype will be an instance of at most one subtype in each category[13] (that is, a given employee cannot be both a manager and a nonmanager, and cannot hold more than one of the three jobs engineer, secretary, and programmer; similarly, a given engineer cannot be both an electronics engineer and a mechanical engineer). Note that an instance of the supertype might not be an instance of *any* subtype in a given category (a given employee might not hold any of the three indicated jobs). If it *is* the case that, with respect to a given category, every instance of the supertype does have to be an instance of some subtype in that category, then we say that the set of subtypes *spans* the supertype per that category—or, more succinctly, that the category spans (or partitions) the supertype. For example, the set of subtypes (MANAGER,NON_MANAGER) spans the supertype EMPLOYEE per the category STATUS. On the other hand, the set of subtypes (ENGINEER,SECRETARY,PROGRAMMER) does not span the supertype EMPLOYEE per the category JOB.

---

13. This restriction is not absolutely necessary (though it will often be satisfied in practice). A given engineer *could* be both an electronics engineer and a mechanical engineer, for example. But in this book we will generally consider only the simple case in which the restriction is satisfied. For discussion of the more general case, see [6.1].

We now show a possible set of relation definitions corresponding to Fig. 6.1. For simplicity we assume throughout that each E-relation has exactly one corresponding P-relation. Also, we ignore the fact that in practice EMPLOYEE would probably be a designative entity type also, involving designations for departments and managers (for example).

```
CREATE E_RELATION EMPLOYEE ;

CREATE P_RELATION EMPLOYEE_PROPERTIES
       FOR E_RELATION EMPLOYEE
       PROPERTIES ( ..... ,
                    JOB     DOMAIN ( ... ) ,
                    SALARY DOMAIN ( ... ) ,
                    ..... ) ;
```

One reason for structuring entity types into a type hierarchy is to avoid explicit occurrences of the "property inapplicable" null value as far as possible. Hence, for example, we place the BUDGET property (see the MANAGER_PROPERTIES P-relation below) at the MANAGER position in the hierarchy, rather than at the EMPLOYEE position, because BUDGET is a property that does not apply to nonmanagers. (If BUDGET did appear at the EMPLOYEE position, then EMPLOYEE_PROPERTIES tuples for nonmanagers would have to show the value of that attribute explicitly as the "property inapplicable" null.) By contrast, we place the SALARY property at the EMPLOYEE position, because salaries do apply to all employees, regardless of their status (and regardless of their job). Note, however, that the choice of where in the tree to place a particular property is left to the database designer; RM/T does not insist that explicit nulls be avoided, it merely provides the type mechanism to assist in achieving that objective if it is considered desirable to do so.

Note also that we include a property at the EMPLOYEE position corresponding to one of the two subtype categories (JOB) but not the other (STATUS). The reason for this choice has to do with the fact that the STATUS category spans the EMPLOYEE type whereas the JOB category does not. The JOB *property,* an attribute of the P-relation EMPLOYEE_PROPERTIES, can take on the values 'ENGINEER', 'SECRETARY', 'PROGRAMMER', *and other values besides*—say, 'ACCOUNTANT', 'GARDENER', and so on. For a given employee, if the JOB property is 'ENGINEER', 'SECRETARY', or 'PROGRAMMER', then of course that employee will be represented as an instance of the appropriate subtype also; but if the JOB property is something else, then that employee will not appear at the next level at all. Now suppose we were to include a STATUS property at the EMPLOYEE position, with possible values 'MANAGER' and 'NON_MANAGER'. Then a given employee will be represented as an instance of the MANAGER subtype if and only if the value of the STATUS property for that employee is 'MANAGER'; and similarly for NON_MANAGER, *mutatis mutandis.* In other words, the STATUS property would be redundant; the status of a given employee could always be determined by seeing which of the two subtype E-relations (per the STATUS category) the employee appears in. From this example, we conclude that a property corresponding to a given category is required at the supertype position when the category in question does not span the supertype, but not otherwise (though again the choice in the latter case is left to the database designer).

Even if STATUS is not included as a property at the EMPLOYEE position (in the P-relation EMPLOYEE_PROPERTIES), an external user can still be provided with a view of employees as an *n*-ary relation that does include a STATUS attribute (with values 'MANAGER', 'NON_MANAGER'). That attribute will be *derived* from the categorization in the type hierarchy, using certain of the new RM/T operators. See Example 6.12.5.

To continue with the definitions corresponding to Fig. 6.1:

```
CREATE E_RELATION MANAGER SUBTYPE OF EMPLOYEE
                           PER CATEGORY STATUS ;
```

The "SUBTYPE OF . . . PER CATEGORY . . ." entry defines a subtype/supertype relationship. In general it would be desirable to indicate whether or not the specified category spans the supertype, but we omit any such specification from the hypothetical syntax shown here.

```
CREATE P_RELATION MANAGER_PROPERTIES
        FOR E_RELATION MANAGER
        PROPERTIES ( ..... ,
                    BUDGET  DOMAIN ( ... ) ,
                    ..... ) ;

CREATE E_RELATION NON_MANAGER SUBTYPE OF EMPLOYEE
                              PER CATEGORY STATUS ;

CREATE P_RELATION NON_MANAGER_PROPERTIES
        FOR E_RELATION NON_MANAGER
        PROPERTIES ( ..... ) ;

CREATE E_RELATION ENGINEER SUBTYPE OF EMPLOYEE
                           PER CATEGORY JOB ;

CREATE P_RELATION ENGINEER_PROPERTIES
        FOR E_RELATION ENGINEER
        PROPERTIES ( ..... ,
                    SPECIALTY  DOMAIN ( ... ) ,
                    ..... ) ;

CREATE E_RELATION SECRETARY SUBTYPE OF EMPLOYEE
                            PER CATEGORY JOB ;
```

```
CREATE P_RELATION SECRETARY_PROPERTIES
       FOR E_RELATION SECRETARY
       PROPERTIES ( ..... ) ;

CREATE E_RELATION PROGRAMMER SUBTYPE OF EMPLOYEE
                           PER CATEGORY JOB ;

CREATE P_RELATION PROGRAMMER_PROPERTIES
       FOR E_RELATION PROGRAMMER
       PROPERTIES ( ..... ) ;

CREATE E_RELATION ELECTRONICS_ENGINEER SUBTYPE OF ENGINEER
                                    PER CATEGORY SPECIALTY ;

CREATE P_RELATION ELECTRONICS_ENGINEER_PROPERTIES
       FOR E_RELATION ELECTRONICS_ENGINEER
       PROPERTIES ( ..... ) ;

CREATE E_RELATION MECHANICAL_ENGINEER SUBTYPE OF ENGINEER
                                    PER CATEGORY SPECIALTY ;

CREATE P_RELATION MECHANICAL_ENGINEER_PROPERTIES
       FOR E_RELATION MECHANICAL_ENGINEER
       PROPERTIES ( ..... ) ;
```

We introduce another naming convention (needed for the new RM/T operators discussed in Section 6.12). Let X be an entity type, and let Y be an entity type that is a subtype (at any level) of entity type X. The sole attribute of the E-relation corresponding to X has attribute-name X¢. Likewise, the sole attribute of the E-relation corresponding to Y has attribute-name Y¢. In addition, attribute Y¢ has an *alias* that is inherited from X, namely X¢. For example, referring to Fig. 6.1, attribute ELECTRONICS_ENGINEER¢ of the E-relation ELECTRONICS_ENGINEER can be referred to by any of the following (qualified) names:

```
ELECTRONICS_ENGINEER . ELECTRONICS_ENGINEER¢
ELECTRONICS_ENGINEER . ENGINEER¢
ELECTRONICS_ENGINEER . EMPLOYEE¢
```

Multiple Supertypes

So far we have tacitly assumed that a given subtype is a subtype of exactly one immediate supertype. It is also possible that a given subtype may generalize to multiple independent immediate supertypes (per multiple categories), in which case a given instance of the subtype will simultaneously be an instance of each of those supertypes. In other words, type hierarchies are not necessarily disjoint. An illustration is given in Fig. 6.2 (the categorization is vastly oversimplified for the sake of the example). Another example might be obtained by extending Fig. 6.1 to show (for

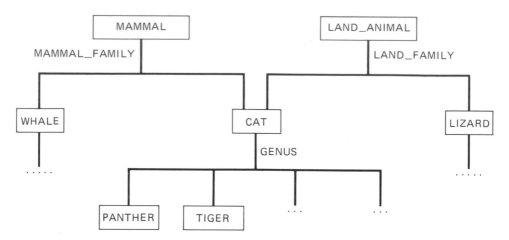

Fig. 6.2 Type hierarchies are not necessarily disjoint.

example) ENGINEERING_MANAGER as a subtype of both MANAGER and ENGINEER. Note carefully that the only reason for introducing a subtype that generalizes to multiple independent supertypes is to allow that subtype to inherit properties from all those supertypes (as well as having properties of its own).

Subtype Integrity

We have already mentioned (Section 6.9) that a reference from an E-relation for a subtype to the E-relation for an immediate supertype of that subtype is a *subtype reference*. Subtype references are constrained by the following integrity rule.

Integrity Rule 8 (Subtype Integrity)

> Whenever a surrogate (say e) belongs to the E-relation for an entity of type E, e must also belong to the E-relation for each entity type for which E is a subtype.

The effect of this rule on the external-level user will of course depend on how entity subtypes and supertypes are materialized to that user. For example, if STATUS ('MANAGER' or 'NON_MANAGER') is represented to the user as an attribute of EMPLOYEE, then (a) that attribute must be specified as "nulls not allowed," and (b) creating an instance of EMPLOYEE must cause the system to enter the new surrogate into the appropriate subtype E-relation as well as into the EMPLOYEE E-relation. (Also, updating that attribute for a given employee must cause that employee to move from one of the subtype E-relations to the other.) Further operational implications of Rule 8 are left as another exercise for the reader.

Alternative Generalization

We conclude this section by mentioning the fact that reference [6.1] also introduces the notion of *alternative generalization* (as opposed to unconditional generalization, which is what we have been discussing so far). "Alternative generalization" refers to the possibility that a given entity type Y may be a *conditional* subtype of a *set* of supertypes X1, X2, . . . , Xn, in the sense that every instance of Y is also an instance of exactly one of the Xi (i = 1, . . . , n), but not every instance of the Xi is an instance of Y. (Without this latter condition, we could treat the Xi as subtypes of Y instead of as supertypes.) We exclude this topic from detailed examination here because it is our belief that it requires considerably more study; it is not clear that the slight increase in function provided justifies the accompanying increase in complexity (which is significant).

6.11   THE RM/T CATALOG

In this section we attempt to pull together some of the many ideas presented in the preceding sections by describing a possible catalog structure for RM/T. The following design should clearly be regarded as preliminary, and indeed as minimal, in the sense that any real implementation would certainly have to introduce numerous further attributes and further relations in addition to those that we show here. Also, the arguments that justify the overall RM/T approach to representing information—for example, the fact that user keys are subject to change, which leads to the need for surrogates—apply with equal force to the catalog itself; for instance, relations should be identified in the catalog by surrogate, not by their external name; but for brevity and simplicity we show the catalog as if it were a collection of "external" (n-ary) relations, with all surrogates hidden and without any explicit separation into E-relations and P-relations. Whether the catalog should physically be represented in this manner is an implementation issue that is beyond the scope of this chapter. (For simplicity, again, we omit all mention of underlying domains in our definitions of the catalog relations. Similarly, we also omit any specification of the various referential constraints that hold among those relations.)

The first three relations we need are DOMAINS, RELATIONS, and ATTRIBUTES (with the obvious intuitive interpretation):

```
DOMAINS      ( DOMNAME, DATATYPE, ORDERING )
             PRIMARY KEY ( DOMNAME )

RELATIONS    ( RELNAME, RELTYPE )
             PRIMARY KEY ( RELNAME )

ATTRIBUTES ( RELNAME, ATTNAME, DOMNAME, PKEY, UKEY, NULLS )
             PRIMARY KEY ( RELNAME, ATTNAME )
```

■   The DOMAINS relation contains a tuple for each domain in the database, giving the name (DOMNAME) and data-type (DATATYPE) for the domain in question and indicating whether that domain is ordered (ORDERING is either YES or NO).

■   The RELATIONS relation contains a tuple for every relation in the database, giving the name (RELNAME) and type (RELTYPE) of the relation in question. The type of a relation is one of the following:

catalog relation:

E-relation;

P-relation.

In the case of an E-relation, the relation type is further qualified to indicate

whether the entity type is kernel, characteristic, or associative;

whether the entity type is designative;

whether the entity type is a subtype (if it is not, it is referred to as "inner").

■   The ATTRIBUTES relation contains a tuple for each attribute of each relation in the database, giving the relation-name, attribute-name, and underlying domain-name, and indicating also: (a) whether the attribute participates in the primary key of the relation concerned (PKEY is YES or NO); (b) whether it participates in a user key for the entity type concerned (UKEY is YES or NO); and (c) whether it can accept null values (NULLS is YES or NO).

The catalog also includes a set of *graph relations,* whose function is to represent the various connections among relations in the database—for example, the connection between an E-relation and its corresponding P-relation(s). The graph relations are as follows:

PG   :   the property graph relation

CG   :   the characteristic graph relation

AG   :   the association graph relation

DG   :   the designation graph relation

SG   :   the subtype graph relation

With respect to the subtype graph relation SG, we should explain that we are considering only unconditional generalization here. Reference [6.1] has two graph relations in place of relation SG, one for unconditional generalization and one for alternative generalization. Also, reference [6.1] does not mention the designation graph relation (DG) at all.

The Property Graph

Relation PG contains a tuple for every P-relation in the database, giving the name of that P-relation and the name of the corresponding E-relation:

```
PG ( P_RELNAME, E_RELNAME )
    PRIMARY KEY ( P_RELNAME )
```

For example, relation PG for the suppliers-and-parts database would look like this (in part):

PG

P_RELNAME	E_RELNAME
SKN	S
ST	S
SC	S
PKN	P
.	.
.	.
.	.
SPSP	SP
.	.

The property graph is a collection of disjoint trees, in the sense that no two E-relations have a P-relation in common. Each of those trees consists of a "parent" (the E-relation) and a set of "children" (the P-relations), and thus involves exactly two levels.

The Characteristic Graph

Relation CG contains a tuple for every characteristic E-relation in the database, giving the name of that E-relation and the name of the immediately superior E-relation:

```
CG ( CHARACTERISTIC_E_RELNAME, SUPERIOR_E_RELNAME )
    PRIMARY KEY ( CHARACTERISTIC_E_RELNAME )
```

For example:

CG

CHARACTERISTIC_ E_RELNAME	SUPERIOR_ E_RELNAME
ORDLINE	ORDER
.	.
.	.

The characteristic graph, like the property graph, is a collection of disjoint trees. Individual trees are not necessarily restricted to two levels (superior entity type T1 may have a characteristic entity type T2, which in turn may have a lower-level characteristic entity type T3, and so on).

The Association Graph

Relation AG contains a tuple for every participant in every association in the database (as usual, we are ignoring nonentity associations). Each such tuple gives the names of the E-relations for the participant and the association, together with the name of the property (attribute) of the association that identifies the participant:

```
AG ( ASSOCIATION_E_RELNAME ,
        ASSOCIATION_P_ATTNAME ,
           PARTICIPANT_E_RELNAME )
    PRIMARY KEY ( ASSOCIATION_E_RELNAME, ASSOCIATION_P_ATTNAME )
```

For example:

AG

ASSOCIATION_ E_RELNAME	ASSOCIATION_ P_ATTNAME	PARTICIPANT_ E_RELNAME
SP SP . .	S¢ P¢ . .	S P . .

(Exercise for the reader: Why were no attribute-names needed in relations PG and CG?)

The association graph is not a collection of disjoint trees, in general (a given entity type can participate multiple times in a given association and/or in multiple associations).

The Designation Graph

Relation DG contains a tuple for every designation in the database. Each such tuple gives the names of the E-relations for the designated and designative entity types, together with the attribute-name for the designative property:

```
DG ( DESIGNATIVE_E_RELNAME ,
        DESIGNATIVE_P_ATTNAME ,
           DESIGNATED_E_RELNAME )
    PRIMARY KEY ( DESIGNATIVE_E_RELNAME, DESIGNATIVE_P_ATTNAME )
```

For example:

DG

DESIGNATIVE_ E_RELNAME	DESIGNATIVE_ P_ATTNAME	DESIGNATED_ E_RELNAME
S	CITY¢	CITY
P	CITY¢	CITY
.	.	.
.	.	.

The designation graph is not a collection of disjoint trees, in general.

The Subtype Graph

Relation SG contains a tuple for every immediate subtype/supertype relationship in the database. Each such tuple gives the names of the E-relations for the subtype and the supertype, together with the name of the applicable category:

```
SG ( SUBTYPE_E_RELNAME, SUPERTYPE_E_RELNAME, CATEGORY )
    PRIMARY KEY ( SUBTYPE_E_RELNAME, SUPERTYPE_E_RELNAME )
```

For example:

SG

SUBTYPE_ E_RELNAME	SUPERTYPE_ E_RELNAME	CATEGORY
MANAGER	EMPLOYEE	STATUS
NON_MANAGER	EMPLOYEE	STATUS
ENGINEER	EMPLOYEE	JOB
SECRETARY	EMPLOYEE	JOB
PROGRAMMER	EMPLOYEE	JOB
ELECTRONICS_ ENGINEER	ENGINEER	SPECIALTY
MECHANICAL_ ENGINEER	ENGINEER	SPECIALTY
.	.	.
.	.	.

The subtype graph is not a collection of disjoint trees, in general.

We note that the system will also need to know when two independent entity types (such as CUSTOMER and STOCKHOLDER) can "overlap," in the sense that a given entity can simultaneously be an instance of both. This information can be represented by introducing yet another catalog relation. The details are left as an exercise for the reader.

6.12   RM/T OPERATORS

What distinguishes RM/T from most other proposals in the semantic modeling area is that it provides, not only a set of objects and rules as described in the foregoing sections,[14] but also a corresponding set of high-level *operators*. Those operators permit (among other things) the definition of widely varying user views over a common underlying database,[15] and moreover allow those definitions to be comparatively independent of the precise structure of that underlying database. Let us consider an example. Suppose that suppliers, parts, and shipments are represented by the E-relations and P-relations discussed in Sections 6.4 and 6.5. Using only the operators of the basic relational model, we could provide user views of these three entity types as the familiar three *n*-ary relations S (degree 4), P (degree 5), and SP (degree 3). However, each of the three view definitions would have to be thought out and formulated independently; each would involve several distinct algebraic operations, and moreover each would be highly sensitive to changes in the RM/T-level definition of the database (consider the effect of breaking the supplier P-relation SKN into two, one each for S# and SNAME, for example). RM/T, however, provides a single operator, the PROPERTY operator, whose effect is to gather together *all* the immediate properties for a specified entity type into a single *n*-ary relation, regardless of how many properties there are, regardless of how those properties are grouped into P-relations, and regardless of the naming structure of those P-relations. We discuss this operator following Example 6.12.1 below.

We do not attempt a comprehensive description of all the operators defined in [6.1] here. In any case, the definitions of [6.1] should to some extent be regarded as preliminary; there are certainly other useful operations that could be defined in addition to those of [6.1], and those that are defined in [6.1] could do with some refinement. We therefore content ourselves with a set of examples indicating the general range of applicability of the operations, giving informal definitions as we go of those particular ones we need. For further information and further examples, the reader is referred to [6.1].

The syntax used in these examples is for expository purposes only and requires further work.

Example 6.12.1   Given an E-relation and a set of P-relations for suppliers (for example, as defined in Sections 6.4 and 6.5), construct a single *n*-ary relation S having as attributes the set of all supplier properties. Do not make any assumptions regarding the number or structure of those P-relations. Do not include the S¢ attribute in the final result.

---

14. Indeed, the objects per se are not even particularly new (though RM/T does tend to be rather more specific about their formal representation than do most comparable proposals). Reference [6.1] identifies the work of Hall, Owlett, and Todd [6.12], Smith and Smith [6.13], Schmid and Swenson [6.14], and Hammer and McLeod [6.15] as all being major influences on this aspect of RM/T.

15. Examples 6.12.1–6.12.6 on the next few pages illustrate this aspect very clearly.

Step 1: Find the names of all P-relations for entity type S.

```
TEMP1   :=   THETA_SELECT ( PG, E_RELNAME = 'S' ) ;
TEMP2   :=   PROJECT ( TEMP1, P_RELNAME ) ;
```

Step 2: Append the E-relation name 'S' to the result of Step 1.

```
TEMP3   :=   UNION ( TEMP2, 'S' ) ;
```

Step 3: Collect together all the relations whose names appear in TEMP3.

```
TEMP4   :=   DENOTE ( TEMP3 ) ;
```

Step 4: Form the outer natural join of all relations in TEMP4 over their common attribute S¢.

```
TEMP5   :=   COMPRESS ( TEMP4, ( OUTER_NATURAL_JOIN, 'S¢' ) ) ;
```

Step 5: Eliminate attribute S¢ from the result of Step 4.

```
S       :=   PROJECT ( TEMP5, BAR ( TEMP5, S¢ ) ) ;
```

Explanations

First note that we have shown the example as constructing a *separate copy* of the data (each step involves one or more *assignment* operations). Of course, it is also possible to use essentially the same sequence of operations to define a virtual relation (view) instead, as in the basic model. It is not our purpose to get involved in such refinements here.

   Step 1 uses the property graph relation PG and the normal relational algebra operators THETA_SELECT and PROJECT to build a unary relation TEMP2 that contains the set of P-relation names for the E-relation S. (If the P-relations are as shown in Section 6.5, then TEMP2 will now contain the names 'SKN', 'ST', and 'SC'.)

   Step 2 appends the E-relation name 'S' to the set of names in TEMP2 and places the result in TEMP3.

   Step 3 uses the operator DENOTE to form in TEMP4 the set of corresponding relations themselves (DENOTE applied to a relation-name returns the relation denoted by that name; DENOTE applied to a set—actually a unary relation—of relation-names returns the set of relations denoted by those names.) Note that TEMP4 itself is not a relation.

   Step 4 uses the COMPRESS operator to reduce the set of relations in TEMP4 to a single relation and then to place that single relation in TEMP5. COMPRESS applied to a set of relations returns a single relation, obtained by repeatedly replacing pairs of relations in the set by a single relation until only one relation is left. The replacement involves applying the operation specified in the COMPRESS—in the example, outer natural join over S¢—to an arbitrary pair of relations in the set and then substituting the result of that application for that pair. The operation specified within the COMPRESS must be both associative and commutative.

Finally, *Step 5* eliminates the S¢ attribute from the result of Step 4 by means of the normal PROJECT operator, and assigns the result to relation S. If R is a relation and A is an attribute (possibly composite) of R, the notation BAR(R,A) refers to the set of attributes of R not included in A. Thus PROJECT(TEMP5,BAR (TEMP5,S¢)) forms the projection of TEMP5 over all attributes *except* S¢.

As suggested at the beginning of the section, it is possible to extrapolate from this example to define a general PROPERTY operator (effectively a kind of macro), whose argument is an entity type name (shown below as &X), and whose result is "the comprehensive P-relation" for that entity type:

```
PROPERTY ( &X ) ≡
   COMPRESS ( DENOTE
                ( UNION
                    ( PROJECT
                        ( THETA_SELECT
                            ( PG, E_RELNAME = '&X' ),
                              P_RELNAME ), '&X' ) ),
                          ( OUTER_NATURAL_JOIN,
                              '&X'||'¢' ) )
```

The operator || represents concatenation (as in PL/I). Note that we define "the comprehensive P-relation" for a given entity type T to be the outer join of all individual P-relations and the E-relation for T, taken over the primary key attribute T¢. It thus includes that T¢ attribute. By contrast, the primary key attribute S¢ was eliminated from the final result in Example 6.12.1 (see Step 5).

Example 6.12.2 Let T be an entity type with immediate characteristic entity types A, B, C, ... Let PT, PA, PB, PC, . . . be the comprehensive P-relations for T, A, B, C . . . , respectively. Form the relation CT consisting of the outer natural join of PT, PA, PB, PC, . . . over T¢ (that is, the relation showing all properties of T, including those of its immediate characteristics).

Step 1: Find the names of all immediate characteristic E-relations for entity type T.

```
TEMP1   :=   THETA_SELECT ( CG, SUPERIOR_E_RELNAME = 'T' ) ;
TEMP2   :=   PROJECT ( TEMP1, CHARACTERISTIC_E_RELNAME ) ;
```

Step 2: Append the E-relation name 'T' to the result of Step 1.

```
TEMP3   :=   UNION ( TEMP2, 'T' ) ;
```

Step 3: Form the set of comprehensive P-relations for the entity types whose names (E-relation names) appear in TEMP3.

```
TEMP4   :=   APPLY ( PROPERTY, TEMP3 ) ;
```

Step 4: Form the required outer natural join.

```
CT      :=   COMPRESS ( TEMP4, ( OUTER_NATURAL_JOIN, 'T¢' ) ) ;
```

The only step requiring any additional explanation here is *Step 3*. APPLY is an operator that takes as arguments an operator *f* and a set X, and produces as result the set of all objects *f(x)* obtained by applying *f* to *x* where *x* is a member of X. Thus APPLY(PROPERTY,TEMP3) generates the set of comprehensive P-relations for the set of entity types whose names are given in TEMP3.

Suppose we had wanted, not the complete outer join CT, but simply the set of all tuples (T¢:t,A¢:a,B¢:b,C¢:c, . . .) such that the entities identified by a, b, c, . . . are all immediate characteristics of the entity identified by t. This relation is a projection of relation CT; it can be obtained by evaluating

```
PROJECT ( CT, ( TEMP3 || '¢' ) ) ,
```

where we assume that the expression TEMP3||'¢' causes the symbol "¢" to be appended to each name in the set TEMP3.

Example 6.12.3 Let T be an associative entity type, with property attributes TX¢, TY¢, TZ¢, . . . identifying participants X, Y, Z, ... Let PT, PX, PY, PZ, . . . be the comprehensive P-relations for T, X, Y, Z, . . . , respectively. Form the relation AT consisting of the outer natural join of PT, PX, PY, PZ, . . . , where the join is taken over TX¢ and X¢ for relations PT and PX, over TY¢ and Y¢ for relations PT and PY, over TZ¢ and Z¢ for relations PT and PZ, and so on. Do not make any assumptions concerning the actual names of the association reference attributes (we used the names TX¢, TY¢, TZ¢, . . . purely as examples).

We include this problem as a challenge for the reader. RM/T as currently defined does not include all the operators needed to handle this problem. As indicated at the beginning of the section, the RM/T operators are still in need of further definition and refinement.

Example 6.12.4 Construct a relation giving all properties of the entity type ENGINEER, including those of its immediate supertype (per category JOB) EMPLOYEE (see Fig. 6.1).

```
TEMP1   :=   PROPERTY ( 'EMPLOYEE' ) ;
TEMP2   :=   PROPERTY ( 'ENGINEER' ) ;
RESULT  :=   NATURAL_JOIN ( TEMP1, TEMP2, EMPLOYEE¢ = ENGINEER¢ ) ;
```

Note that we need the regular natural join, not the outer natural join, in this example (why?). Note also that the joining condition could equally well have been expressed in the form

```
EMPLOYEE¢ = EMPLOYEE¢   ,
```

since EMPLOYEE¢ is an alias for ENGINEER¢ (see Section 6.10).

Example 6.12.5 Construct a relation (EMPLOYEE¢,STATUS) consisting of all pairs (e,s) such that e is the surrogate of an employee and s is the status of that employee (see Fig. 6.1). Assume that the STATUS category partitions the EMPLOYEE type, but do not make any assumptions regarding the status values (that is, the names of the subtypes).

```
TEMP1   :=  THETA_SELECT ( SG, SUPERTYPE_E_RELNAME = 'EMPLOYEE'
                              AND CATEGORY          = 'STATUS' ) ;
TEMP2   :=  PROJECT ( TEMP1, SUBTYPE_E_RELNAME ) ;
TEMP3   :=  DENOTE ( TEMP2 ) ;
TEMP4   :=  APPLY ( TAG, TEMP3 ) ;
RESULT  :=  COMPRESS ( TEMP4, UNION ) ;
```

The only new operation introduced here is TAG. TAG applied to a relation R returns a relation that is a copy of R extended to include one additional attribute; the value of that attribute in every tuple is the character string representation of the name of R. Thus TAG "tags" the tuples of a relation with the name of that relation. In the example, TEMP3 is a *set* of relations, containing in fact the two E-relations MANAGER and NON_MANAGER; TEMP4 therefore contains two binary relations, one consisting of the set of all tuples (e,'MANAGER') where e identifies a manager, and the other consisting of the set of all tuples (e,'NON_MANAGER') where e identifies a nonmanager. We then compress these two relations into a single relation by means of UNION.

Example 6.12.6 Given the representation of suppliers shown in Sections 6.4 and 6.5, construct a set of relations (in effect, subtype E-relations) such that

a) there is one such relation for each distinct supplier city;

b) each such relation contains precisely the surrogates for suppliers located in the applicable city.

```
TEMP1   :=  PARTITION ( SC, CITY ) ;
RESULT  :=  APPLY ( ( PROJECT, S¢ ), TEMP1 ) ;
```

Let R be a relation and let A be an attribute of that relation. Then PARTITION(R,A) is the set of relations obtained by partitioning R in accordance with the set of all distinct values of A. (PARTITION is essentially identical to the GROUP BY operator of SQL.)

6.13 SUMMARY

We have devoted this chapter to a detailed discussion of one particular extended model, RM/T. The reader should realize that an extended model such as RM/T can be used as a discipline and an aid to systematic database design, even in the absence of direct system support for that model—just as the basic relational model has similarly been used for some time as a (more primitive) design aid in systems that do not directly support relational databases at all. The study of such models should thus not be regarded as just an academic exercise.

In this final section we summarize the major aspects of RM/T (as we have presented them in this chapter) by giving short reference lists for each of the following:

- the new objects;
- the new operators;
- the new integrity rules;
- the naming conventions;
- the catalog relations.

We also give a summary BNF definition for the (incomplete) hypothetical syntax we have been using to illustrate the manner in which the RM/T-level objects might be defined (CREATE E_RELATION, etc.).

Objects

Informal

- entity, entity type
- kernel, characteristic, association
- designation
- subtype, supertype

Formal

- surrogate
- E-null
- E-domain
- E-attribute
- E-relation
- P-relation
- characteristic relation
- catalog relations
- set of relations

Operators

DENOTE
COMPRESS
BAR
PROPERTY
APPLY
TAG
PARTITION
(plus others, not discussed in this chapter)

Integrity Rules

Integrity Rule 3 (Entity Integrity in RM/T): E-relations accept insertions and deletions but not updates.

Integrity Rule 4 (Property Integrity): If a tuple t appears in a P-relation P, then the (surrogate) primary key value of t must appear in the E-relation corresponding to P.

Integrity Rule 5 (Characteristic Integrity): A characteristic entity cannot exist in the database unless the entity it most immediately describes is also in the database.

Integrity Rule 6 (Association Integrity): Let A be an associative entity type, and let E be the set of E-attributes whose function is to identify the participants in A. Then a given instance of A can exist in the database only if, for that instance, each E-attribute in E either (a) has the value E-null, or (b) identifies an existing entity of the appropriate type.

Integrity Rule 7 (Designative Integrity): Let D be a designative entity type, and let E be the set of E-attributes representing designations by D. Then a given instance of D can exist in the database only if, for that instance, each E-attribute in E either (a) has the value E-null, or (b) identifies an existing entity of the appropriate type.

Integrity Rule 8 (Subtype Integrity): Whenever a surrogate (say e) belongs to the E-relation for an entity of type E, e must also belong to the E-relation for each entity type for which E is a subtype.

Naming Conventions

1. The symbol "¢" is used as the name of the E-domain.

2. Every E-attribute has a name that ends in "¢" (and no other attributes have such a name).

3. The E-relation for a given entity type is given the same name as that entity type.

4. The single attribute of an E-relation is given a name that is obtained by appending a trailing "¢" to the relation-name.

5. The primary key of every P-relation is an E-attribute with the same name as the single attribute of the corresponding E-relation.

6. No two P-relations for a given E-relation have any attribute-names in common except as specified under paragraph 5.

7. The P-relations for a given entity type do not have any attribute-names in common with the P-relations for any supertype (at any level) of that entity type.

8. The P-relations for a given characteristic entity type include exactly one attribute whose name is the same as that of the sole attribute of the E-relation for the immediate superior type of that characteristic type.

9. No property of a characteristic entity type can have the same attribute-name as any property of any superior entity type, at any level.

10. Let X be an entity type, and let Y be an entity type that is a subtype (at any level) of entity type X. The sole attribute of the E-relation corresponding to X has attribute-name X¢. Likewise, the sole attribute of the E-relation corresponding to Y has attribute-name Y¢. In addition, attribute Y¢ has an *alias* that is inherited from X, namely X¢.

Catalog Relations

Domain List

```
DOMAINS     ( DOMNAME, DATATYPE, ORDERING)
            PRIMARY KEY ( DOMNAME )
```

Relation List

```
RELATIONS   ( RELNAME, RELTYPE )
            PRIMARY KEY ( RELNAME )
```

Attribute List

```
ATTRIBUTES ( RELNAME, ATTNAME, DOMNAME, PKEY, UKEY, NULLS)
            PRIMARY KEY ( RELNAME, ATTNAME )
```

Property Graph

```
PG ( P_RELNAME, E_RELNAME )
   PRIMARY KEY ( P_RELNAME )
```

Characteristic Graph

```
CG ( CHARACTERISTIC_E_RELNAME, SUPERIOR_E_RELNAME )
   PRIMARY KEY ( CHARACTERISTIC_E_RELNAME )
```

Association Graph

```
AG ( ASSOCIATION_E_RELNAME ,
        ASSOCIATION_P_ATTNAME ,
            PARTICIPANT_E_RELNAME )
   PRIMARY KEY ( ASSOCIATION_E_RELNAME, ASSOCIATION_P_ATTNAME )
```

Designation Graph

```
DG ( DESIGNATIVE_E_RELNAME ,
        DESIGNATIVE_P_ATTNAME ,
            DESIGNATED_E_RELNAME )
   PRIMARY KEY ( DESIGNATIVE_E_RELNAME, DESIGNATIVE_P_ATTNAME )
```

Subtype Graph

```
SG ( SUBTYPE_E_RELNAME, SUPERTYPE_E_RELNAME, CATEGORY )
   PRIMARY KEY ( SUBTYPE_E_RELNAME, SUPERTYPE_E_RELNAME )
```

Hypothetical Syntax

```
create-e-relation
    ::=    CREATE E_RELATION entity-type-name
              [ characteristic-spec
              | association-spec
              | subtype-spec ]
              [ designation-spec ]
              [ USER KEY ( attribute-name-commalist ) ] ;

characteristic-spec
    ::=    CHARACTERISTIC OF entity-type-name

association-spec
    ::=    ASSOCIATING ( participant-spec ,
                         participant-spec-commalist )

participant-spec
    ::=    entity-type-name VIA e-attribute-name

subtype-spec
    ::=    SUBTYPE OF entity-type-name PER category-name

designation-spec
    ::=    DESIGNATING ( participant-spec-commalist )

create-p-relation
    ::=    CREATE P_RELATION property-list-name
              FOR E_RELATION entity-type-name
              PROPERTIES ( property-spec-commalist ) ;

property-spec
    ::=    superior-defn | participant-defn | simple-attribute-defn

superior-defn
    ::=    SURROGATE FOR entity-type-name

participant-defn
    ::=    e-attribute-name SURROGATE FOR entity-type-name
                               [ NULLS ALLOWED ]

simple-attribute-defn
    ::=    attribute-name DOMAIN ( domain-name )
                               [ NULLS ALLOWED ]
```

For brevity, syntactic categories terminating in "-name" (for example, entity-type-name) are not further elaborated here.

We conclude by remarking that, in addition to the topics discussed in this chapter so far, reference [6.1] also gives some suggestions for the handling of *events* (entities that involve a start time or stop time or time of occurrence). Proposals for dealing with the time dimension in a database can also be found in references [6.7-6.11]. The reader is referred to those papers for more information. Likewise, reference [6.1] also discusses the concept of *aggregation* (see Chapter 5), and divides it into *Cartesian* aggregation and *cover* aggregation. Cartesian aggregation refers to such simple cases as the aggregation of an entity and all its properties, or an association and all its participants, and has tacitly been discussed in this chapter already. Cover aggregation refers to the grouping together of a possibly heterogeneous collection of entities into a higher-level object, in accordance with some kind of *membership* criterion (for example, a lending library may contain books, disks, and tapes). For more details, again, the reader is referred to [6.1], also to [6.15].

EXERCISES

6.1 Give an RM/T version of the education database of Exercise 5.1.

6.2 Assume that the suppliers-and-parts example is extended to allow parts to have multiple colors. Give (a) a suitable representation for part information, using only the basic relational model; (b) the same, using the constructs of RM/T. Ignore domains throughout. [Note: Your solution to part (a) could serve as an external-level view of your solution to part (b). Discuss the differences between the two solutions.]

6.3 It is sometimes suggested that the notion of a surrogate is essentially the old familiar DBTG notion of a database-key under a new name. Discuss.

6.4 What does "E-null" signify?

6.5 Can a characteristic entity be a participant in an association?

6.6 Can an associative entity also be designative?

6.7 Give an example of an association in which at least one of the participants is also an association.

6.8 Must a supertype of a characteristic entity type itself be a characteristic? Must a supertype of an associative entity type be associative? Must a supertype of a designative entity type be designative?

6.9 Redo Exercise 5.7 (subtypes and supertypes).

6.10 (Requires a knowledge of IMS.) A data dictionary for an IMS installation needs to keep track of numerous objects (for example, databases, segments, fields, indexes) and numerous relationships among those objects (for example, which segments are referenced in which DBDs, which PSBs refer to which DBDs, which databases are indexed by which other databases, which logical segments derive from which physical segments, which segments are parents to which segments). Define an appropriate dictionary structure for such information, using the constructs of RM/T.

6.11 Consider the SQL query

```
SELECT  S#
FROM    SP
WHERE   P# = 'P2'
```

("Find supplier numbers for suppliers who supply part P2"). Show the more primitive operations involved in executing this external-level operation, if the underlying RM/T-level representation of suppliers and parts is as defined in Sections 6.4 and 6.5.

6.12 Merge the association graph and designation graph (relations AG and DG) into a single degree-4 relation RG, such that the tuple (rn1,att,rn2,label) appears in RG if and only if the tuple (rn1,att,rn2) appears in AG (in which case the value of "label" is 'AG') *or* the tuple (rn1,att,rn2) appears in DG (in which case the value of "label" is 'DG').

6.13 Given an entity type T, construct a relation that lists all characteristic entity types of T, to all levels, and shows in each case the relative level of that characteristic below T. [Note: This exercise requires certain operators not discussed in Section 6.12. You may like to consider what those operators might be, before referring to the discussion given in the Answers section.]

6.14 Write a suitable set of referential and other integrity constraints for the relations of the RM/T catalog.

REFERENCES AND BIBLIOGRAPHY

References [6.12–6.14] are discussed in Chapter 5 (Section 5.6). Reference [6.5] is discussed in Chapter 2 (answer to Exercise 2.3).

6.1 E. F. Codd. "Extending the Database Relational Model to Capture More Meaning." *ACM TODS* **4**, No. 4 (December 1979).

6.2 W. Kent. "The Entity Join." *Proc. 5th International Conference on Very Large Data Bases* (October 1979).

6.3 F. Saltor. "Reflexio Critica Sobre RM/T (A Critique of RM/T)." *Prov. Convencio Informatica Llatina,* Barcelona, Spain, June 1981.

An analysis and critique of some aspects of [6.1]. The author is very critical of the fact that RM/T rests on an undefined notion, the notion of entity: ". . . there are no criteria strong and stable enough to determine which objects, facts, and abstractions should be considered entities and which not." He quite rightly observes that, if a "nonentity" in the database is elevated to entity status, then there will be serious repercussions on the RM/T-level design of the database; and similarly if an entity classification changes, for example, from characteristic to associative. He also suggests that such changes are comparatively painless in the basic relational model. Two points should be made, however:

a) While such changes can be accommodated quite straightforwardly *in the database* (schema) in the basic model, the effect on users might not be quite so painless. The point is, such changes correspond to changes in the perception of the real world, with corresponding changes in integrity constraints and the like. Those changes are likely to affect users and user programs rather than the database, precisely because users understand them and the database does not. The basic model is simply not sophisticated enough to understand, and hence react to, such changes. By contrast, the extended model does understand the significance of what is going on, at least to a greater degree, and is therefore necessarily more sensitive to change.

b) Though it is true that the RM/T-level design may have to change quite drastically (precisely because it is necessary to inform the system of the new state of affairs), the effects on the *external-level* user should be no more and no less than they were under the basic model. (By "external-level user" here we mean a user who is continuing to view the database by means of the familiar basic model, not one who is conscious of surrogates and the other new mechanisms introduced by RM/T.)

6.4 C. J. Date. "The Outer Join." Submitted to 8th International Conference on Very Large Data Bases (September 1982).

6.5 C. J. Date. "Referential Integrity." *Proc. 7th International Conference on Very Large Data Bases* (September 1981).

6.6 C. J. Date. "A Relational Dictionary Structure for IMS Databases and Related Objects." In preparation.

This paper will provide an answer to Exercise 6.10.

6.7 B. -M. Schueler. "Update Reconsidered." In G. M. Nijssen (ed.), *Architecture and Models in Data Base Management Systems.* North-Holland (1977).

Argues forcefully that delete and destructive (overwriting) update operations should be outlawed. Instead, every item in the database is perceived as a chronologically ordered stack: The top entry in the stack represents the current value of the item, previous values are represented by entries lower down (an update operation thus places a new entry on the top of the stack and pushes all existing entries one place down). Each entry is time-stamped, and all entries are accessible at all times. The author claims that such a scheme can dramatically simplify the structure of the system (in such areas as recovery, auditability, locking, archiving, understandability, usability, and so on), and hence reduce system costs and system limitations in a variety of ways. Moreover, the availability of new, cheap, high-capacity, write-once media, such as the optical disk, may make such a scheme quite practical to implement.

6.8 S. Jones and P. J. Mason. "Handling the Time Dimension in a Data Base." In S. M. Deen and P. Hammersley (eds.), *Proc. International Conference on Data Bases,* Aberdeen, Scotland (July 1980). Heyden and Son Ltd. (1980).

Describes a system that implements the "nondestructive update" ideas of Schueler [6.7]. Every tuple includes "start" and "end" attributes defining the period of validity of that tuple (a null "end" value means that the information is still current). A special form of join is provided that understands the concept of overlapping time periods.

6.9 K. A. Robinson. "An Entity/Event Data Modelling Method." *Comp. J.* **22,** No. 3 (August 1979).

6.10 B. Breutmann, E. Falkenberg, and R. Mauer. "CSL: A Language for Defining Conceptual Schemas." In G. Bracchi and G. M. Nijssen (eds.), *Data Base Architecture.* North-Holland (1979).

6.11 J. A. Bubenko, Jr. "The Temporal Dimension in Information Modeling." In G. M. Nijssen (ed.), *Architecture and Models in Data Base Management Systems.* North-Holland (1977).

6.12 P. Hall, J. Owlett, and S. J. P. Todd. "Relations and Entities." In G. M. Nijssen (ed.), *Modelling in Data Base Management Systems.* North-Holland (1976).

6.13 J. M. Smith and D. C. P. Smith. "Database Abstractions: Aggregation and Generalization." *ACM TODS* **2,** No. 2 (June 1977).

6.14 H. A. Schmid and J. R. Swenson. "On the Semantics of the Relational Data Model." *Proc. 1975 ACM SIGMOD International Conference on Management of Data.*

6.15 M. M. Hammer and D. J. McLeod. "The Semantic Data Model: A Modelling Mechanism for Database Applications." *Proc. 1978 ACM SIGMOD International Conference on Management of Data.*

ANSWERS TO SELECTED EXERCISES

6.1 *Kernel entity types:*

```
CREATE E_RELATION COURSE ;

CREATE E_RELATION EMPLOYEE ;

CREATE P_RELATION COURSE_PROPS
        FOR E_RELATION COURSE
        PROPERTIES ( COURSE# DOMAIN ( ... ) ,
                     TITLE   DOMAIN ( ... ) ) ;

CREATE P_RELATION EMPLOYEE_PROPS
        FOR E_RELATION EMPLOYEE
        PROPERTIES ( EMP#    DOMAIN ( ... ) ,
                     NAME    DOMAIN ( ... ) ) ;
```

Characteristic entity type:

```
CREATE E_RELATION OFFERING
        CHARACTERISTIC OF COURSE ;

CREATE P_RELATION OFFERING_PROPS
        FOR E_RELATION OFFERING
        PROPERTIES ( SURROGATE FOR COURSE ,
                     OFF#      DOMAIN ( ... ) ,
                     DATE      DOMAIN ( ... ) ,
                     LOCATION  DOMAIN ( ... ) ) ;
```

Associative entity types:

```
CREATE E_RELATION PREREQ
        ASSOCIATING ( COURSE VIA COURSE¢ ,
                      COURSE VIA PRE¢ ) ;

CREATE E_RELATION TEACHER
        ASSOCIATING ( OFFERING VIA OFFERING¢ ,
                      EMPLOYEE VIA EMPLOYEE¢ ) ;

CREATE E_RELATION STUDENT
        ASSOCIATING ( OFFERING VIA OFFERING¢ ,
                      EMPLOYEE VIA EMPLOYEE¢ ) ;

CREATE P_RELATION PREREQ_PROPS
        FOR E_RELATION PREREQ
        PROPERTIES ( COURSE¢ SURROGATE FOR COURSE ,
                     PRE¢     SURROGATE FOR COURSE ) ;

CREATE P_RELATION TEACHER_PROPS
        FOR E_RELATION TEACHER
        PROPERTIES ( OFFERING¢ SURROGATE FOR OFFERING ,
                     EMPLOYEE¢ SURROGATE FOR EMPLOYEE ) ;
```

```
CREATE P_RELATION STUDENT_PROPS
        FOR E_RELATION STUDENT
        PROPERTIES ( OFFERING¢ SURROGATE FOR OFFERING ,
                     EMPLOYEE¢ SURROGATE FOR EMPLOYEE ,
                     GRADE     DOMAIN ( ... ) ) ;
```

This is of course not the only possible design.

6.2 (a) Basic relational model solution:

Relations:

```
P       ( P#, PNAME, WEIGHT, CITY )
        PRIMARY KEY ( P# )
PC      ( P#, COLOR )
        PRIMARY KEY ( P#, COLOR )
```

Referential constraint:

```
PC.P# ->> P.P# /* PC.P# is a foreign key */
        DELETING CASCADES
        UPDATING CASCADES
```

Note that PC.P# cannot accept null values (why not?). Each PC tuple is existence-dependent on the corresponding P tuple.

  b) RM/T solution:

E-relations:

```
P       ( P¢ )                  /* kernel */
        PRIMARY KEY ( P¢ )
PC      ( PC¢ )                 /* characteristic */
        PRIMARY KEY ( PC¢ )
        CHARACTERISTIC OF P
```

P relations:

```
P_PROPS   ( P¢, P#, PNAME, WEIGHT, CITY )
            PRIMARY KEY ( P¢ )
PC_PROPS  ( PC¢, P¢, COLOR )
            PRIMARY KEY ( PC¢ )
```

Discussion:

Solution (b) seems much clumsier than solution (a). The idea of having to treat something so trifling as the color of a part as an entity is rather cumbersome, to say the least. In place of the characteristic relations PC and PC_PROPS, why not simply allow a relation of the form

```
P_COLORS ( P¢, COLOR )   ?
```

But consider the consequences of such an approach. First, relation P_COLORS represents a new kind of object so far as RM/T is concerned (it is neither an E-relation nor a P-relation).

Let us agree to call it a C-relation. A C-relation must

- contain exactly one E-attribute;
- have a composite primary key, involving the single E-attribute and one or more of the other attributes;
- satisfy certain naming conventions (details of which are left as an exercise for the reader).

The second point above shows that C-relations would share with "nonentity associations" (see Section 6.8) the doubtful honor of being the only kind of object to require a composite primary key. In fact, the situation is even worse (even less disciplined) than with nonentity associations, since the components of the primary key of a C-relation might not even be surrogates.

Furthermore, C-relations would require additional integrity rules and additional operators (details left to the reader's imagination).

Finally, there would now be two ways of representing multivalued properties, with no obvious reason for preferring one over the other in any given situation. This fact in turn would considerably complicate the question of providing high-level operators (to be used in, for example, the definition of external-level views) that are independent of the precise nature of the RM/T-level representation. In sum, the slight clumsiness referred to earlier seems a small price to pay to avoid all this extra complexity.

6.3 The two notions are significantly different.

a) Surrogates identify entities, database-keys identify records. There is not necessarily any well-defined correspondence between entities and records: One entity may correspond to many records, and/or one record may correspond to many entities.

b) Database-keys have performance connotations, surrogates do not (access to a record via its database-key is assumed to be fast).

c) Database-keys are local to a run-unit and transient, surrogates are global and permanent. There is no guarantee that the same database-key will identify the same record in two distinct run-units (regardless of whether those run-units execute in parallel or serially). In fact, it is intended that database-keys be closely related to physical addresses, and hence that they be allowed to change whenever records change position (for example, as the result of a database reorganization).

d) It is not possible to store a database-key as a field value in a database record, whereas it very definitely is possible to store a surrogate as an attribute value in a tuple. Thus database-keys do not provide the general entity referencing function that is so crucial to any database. (The "fanset" construct provides a very limited form of such referencing, essentially by storing database-keys in *hidden* fields; but that construct also bundles in a lot of additional function that would be better kept separate. See Volume I.)

In a nutshell: Surrogates are a logical concept; database-keys are a physical concept.

6.5 Yes. See entity type OFFERING in the answer to Exercise 6.1, above.

6.6 Yes (although we stress once again that all such classifications are rather subjective). As an example, let us extend entity type SP to include a property DRIVER¢, whose purpose is to identify the driver responsible for delivering the shipment. Let us further assume that EMPLOYEEs are another entity type in the database, and that the value of DRIVER¢ is required to be equal to EMPLOYEE¢ for some known employee. Then we can regard SP as an *associative* entity type (with participant entity types S and P) that additionally *designates* entities of type EMPLOYEE. We could not reasonably regard it as an associative entity type with three participants (because a given driver is presumably allowed to deliver any number of shipments.)

6.7 We amend our answer to Exercise 6.6 as follows. Define ES to be an association between drivers (employees) and shipments:

```
CREATE E_RELATION ES
          ASSOCIATING ( EMPLOYEE VIA DRIVER¢ ,
                        SP VIA SP¢ ) ;
```

Then ES is an associative entity type for which one of the participants (SP) is also an associative entity type. This design will permit a single shipment to have multiple drivers.

6.8 The answer to all three questions is "not necessarily." For example, suppose that some but not all employees are assigned to projects, but that no employee is assigned to more than one project at a time. Then "assigned employees" are a subtype of "employees"; moreover, "assigned employees" constitute a designative entity type, whereas "employees" in general do not.

6.11 Using a pidgin form of SQL, the "more primitive" operations can be represented as a single nested expression:

```
SELECT  S#
FROM    ( SELECT  S#, P#, QTY
          FROM    SKN, PKN, SPSP, SPQ
          WHERE   SKN.S¢ = SPSP.S¢
          AND     PKN.P¢ = SPSP.P¢
          AND     SPSP.SP¢ = SPQ.SP¢ )
WHERE   P# = 'P2'
```

The inner (parenthesized) expression is a SQL definition of the external-level relation SP in terms of the RM/T-level relations. (We remark in passing that it would be extremely convenient if SQL did actually permit such forms of nested expression. See reference [6.4].) We are assuming, however, that every shipment is represented in relation SPQ (because any shipment that is not so represented will not appear in the external-level relation SP by our SQL definition). The problem is that SQL does not support the outer join operation; again, see reference [6.4].

6.12 RG := UNION (TAG (AG), TAG (DG)) ;

6.13 RESULT := PROJECT
                  (STEP (CLOSE (CG)),
                          (CHARACTERISTIC_E_RELNAME, SEP)) ;

CLOSE produces the *transitive closure* of a graph relation. That is, if R(SUP,SUB) is a graph relation, then CLOSE(R) is a superset of R, defined as follows: The tuple (SUP:x,SUB:y) appears in CLOSE(R) if and only if it appears in R or there exists a sequence of values $z1$, $z2$, . . . , zn, such that the tuples (SUP:x,SUB:z1), (SUP:z1,SUB:z2), . . . , (SUP:zn,SUB:y) all appear in R.

STEP expands a graph relation to include the "separation" (SEP) of the two components in each tuple of that graph relation. That is, (SUP:x,SUB:y,SEP:n) appears in STEP(R) if and only if (SUP:x,SUB:y) appears in R and n is the least number of edges in the graph represented by R separating node x from node y.

7
Distributed
Databases

7.1 INTRODUCTION

We begin with a working definition: A distributed database is a database that is not stored in its entirety at a single physical location, but rather is spread across a network of locations that are geographically dispersed and connected via communication links. Of course, this definition is very imprecise; it is difficult to pin down exactly what is meant by terms such as "geographically dispersed" and "single physical location." The following statement is more accurate, if less immediately understandable: A database is "distributed" if it can be divided into distinct pieces, such that for a given user access to some of those pieces is very much slower than access to others. The following example is based on one given by Champine [7.13]. A certain bank, located in the state of California, operates a system in which account records for the Los Angeles area are kept in a database in Los Angeles and account records for the San Francisco area are kept in another in San Francisco, and the two local databases are linked together to form a single "global" or distributed database (Fig. 7.1). The advantages of such an organization are clear: It combines efficiency of processing (the data is stored close to the point where it is most commonly used) with increased accessibility (it is possible to access a Los Angeles account from San Francisco and vice versa, via the communication link). Other advantages will be discussed later.

Let us examine this example a little more closely, because it will help to identify some of the major concepts of distributed systems. In general, a distributed system consists of a collection of *sites* or *nodes,* connected together into a communication *network.* (The network in the example is very simple, of course, and involves only two sites.) Each site, in turn, constitutes a database system in its own right—it has its own database, its own complement of terminals, and its own central processor, run-

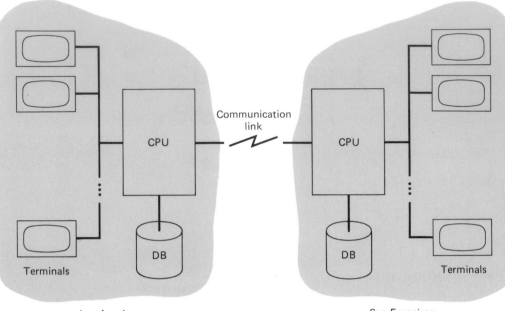

Fig. 7.1 Example of a distributed system.

ning its own local DBMS (complete with DC Manager, Recovery Manager, Log Manager, and so on). In fact, each site enjoys a very high degree of autonomy, and relies scarcely at all on any kind of centralized service or control. It is thus more helpful in many ways to think of a distributed system as a *partnership* among a set of independent but cooperating centralized systems, rather than as some kind of monolithic and indivisible object. By the same token, a "distributed database" can best be thought of as the union of a set of individual centralized databases.

Location Transparency

A major objective of distributed database systems is to provide what is usually called *location transparency*. Location transparency means that users and user programs should not need to know where (that is, at which site) any particular item of data is located. Instead, all such location information should be kept by the system as part of its system catalog, and all user requests for data should be interpreted by the system in accordance with that information. A request to operate on a nonlocal piece of data may cause (a) that data to be moved to the local site for local processing, or (b) processing to occur at the remote site and results moved to the local site, or more generally (c) a combination of both (a) and (b). The advantages of such transparency are obvious: It simplifies the logic of application programs, and it allows data to be moved from one site to another as usage patterns change without necessitating any reprogramming. As an illustration of the first of these points, suppose location transparency were *not* provided in the system of Fig. 7.1, and consider the effect on a program P whose function is to transfer funds from one account to another. Suppose P is to execute at site S. Then P would have to cater for four different cases —both accounts at the local site S, both accounts at the remote site, debit account at site S and credit account remote, and credit account at site S and debit account remote.

Replication Transparency

In our banking example so far we have tacitly been assuming that the data is *partitioned:* Corresponding to any given logical data object (say, any given account), there is precisely one physically stored representative of that object, at precisely one site in the network. A more general example would involve *replicated* stored objects. Data replication means that a given logical data object can have several distinct stored representatives, at several distinct sites. The advantages of such an arrangement are that it can provide both improved performance and improved availability: Applications can operate on local replicas instead of having to communicate with remote sites, and a given data object remains available for processing so long as at least one replica is available, that is, so long as at least one site that holds a copy of that object is accessible. There are some disadvantages too, of course: Updating an object requires the update to be propagated to all copies of that object at all sites, and obviously more storage is required; but the advantages are likely to outweigh the disadvantages, and in general we can say that some degree of support for replication is a prerequisite for achieving the true potential of a distributed system.[1]

In a system that does support replication, however, the details of data access can quickly become quite complex. To be specific, retrieval operations need to be addressed to the nearest available copy, and update operations need to be addressed to *all* copies—with special provision for the case of copies that are currently unavailable because of site or network failures. Moreover, it is desirable to be able to add or remove replicas as usage patterns change, again without necessitating any reprogramming. Consequently, a system that supports replication should also provide *replication transparency:* That is, all details of locating and maintaining replicas should be handled by the system, not by the user. System-supported data replication is thus an important special case of controlled redundancy (see Volume I).

---

1. The phone book provides a good and commonly quoted example of replicated data. Note that this is an example in which almost all transactions are read-only. Replication comes into its own in such a situation.

Location transparency and replication transparency together imply that (ideally) *a distributed system should look like a centralized system to the user.*[2] The user should be able to think purely in terms of logical data objects and should not be concerned with where or how many times those objects are physically stored. It follows that, generally speaking, *the problems of distributed systems are internal-level problems* (to use the terminology of ANSI/SPARC), *not conceptual- or external-level problems* [7.8]. Distribution per se does not have any effect on (for example) the user's view of the data, or on the specific language used, or on logical database design. It does, however, have a very definite effect on such matters as concurrency control, recovery, and physical database design. Solutions to these latter problems in a centralized context are frequently inappropriate in a distributed context because the internal-level structure is so different. We shall consider some of these problems in more detail in subsequent sections of this chapter.

Advantages of Distributed Systems

We conclude this introductory section with a brief summary of the main arguments in favor of distributed systems. Some of these points have already been touched on, but we include them again here for completeness and ease of reference.

Local autonomy

The enterprise the database system serves is very often logically distributed (into divisions, departments, projects, etc.), and is quite likely to be physically distributed as well (into plants, factories, laboratories, etc.). Distributing the system allows individual groups within the enterprise to exercise local control over their own data, with local accountability, and more generally makes them less dependent on some remote data processing center that by definition cannot be so deeply involved in purely local issues. At the same time, of course, it allows those local groups to access data at other locations when necessary.[3]

Capacity and incremental growth

A common reason for installing a distributed system in the first place is simply that there does not exist any single machine with adequate capacity for the application in hand. Once installed, moreover, a distributed system can *grow* more gracefully than

---

2. In fact, of course, location transparency and replication transparency are nothing more than aspects of the familiar concept of physical data independence, as it applies to a distributed system. See Volume I for a discussion of physical data independence in the nondistributed case. Note, however, that most commercially installed (as opposed to experimental) systems today do not provide replication transparency, although some do provide location transparency.

3. We shall assume throughout this chapter that local autonomy is desirable, and hence that the "independent but cooperating centralized systems" are all peers of one another. Other arrangements (for example, one master plus several slaves) are possible, but are beyond the scope of this chapter.

a nondistributed system: If it becomes necessary to expand the system because the volume of data has expanded or the volume of processing against it has increased, then it may be easier to add a new site to an existing distributed system than to replace an existing centralized system by a larger one. What is more, such additions may be made in smaller increments (and typically should involve less disruption of service to the users) than in the nondistributed case.

Reliability and availability

A distributed system offers greater reliability than a centralized system in that it is not an all-or-nothing proposition—it can continue to function (at a reduced level) in the face of failure of an individual site or individual communication link. And if data is replicated, then, as pointed out earlier, availability is improved also—a replicated data object remains available so long as at least one copy of that object is available. Moreover, each replica of a given object can be used as a free backup for any copy of that object that happens to be destroyed by some failure.

Efficiency and flexibility

Data in a distributed system can be stored close to its normal point of use, thus reducing both response times and communication costs (most access is local). And if the pattern of use changes, then data can be dynamically moved or replicated, or existing replicas can be eliminated (we are assuming here of course that the system does provide both location and replication transparency).

7.2 DISTRIBUTED SYSTEM STRUCTURE

In this section we examine the structure of distributed systems in a little more depth. This examination will serve as a basis for our discussion in subsequent sections of more specific aspects of such systems.

A distributed system is most easily visualized as a *graph*, that is, as a collection of nodes and edges (Fig. 7.1 provides an example). The nodes of such a graph represent the sites of the network and the edges represent the communication links among those sites. Each site consists of a central processing unit (with associated primary storage, etc.), a local database, and a set of online terminals. Two sites A and B are *connected* if there is a direct, operational link between them or if there exists a third site C such that A is connected to C and C is connected to B (a recursive definition). In normal operation every site is connected to every other site; however, the possibility of site failure means that any site can become (temporarily) nonoperational, and thus effectively disconnected from the rest of the system for the duration of the failure. Communication links can also fail; a site may therefore become (temporarily) disconnected from the rest of the system, even though it may itself still be operational, if all links to it have failed. More generally, it is possible for the network to degenerate into a *partitioned* state—that is, the total network can split into a collection of subnetworks, each individually operational but (temporarily) out of communication with all the rest. A partition consisting of a single site is just a special case. A major problem with such partitioning lies in having to reconcile any updates made in the various subnetworks after the communication links among them have been reestablished.

Reliable Communications

We shall generally assume, the previous paragraph notwithstanding, that the communication system is *reliable,* even in the face of site or link failures. By "reliable" here we mean that, if the system accepts a message from site A for transmission to site B, then it will eventually deliver that message to site B. Moreover, messages will not be garbled, will not be delivered more than once, and will be delivered in the order sent. (More precisely, messages from a specific site A to some other site B will be delivered to site B in the order that site A sent them. It is not possible to guarantee that messages from *different* sites to the same destination will arrive in the order they were sent, in general.)

Providing communication reliability is the responsibility of the communication control software (beyond the scope of this book).

Data Fragmentation

We have indicated in Section 7.1 that data in a distributed system may be *partitioned* and *replicated* in physical storage. Given a particular logical data collection, say the ACCOUNTS relation of Fig. 7.2 below, that collection may be partitioned into separate *fragments,* and copies of those fragments may then be stored at multiple locations. The question arises, what constitutes a suitable unit for fragmentation purposes?

In a relational system, the basic unit of data storage is (by definition) the *stored relation.* Let us define a "subrelation" to be the result obtained by applying an arbitrary combination of projection and restriction (theta-selection) operations to a given relation. A subrelation is thus an arbitrary row-and-column subset of a given relation. Since subrelations are still relations, they provide the obvious "fragments"

ACCOUNTS	ACCOUNT#	BRANCH	CUSTOMER	TYPE	BALANCE
	272612	SF	Able	Checking	974.15
	490134	SF	Able	Savings	50.00
	499760	LA	Baker	Checking	1210.26
	536179	SF	Clark	Checking	873.40
	588224	SF	Davies	Checking	75.43
	690047	LA	Davies	Savings	4037.91
	756630	SF	Evans	Checking	4.03

Fig. 7.2 The ACCOUNTS relation.

in a relational system. (Exercise: What would constitute a suitable "fragment" in a system involving essential fansets?) Given the ACCOUNTS relation of Fig. 7.2, for example, we might define the following fragments (using a SQL-like language):

```
DEFINE FRAGMENT SF1
    AS SELECT ACCOUNT#, BRANCH, TYPE
       FROM    ACCOUNTS
       WHERE   BRANCH = 'SF'

DEFINE FRAGMENT SF2
    AS SELECT ACCOUNT#, CUSTOMER, BALANCE
       FROM    ACCOUNTS
       WHERE   BRANCH = 'SF'

DEFINE FRAGMENT LA1
    AS SELECT ACCOUNT#, BRANCH, TYPE
       FROM    ACCOUNTS
       WHERE   BRANCH = 'LA'

DEFINE FRAGMENT LA2
    AS SELECT ACCOUNT#, CUSTOMER, BALANCE
       FROM    ACCOUNTS
       WHERE   BRANCH = 'LA'
```

Assuming for simplicity that each of these fragments is stored exactly once, the system can reconstruct the ACCOUNTS relation by joining SF1 and SF2 over ACCOUNT#, joining LA1 and LA2 over ACCOUNT#, and then taking the union of these two joins. If any of the fragments is stored more than once, then another operator ("choose") must be applied to choose one of the replicas of that fragment before the corresponding join is performed. The whole of this reconstruction process will be concealed from the user, of course.

In the ACCOUNTS example, we showed each fragment as retaining the primary key (ACCOUNT#) of the original relation, thus guaranteeing that the overall decomposition was nonloss (as explained in Volume I). In practice it is more likely that a technique based on *tuple identifiers* would be used. That is, the system would (conceptually) add a hidden column to the ACCOUNTS relation, containing a system-generated, globally unique tuple identifier for each tuple of that relation, and those tuple identifiers would then automatically be appended to the tuples of any fragment derived from that relation. This technique is employed in both the systems SDD-1 [7.18] and R* [7.19]. (SDD-1 is an experimental system developed by the Computer Corporation of America in Cambridge, Massachusetts. R* (pronounced "R star") is a distributed version of System R currently under development at the IBM Research Laboratory, San Jose, California.)

We remark in passing that partitioning can make the maintenance of global integrity constraints rather difficult. Consider what is involved in maintaining the global uniqueness of account numbers, for example, given the fragmentation of ACCOUNTS shown above.

Transaction Management

The basic purpose of any database system is to execute transactions. However, the notion of transaction requires careful definition in a distributed environment, because it may involve the execution of code at multiple sites in the system *(distributed transaction processing)*. Following Gray [7.10], we define a transaction (that is, a transaction *instance*) to be a unit of recovery (a logical unit of work), and an *agent* to be a process executing on behalf of some particular transaction at some particular site (that is, a "representative" of that transaction at that site). Initiating a transaction causes an agent to start executing at some site. As that agent executes it may cause other agents to start executing at other sites, and so on. Two agents within the same transaction are said to be *cohorts* of each other. The system must understand that all cohorts in a given transaction are logically related and must treat them as a unit for such purposes as recovery and concurrency control. In particular, two-phase commit protocols must be used to ensure that the cohorts either all commit together or all roll back together, as explained in Chapter 1 (we shall consider this question in some depth in Section 7.8).

Some systems permit parallel processing within a transaction—that is, multiple agents within a transaction may execute simultaneously at multiple sites. Other systems require an agent A that initiates another agent B to wait for B to complete before continuing with its own execution. Regardless of whether parallelism is supported, however, the system should allow the agent B to initiate a third agent C back at the site of the original agent A, if required by the logic of the application and/or by the data distribution.

Homogeneous vs. Heterogeneous Systems

One further point concerning the structure of distributed systems in general is that the database management systems at different sites need not all be of the same family. For example, it is perfectly feasible to connect an IMS site to a CICS site (see Section 7.4). If the DBMSs *are* all of the same kind the system is said to be homogeneous, otherwise it is heterogeneous. We shall normally assume a homogeneous system, unless we specify otherwise.

Problems of Distributed Systems

We are now in a position to understand some of the problem areas in distributed systems. The first point is that communication links are typically rather slow in comparison with local storage devices such as disks. ARPANET, for example, has a bandwidth (data rate) of approximately 25,000 bytes per second, whereas the typical disk drive has a data rate of approximately one *million* bytes per second. Second, communication systems typically also have a high access delay time, say of the order of one tenth of a second. Third, regardless of the speed of the communication system itself, messages are expensive in terms of CPU instructions executed; to send a message and handle the acknowledgment from the recipient typically costs of the order of 5,000–10,000 instructions of operating system and communication control code. Fourth and last, different communication systems have widely differing characteristics; as Rothnie and Goodman point out in [7.11], data rates can vary by as much as three orders of magnitude and access delay by as much as six! Hence design decisions that are acceptable for one system may be quite unacceptable for another; for example, it may or may not be feasible to propagate updates to all copies of an object in real time. The trade-offs differ considerably from one system to another. But it is generally true that, whereas in a centralized system the overriding performance objective is to minimize the number of disk accesses, in a distributed system it is to minimize the volume of data and the number of messages transmitted across the network.[4]

The basic problem just outlined gives rise to further problems in several areas, among them the following:

- Query processing
- Update propagation
- Concurrency control
- Commit protocols
- Catalog management

We will address these problems in Sections 7.5–7.9, respectively. First, however, a word of caution is appropriate. Distributed systems research is a very young field. While considerable effort has already been devoted to the problems listed above, most proposed solutions can only be regarded as speculative at this time—they have typically been implemented, if at all, only in a research environment, and they have not been subjected to any extensive practical tests. Nor is there always consensus on the best approach in many cases (see, for example, the discussion of locking vs. timestamping in Section 7.7). Before discussing the problems in any depth, therefore, we present in Sections 7.3 and 7.4 an outline description of the distributed database functions of IMS and CICS, in order to give some idea of the state of the art in current commercial systems (as opposed to experimental systems). For a brief discussion of some operational installations, see reference [7.13], also reference [7.10].

---

4. One implication of this statement is that if an agent at one site initiates an agent at another, then it is desirable for the initiation request to be at a high semantic level, to reduce the number of such requests and thus the volume of communication traffic. Translating this requirement into user terms, it is desirable for the user's data manipulation language to be at a level at least comparable to that of, for example, QUEL or SQL, rather than at a record-at-a-time level as in, for example, DL/I or DBTG.

7.3   DISTRIBUTED DATABASE AND IMS

The Multiple Systems Coupling feature (MSC) of IMS allows two or more IMS systems to be interconnected in such a way that an end-user or program on one of those systems can invoke a program on another [7.14]. Consider the end-user first. That user will enter an input message to invoke a transaction, and that message will be placed on the input queue at the site of entry, exactly as in the nondistributed case (see Chapter 1). IMS will then examine a local catalog to see whether the program to be executed for this transaction resides at a remote site. If it does, the input message will then be transmitted to that remote site, where it will be processed just as if it had originally been entered directly at that site; in particular, it will be placed on the input queue at that site. Output messages, if any, will be transmitted back to the original site.

The second case, invocation of a remote program by a local program rather than by an end-user, is essentially the same as the first: The local program issues an IMS DC call ("insert to the message queue") that looks effectively like an end-user transaction invocation, and that call is treated as described above (it causes a message to be placed on the input queue at the remote site). The most general situation, therefore, involves an end-user U entering an input message and thus invoking a (local or remote) program A, which then invokes a remote program B, which in turn invokes a remote program C, . . . , which finally invokes a remote program N. Each of A, B, C, . . . , N can access its own local data *only* and (except of course for N) can pass data on to the next program in sequence, via the input message for that next program. Any or all of A, B, C, . . . , N can send output messages back to U.

Let us interpret the foregoing in terms of the general discussions of Sections 7.1 and 7.2. Note first that location transparency *is* provided, but only in a limited form. Specifically, the end-user does not have to know where data or programs reside, but can invoke a transaction from any site. Programs, however, can access only local data; while they do not need to know the precise location of remote data, they do have to know when data is remote and they do have to know the identity of the remote programs involved, and to that extent knowledge of the data distribution is built into the application logic.

Second, any data replication is user-controlled, not system-controlled. There is no replication transparency.

Third, in the example above, *each of the programs A, B, C, . . . , N is considered by IMS as a separate transaction*—that is, as a separate unit of recovery. They are *not* considered as cohorts (agents within a single overall transaction). What is more, each of A, B, C, . . . must complete execution before the next one in sequence can start; there is no parallelism among them, and no return of control from an invoked program to its invoking program. The reason for this state of affairs is that, as explained in Chapter 1, the message from A to invoke B, since it is an output message from A, will not actually be sent until A completes (and similarly for the others). As a consequence, it is possible for the "real-world" transaction (the total sequence A - B - C - · · · · - N) to fail in the middle and for the global database to be left in an inconsistent state. If possible, program N should be the only one in the sequence that is allowed to do any database updating.

It can be seen that Multiple Systems Coupling does not really support distributed transaction processing in the sense of Section 7.2. Instead, it supports what is sometimes called *transaction routing* (the term "transaction" is used in IMS to mean an input message rather than the execution of a program, and the MSC scheme essentially involves the routing of such messages from one system to another).[5]

Multiple Systems Coupling is an IMS-only feature. IMS is also capable of participating in a different distributed scheme known as ISC (InterSystems Communication), which however does not apply only to IMS. Rather, ISC is a set of protocols that will allow *any* systems following those protocols (not just IMS systems, and not necessarily even just IBM systems) to communicate with each other. For example, under ISC, an IMS system can communicate with a CICS system, or two CICS systems can communicate with each other. The facilities of ISC are quite different from those of MSC; we describe those facilities in the context of CICS (Section 7.4), since they were originally developed for use in the CICS environment, and since CICS currently supports a larger subset of the ISC protocols than IMS does.

7.4 DISTRIBUTED DATABASE AND CICS

As indicated at the end of the previous section, ISC (InterSystems Communication) is a set of protocols by which any systems conforming to those protocols can communicate with one another. A significant subset of the ISC protocols is supported by CICS [7.15]. CICS/ISC allows two or more CICS systems to be interconnected in such a way that

1. an application program executing at one site can invoke another at another site, *without* ceasing execution itself;

2. an application program executing at one site can issue a DL/I call against a database that resides at another site.

Both (1) and (2) are genuine distributed transaction processing in the sense of Section 7.2 (complete with parallel execution within a transaction, in case (1)), but CICS reserves the "distributed transaction processing" label for case (1) only; case (2) is called "data request shipping," or alternatively "remote DL/I call." We examine the two cases in turn.

---

5. We remark in passing that transaction routing provides a simple mechanism for connecting heterogeneous systems together; as Gray observes [7.10], all that those systems have to do is agree on certain common message formats for commands and data exchange, and settle accounting and authorization problems, and the rest is—comparatively—straightforward.

Distributed transaction processing (in the CICS sense of the term) allows the total application to be divided into a distributed set of programs, each one accessing its own local data. The end-user will initiate the overall transaction by invoking the first of these programs at that user's local site (in contrast with IMS/MSC, CICS/ISC does not allow an end-user to invoke a transaction directly at a remote site). As it executes, that program, or rather agent, can invoke agents at other sites, which can invoke other agents, and so on. The set of all agents is considered as a unit for recovery purposes. One shortcoming is that CICS does *not* maintain a catalog giving the location of each program; instead, an agent A that wishes to invoke another agent B must specify (at least symbolically) the site at which the program for B resides, and so to that extent knowledge of the data distribution is built into the application logic (location transparency is not provided). On the other hand the invoked agent *can* return a message to the invoking agent without having to know that agent's location.

Data request shipping, by contrast, does provide complete location transparency at the application program level (and application programs in turn can provide such transparency to the end-user; as before, end-users cannot directly invoke transactions at remote sites). The basic idea is that programs can issue DL/I database calls against a remote database exactly as if that database were at the local site, and CICS/ISC will intercept the call and ship it to the appropriate remote site, using a catalog that gives the location of each database. A "mirror transaction" (agent) will automatically be established at the remote site to issue the call on the original program's behalf and to return the result to that program. (There are some restrictions on this facility, beyond the scope of this text.) Again all agents are considered as a unit for recovery purposes.

Comparing the two approaches (distributed transaction processing vs. remote DL/I call), we can see that the second is easier for the programmer but the first is likely to perform better, at least if the transaction involves many DL/I calls. The basic problem with the second approach, as pointed out in Footnote 4, is that DL/I calls tend to be too low-level.

In addition to the functions outlined above, CICS/ISC also supports the following:

- A program at one CICS site *can* invoke another at another site without having to know the identity of that site (contrast distributed transaction processing above), but only if it does not need to obtain any returned messages from the invoked program. A location catalog is used to support this function (again, contrast distributed transaction processing). The programs are not considered as a unit for recovery purposes. The reader will see that this capability is rather similar to that provided by the MSC feature in IMS.

- A CICS/ISC site can be connected to an IMS/ISC site. Distributed transaction processing (in the CICS sense) is supported—*without* coordinated recovery—but remote DL/I call is not. The initial program execution can be at either site.

CICS/ISC, like IMS/MSC, does not offer any system support for data replication.

The reader who is interested in further details of distributed database support in IMS and CICS is referred to [7.14–7.16]. Reference [7.17] is recommended as a useful overview.

7.5 QUERY PROCESSING

In this section we consider what is involved in handling a query in a truly general-purpose distributed system such as SDD-1 or R*. We assume that the query is expressed in a high-level language such as QUEL or SQL, and that the system provides full location and replication transparency. As pointed out in Section 7.1, a query entered at site A against data stored at site B may cause the data to be processed at site B and the result returned to site A, or it may cause the data to be moved to site A and processed there. As a more complex example, a request for a join of a relation RA at site A and a relation RB at site B could be carried out by moving RA to B, or by moving RB to A, or by moving both to a third site C. Rothnie and Goodman [7.11] give an example that dramatically illustrates the importance of choosing a good strategy for processing queries in a distributed environment. The following is an edited version of their example.

Database (suppliers and parts, simplified):

```
S     (S#, CITY)       10,000 tuples, stored at site A
P     (P#, COLOR)     100,000 tuples, stored at site B
SP    (S#, P#)      1,000,000 tuples, stored at site A
```

Assume that every tuple is 100 bits long.

Query (supplier numbers for London suppliers of red parts):

```
SELECT  S.S#
FROM    S, SP, P
WHERE   S.CITY   = 'LONDON'
AND     S.S#     = SP.S#
AND     SP.P#    = P.P#
AND     P.COLOR  = 'RED'
```

Estimates (cardinalities of certain intermediate results):

```
Number of red parts                        =        10
Number of shipments by London suppliers    =   100,000
```

Communication assumptions:

```
Data rate      = 10,000 bits per second
Access delay   = 1 second
```

We now briefly examine six possible query processing strategies, and for each strategy i calculate the total communication time T[i] from the formula

T[i] = total access delay + (total data volume / data rate)
   = (number of messages * 1) + (total number of bits / 10000)

(measured in seconds).

1. Move relation P to site A and process the query at A.

$$T[1] = 1 + (100000 * 100) / 10000$$
$$= 1000 \text{ seconds approx. (16.7 minutes)}$$

2. Move relations S and SP to site B and process the query at B.

$$T[2] = 2 + ((10000 + 1000000) * 100) / 10000$$
$$= 10100 \text{ seconds approx. (2.8 hours)}$$

3. Join relations S and SP at site A, select tuples from the join for which the city is London, and then, for each of those tuples in turn, check site B to see whether the indicated part is red. Each of these checks will involve two messages, a query and a response. The transmission time for these messages is small compared with the access delay.

$$T[3] = 200000 \text{ seconds approx. (2.3 days)}$$

4. Select tuples from relation P at site B for which the color is red, and then, for each of those tuples in turn, check site A to see whether there exists a shipment relating the part to a London supplier. Each of these checks will involve two messages. The transmission time for these messages is small compared with the access delay.

$$T[4] = 20 \text{ seconds approx.}$$

5. Join relations S and SP at site A, select tuples from the join for which the city is London, project the result over S# and P#, and move the projection to site B. Complete the processing at B.

$$T[5] = 1 + (100000 * 100) / 10000$$
$$= 1000 \text{ seconds approx. (16.7 minutes)}$$

(We are assuming that tuples in the projection are 100 bits long.)

6. Select tuples from relation P at site B for which the color is red and move the result to A. Complete the processing at A.

$$T[6] = 1 + (10 * 100) / 10000$$
$$= 1 \text{ second approx.}$$

Figure 7.3 summarizes the foregoing results. The significant points are as follows (see reference [7.11]):

- Each of the six strategies represents a plausible approach to the problem, yet the variation in communication time is enormous.

- Data rate and access delay are both important factors in choosing an appropriate strategy.

- Computation time is likely to be negligible compared with communication time for the poor strategies. (This may also be the case for the better strategies, though not necessarily; see the discussion of reference [7.21] below.)

Strategy	Technique	Communication time
1	Move P to A	16.7 min
2	Move S and SP to B	2.8 hr
3	For each London shipment, check corres. part	5.6 hr
4	For each red part, check for London supplier	33.3 min
5	Move London shipments to B	1.7 min
6	Move red parts to A	11 sec

Fig. 7.3 Example of distributed query processing (summary).

In addition, some strategies permit parallel processing at the two sites. Strategy (6), for example, allows the selection of London shipments to be performed at site A concurrently with the selection of red parts at site B. Thus the total elapsed processing time may actually be less than in a centralized system for some queries. Note, however, that we have totally ignored the question of where (at which site) the final result is to be materialized.

The issue of query processing in a distributed environment is also explored in Selinger and Adiba [7.21]. Their approach is an extension of the techniques used for query processing in System R (which is of course a centralized system), and is currently being incorporated into the distributed system R*. In outline the approach works as follows. As in System R, the SQL compiler chooses an *access plan* for a given query by generating a set of possible strategies for that query, estimating the work involved in each strategy and assigning a cost to it accordingly, and then selecting the plan having the lowest cost. For System R the cost formula is essentially

I/O cost + CPU cost.

For R* it is

I/O cost + CPU cost + communication cost.

The paper shows that in the case of queries involving a join among relations stored at different sites, the cost of the query—perhaps rather surprisingly—is *not* necessarily dominated by the communication cost. (However, we should point out that the major examples in the paper assume a communication system with access delay one tenth of a second and data rate 50,000 bits per second. Contrast the assumptions in the Rothnie and Goodman example sketched earlier.) For "extremely simple" joins—see [7.21] for an explanation of "extremely simple" in this context—the communication cost *is* the most significant factor, but the other factors become increasingly important as the joins become more complex, and the crossover point occurs quite quickly. The obvious conclusion is that both aspects (local costs and communication costs) must be considered in choosing a strategy.

Wong [7.20] describes a query processing technique that has been implemented in SDD-1. Essentially this technique represents an adaptation of the query decomposition approach used in the centralized version of INGRES (see Volume I); however, it replaces the *tuple substitution* operation of that approach (again, see Volume I) by a *subrelation move* operation, with the objective of reducing the number (as opposed to volume) of messages involved. (A more straightforward adaptation of the original decomposition approach that retains tuple substitution as a basic operation is described in [7.22]. That adaptation is vulnerable to the problems illustrated by strategies (3) and (4) of the Rothnie and Goodman example.) In outline the SDD-1 scheme works as follows.

Step 1: Perform all the local processing that can be done without any data movement at all.

Step 2: Choose the cheapest set of moves, M say, that will collect all the results of Step (1) together at a single site.

Step 3: Replace M by two sets of moves, M1 and M2 say, that can be executed in sequence with additional local processing between them, such that the costs of M1 and M2 and that extra local processing are together less than the cost of M.

Step 4: Repeat Steps (3) and (4) with M1 replacing M, then M2 replacing M, until no further improvements are obtained.

A basic difference between the SDD-1 approach and that of R* is that the SDD-1 approach starts by choosing a workable strategy and then tries to improve on it, whereas the R* approach attempts to generate a whole set of workable strategies and then selects the cheapest one. The SDD-1 scheme can be characterized as "greedy," in that it always looks for *immediate* improvements; it will find a solution that is locally optimal, but not necessarily one that is globally optimal.

For more details of Wong's scheme, see the annotation to reference [7.20] at the end of the chapter. A futher refinement of that scheme, planned for implementation in the distributed version of INGRES ("Distributed INGRES"), is described in [7.23]. Reference [7.24] presents a comparative analysis of various query processing strategies.

7.6 UPDATE PROPAGATION

The basic problem with data replication, as pointed out in Section 7.1, is that an update to any given logical data object must be propagated to all stored copies of that object. Note that this problem would exist even in a single-user system, that is, even if there were no transaction concurrency. We therefore defer discussion of concurrency control questions to Section 7.7, and concentrate here on the single-user case.

A difficulty that arises immediately is that one or more of the sites holding a copy of the object may be disconnected (because of site or link failures) at the time of the update. The obvious strategy of propagating updates immediately to all copies may thus be unacceptable, because it implies that the update (and hence the transaction) will fail if any one of those copies is currently unavailable. If there are n sites holding copies of the object, and if p is the probability ($p < 1$) that a given site is connected at any given time, then the probability of the update succeeding is p^n, which decreases towards zero as n increases. In other words, data is *less* available under this strategy than in the nonreplicated case, at least for update transactions.

An obvious improvement on the foregoing strategy is to apply updates at all *available* sites immediately, and to keep a list for each unavailable site of updates that need to be applied at that site as soon as it becomes available again. (In practice there would probably be several such lists. Any such list(s) will of course have to be maintained at some available site or sites.) When a site that has been disconnected becomes reconnected to the rest of the system, the restart procedure for that site will have to examine the appropriate list(s) and apply any pending updates before normal operation can be resumed.

Another improvement (one offering increased parallelism) involves designating exactly one copy of each object as the *primary* copy of that object. The primary copies of different objects will be at different sites, in general. Update operations are directed to the primary copy in the first instance. An update is deemed complete as soon as it has been applied to the primary copy (control is returned and the transaction can continue execution). The site holding the primary copy is responsible for broadcasting the update to all other sites after applying the initial update; those other sites can then update their copies in parallel with the continuing transaction execution. A problem with this approach is that the transaction may update an object X for which the primary copy is at some remote site, and may then issue a read for X which is directed to a secondary copy that has not yet been updated. If replication transparency is to be preserved, then the system must recognize this situation and either (a) make the transaction wait until the update has occurred, or (b) redirect the read to a copy of X that *has* already been updated. By the same token, care must be taken to ensure that some distinct transaction does not see an inconsistent version of the database (for example, an updated copy of X and a nonupdated copy of some related object Y).

The primary copy scheme also suffers from an availability problem—namely, if the site containing the primary copy of X is unavailable, then X is unavailable (at least for update), even if other copies of X are still accessible. The "moving primary copy" strategy is intended to overcome this drawback. Under this strategy, update operations may be directed to any copy of the object in question. If an update request for X is initially directed to a secondary copy, the site holding that copy will forward the request to the primary copy; and if it then discovers that the site holding that copy is disconnected, it will act in concert with the other secondaries to elect a new primary. When the site holding the old primary copy is reconnected, it will discover that it has been deposed, and will henceforth act as a secondary for this particular object. However, an update request will still fail if it is initially directed to the primary copy, rather than to one of the secondaries, and the site holding that primary copy is currently disconnected.

The simpler strategies—those not involving a primary copy—are also vulnerable to network partitioning problems (even in a single-user system, though the assumption of a single user may seem particularly unrealistic in this context). Suppose the network becomes temporarily partitioned into two subnetworks, A and B, each containing at least one copy of an object X. Then it is clear that X could be updated to a value X1 in A and to a value X2 in B, and that there might be no obvious way—probably *no* way, short of human intervention—of reconciling the two updates when A and B are reconnected to each other.

In the light of the foregoing difficulties, it seems worthwhile to investigate the possibility of abandoning the notion of replicas entirely. Adiba and Lindsay [7.25] propose an approach (essentially a modified version of the primary copy scheme) based on the notion of *snapshots*. A snapshot is a derived relation, like a view; however, unlike a view, it is actually stored in the database. Here is an example:

```
DEFINE SNAPSHOT LONDON_SUPPLIERS
    AS SELECT S#, SNAME, STATUS
       FROM   S
       WHERE  CITY = 'LONDON'
    REFRESH EVERY DAY
```

Executing a DEFINE SNAPSHOT statement is much like executing a query; however, the result of that execution is stored in the database under the specified name (LONDON_SUPPLIERS in the example) as a *read-only* relation. The definition of that relation and the time of its creation are entered into the system catalog. Periodically (EVERY DAY in the example) the snapshot is "refreshed"—that is, the current value is discarded, the query is reexecuted, and the result of that execution becomes the new value (the "time of creation" entry in the catalog is also updated appropriately, of course). In addition, users can force a refresh whenever they desire by means of an explicit REFRESH statement; for example,

```
REFRESH SNAPSHOT LONDON_SUPPLIERS
```

The point of the snapshot concept is that many applications—probably a majority—can tolerate, or may even require, data "as of" some particular earlier point in time. For example, reporting and accounting applications would normally fall into this category; such applications typically require the data to be "frozen" at an appropriate moment (for example, the end of an accounting period), and snapshots allow such freezing to occur without preventing other transactions from performing updates on the data in question. Similarly, it may be desirable to freeze large amounts of data for a complex query application, again without locking out updates. In fact, it is quite difficult to think of an application that genuinely requires up-to-the-millisecond information.

The proposal, then, is *not* to support replicated data as such, but rather to have a single "master" copy of each logical data object, together with an arbitrary number of snapshots defined over those master objects. Of course, a snapshot may be defined to be a direct copy of some master object, though it will actually be identical to that master object only between the time it is refreshed and the time of the next update to the master. Snapshots (as opposed to master objects) *can* be replicated by the system. Transactions will refer to snapshots or master objects by name—that is, the snapshot concept is *not* totally "transparent to the user." Update operations must be directed to master objects, of course, since snapshots are read-only, but read operations will normally be directed to snapshots (and the system can then apply the read to any available replica).

The foregoing scheme does suffer from the update availability problem associated with the primary copy strategy. However, it overcomes certain other difficulties (in particular, it avoids some of the concurrency control overheads described in the next section), it preserves most of the advantages of replication, and it has the virtue of simplicity. A snapshot scheme along these lines is planned for incorporation into R*.

We mention one further update problem, not connected with update propagation as such. Suppose in the suppliers-and-parts database that the supplier relation is fragmented and distributed on the basis of city values, so that London suppliers are stored at one site, Paris suppliers at another, and so on; and consider the effect of updating the city value for supplier S1 from London to Paris. It is clear that the system must not only perform the update, but must also recognize that the record concerned should migrate from one site to another. (This is a problem of location transparency rather than replication transparency. It is reminiscent of the problem of updating a record through a view in such a way that the record no longer satisfies the view-defining predicate, or conversely of updating a record in such a way that the record now does satisfy some view-defining predicate that it did not satisfy before. See Volume I.)

7.7 CONCURRENCY CONTROL

The reader of this section is assumed to be broadly familiar with the concepts of concurrency control in the centralized case, as discussed in Chapter 3. In that chapter we defined *serializability* as the formal criterion for correct execution of a set of concurrent transactions, and we presented two general strategies for achieving it, one based on *locking* and the other on *timestamping*. (Most of that chapter was concerned with locking rather than timestamping, however, for reasons explained in the text.) Two significant general properties of the two approaches are the following:

- Given a set of transactions to be executed concurrently:

    a) Locking will guarantee that the concurrent execution is equivalent to *some* (unpredictable) serial execution of those transactions;

    b) Timestamping will guarantee that the concurrent execution is equivalent to a *specific* serial execution of those transactions—namely, that defined by the order of the timestamps.

- Locking is susceptible to deadlock, timestamping is not.

Both techniques can be used in a distributed system as well as in a centralized one; however, as indicated in Chapter 3, the trade-offs are different in the two cases, and at least some researchers feel that timestamping is the technique of choice in the distributed case—see, for example, references [7.34–7.40]. The point is not universally accepted, however; on the contrary, reference [7.12] suggests that locking allows more concurrency than timestamping. Reference [7.39] presents a theoretical analysis of the two approaches, including numerous variations on each of them. We also draw the reader's attention to a third possibility, the so-called optimistic methods described by Kung and Robinson [7.42] (see Chapter 3). It is our feeling that more experience is needed with actual implementations before we can say with any certainty which techniques are most appropriate in which situations.

Locking

A paper by Traiger et al. [7.27] extends the authors' earlier work on two-phase locking (see Chapter 3) to the distributed case. Basically, the paper shows that, if all transactions in a distributed system (a) lock every object they access and (b) retain all locks until end-of-transaction, then all concurrent executions of those transactions will be serializable—that is, equivalent to some serial execution of those transactions *in a system consisting of a single site.* (It is assumed that there is no parallelism within transactions.) In other words, a system in which the following protocols are enforced will always be correct:

- Before executing a read operation, the transaction concerned must acquire a shared lock (S lock) on *at least one* replica of the object to be accessed.

- Before executing an update operation, the transaction concerned must acquire an exclusive lock (X lock) on *every* replica of the object to be accessed.

- Once it has acquired a lock, the transaction concerned must not release that lock until COMMIT.

These protocols will need some refinement to cater for the possibility that some replicas may be currently unavailable. Also, note that an update transaction cannot complete its commit processing until every affected site has installed (or at least agreed to install) that transaction's updates, as explained in the discussion of two-phase commit in Chapter 1; again, complications arise because of the fact that some of those sites may not be available at commit time. We shall return to this topic in Section 7.8.

The problem with locking in a distributed environment is the amount of message traffic (and hence overhead) it generates. Consider a transaction T that needs to update an object for which there exist replicas at n remote sites. If every site has its own Lock Manager to control access to objects at that site (this assumption is consistent with our view of a distributed system as a partnership among a set of autonomous centralized systems), then a straightforward implementation of the protocols above will require $5n$ messages:

   n lock requests
   n lock grants
   n update messages
   n acknowledgments
   n unlock requests

   The total time to perform the update could easily be two or more orders of magnitude greater than in a centralized system. Various techniques are available for reducing the message volume somewhat—for example, the unlock requests would in practice be bundled together with the commit messages at end-of-transaction, thus reducing the 5*n* to 4*n*—but in general it does seem that a system in which each site is highly autonomous will incur lengthy delays and/or a high degree of overhead if there are many updates to nonlocal data.

   Numerous techniques have been proposed for improving matters. One strategy is to give up some of the local autonomy by introducing a degree of centralized control into the system. The obvious technique is to have just one Lock Manager, at one site, and to let that site handle locking for the entire system (the set of all replicas of a given object can be considered as a single object for locking purposes under this scheme). The effect of this approach on the example above would be to reduce the number of messages from 5*n* to 2*n* + 3. However, there are some obvious drawbacks: First, the locking site is likely to become a system bottleneck; and second, the system is rather vulnerable—if the locking site fails, then the entire system will fail.

   A slightly better approach is to adopt the "primary copy" technique discussed in Section 7.6: For a given object X, the Lock Manager at the site containing the primary copy of X will handle all lock requests on X (remember that the primary copies of different objects will be at different sites, in general). Again the set of all copies of a given object can be considered as a single object for locking purposes. The snapshot scheme described in Section 7.6 represents a further improvement on this technique. These "primary copy" approaches overcome the drawbacks of the single locking site scheme discussed above, but they also reintroduce the possibility of *global deadlock* (not possible in the single Lock Manager scheme), which we now discuss.

Global Deadlock

A global deadlock is a deadlock involving two or more sites. It can arise if, for example, transaction T1 has a lock on object X at site A and requests a lock on object Y at site B, and transaction T2 has a lock on object Y at site B and requests a lock on object X at site A. (For simplicity we assume that all locks are exclusive.) Let us make the example more specific. Consider the following sequence of events:

■   Transaction T1 starts executing at site A. Let the agent representing T1 at A be $T1_A$. Assume $T1_A$ acquires a lock on object X_A at site A.

■   Transaction T2 starts executing at site B. Let the agent representing T2 at B be $T2_B$. Assume $T2_B$ acquires a lock on object Y_B at site B.

- Agent $T1_A$ invokes a cohort $T1_B$ at site B and enters the wait state, waiting for $T1_B$ to complete.
- Agent $T2_B$ invokes a cohort $T2_A$ at site A and enters the wait state, waiting for $T2_A$ to complete.
- Agent $T1_B$ requests a lock on Y_B and so enters the wait state, waiting for $T2_B$ to release its lock on Y_B.
- Agent $T2_A$ requests a lock on X_A and so enters the wait state, waiting for $T1_A$ to release its lock on X_A. Deadlock!

Figure 7.4 illustrates the situation at this point.

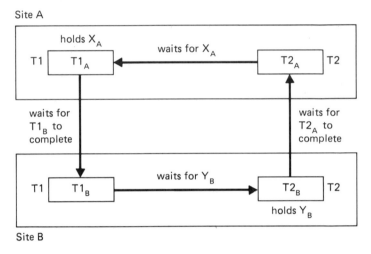

Fig. 7.4 Example of global deadlock.

The problem with the deadlock in this example is that the individual Lock Managers at A and B cannot *detect* the deadlock using only the information that is internal to their own site. The Lock Manager at A knows only that agent $T2_A$ is waiting for agent $T1_A$ and that agent $T1_A$ is waiting for some agent at B to complete, but it does not know that the agent at B is in turn waiting for another which is waiting for $T2_A$ to complete; and similarly for the Lock Manager at B. In other words, there are no cycles in the two *local* Wait-For graphs, but a cycle will appear if those two graphs are joined together. It follows that global deadlock detection incurs further communication overhead, because it requires the joining together of individual local graphs (or at least pieces of them).

One way to handle global deadlock detection is to do it in a centralized manner: that is, assign the responsibility to one specific site, and have all other sites transmit their local Wait-For graph to that site on some periodic basis. But this approach is vulnerable to failure of the deadlock detection site, and moreover involves a loss of autonomy on the part of all other sites. Obermarck [7.28] presents a distributed algorithm for deadlock detection that avoids the need for any distinguished detection site. The method works by introducing a special node EXT into the graph at each site, representing (in effect) all agents at all other sites. Consider some specific site, say site S. If agent $T1_S$ executing at S initiates an agent at some remote site, then an edge is added to the local graph from the $T1_S$ node to the EXT node ($T1_S$ is waiting for a remote agent to complete). If agent $T2_S$ is initiated at S by an agent at some remote site, then an edge is added to the local graph from the EXT node to the $T2_S$ node (a remote agent is waiting for $T2_S$ to complete). In the example of Fig. 7.4, the graph at site A would include the path

$$EXT \rightarrow T2_A \rightarrow T1_A \rightarrow EXT$$

and the graph at site B would include the path

$$EXT \rightarrow T1_B \rightarrow T2_B \rightarrow EXT$$

A global deadlock potentially (but not necessarily) exists whenever a local graph includes a path of the form

$$EXT \rightarrow Ti \rightarrow Tj \rightarrow \cdots \rightarrow Tk \rightarrow EXT$$

(for simplicity we now drop the site IDs and show the transaction IDs only). This path does not necessarily represent a genuine cycle in the *global* Wait-For graph, since it is not necessarily the case that Tk is waiting for Ti, either directly or indirectly. But it *is* true that if no such "potential" cycles exist in the local graphs, then no global deadlock exists. In what follows we reserve the term "cycle" for a genuine cycle, that is, a path that is definitely known to correspond to a deadlock.

Let S be the site whose local graph includes the "potential deadlock" path

$$EXT \rightarrow Ti \rightarrow Tj \rightarrow \cdots \rightarrow Tk \rightarrow EXT$$

shown above. On discovering this situation, site S will transmit a copy of the path to the site S' for which Tk is waiting (the identity of site S' is of course known to site S). Site S' can then add this information to its local graph and check for cycles in the expanded graph so formed. There are two possibilities:

a) The local graph at S' already includes a path of the form

$$EXT \rightarrow Tk \rightarrow \cdots \rightarrow Ti \rightarrow EXT$$

In this case, adding the path information from site S will cause a cycle to appear, of the form

$$Ti \rightarrow Tj \cdots \rightarrow Tk \rightarrow \cdots \rightarrow Ti$$

Site S' can then break the deadlock in the usual manner—that is, by choosing a victim and arranging for (all agents of) that victim to be backed out.

b) The local graph includes a path of the form

$$EXT \to Tk \to \cdots \to Tn \to EXT$$

(Tn distinct from Ti). In this case, site S′ can send a copy of the extended path

$$EXT \to Ti \to Tj \to \cdots \to Tk \to \cdots \to Tn \to EXT$$

to the site for which Tn is waiting. That site in turn can then go through a simi-lar process. Obermarck proves in [7.28] that, if a global deadlock really does exist, then this procedure will eventually cause a cycle to appear at some site, and hence that the deadlock will be detected and broken.

Obermarck also presents an optimization that reduces the communication traf-fic involved by approximately 50 percent. Consider the deadlock of Fig. 7.4 once again, and note that there is no need to transmit *both* the path information from site A to site B *and* the path information from site B to site A in order to detect the dead-lock. We can modify the algorithm described above accordingly: Site S should trans-mit its path information to site S′ only if the transaction ID for Ti is greater than that for Tk (the "greater than" is arbitrary, of course).

Further work on global deadlock detection is reported in [7.29] and [7.30].

Several researchers have proposed techniques that eliminate the possibility of deadlock entirely, at the cost of providing less concurrency. Such techniques avoid the overhead of having to ship Wait-For information around the network. The *transaction retry* schemes Wait-Die and Wound-Wait of Rosenkrantz et al. [7.31] provide one example, in which any lock request from one transaction for an object that is already locked by another and that *might* (eventually) lead to a deadlock causes one of the two transactions to be rolled back and restarted (see Chapter 3 for more details). Another approach, called *transaction scheduling* in Chapter 3, is simply not to schedule transactions for simultaneous execution if their data require-ments can possibly conflict. As pointed out in Chapter 3, such an approach may produce a rather low level of concurrency; however, it does have its advantages, and a more sophisticated version of the scheme, based on "transaction classes" and "conflict graph analysis," is used in SDD-1. We defer discussion of this approach to a later subsection. The third and last of the deadlock-avoidance schemes we mention here is the "majority consensus" technique of Thomas [7.32]. This technique assumes a fully redundant database—that is, a database in which every site contains a replica of every logical data object in the system. We give an outline description of this technique in the References and Bibliography section at the end of the chapter.

Timestamping

An introduction to timestamp-based concurrency control techniques was given in Chapter 3, Section 3.14. The basic idea is as follows.

1. Every transaction is assigned a globally unique timestamp.

2. Updates are not physically applied to the database until (successful) end-of-transaction.

3. Every object in the database carries the timestamp of the transaction that last read it and the transaction that last updated it (at least conceptually, although several optimizations are possible [7.38]).

4. If a transaction T1 requests a database operation that conflicts with some other database operation already executed on behalf of a *younger* transaction T2, that transaction T1 is restarted. An operation from T1 is in *conflict* with T2 if and only if

   a) It is a read, and the object in question has already been updated by T2; or

   b) It is an update, and the object in question has already been read or updated by T2. This case can occur only during T1's commit processing, by virtue of (2) above.

   By "object" here we mean a physically stored object (that is, one of possibly many replicas of a logical object).

5. If a transaction is restarted it is assigned a new timestamp.

The advantages of this approach are that no locks are set, and hence that deadlock is impossible and the communication overheads of locking and deadlock detection are avoided. Many variations on the basic scheme can be devised [7.38]. We describe one, *conservative* timestamping, in the next subsection; two further extensions of that technique will then be sketched briefly in the following two subsections. First, however, we examine the nature of the timestamps themselves.

The basic point is that timestamps must obviously be globally unique. In a distributed system, however, since there are multiple sites and those sites are all performing work in parallel, it is possible for two or more discrete events—in particular, the initiation of two distinct transactions—to occur simultaneously. Therefore timestamps cannot be simple clock readings. Instead, they consist of two components, a *clock value* (major component) and a *site ID* (minor component). The clock value is the clock reading of the local clock at the site S at which the event in question occurs; the site ID is the identifier of that site S, which must in turn be globally unique. (We are assuming of course that each site maintains its own independent local clock.) Exercise: Why do we use clock value as the more significant portion of the timestamp and site ID as the less significant portion, rather than the other way around?

We also require that timestamps do actually increase with time—that is, if two events i and j occur in the system, and i not only occurs before j but actually or potentially has some influence on j, then we require the timestamp for i to be less than that for j. More specifically, we require that, for any two events i and j:

1. If event *i* precedes event *j* and both events occur at the same site S, then the clock value at site S corresponding to event *i* must be strictly less than that corresponding to event *j;*
2. If event *i* is the sending of a message *m* from site S1 and event *j* is the receipt of that message *m* at site S2, then the clock value at site S1 corresponding to event *i* must be strictly less than the clock value at site S2 corresponding to event *j*.

Reference [7.33] presents a technique for satisfying these requirements. The technique involves

1. ensuring that each site S increments its local clock between every pair of consecutive events at that site;
2. timestamping messages with the clock value t1 of the sending site S1 when the message is sent, and setting the clock value at the receiving site S2 equal to MAX(t1,t2) when the message is received (where t2 is the previous value of the local clock at S2).

This technique imposes a total ordering on all events in the system.

Conservative Timestamping

Now we turn to "conservative timestamping" [7.38]. Conservative timestamping is a technique for eliminating the possibility of conflicting operations, and hence eliminating the need to restart transactions because of such conflicts. Eliminating restarts means less work done twice (less work wasted) and less communication traffic; on the other hand, the approach provides considerably less concurrency than the basic timestamp scheme.

The fundamental idea underlying conservative timestamping is simple: No database operation is ever performed until it can be guaranteed that it cannot possibly cause a conflict (and therefore a restart) at some time in the future. In other words, when a request for a database operation is received from transaction T, that request is delayed (and transaction T waits) until the system knows it cannot receive any conflicting requests from older transactions (that is, transactions having a smaller timestamp than T).

We assume first that each transaction has a "home site," namely the site at which the transaction originates, which oversees the execution of that transaction. The home site for transaction T is responsible for directing all data access requests from T to other sites as appropriate. For the conservative timestamping scheme to work, it is necessary for each site to guarantee that it will handle COMMITs for transactions originating at that site *in timestamp order* (for otherwise an update request for a younger transaction could be received and processed by a remote site before an update request for an older transaction, and hence the older request would have to be rejected and the older transaction restarted). Thus, if transactions T1 and

T2 originate in that order at site S, then site S must perform the commit processing for T1 before that for T2, even if T2 actually reaches its commit point first. Suppose transaction T originates at site S. Then read requests from T will be directed by S to the appropriate site at the time they occur (however, they may still be delayed when they reach that site, as explained below). Update requests from T will be directed by S to the appropriate site or sites during S's commit processing for T. Taken together, the foregoing statements are almost but not quite equivalent to saying that site S can handle only one transaction at a time.

Now consider some other site S'. For each site in the system, S' will maintain a queue of read requests (for objects stored at S') and a queue of update requests (again, for objects stored at S'). All requests will be timestamped with the timestamp of the requesting transaction, and all queues will be maintained in ascending timestamp order (oldest transactions first).

■   When S' receives a read request from site S, it delays that request until every update queue at S' is nonempty *and* the first entry in each of those update queues has a timestamp greater than that of the read request. It then executes the read.

■   When S' receives an update request from site S, it delays that request *at least* until every update queue at S' is nonempty. When that condition is satisfied, it executes that update having the smallest timestamp (which may or may not be the one originating from S).

The net effect of these rules is that (a) update operations are executed in strict timestamp order, and (b) if U1 and U2 are consecutive updates to some object X, with timestamps t1 and t2 respectively (t1 < t2), then all reads against X having a timestamp t between t1 and t2 (t1 < t < t2) are executed between U1 and U2.

A problem with the scheme just described is that site S' may do no work at all over a long period if some other site S does not send any update requests during that period (that is, an empty update queue can cause the system to "get stuck"). In order to overcome this problem, a site S that does not have any genuine requests to send to a site S' can periodically send a timestamped "null request" to that site. The null request indicates that site S will not send any future requests with a timestamp less than that of the null request, and so enables site S' to continue with useful work. It must also be possible for site S' to demand such a null request if it gets impatient (for example, in case the other site has failed).

An advantage of conservative timestamping is that the timestamps in the database are no longer needed (except that they *are* still required if the "Thomas write rule" is in force; see the annotation to reference [7.32] at the end of the chapter). A disadvantage is that it involves a lot of intersite communication (basically, every site has to be in communication with every other at all times; imagine a 100-site system). Another disadvantage is that it is *very* conservative; essentially it eliminates conflicts by *actually serializing all operations* at each site, not just those operations that would otherwise conflict. This is why we suggested earlier that the technique does not provide very much concurrency. We can improve the situation considerably by introducing the concept of *transaction classes* (in fact, it is doubtful whether conservative timestamping would ever be used in practice without some such improvement). Transaction classes are discussed in the next subsection.

Transaction Classes

The basic problem with conservative timestamping, as just pointed out, is that it is a very pessimistic technique. Effectively, it assumes that every request is potentially in conflict with an unknown number of requests still to come, and so it delays execution of every request until all danger of such conflict is past. In practice, of course, it is likely that most requests will never be in actual conflict at all. The notion of transaction classes is intended to help the system to recognize cases where conflict cannot possibly occur, and thus cases where requests can be executed immediately with impunity. So the basic idea is to apply the run-time concurrency control mechanism only to those requests that need it, and to let others run quite unimpeded.

To explain how the technique works, we first need some definitions. A transaction's *readset* is the set of (logical) data objects it reads. Similarly, a transaction's *writeset* is the set of logical data objects it writes (updates). For example, if T is the transaction "Add 5% interest to San Francisco savings account balances" (refer back to Fig. 7.2), then T's readset and writeset both consist of the set defined by

```
SELECT  *
FROM    ACCOUNTS
WHERE   BRANCH = 'SF'
AND     TYPE   = 'SAVINGS'
```

(We assume for simplicity that the "granularity" of readset and writeset definitions—that is, the unit of data in terms of which such definitions can be expressed—is the individual record. In practice the system might support a field-level granularity, in which case the definitions given above for T's readset and writeset could clearly be refined somewhat.)

A transaction *class* is defined by a (maximum) readset and a (maximum) writeset. For example, the transaction class ADD_SAVINGS_INTEREST might be defined as

```
ADD_SAVINGS_INTEREST readset          :    SELECT  *
                                            FROM    ACCOUNTS
                                            WHERE   TYPE = 'SAVINGS'

ADD_SAVINGS_INTEREST writeset         :    SELECT  *
                                            FROM    ACCOUNTS
                                            WHERE   TYPE = 'SAVINGS'
```

That is, any transaction of the ADD_SAVINGS_INTEREST class will read and update some subset of the savings account records. The sample transaction T mentioned above ("Add 5% interest etc.") is a member of this class. As a second example, the transaction class PRINT_CHECKING_STATEMENT might be defined as

```
PRINT_CHECKING_STATEMENT readset     :   SELECT *
                                         FROM    ACCOUNTS
                                         WHERE   TYPE = 'CHECKING'

PRINT_CHECKING_STATEMENT writeset    :   empty set
```

An individual transaction is a *member* of a given transaction class if and only if its readset is a subset of the class readset and its writeset is a subset of the class writeset. Transaction T above, for example, is a member of the ADD_SAVINGS_ INTEREST class, as already indicated. A given transaction can simultaneously be a member of several classes.

Two transaction classes are said to conflict with each other if and only if it is possible for some individual transaction in one class to conflict with some individual transaction in the other—that is, if and only if it is possible for some record to belong simultaneously to both the writeset of the one transaction and the readset or writeset of the other transaction. Loosely, we say that two classes conflict if the writeset of either *intersects* the readset or writeset of the other. Classes ADD_SAVINGS_INTEREST and PRINT_CHECKING_STATEMENT above are not in conflict. As a consequence, transactions in either one of these classes can run concurrently with transactions in the other without any need for mutual synchronization. (However, transactions in the ADD_SAVINGS_INTEREST class do need synchronization *among themselves.*)

We assume, therefore, that the database administrator initially defines an appropriate set of transaction classes, and that the system knows, for every individual transaction, the class or classes to which that transaction belongs (*before* that transaction executes). It is desirable to define transaction classes in as tight a manner as possible, that is, with as small a readset and a writeset as possible, to minimize the number of conflicts. For simplicity, we assume a one-to-one correspondence between sites and classes—each site is the home site for transactions in one class only, and each class has only one home site. These assumptions do not really restrict the system in any way: A site that physically handles several distinct classes can be logically considered as several distinct sites, and a given class can physically be handled by several distinct sites by defining several distinct classes all identical to the given class. If a site is asked to execute a transaction that does not belong to its class, it can simply forward that transaction to a site that can handle it.

Finally, we assume that each site handles transactions in its class one at a time, in timestamp order, without any interleaving. (Actually a limited amount of interleaving may be possible, just so long as the property is preserved that each site transmits all requests to other sites in timestamp order.)

Now consider some site S that receives a request with timestamp t for a database operation on an object X stored at S.

- If the request is a read, S delays the request only until all update queues *for sites whose class writeset includes X* begin with an entry with timestamp greater than t. It then executes the read.

- If the request is an update, S again delays the request only until all update queues *for sites whose class writeset includes X* begin with an entry with timestamp greater than t. It then executes that pending update having the smallest timestamp (which may or may not be the one just received).

It is not necessary to involve any other queues (queues for sites whose class writeset does not include X) at all. The net effect is thus to reduce delays and hence to increase concurrency.

We conclude this subsection with three observations.

- First, the transaction class concept could be used in conjunction with locking as well as with conservative timestamping (locking is also a pessimistic technique, inasmuch as it normally assumes that every operation is subject to possible conflict).

- Second, *the scheme as described above is crucially dependent on a correct assignment of transactions to transaction classes*—for otherwise the system may produce incorrect results, and moreover may do so in a manner that is highly unpredictable, subtle, and difficult to detect. For example, if transaction T updates an object that is not within the writeset of the class to which T has been assigned, then that update will not be synchronized by the concurrency control mechanism, and T—or some unfortunate concurrent transaction—may therefore produce the wrong answer.[6] These observations suggest that the authorization subsystem should be used to ensure that transactions are genuinely restricted to the readset and writeset of their assigned class.

- Third, the system must be ready to handle unanticipated transactions—that is, transactions that do not fit into any of the predefined classes (consider the case of an ad hoc query). The obvious approach to this problem is to define a "global class," whose readset and writeset are each the entire database, and to treat unanticipated transactions as members of that global class. Unfortunately, however, that global class conflicts with every other class, which means that every transaction in the system must be synchronized against "global" transactions. Since global transactions are presumably infrequent, the conservative timestamping scheme as described in the previous subsection would require the site handling the global class to transmit a high proportion of null requests, to allow other sites to get on with useful work.

---

6. In SDD-1 (which supports the notion of transaction classes), this problem is avoided because transactions are assigned to transaction classes by the system itself; that is, the system itself determines the (potential) readset and writeset of each individual transaction, and then compares the results of its determinations with the class definitions previously provided by the DBA. But it seems likely that any such automatic procedure must necessarily be rather pessimistic in its assumptions.

Conflict Graph Analysis

Conflict graph analysis represents a refinement of the transaction class idea introduced in the previous subsection. It allows the degree of possible conflict among transaction classes to be pinned down a little more precisely, and hence the degree of interference on the part of the concurrency control mechanism to be reduced a little further. Conflict graph analysis has been implemented in SDD-1 [7.35] in conjunction with a timestamp mechanism, but there is no reason in principle why the same ideas should not also be applicable in a system using locking instead.

The basic point is that synchronization may be unnecessary even when two transactions are actually—not just potentially—in conflict. For example, let transactions T1 and T2 be as follows:

T1: Deposit $100 in Able's savings account	T2: Display Able's savings account balance
READ Able's savings record add $100 WRITE Able's savings record	READ Able's savings record . . . . . print

T1 and T2 are in conflict—the readset of T2 intersects the writeset of T1—and the conservative timestamping mechanism (or a conventional locking mechanism) would synchronize them accordingly. In fact, however, *all possible interleaved executions of these two transactions are serializable* (Exercise: Do you agree with this statement?), and no synchronization is needed at all. The only effect of such synchronization would be to introduce unnecessary delay. The purpose of conflict graph analysis is to attempt to identify situations such as this one, and hence to eliminate the unnecessary delays.

Conflict graphs are defined as follows. The conflict graph for a given system contains two nodes, a read node and a write node, for each transaction class in that system. The read node for a given class is placed above the write node for that class and is connected to that write node by a *vertical* edge. Further edges are defined as follows: (1) If the writeset of class Ci intersects the writeset of class Cj, then there is a *horizontal* edge connecting the write node for Ci and the write node for Cj; (2) if the readset of class Ci intersects the writeset of class Cj, then there is a *diagonal* edge connecting the read node for Ci and the write node for Cj. Intuitively, the horizontal and diagonal edges indicate situations where synchronization *may* be required—that is, situations in which transactions from the two classes concerned may require such synchronization. If there are no horizontal or diagonal edges connecting two classes, those classes do not require synchronization at all. The object of conflict graph analysis is to decide for every pair of transaction classes (a) whether that pair requires synchronization, and (b) if it does, what *level* of synchronization is required (see later). In particular, it identifies situations in which synchronization is *not* required.

Let us consider an example. Let the transaction classes ADD_SAVINGS_
INTEREST, MAKE_SAVINGS_DEPOSIT, DISPLAY_SAVINGS_BALANCE,
and PRINT_CHECKING_STATEMENT be defined as follows:

```
ADD_SAVINGS_INTEREST readset        :  SELECT *
                                       FROM    ACCOUNTS
                                       WHERE   TYPE = 'SAVINGS'

ADD_SAVINGS_INTEREST writeset       :  SELECT *
                                       FROM    ACCOUNTS
                                       WHERE   TYPE = 'SAVINGS'

MAKE_SAVINGS_DEPOSIT readset        :  SELECT *
                                       FROM    ACCOUNTS
                                       WHERE   TYPE = 'SAVINGS'

MAKE_SAVINGS_DEPOSIT writeset       :  SELECT *
                                       FROM    ACCOUNTS
                                       WHERE   TYPE = 'SAVINGS'

DISPLAY_SAVINGS_BALANCE readset     :  SELECT *
                                       FROM    ACCOUNTS
                                       WHERE   TYPE = 'SAVINGS'

DISPLAY_SAVINGS_BALANCE writeset :     empty set

PRINT_CHECKING_STATEMENT readset :     SELECT *
                                       FROM    ACCOUNTS
                                       WHERE   TYPE = 'CHECKING'

PRINT_CHECKING_STATEMENT writeset:     empty set
```

(ADD_SAVINGS_INTEREST and PRINT_CHECKING_STATEMENT are as defined in the subsection on "Transaction classes" earlier. Transactions T1 and T2
above are members of the classes MAKE_SAVINGS_DEPOSIT and DISPLAY_
SAVINGS_BALANCE, respectively.) The conflict graph for these four classes is
shown in Fig. 7.5.

In this example, transactions in the ADD_SAVINGS_INTEREST, MAKE_
SAVINGS_DEPOSIT, and DISPLAY_SAVINGS_BALANCE classes do require
synchronization with each other. By contrast, transactions in the PRINT_
CHECKING_STATEMENT class do not require synchronization with transactions
in any of the other three classes. Inspection of the conflict graph shows that the difference between the two cases (fairly obviously) is that there are no edges connecting
PRINT_CHECKING_STATEMENT nodes to other nodes, whereas each of the remaining classes has at least one edge connecting its read node to the write node of
some other class. It is also possible, though the example does not illustrate this case,
for two classes to be connected just by a horizontal edge joining the two write
nodes.[7] *Two classes Ci and Cj require synchronization if and only if there is an edge*

7. Two classes can be connected by zero, one, two, or three edges. There are no other possibilities.

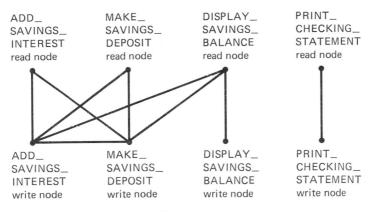

ADD_	MAKE_	DISPLAY_	PRINT_
SAVINGS_	SAVINGS_	SAVINGS_	CHECKING_
INTEREST	DEPOSIT	BALANCE	STATEMENT
read node	read node	read node	read node

ADD_	MAKE_	DISPLAY_	PRINT_
SAVINGS_	SAVINGS_	SAVINGS_	CHECKING_
INTEREST	DEPOSIT	BALANCE	STATEMENT
write node	write node	write node	write node

Fig. 7.5 Example of a conflict graph.

connecting the read node of Ci and the write node of Cj. Furthermore, the precise *level* of synchronization required between classes Ci and Cj depends upon the precise structure of the graph in the region of Ci and Cj (different structures require different degrees of synchronization and hence different concurrency control protocols at run time; see [7.35] for details of these differences).

Conflict graph analysis is supported by the system SDD 1 as follows [7.35]. Transaction classes are statically predefined as explained in the previous subsection, and are statically analyzed (by the system) to produce a *protocol table.* That table indicates (a) for each pair (*Ci, Cj*) of transaction classes, whether those two classes need to be synchronized with each other, and (b) for those cases where synchronization is needed, the level of synchronization required (as mentioned earlier). At run time the system automatically assigns each individual transaction to an appropriate class and hence decides which protocols to apply.

We remark that the transaction class technique outlined in the previous subsection amounts to a limited form of *run-time* conflict graph analysis.

7.8 COMMIT PROTOCOLS

The reader will recall that the notion of *two-phase commit* was introduced toward the end of Chapter 1. Briefly, two-phase commit protocols are required whenever a transaction interacts with multiple autonomous resource managers; the purpose of such protocols is to ensure that all the resource managers concerned "go the same way" on the transaction—that is, either they all accept it (commit it) or they all reject it (roll it back), thus guaranteeing that the transaction is genuinely all-or-nothing. Two-phase commit is particularly important in a distributed system, where distinct resource managers are typically at distinct sites and are hence particularly vulnerable to independent failure, and where in addition we would like to provide as much local site autonomy as possible. In this section we examine the concept of two-phase commit in the context of a distributed system in a little more depth.

We begin by reviewing the basic idea. (For simplicity we will describe all algorithms, etc., exclusively in distributed system terms. Also, we will assume that there is a one-to-one correspondence between resource managers and sites, again for reasons of simplicity.) Let T be a transaction, and let the agents (cohorts) representing that transaction be A1, A2, . . . , An, A(n + 1), executing at sites S1, S2, . . . , Sn, S(n + 1), respectively. One of those sites, call it C, will be appointed as the Coordinator site for T. Site C is required to know the identity of all of the sites S1, S2, . . . , Sn, S(n + 1). Events proceed as follows:

Step 1: As T executes, any given Ai can unilaterally decide to fail the transaction, and hence to roll it back at Si. An uncorrectable error condition such as overflow at Si would be sufficient justification for such a decision.

Step 2: When T completes (that is, all Ai's have completed), control is given to C, which then broadcasts a "get ready to terminate" message to all Si's.

Step 3: On receipt of this message, site Si proceeds as follows: If it has already failed T, it returns a "not OK" message to C; otherwise, it forces all log records involving T and local resources to its local log, thus becoming "ready to go either way," and returns an "OK" message to C.

Step 4: Site C collects the responses from the Si's. If all responses are "OK," site C forces a "broadcasting commit" message to its local log and transmits a "commit" command to all Si's. If any response is "not OK," site C forces a "broadcasting rollback" message to its local log and transmits a "rollback" command to all Si's.

Step 5: On receipt of the broadcast command, site Si either commits T or rolls it back, as instructed (unless of course it has already rolled it back, in which case the broadcast command *must* be "rollback"), and releases T's resources at that site. It also returns an acknowledgment to site C.

Step 6: When all acknowledgments have been received, the Coordinator terminates.

As indicated (Step 1), this protocol has the important property that any site can unilaterally decide to fail a transaction at any time up to the point when it agrees to commit. At that point, however, the site suffers a *loss of autonomy*—once it has agreed to commit if instructed to do so (Step 3), it is not allowed to change its mind, and all local resources needed to perform the commit are sequestered until Step 5. While such loss of autonomy is undesirable, it is a fact that there is no known method of guaranteeing the required transaction atomicity while preserving local autonomy at all times. The best that can be done is to reduce the duration of the period from Step 3 to Step 5 to a minimum.

Before proceeding further, we draw the reader's attention to an illuminating analogy, apparently first noted by Gray [7.43]. The fact is, two-phase commit is nothing more than a formalized version of a protocol that has been employed in civil contract law and similar contexts since time immemorial. A good example is provided by the Christian marriage ceremony:

1. . . . then shall the Minister say unto the Man,
    Wilt thou have this Woman to thy wedded wife?
2. The Man shall answer,
    I will.
3. Then shall the Minister say unto the Woman,
    Wilt thou have this Man to thy wedded husband?
4. The Woman shall answer,
    I will.

        ....

5. Then shall the Minister speak unto the people . . .
    I pronounce that they be Man and Wife together.

In this transaction, the Man and the Woman are the agents (cohorts) and the Minister is the Coordinator. The Man surrenders autonomy and agrees to abide by the Minister's decision at Step 2, and the Woman does likewise at Step 4. Step 5 is the commit. Note that the Man can unilaterally cancel the contract at any time prior to Step 2, and the Woman likewise prior to Step 4; if either agent exercises such a "cancel" option, then the effect—at least to a first approximation—is as if the transaction had never started in the first place.

To return to more technical matters, we observe that two-phase commit is likely to be very expensive in terms of performance. Consider transaction T once again, with agents executing at n sites (not counting the Coordinator site). If two-phase commit were not in effect, the total number of messages for T would be $2n$:

n agent invocations
n "agent complete" messages

With the two-phase commit protocol as described above, however, the number goes up to $6n$:

n agent invocations
n "agent complete" messages
n "get ready" messages
n responses (OK or not OK)
n "commit" or "rollback" commands
n acknowledgments

In practice the "get ready" messages can be included with the agent invocations, and the responses can be included with the "agent complete" messages, thus reducing the $6n$ to $4n$. But this still represents a 100-percent increase in the total number of messages, and hence quite possibly a 100-percent increase in total execution time. It is clearly highly desirable that as many transactions as possible access (or at least update) data at a single site only.

Note: The protocol we have described is known as *centralized* two-phase commit. There is some possibility of reducing the total number of messages, at the cost of increasing the total message delay (and hence the length of the period during which sites must give up their local autonomy), by adopting a variation known as *linear* two-phase commit [7.12]. In this protocol the sites involved in the transaction are first arranged in a linear sequence. When the transaction completes execution, the first site in the sequence gets ready to "go either way" itself, then transmits "get ready" to the second site, which in turn gets ready and passes the message on to the third site, and so on. The last site then acts as the Coordinator; it makes the overall decision, acts on that decision itself, then transmits the decision to the previous site in sequence, which in turn acts on it and passes it on to its predecessor, and so on. (In this second phase each site must also send an acknowledgment back to the site from which it received the overall decision.) This protocol will reduce the number of messages required *by the protocol itself* from $4n$ to $3n$; however, it is not clear that there will be any real saving compared with the centralized protocol if messages can be combined as suggested earlier.

So far we have largely ignored the possibility of site and link failures. It is easy to see that the basic protocol as we have presented it is vulnerable to a variety of such failures. For example, there is a problem if site C (the Coordinator site) fails after sending the "commit" command to some sites but before it has sent it to all of them. Therefore, of course, it is necessary to extend the protocol appropriately to cater for such eventualities. Ideally we would like to make it resilient to every possible kind of failure. The question is, how?

Unfortunately, this problem is fundamentally unsolvable, as can easily be shown. That is, there does not exist any finite protocol that will guarantee the desired result—namely, that all cohorts commit or roll back in unison—in the face of arbitrary failures. For suppose conversely that such a protocol does exist. Let M be the minimum number of messages required by such a protocol (M > 0). Suppose the last of these M messages is lost because of some failure. Then either this message is unnecessary, which is contrary to the assumption that M is minimal, or the protocol now does not work. Either way we have a contradiction, from which we deduce that there is no such protocol.

A further negative result is given in a paper by Skeen and Stonebraker [7.45]. The paper first introduces the notion of *independent recovery*. A system is said to support an independent recovery protocol if, during the restart process that follows a local site failure, the Recovery Manager at that site does not attempt to communicate with any other site in the system. The paper then goes on to show that there does not exist any independent recovery protocol that is resilient to the simultaneous failure of two or more sites. (On the other hand, the paper also shows that independent recovery protocols do exist that are resilient to failure of any single site.)

Despite these depressing results, of course, *something* must be done. In practice, therefore:

a) The Coordinator portion of the two-phase commit protocol must be extended to perform appropriate timeout checks and to retransmit messages as many times as necessary to ensure that those messages eventually reach their intended destination. (It may be possible to delegate this responsibility to the communication control software.)

b) If a site failure occurs at any point during the commit process (either at the Coordinator site or at one of the participant sites), the Recovery Manager at that site must communicate with other sites to determine what must be done in order to ensure that the commit process is completed correctly.

Both of these extensions were incorporated into the protocols as discussed in Chapter 1, and the reader is referred to that chapter for details. Observe how the extensions relate to the two negative results discussed above. Point (a) means that the protocol is now potentially of infinite length (in practice, of course, it is "never" *actually* infinite, but it may certainly take a long time if, for example, one of the participants fails after sending its "OK" message and before receiving the Coordinator's broadcast command—for then the Coordinator will continually retransmit that command until the participant revives). Point (b) means that the system is not supporting an independent recovery protocol.

7.9 CATALOG MANAGEMENT

The system catalog (also known as the system dictionary or system directory) is the repository of a variety of control information concerning objects of interest to the system—for example, domains, relations, attributes, users, programs, access privileges, integrity constraints. One of the main purposes of the catalog is to enable the system to transform high-level user requests for data into appropriate low-level operations on stored objects, and hence to satisfy the objectives of data independence, as explained in Volume I. In the case of a distributed system in particular, the catalog entry for a given object must specify the site(s) at which that object is stored, in addition to all the more usual information; such site specifications allow the system to provide the desired replication and location transparency, as discussed in Section 7.1. The question arises, where and how should the catalog itself be stored?

As Rothnie and Goodman point out in [7.11], there are many possible answers to this question, and it may well be that the answer is different for different portions of the catalog (because the pattern of use is different for different portions). The following are some of the possible approaches.

1. *Centralized:* The total catalog is stored exactly once, at a single central site.

2. *Fully replicated:* The total catalog is stored in its entirety at every site.

3. *Partitioned:* Each site maintains its own catalog for objects stored at that site. The total catalog is the union of all those disjoint local catalogs.

4. *Combination of (1) and (3):* Each site maintains its own local catalog, as in (3); in addition, a single central site maintains a unified copy of all of those local catalogs, as in (1).

5. *Other combinations:* Other combinations are clearly possible. Some of the possibilities are discussed below.

Before expanding on approach (5), let us examine the first four approaches in a little more detail. Approach (1) (centralized) suffers from some obvious disadvantages: There is a severe loss of local autonomy (even access to purely local data requires remote access to the catalog), and the entire system is critically dependent on the availability of the catalog site. Approach (2) (fully replicated) has the drawback that every catalog update must be propagated to every site—counter once again to the objective of local autonomy—and in particular makes the addition of a new site to the network a highly nontrivial operation. Further arguments against these two approaches can be found in [7.47].

Approach (3) (partitioned) does have the advantage that purely local operations do not involve any remote access. However, requests for nonlocal operations must cause a broadcast to all sites in order to locate the required catalog entries. Approach (4) (combination of 1 and 3) is an improvement, in that request for nonlocal operations involve, not a broadcast, but an access only to the central catalog site; but, as with approach (1), that central site is now crucial to the overall operation of the system.

So we are left with approach (5) (other combinations). Clearly, the most general possibility is to allow an arbitrary subset of the total catalog to be stored at each site. (Given this flexibility, however, any arrangement in which some site does not store at least the complete local catalog for that site does not seem particularly sensible.) The systems SDD-1, Distributed INGRES, and R* all support some version of approach (5). We discuss the SDD-1 and R* approaches here; for a discussion of Distributed INGRES, see [7.22].

In SDD-1 [7.18] the entire catalog consists (logically) of a single relation. That relation is treated exactly like any other relation in the database: It can be fragmented in an arbitrary manner, and fragments can be distributed and possibly replicated in an arbitrary manner, just as if it contained user data instead of catalog information. This scheme is very attractive for a number of reasons:

- Users can interrogate the catalog using their normal data access interface.

- The catalog management component can rely on the concurrency control and two-phase commit mechanisms of the underlying system to ensure that catalog fragments and the objects they describe are always mutually consistent, instead of having to supply its own special code for this purpose.

- In a similar fashion, security requirements with respect to the catalog can be handled by the authorization mechanism of the underlying system.

- The problem of physically allocating portions of the catalog to specific sites can be treated as part of the physical database design problem and can be solved on an installation-by-installation basis, instead of having to be solved in a comparatively inflexible manner at the time the DBMS software is designed.

(All but the last of these points also apply to a nondistributed system, of course, though perhaps they carry more weight in the distributed case.) However, it can be argued that SDD-1 is *too* flexible in its catalog management scheme. For one thing, it is possible for a local object to have its catalog entry at a remote site, which (as we have already suggested) is unnecessarily inefficient. More significantly, since the system has no a priori knowledge of the location of any given catalog entry, it is necessary to maintain a higher-level catalog to provide that information. Such a higher-level catalog, the "directory locator," is included in SDD-1, and is *fully replicated* (that is, a copy is stored at every site). As a consequence, any change to the physical distribution of the catalog (presumably an infrequent operation) will require directory locator updates at every site.

SDD-1 also provides a *caching* mechanism to improve the efficiency of repeated access to remote catalog entries. Briefly, a reference from a local site L to a catalog entry E stored at a remote site R causes a copy of E to be retrieved from R and kept in a cache at L; subsequent references to E from L can be directed to that copy instead. However, the caching mechanism itself leads to additional overhead, because the cached copy at L must be discarded if the original remote entry at R is updated. See [7.47] for further discussion of this point.

We turn now to R*. Before describing the R* catalog management scheme per se, however, we must first say something about *object naming* in that system [7.47]. (By "object" here we mean a user-perceivable object, that is, an object that is visible through the SQL interface, such as a base table or an index.) R* distinguishes between an object's *printname,* which is a name by which the object can be referenced in, for example, a SQL SELECT statement, and its *system-wide name,* which is a globally unique identifier for the object. An object can have many printnames (so that different users can refer to the same object by different names), but it always has exactly one system-wide name. Moreover, different objects can have the same printname; for example, the object known as MYDATA by user U1 and the object known as MYDATA by user U2 may be different.

System-wide names have four components:

- creator ID   - the ID of the user who created the object (unique within site)
- creator site ID - the ID of the site from which the object was created (unique across all sites)
- local name   - the name of the object as assigned by its creator (unique within objects of this type created by this user from this creator site at this birth site)

- birth site ID   -   the ID of the site at which the object is initially stored (unique across all sites)

For example, the system-wide name

```
ARTHUR @ HURSLEY . STATS @ GREENOCK
```

identifies an object with local name STATS, created by the user called ARTHUR at the HURSLEY site and first stored at the GREENOCK site. That object may subsequently be moved to some other site, say the CROYDON site; however, its system-wide name will not change as a consequence. System-wide names never change so long as the object they identify remains in existence.

As already indicated, users refer to objects by printnames. Usually a printname consists of a simple unqualified name—either the "local name" component of the system-wide name (for example, STATS), or a *synonym* for the system-wide name, introduced via the SQL statement DEFINE SYNONYM. In the first case, default name completion rules allow the system to expand the local name to its full system-wide form (the details of this process are straightforward and are given in [7.47]). As an example of the second case, the statement

```
DEFINE SYNONYM DETAILS
        AS ARTHUR @ HURSLEY . STATS @ GREENOCK
```

will allow the user issuing it henceforth to use the name DETAILS as a printname for the STATS object. Note: It is also possible, though unusual, for users to refer to system-wide names explicitly; that is, a printname can be identical to the corresponding system-wide name. But normally users would and should be unaware of the complete system-wide name of an object.

The first component of the system catalog, then, is a set of *synonym tables*. Each site will maintain a set of local synonym tables for each user known at that site, mapping the synonyms available to that user to their corresponding system-wide names.

Now consider some site S. Site S will maintain a local catalog entry for every object X for which S is the *birth* site, and a local catalog entry for every object Y for which S is the *current* site (that is, the site at which Y is currently stored; for the moment we ignore the possibility that Y may be partitioned and/or replicated). Consider also a user reference to some printname Z. By the name completion rules or by reference to the local synonym tables, the system is able to determine the system-wide name for Z, and hence can identify Z's birth site. It can then interrogate the local catalog at that birth site. If Z is still stored at that site, then the required object has been located. Otherwise, the catalog entry for Z at the birth site will point to Z's current site, and the system can then go to that site for the desired object. Thus any desired object can be located in at most two remote accesses.

Extensions to the foregoing scheme to handle replicated and partitioned data are straightforward, and are described in detail in [7.47].

Like SDD-1, R* employs a caching scheme for recently referenced remote catalog entries. Unlike SDD-1, however, it does not attempt to discard those entries if the original entries are updated. Instead, what happens is the following. Catalog entries (both cached and original) are tagged with *version numbers*. When compiling a SQL statement, the system makes a note of the version numbers of all catalog entries used in that compilation. Then, when the compiled statement is executed, the system checks those version numbers against the current values. If any catalog entry has been updated in the interim, its version number will have changed, and the discrepancy will be noted; the system can then automatically recompile the original SQL statement.

We conclude this section with a brief description of the SQL compilation process in R*, since that process is heavily dependent on the catalog structure outlined above. Suppose a SQL statement is submitted at site S. Compilation proceeds as follows.

1. The SQL compiler at site S parses the statement in the usual way and gathers together the catalog entries (both local and remote) for all objects referenced by that statement, locating those entries as explained above under the discussion of object naming.

2. It then generates an overall access strategy for the statement, using the techniques described in reference [7.21]. In general that strategy will involve processing on the part of several sites, say S1, S2, . . . , Sn. Site S therefore sends each of those sites the relevant portion of its overall processing plan, thus allowing each of those sites to complete the compilation process for its own portion.

3. Local completion of the compilation process at site S*i* includes checking that the user is authorized to access the objects requested at S*i*, and storing the compiled code to perform all such access in the database at S*i*.

4. In addition, site S*i* makes entries in its local catalog to record the dependency of that stored code on those local objects.

This last step is necessary for reasons (once again) of local autonomy: It must be possible to drop a local object, say an index, or to revoke a local access privilege, without having to refer to any remote sites; hence all dependencies on a given object must be known at the site at which that object is stored, for otherwise the ability to drop the object might depend on the availability of some remote site. As it is, however, dropping an object is a purely local operation, and can result in the invalidation of some *local* compiled code. An attempt at run-time to execute an invalidated piece of code will cause an automatic recompilation. That recompilation will involve only the local code if it is merely a local access path that has changed (for example, an index has been dropped), the entire original SQL statement otherwise.

7.10   CONCLUSION

Distributed database research is a flourishing area within the database technology field, and seems likely to remain so for some time to come. In this chapter we have surveyed some—by no means all—of the major problems in this area, and we have indicated some of the approaches currently being taken to solving those problems. In particular we have used two experimental systems, SDD-1 and R*, as the basis for much of our discussion. The problem areas we have examined in depth are the following:

- distributed query processing,
- data replication and update propagation,
- distributed concurrency control,
- two-phase commit,
- distributed catalog management.

In passing we have also touched on numerous additional problems, such as the problem of heterogeneous systems. We have also sketched the distributed system capabilities of IMS and CICS, in order to provide some indication of the state of the art in commercially available (as opposed to experimental) systems. A comparison of Sections 7.3 and 7.4 with the remainder of the chapter will show that we still have a long way to go.

EXERCISES

7.1 Define (a) location transparency, (b) replication transparency.

7.2 Summarize the major differences between MSC and ISC.

7.3 Refer to the query processing example in Section 7.5. Compute the communication time for each of the six strategies presented in that example under the revised estimates:

> Number of red parts   = 1,000
> Number of shipments by London suppliers   = 10,000

7.4 Explain the method for guaranteeing that timestamps are globally unique in a distributed system.

7.5 Define the notion of *conflicting transactions* as the term is used in conjunction with timestamp-based concurrency control algorithms. Give an example of two transactions that are in conflict with each other and yet may safely be run without any synchronization.

7.6 Sketch a concurrency control mechanism that is based on locking but takes advantage of the concept of transaction classes.

7.7 Discuss strategies for managing the catalog in a distributed system.

REFERENCES AND BIBLIOGRAPHY

Refcrences [7.1–7.6] are the proceedings of the first six of a continuing series of conferences devoted to the topic of distributed systems. Many of the references listed subsequently first appeared in one or other of these first six.

7.1 *Proc. 1st Berkeley Conference on Distributed Data Management and Computer Networks.* Lawrence Berkeley Laboratory (1976).

7.2 *Proc. 2nd Berkeley Conference on Distributed Data Management and Computer Networks.* Lawrence Berkeley Laboratory (May 1977).

7.3 *Proc. 3rd Berkeley Conference on Distributed Data Management and Computer Networks.* Lawrence Berkeley Laboratory (August 1978).

7.4 *Proc. 4th Berkeley Conference on Distributed Data Management and Computer Networks.* Lawrence Berkeley Laboratory (August 1979).

7.5 *Proc. 5th Berkeley Conference on Distributed Data Management and Computer Networks.* Lawrence Berkeley Laboratory (February 1981).

7.6 *Proc. 6th Berkeley Conference on Distributed Data Management and Computer Networks.* Lawrence Berkeley Laboratory (February 1982).

7.7 A. L. Scherr. "Distributed Data Processing." *IBM Sys. J.* **17**, No. 4 (October 1978).

A useful introductory paper. It discusses motivations for adopting the distributed approach, compares and contrasts possible distributed system architectures (that is, designs for installed systems, not for the software itself), and considers factors involved in choosing one design over another.

7.8 P. A. Bernstein, J. B. Rothnie, Jr., and D. W. Shipman (eds.). Tutorial: Distributed Data Base Management. IEEE Computer Society, 5855 Naples Plaza, Suite 301, Long Beach, California 90803 (1978).

A collection of papers from various sources, grouped under the following headings:

- Overview of relational database management
- Distributed database management overview
- Approaches to distributed query processing
- Approaches to distributed concurrency control
- Approaches to distributed database reliability

7.9 Various authors. "Distributed Data Base Management." In H. Weber and A. I. Wasserman (eds.): *Issues in Data Base Management (Proc. 4th International Conference on Very Large Data Bases, September 1978).* North-Holland (1979).

Contains a paper entitled "Issues in Distributed Data Base Management Systems," by M. Adiba, J. C. Chupin, R. Demolombe, G. Gardarin, and J. le Bihan, followed by comments from P. A. Bernstein, M. Edelberg, E. J. Neuhold, J. B. Rothnie, Jr., and H.-J. Schneider.

7.10 J. N. Gray. "A Discussion of Distributed Systems." *Proc. Congresso AICA* **79**, Bari, Italy (October 1979). Also available as IBM Research Report RJ2699 (September 1979).

A sketchy but good overview/tutorial. As an illustration of the state of the art in installed systems, it quotes the airlines as having ". . . probably the most sophisticated system currently in operation, involving as it does:

- multiple corporations,
- diverse data management systems,
- diverse terminal types,
- diverse computer architectures,
- diverse operating systems, and
- activity on six continents.

The system is continuously available (24-hour operation) and supports quite high transaction rates. A typical node has duplexed processors, upward of ten billion bytes of disk (over 100 spindles), and runs about 100 transactions a second (average). Large systems and peak loads double these figures. The nodes are connected via a special network that carries over 30 messages per second among them." (Slightly paraphrased.)

7.11 J. B. Rothnie, Jr., and N. Goodman. "A Survey of Research and Development in Distributed Database Management." *Proc. 3rd International Conference on Very Large Data Bases* (October 1977). Also published in [7.8].

A very useful survey. The field is discussed under the headings of

- Synchronizing update transactions
- Distributed query processing
- Handling component failures
- Directory management
- Database design

Of these, all but the last have been covered in some depth in the body of the chapter. For completeness, we summarize below the authors' comments on the last topic, "database design" (the authors are referring here to *physical* design, and in particular to the problem of how data files should be assigned to individual sites in the network—the so-called file allocation problem). While it is the case that useful work has been done in this area, the authors suggest that the assumptions underlying that work are typically too much oversimplified for the solutions to be directly applicable to distributed systems such as SDD-1 and R*. Those assumptions are basically as follows:

1. The network configuration, link capacities and costs, and site capacities and costs are all known.

2. The volume of reads and volume of writes from each site to each file are also known.

Under these assumptions, it is possible to apply mathematical techniques to find a file allocation scheme that does not violate any capacity constraint and minimizes the total cost function. However, as the authors point out, such approaches

a) do not consider the possibility of a single access request involving multiple files, and hence do not allow for the cost of moving data from one file to another (and, as we saw in Section 7.5, such costs may easily dominate every other factor);

b) do not consider the possibility of data replication and the costs of concurrency control and update propagation (again, such costs may outweigh all other considerations);

c) do not help to determine data partitioning (taking the file as the unit of allocation effectively assumes that any such partitioning has already been done).

The conclusion is that there does not yet exist any completely adequate physical design methodology for distributed systems.

7.12 B. G. Lindsay et al. "Notes on Distributed Databases." IBM Research Report RJ2571 (July 1979).

This paper is divided into five chapters:

1. Replicated data

2. Authorization and views

3. Introduction to distributed transaction management

4. Recovery facilities

5. Transaction initiation, migration, and termination

Chapter 1 discusses update strategies, along the lines of Section 7.6 of the present chapter. Chapter 2 is almost totally concerned with authorization in a *non*distributed system (in the style of System R), except for a few remarks at the end. Chapter 3 considers transaction initiation and termination, concurrency control, and recovery, all rather briefly. Chapter 4 is devoted to a discussion of recovery in the *non*distributed case (again). Finally, Chapter 5 discusses certain aspects of distributed transaction management in considerable detail; in particular, it gives a very careful presentation of two-phase commit.

7.13 G. A. Champine. "Six Approaches to Distributed Databases." *Datamation* (May 1977). Also published in [7.8].

7.14 IBM Corporation. IMS/VS Version 1 System Administration Guide. IBM Form No. SH20-9178.

Describes IMS/MSC.

7.15 IBM Corporation. CICS/VS System/Application Design Guide. IBM Form No. SC33-0068.

Describes CICS/ISC.

7.16 IBM Corporation. IMS/VS Version 1 Programming Guide for Remote SNA Systems. IBM Form No. SH20-9054.

Describes IMS/ISC.

7.17 R. G. Ross. "IBM's Distributed Processing Capabilities for Large-Scale Data Base Systems." *Performance Development Corporation Data Base Newsletter* **9**, No. 2 (March 1981).

7.18 J. B. Rothnie, Jr., et al. "SDD-1: A System for Distributed Databases" (revised version). In *Database: Proc. 74th Infotech State of the Art Conference,* London, England (October 1980). An earlier version of this paper, under the title "Introduction to a System for Distributed Databases (SDD-1)," appears in *ACM TODS* **5**, No. 1 (March 1980).

7.19 R. Williams et al. "R*: An Overview of the Architecture." IBM Research Report RJ3325 (December 1981).

7.20 E. Wong. "Retrieving Dispersed Data from SDD-1: A System for Distributed Databases." In [7.2].

Wong's algorithm is described in outline in the body of the present chapter. We describe one important aspect of it in more detail here. That aspect is based on what we may call *joinable subsets* (the more usual, though less descriptive, term is "semijoins"). Let X and Y be two relations having a natural join J. Then the joinable subset of X with respect to J is the subset of X that participates in J—that is, the set of tuples of X that "match" at least one tuple in Y, according to the defining condition for J. For example, if X is the supplier relation S, Y is the shipment relation SP, and J is the natural join of S and SP over S#, then the joinable subset of X (that is, S) with respect to J is the set of S tuples for suppliers that supply at least one part (tuples for suppliers that do not supply any parts are excluded).

Now suppose that S and SP are stored at sites A and B, respectively, and that it is necessary to compute the join J. Instead of shipping the entire relation S to B (say), we can do the following:

- Compute the projection of SP over S# at B; call the result TEMP1.
- Ship TEMP1 to A.
- Compute the natural join of S and TEMP1 over S# at A; call the result TEMP2. TEMP2 is the joinable subset of S with respect to J.
- Ship TEMP2 to B.
- Compute the natural join of TEMP2 and SP over S# at B. The result is the natural join J of S and SP over S#.

This procedure will reduce the total amount of data movement if and only if

```
SIZE ( TEMP1 ) + SIZE ( TEMP2 ) < SIZE ( S )
```

where the "size" of a relation is the cardinality of that relation multiplied by the width of an individual tuple (in bits, say). In practice this condition may frequently be satisfied.

7.21 P. G. Selinger and M. E. Adiba. "Access Path Selection in Distributed Data Base Management Systems." In S. M. Deen and P. Hammersley (eds.): *Proc. International Conference on Data Bases,* Aberdeen, Scotland (July 1980). Heyden and Sons Ltd. (1980).

7.22 M. R. Stonebraker and E. J. Neuhold. "A Distributed Data Base Version of INGRES." In [7.2].

7.23 R. Epstein, M. R. Stonebraker, and E. Wong. "Distributed Query Processing in a Relational Data Base System." *Proc. 1978 ACM SIGMOD International Conference on Management of Data* (June 1978).

Presents the query processing algorithm for Distributed INGRES. This algorithm represents a refinement of the algorithm described in [7.20] and [7.22]. The algorithm works by choosing data *not* to be moved and then choosing the set of sites to do the processing. The choices take into account the kind of network available, *site-to-site* (for example, ARPANET), in which the cost of sending a message to n sites is assumed to be n times the cost of sending it to a single site, or *broadcast* (for example, ETHERNET), in which the cost for n sites is assumed to be the same as for one site. It is suggested that a broadcast network is particularly suited to a relational system like Distributed INGRES.

7.24 R. Epstein and M. R. Stonebraker. "Analysis of Distributed Data Base Processing Strategies." *Proc. 6th International Conference on Very Large Data Bases* (October 1980).

A report on a set of distributed query processing simulation experiments. The experiments compared the strategies produced by a number of different algorithms on the basis of the amount of data movement involved. The general conclusions were that (1) Limited search algorithms do not perform very well (that is, do not usually select the best strategy) compared with algorithms that exhaust all possibilities; (2) Reliable estimates of intermediate result sizes are crucial (the System R estimate of "worst case divided by 10" seems to be quite satisfactory); and (3) Run-time methods do not perform significantly better than compile-time methods (by "run-time method" we mean a method that makes its choice of strategy dynamically as the query executes, when relation sizes are known accurately; by "compile-time method" we mean a method like that of System R, in which all such choices are made at compile time).

7.25 M. E. Adiba and B. G. Lindsay. "Database Snapshots." *Proc. 6th International Conference on Very Large Data Bases* (October 1980).

7.26 M. E. Adiba. "Derived Relations: A Unified Mechanism for Views, Snapshots, and Distributed Data." IBM Research Report RJ2881 (July 1980).

Defines some extensions to relational algebra to permit the definition of (among other things) snapshots and replicated data.

7.27 I. L. Traiger, J. N. Gray, C. A. Galtieri, and B. G. Lindsay. "Transactions and Consistency in Distributed Database Systems." IBM Research Report RJ2555 (June 1979).

7.28 R. Obermarck. "Global Deadlock Detection Algorithm." IBM Research Report RJ2845 (June 1980).

7.29 R. Obermarck. "Deadlock Detection for All Resource Classes." IBM Research Report RJ2955 (October 1980).

Lockable resources can be classified into three categories, referred to in this paper as

1. uniquely named,

2. M-of-N, and

3. pool.

A request for a *uniquely named* resource is a request for a specific object (for example, a specific database record). A request for an *M-of-N* resource is a request for some number (M) of effectively interchangeable objects from a set of N such objects (for example, a request for three tape drives out of a possible ten). A request for a *pool* resource is also a request for M indistinguishable objects from a set of N, but those M are required to satisfy some specific constraint, such as their all being contiguous (for example, a request for M contiguous bytes of main storage). Centralized systems use *locking* to control access to uniquely named resources, but *scheduling* to control access to M-of-N and pool resources (thus requests for these latter two kinds of resource cannot cause a deadlock in a centralized system). In a distributed system, however, an agent at one site may initiate another at a remote site, and that remote agent may then require some M-of-N or pool resources. The deadlock avoidance protocols do not work very well in such an environment. What is needed, therefore, is a scheme for handling all resource classes in a uniform manner, and a corresponding deadlock detection mechanism. This paper proposes such a scheme. (See also [7.30].)

7.30 C. Beeri and R. Obermarck. "A Resource Class Independent Deadlock Detection Algorithm." *Proc. 7th International Conference on Very Large Data Bases* (September 1981).

Corrects some deficiencies in (and effectively supersedes) reference [7.29].

7.31 D. J. Rosenkrantz, R. E. Stearns, and P. M. Lewis II. "System Level Concurrency Control for Distributed Database Systems." *ACM TODS* **3**, No. 2 (June 1978).

See Chapter 3 for a description of the proposals of this paper.

7.32 R. H. Thomas. "A Majority Consensus Approach to Concurrency Control for Multiple Copy Data Bases." *ACM TODS* **4**, No. 2 (June 1979). An earlier version of this paper, under the title "A Solution to the Concurrency Control Problem for Multiple Copy Data Bases," was published in *Proc. 16th IEEE Computer Society International Conference* (1978), and also in [7.8].

Describes a deadlock-free concurrency control mechanism for the fully redundant case. In outline the scheme works as follows.

- Transactions are assigned globally unique timestamps.
- Every stored object (replica) in the database carries the timestamp of the transaction that last updated it.
- Each transaction T executes at a single site and directs all its read operations, *without* any locking, to the replicas at that site. The read operations are recorded in an *action list* for T at T's site. The entry in the action list for an object X read by T gives the timestamp associated with X, as read from the database at T's site.
- Updates by T are not installed in the database as T executes but are instead also recorded in T's action list. The entry in the action list for an object X to be updated by T gives the timestamp associated with X (as read from the database at T's site), together with the updated value X'.
- When T completes, its action list is broadcast to all sites, and the sites then *vote* on it. If a majority of sites vote "yes," T is accepted, and its updates (if any) are applied at all sites; otherwise, T is restarted (observe that no rollback is necessary).
- *The voting procedure.* Site S votes "yes" on action list L (from transaction T) if and only if the following conditions (1) and (2) both hold.

  1. No object X in L has been updated at S since T read it (that is, the timestamp of X at S is less than or equal to the timestamp of X in L).
  2. No object X in L is scheduled for update at S in some other action list L' (from transaction T') that is "pending" at S (an action list is pending at S if S voted "yes" on it but S has not yet been informed of the system's overall decision regarding it).

  If condition (1) is violated, site S votes "no."

  If condition (1) holds but condition (2) does not hold, site S votes "pass" if T is younger (has a smaller timestamp) than T', and defers its vote to a later time otherwise. (Note: If site S were to wait instead of voting "pass," deadlock would be possible.)

  For an explanation of why this voting procedure guarantees correctness, see the paper.

- *The update application procedure.* On being instructed to apply the updates in action list L from transaction T, site S actually updates a given object X only if the timestamp of X at S is less than the timestamp of T. (For if this condition does not hold, then T's update has been superseded by a more recent one that S has already applied.)

Reference [7.39] suggests that, although many of the ideas in the majority consensus approach are useful in themselves—for example, the update application procedure described above is used in SDD-1, under the name of the "Thomas write rule"—the overall approach does not generalize to the case in which the database is less than fully redundant.

7.33 L. Lamport. "Time, Clocks, and the Ordering of Events in a Distributed System." *CACM* **21,** No. 7 (July 1978).

7.34 P. A. Bernstein and N. Goodman. "Approaches to Concurrency Control in Distributed Database Systems." *Proc. 1979 ACM National Conference* (June 1979).

7.35 P. A. Bernstein, D. W. Shipman, and J. B. Rothnie, Jr. "Concurrency Control in a System for Distributed Databases (SDD-1)." *ACM TODS* **5,** No. 1 (March 1980).

7.36 P. A. Bernstein and D. W. Shipman. "The Correctness of Concurrency Control Mechanisms in a System for Distributed Databases (SDD-1)." *ACM TODS* **5,** No. 1 (March 1980).

7.37 G. McLean, Jr. "Comments on SDD-1 Concurrency Control Mechanisms." *ACM TODS* **6,** No. 2 (June 1981).

Points out some errors in the SDD-1 concurrency control mechanism [7.35, 7.36]. In particular, the author shows that deadlock is possible, and proposes a simple extension to the mechanism for resolving such deadlocks.

7.38 P. A. Bernstein and N. Goodman. "Timestamp-Based Algorithms for Concurrency Control in Distributed Database Systems." *Proc. 6th International Conference on Very Large Data Bases* (October 1980).

7.39 P. A. Bernstein and N. Goodman. "Fundamental Algorithms for Concurrency Control in Distributed Database Systems." Computer Corporation of America Technical Report CCA-80-05 (February 1980).

7.40 P. A. Bernstein and N. Goodman. "Concurrency Control in Distributed Database Systems." *ACM Comp. Surv.* **13,** No. 2 (June 1981).

References [7.34–7.40] overlap considerably. [7.34] is recommended as a gentle introduction to the overall topic; it covers both locking and timestamping. [7.40] is an extended treatment of the same material, still fairly tutorial in style. [7.39] is a very formal treatment. [7.38] is a useful summary of timestamp algorithms only. [7.35–7.37] are of course specifically concerned with SDD-1.

7.41 M. R. Stonebraker. "Concurrency Control and Consistency of Multiple Copies in Distributed INGRES." *IEEE Transactions on Software Engineering* Vol. SE-5, No. 3 (May 1979).

7.42 H. T. Kung and J. T. Robinson. "On Optimistic Methods for Concurrency Control." *ACM TODS* **6,** No. 2 (June 1981).

The reader is referred to the annotated bibliography in Chapter 3 for a description of the proposals of this paper.

7.43 J. N. Gray. "The Transaction Concept: Virtues and Limitations." *Proc. 7th International Conference on Very Large Data Bases* (September 1981).

7.44 W. H. Kohler. "A Survey of Techniques for Synchronization and Recovery in Decentralized Computer Systems." *ACM Comp. Surv.* **13,** No. 2 (June 1981).

7.45 D. Skeen and M. R. Stonebraker. "A Formal Model of Crash Recovery in a Distributed System." University of California, Berkeley: Report UCB/ERL M80/48 (December 1980).

7.46 M. M. Hammer and D. W. Shipman. "Reliability Mechanisms for SDD-1: A System for Distributed Databases." *ACM TODS* **5,** No. 4 (December 1980).

> In an attempt to avoid the lengthy delays that may theoretically occur with the normal two-phase commit protocol (see Section 7.8), SDD-1 uses a *four*-phase protocol, in which the Coordinator site first establishes one or more secondary Coordinator sites that can take over if the primary Coordinator fails at an inopportune moment. An obvious disadvantage of this scheme is that it imposes significant additional overhead on every transaction, even in the normal case; moreover, it is still susceptible to certain (unlikely) failure combinations, as is only to be expected.

7.47 B. G. Lindsay. "Object Naming and Catalog Management for a Distributed Database Manager." IBM Research Report RJ2914 (August 1980).

7.48 B. G. Lindsay and P. G. Selinger. "Site Autonomy Issues in R*: A Distributed Database Management System." IBM Research Report RJ2927 (September 1980).

> This paper outlines the problems inherent in preserving maximum local autonomy in a distributed system, and sketches the approach being taken to those problems in R*. The problems are discussed under the following headings: Authorization; Query Compilation and Binding; Catalog Management; and Commit Protocols.

ANSWERS TO SELECTED EXERCISES

7.3

Strategy	Technique	Communication time
1	Move P to A	16.7 min
2	Move S and SP to B	2.8 hr
3	For each London shipment, check corres. part	2.3 day
4	For each red part, check for London supplier	20 sec
5	Move London shipments to B	16.7 min
6	Move red parts to A	1 sec

8
Database
Machines

8.1 INTRODUCTION

Database machines have been the subject of considerable research for quite some time (at least ten years at the time of writing). Until recently, however, that activity has had little impact on the database field as a whole; but within the past couple of years we have begun to see the first product announcements in this area, and it seems likely that we shall see more in the near future. It is also certain that research into database machines will continue in a number of directions.

So what exactly is a database machine? Before trying to answer this question, let us first consider the structure of a conventional database system (Fig. 8.1).

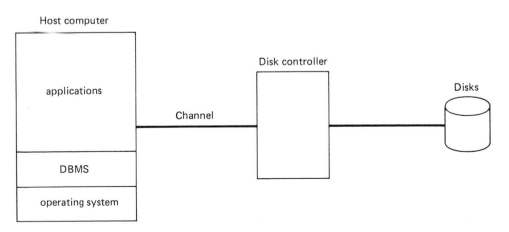

Fig. 8.1 Structure of a conventional system.

It is well known that there is a severe mismatch between the capabilities of conventional computer hardware on the one hand, and the requirements of data storage and retrieval applications on the other. In a nutshell, the hardware is designed to access data by physical address, whereas applications need to access it by value (that is, associatively). This mismatch leads to a heavy reliance on the use of *pointers* on the part of the DBMS. For example, a user request for the S record for supplier S4 will typically involve

- searching the catalog for the entry for the supplier number index;
- following a pointer from that catalog entry to that index;
- following pointers through the levels of that index, starting at the top level and working down until the entry for supplier S4 is found at the bottom level;
- following a pointer from that index entry to the desired S record; and finally
- retrieving that record.

If the access mechanism is not indexing but (say) hash-addressing or stored fansets, it is still pointers that provide the basis of that mechanism (in hashing, for example, the hash procedure converts a user-supplied key into a pointer (the hash address), and pointers are also used to chain together records that generate the same hash address). Thus, regardless of the particular mechanism in use, a single data request at the application level will typically involve numerous accesses to the disk at the hardware level. Moreover, if the original request involves not just an equality condition on a primary key but some more complex selection condition, then the pointer mechanisms will probably not be adequate in themselves; rather, the DBMS will have to retrieve a superset of the records actually required and then perform some additional processing to eliminate those that do not qualify. All of this activity—following pointers on the disk, analyzing records in the host CPU—amounts to a *software implementation of associative addressing.*

Given all of the above, it is hardly surprising that the tables (catalogs, indexes, etc.) needed to locate data can easily occupy more storage than the data itself, and that the DBMS can easily account for a higher percentage of the total CPU activity than the rest of the system put together. (It is a fact, incidentally, that database management systems tend to be CPU-bound rather than I/O-bound.) So the question is: Can we offload some or all of the DBMS activity (in particular the associative addressing function) from the host machine to some backend system—that is, a "database machine"? If we can, then resources at the host can be freed and made available for other activities not directly connected with database access per se. See Fig. 8.2.

The system of Fig. 8.2 works as follows (in outline). An application program executing in the host computer issues a database request in the usual way. That request is then sent across the channel from the host to the database machine, which executes it and sends the result back across the channel to the host. The link between the host and the backend machine would normally be an I/O channel, but may be a

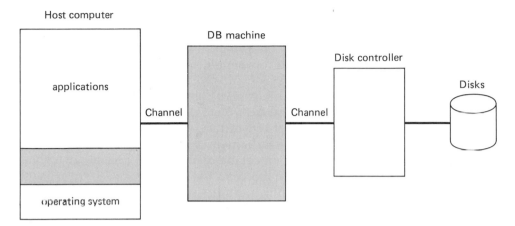

Fig. 8.2 Structure of a system with a database machine.

communications line. The backend machine itself may be a conventional (but dedicated) system running conventional DBMS software, or it may involve specialized hardware such as an "associative disk," or it may be a combination of both. We deliberately leave unspecified for the time being all details of the precise distribution of function between the host and the backend system (note that the "DBMS" is not shown in Fig. 8.2).

Before going any further, we remark that the system of Fig. 8.2 is actually a very special case of a distributed database system, in which the entire database happens to be stored at one node and applications execute at another. The outline description just given of the way the system operates is very similar to the description of "data request shipping" in Section 7.4. As we proceed through the present chapter we shall see many instances of such parallels between systems that incorporate a database machine and systems that support a distributed database. The fact is, the two classes of system share a lot of common problems, and may thus potentially also share some common solutions. We shall touch on this point several times in what follows.

What Is a Database Machine?

We are now in a position to examine the question "What exactly is a database machine?" Unfortunately, it is very difficult to give a precise answer to this question, or indeed any answer that will be universally accepted by all workers in the field. There is simply no consensus. Hsiao, for example, defines a database machine as "specialized hardware supporting basic DBMS functions found in most contemporary software database management systems" [8.6]. But this definition excludes the case of a dedicated but conventional backend system, running a conventional software DBMS. Other people reserve the term to mean, specifically, a storage device that incorporates some new hardware technology (for example, magnetic bubble memory) and/or hardware associative addressing. Still others use the term to mean a CPU that includes microcoded support for common database constructs such as indexes and cursors [8.16]. Perhaps the most satisfactory definition is simply "any special-purpose hardware/software combination that is specifically intended to make the database system go faster"—except that, as we shall see, some proposals are more likely to have the opposite effect. In fact, the following point should be made at the outset: Not only is there no consensus on what a database machine is—there is not even any consensus that database machines in general are a good idea. We shall see why this is so as we proceed.

One consensus that does exist is that most on-line storage will continue to be based on conventional moving-head disk technology for many years to come. The newer technologies—magnetic bubbles, charge-coupled devices (CCDs), and so forth—though they may have some specialized role to play within the overall system, simply cannot compete, in terms of either capacity or cost, with moving-head disk technology for the role of principal data storage medium. Thus, most of the database machine hardware proposals concentrate on either (a) finding a suitable role for the newer technologies (for example, using them for a cache memory between main storage and the disks), or (b) enhancing the moving-head disk technology (for example, adding search logic to the read/write heads), or (c) a combination of both. We shall discuss some of these proposals in Sections 8.3 and 8.4.

Advantages and Disadvantages

We conclude this section by considering briefly some of the potential gains and drawbacks of a database machine.

Performance

Improving performance is of course the primary motivation for introducing a database machine in the first place. Note carefully, however, that the performance of any individual database request will almost certainly be *worse* than in a conventional system, because the execution of that request now involves two messages in addition to everything that had to be done before (compare Figs. 8.1 and 8.2). "He travels the fastest who travels alone." It is the *parallelism* inherent in a system such as that of Fig. 8.2—that is, the fact that there are two machines doing work simultaneously where there was only one before—that can yield improved performance. Hence, "improved performance" in a database machine system must be understood to mean "increased *throughput*," not improved response time. The hope is that the gains from parallel execution will outweigh the losses from host/backend communication; if they do not, then the installation would do better simply to upgrade the host CPU or to invest in additional channels or disks.

Reliability

It is a fact that conventional software database management systems are large and complex, and that large and complex software systems are both prone to failure and exceedingly difficult to verify. Some people (but this writer is not among them) feel that the situation with hardware is more satisfactory: The construction of large, sophisticated hardware systems that are guaranteed to be logically correct is a much more viable proposition (see, for example, Hsiao [8.6]). Thus, by incorporating some of the basic database functions into hardware, it *may* be possible to achieve greater reliability for those functions; it may even be possible to improve the reliability of the software at the same time, since that software will now be smaller and less complex than it would otherwise be. Even if these possibilities can be realized, however, a system with a database machine involves more components than one without (compare Figs. 8.1 and 8.2 again), and is thus likely to fail more often.

Security

Data security may be enhanced, because the backend machine is dedicated to database functions (no user programs execute on that machine), and hence the *only* access to the data is via the system. In a conventional system, by contrast, it may be possible to bypass the DBMS and access the database directly, using standard operating system facilities. Note, however, that a database machine system is not *intrinsically* more secure than a conventional system—it is just that most conventional systems happen to be defective in this respect.

Database sharing

An advantage of the architecture shown in Fig. 8.2 is that it is comparatively easy to extend it to one in which a single database machine serves as backend to multiple hosts, thus permitting those hosts to share data and database management functions. This arrangement can have concomitant security and operational advantages also. However, there is also the possibility that the shared machine may become a system bottleneck. Also, of course, if the database machine fails, then the entire system will fail. (Observe the several parallels here with distributed systems.)

Multiple database machines

This point is the complement of the previous one. Just as it may be possible for several hosts to share a single database machine, so it may also be possible for several database machines to be attached to a single host. Such an arrangement may be desirable if the overall system is very heavily database-oriented; for example, if 80 percent of the host would otherwise be dedicated to DBMS functions, it may be possible to offload 40 percent to one database machine and 40 percent to another. But note clearly that such a structure is closer than ever to a distributed system, and hence that the problems of distributed recovery (two-phase commit), distributed deadlock detection, etc., etc., must now all be taken into consideration.

Load balancing

A system in which processor A is dedicated to one function and processor B to
another is necessarily less flexible in its ability to distribute work than one in which
there is a single general-purpose processor that does everything. There is thus a risk
of system imbalance: For example, the host may be saturated with work and still be
unable to generate database requests fast enough to keep the backend busy.

We now proceed to examine (in Sections 8.2 and 8.3) what we perceive to be the
two major categories of database machine—namely, the dedicated but conventional
backend computer (Section 8.2), and the specialized hardware device or "associative
disk" (Section 8.3). In Section 8.4 we present some conclusions, the most significant
of which is that (in our opinion) database machines have only a very limited sphere
of application. The References and Bibliography section includes several papers that
support this position, as well as many that argue strongly in favor of one particular
kind of machine or another.

8.2   THE DEDICATED CONVENTIONAL MACHINE APPROACH

In this section we discuss the case in which the database machine consists of a conventional general-purpose computer, running a conventional software DBMS. See
Fig. 8.3.

We have already indicated in outline how such a system operates:

1. An application program executing in the host issues a database request in the
   normal manner.
2. The host interface code intercepts that request and ships it to the backend machine.
3. The backend interface code receives the request and passes it to the DBMS.
4. The DBMS executes the request and produces a result.
5. The backend interface code intercepts the result and ships it back to the host.
6. The host interface code receives the result and passes it to the application.

We have also indicated that this overall process is likely to take longer than
simply executing the original request on a conventional (single-machine) system,
though it is true that there will now be less data flowing across the channel into the
host than before. Let us examine this performance issue in a little more detail.

Performance

Suppose the application consists of the query "Get part numbers for parts supplied
by supplier S1." Suppose there are 100 such parts. Suppose also that the data manipulation language (DML) is record-at-a-time, as in DL/I or DBTG. Then there
will be 100 DML statements executed, that is, 100 calls on the DBMS.

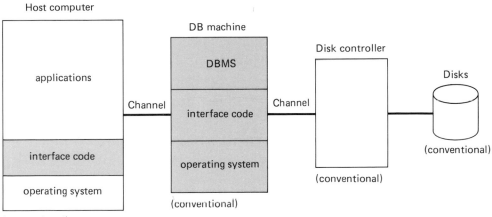

Fig. 8.3 The dedicated conventional machine approach.

- In a conventional system this means

  100 DBMS calls
  100 I/O operations (assume access is via physical sequential
                         scan or by following a pointer chain, and
                         records are not physically clustered)

- In a system such as that of Fig. 8.3 it means

  100 messages to the backend
  100 DBMS calls
  100 I/O operations
  100 messages to the host

The following figures are typical:

  10 msec per DBMS call
  30 msec per I/O operation
   5 msec per message

With these figures, the total application execution time is

- Conventional system :   4 seconds

- Fig. 8.3:   5 seconds

Suppose now, by contrast, that the DML is set-at-a-time, as in, for example, QUEL or SQL. We now have

- Conventional system :

    1   DBMS call
  100 I/O operations

Total time = 3.01 seconds

- Fig. 8.3:

    1   message
    1   DBMS call
  100 I/O operations
    1   message

Total time = 3.02 seconds

From this example we conclude that set-at-a-time DMLs are even more desirable in a database machine environment than in a conventional system—just as they are more desirable in a distributed system also, and for the same reason. In fact, most researchers in the field would agree that a set-at-a-time DML—probably a *relational* DML—is a sine qua non for the success of a database machine system. The following commonly quoted rule of thumb (which is sometimes referred to, informally, as *the offloading theorem*) amounts more or less to a restatement of the same point:

> For offloading to be cost-effective, the amount of work offloaded should be an order of magnitude greater than the amount of work involved in doing the offloading.

If we agree for the sake of our example that work can be measured in terms of the time it takes to perform it, then in the record-level version the amount of work offloaded is 4 seconds-worth and the work in doing the offloading is 1 second-worth; the conditions of the "theorem" are thus violated. In the set-level version the figures are 3.01 and 0.01, respectively, so the offloading is deemed to be cost-effective.

Aside: As stated above, relational DMLs are particularly attractive in a database machine environment. In fact, relational *systems* are the most attractive anyway, because the regularity of the relational data structure makes it the most amenable to parallel processing. Consider the query "Get part numbers for parts supplied by supplier S1" once again. If the tuples of relation SP are partitioned and spread equally across n backend processors (either conventional or special-purpose), then the system can respond to the query in approximately one nth of the time a single processor would take. (This is basically a restatement of the point made in Chapter 7 to the effect that it is easy to see how data might be "fragmented" in a relational system. Once again we are touching on the issue of commonality between database machines and distributed databases.)

Backend Software

So far we have assumed that the DBMS in the backend machine is running on a conventional operating system. That assumption may well be valid in practice, but in fact a conventional operating system is not totally appropriate, for the following two basic reasons:

1. The DBMS is the only "application program" in the system, and is permanently resident in main storage. Many of the functions of a conventional operating system—for example, dynamic program loading, virtual memory management, job stream management—are thus simply not applicable and could profitably be dispensed with.

2. Even where the operating system does provide an applicable function, it may well be the case that the general-purpose algorithms it uses are not the most suitable for the special-purpose application that is the DBMS. For example, the file system supported by the operating system may not provide the right building-blocks for implementing a database (this is one of the reasons that System R, for example, did not use VSAM).

Ideally, then, the backend machine will run a database management system *only*. That DBMS will directly support its own "file system," in a form tailored to its own needs. That portion of main storage not occupied by the DBMS will be dedicated to buffers, which will be managed by the DBMS using algorithms that exploit the DBMS's knowledge of data access patterns (for example, buffer pages containing catalog data should be overwritten as infrequently as possible; buffer pages containing data accessed as a result of an "out-of-the-blue" user request should be discarded immediately after use). The DBMS should be capable of supporting a wide variety of disk devices for the database; however, the only "genuine" I/O (contact with the outside world) it need be capable of is (1) acceptance of an input message carrying a database request and (2) transmission of an output message carrying the result of such a request (we are of course ignoring I/O having to do with system initialization, instrumentation, and the like).

For further discussion of the foregoing ideas, see references [8.10] and [8.58].

Some Implemented Systems

The first backend system to be implemented (and the one that sparked interest in the whole approach) was the Experimental Database Management System XDMS [8.11], a prototype system built in the early 1970s at Bell Laboratories in Piscataway, New Jersey. In that system the host machine was a Univac 1108, the backend was a Digital Scientific META-4 minicomputer; the two machines were connected by a 2000-bit-per-second communication line, not an I/O channel. A DBTG system was written for the backend machine, and a personnel application (already running on the host using the Univac DMS 1100 system) ran successfully using that new DBMS. No performance figures for the system are available, but reference [8.11] suggests that faster communications (at least 50,000 bits per second) would be required in practice. The offloading theorem suggests that a higher-level DML would also be helpful.

Several other prototype systems have been built since the pioneering XDMS effort; see Maryanski [8.9] for a discussion of some of these.

The first commercial implementation of these ideas seems to be the ADABAS Database Machine, from Software AG [8.13], which supports ADABAS running on a 370-compatible backend machine and attached via an I/O channel to a 370 host. A single backend machine can serve multiple host computers; equally, a single host computer can connect to multiple backend machines. The backend machine runs a specially streamlined version of the operating system and up to eight copies of the ADABAS software. However, most communication from the host to the backend machine is in terms of a rather low-level (record-at-a-time) DML.

More recently, Britton Lee, Inc., has produced a system called the IDM 500 (the Intelligent Database Machine) [8.14]. The IDM is actually a hybrid system: It consists of a backend machine, basically along the lines we have been discussing in this section except that it is a (fast) special-purpose processor, running a more or less conventional DBMS, together with some optional "associative disk" hardware (it is one of the first commercial systems to incorporate such hardware). Input to the IDM is a database request, such as "List details of parts supplied by supplier S1." The level of such requests is comparable to that of QUEL or SQL, but the IDM requires them to be submitted in a special encoded ("parsed") form. The frontend machine issuing the request may be either a conventional host or a programmable terminal. Whichever it is, software in that frontend machine is responsible for

1. accepting a user-level request in some high-level language such as QUEL or SQL or an IDM-specific language (very similar to QUEL) called IDL;

2. translating such user-level requests into the appropriate encoded form;

3. sending the encoded request to the IDM for execution;

4. receiving the result back from the IDM;

5. formatting the result and displaying it to the user.

Software in the IDM provides the following functions, among others:

- relational data management (including aggregate function and view support);
- dynamic data definition (databases, relations, views, and indexes can be created and destroyed at any time);
- transaction processing (BEGIN TRANSACTION, END TRANSACTION, and ABORT TRANSACTION commands);
- logging and recovery;
- concurrency control;
- security (PERMIT and DENY commands);
- optimized access path selection;
- random access file system.

According to Britton Lee, the IDM can achieve transaction rates of the order of 20 to 30 a second. It supports up to 32 billion bytes of on-line data (stored relations); data can have any of the usual data-types (binary integer, floating point, packed decimal, character string). The primary access mechanism is the B-tree.

We conclude this section by noting that MSC or ISC could be used to run a backend IMS "database machine"—yet another illustration of the close relationship between database machines and distributed databases. Incidentally, MSC and ISC do support channel-to-channel connections as well as the slower communication lines discussed in Chapter 7.

8.3   THE ASSOCIATIVE DISK APPROACH

We begin by briefly reviewing the terminology associated with the conventional magnetic disk (see Figs. 8.4 and 8.5). Such a "disk" actually consists of several (typically 11) physical disks, arranged in a vertical stack and rigidly attached to a common central hub. It thus provides a number of *surfaces* for recording data—basically two surfaces per physical disk, except that the two outermost surfaces are not used, so that (for example) a stack of 11 disks will provide 20 usable surfaces, numbered 0, 1, . . . , 19. Each surface contains a large number (several hundred) of concentric circular *tracks* along which the data is physically recorded. The tracks are numbered 0, 1, 2, . . . on each surface. The set of all tracks, one from each surface, sharing a common track number i constitute the ith *cylinder* of the device. The device also provides a set of *read/write heads* (R/W heads). In a moving-head disk (Fig. 8.4), there is one R/W head per surface; at any given time, the set of all such R/W heads will all be positioned within the same cylinder, and moving them to another cylinder will require a *seek* operation. In a fixed-head disk (Fig. 8.5), there is one R/W head per track per surface; thus each individual track has its own dedi-

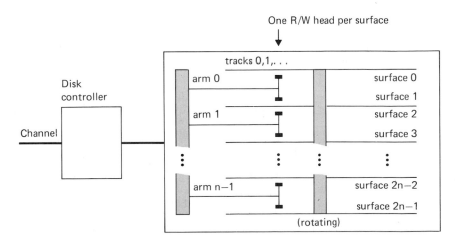

Fig. 8.4   Structure of a moving-head disk device.

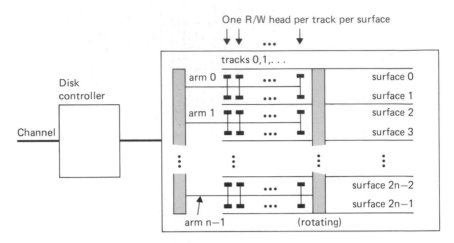

Fig. 8.5   Structure of a fixed-head disk device.

cated R/W head, and seek operations are never needed. In either case, data is brought under a R/W head by the *rotation* of the disk stack. On each revolution of the disk, therefore, the entire data content of any given track can be scanned by the R/W head for that track (assuming in the case of the moving-head disk that the R/W head has first been brought into position over that track).

Now we turn to associative disks. The basic idea in an associative disk is to apply some hardware search logic directly to the data as it is read from the disk, with the intent of reducing the amount of data that has to be transmitted across the channel to the host and reducing the amount of processing the software has to do. For example, the conventional disk might be extended to incorporate a microprocessor with each R/W head; each such processor could then apply some simple selection logic to the data as it passes under the corresponding R/W head. Moreover, those processors might all operate in parallel, thus allowing several tracks of data to be searched simultaneously.

Note 1:   The "disk" may actually be a conventional magnetic disk, as we have been implying, or it may involve bubble memories, CCDs, or some other new technology. Architecturally, however, these latter devices still look like (faster) disks. It is not our purpose here to get into hardware technology details per se; the interested reader is referred to (for example) references [8.17–8.26] for such information. Equally, it is not our purpose to get into too much detail regarding specific individual proposals; rather, what we will do is divide those proposals into various categories, and compare and contrast the properties of those different categories. A few details of individual machines are given in the References and Bibliography section at the end of the chapter.

Note 2: Recent advances in microelectronics make associative disks economically feasible. Observe, however, that each of the microprocessors has to perform many of the functions performed by the disk controller in a conventional system (error detection and automatic retry, for example). There is thus considerable duplication of function, which means that the overall device may still be comparatively expensive; reference [8.1] suggests a typical figure of six or seven times the cost of a conventional disk. Note also that the microprocessors must be quite fast if they are to keep up with the speed of the disk. A typical disk has a data rate of the order of one million bytes per second. Typical software DBMSs average ten instructions per byte in evaluating a given selection condition on a given record. Hence each microprocessor needs to be capable of executing about ten million instructions per second (10 MIPS) to handle the search logic alone—and this figure does not include any of the other functions that the microprocessor is responsible for (for example, the error detection function mentioned above).

Note 3: A system that includes two or more associative disks possesses (once again) some of the characteristics of a distributed system.

The hardware search capability in an associative disk varies in detail from device to device. Typically, however, it involves the ability to select or reject an individual record on the basis of an arbitrary restriction predicate—that is, a predicate consisting of an arbitrary Boolean combination of simple comparisons involving fields of that record and constants. In other words, the search logic represents a hardware implementation of the extended selection operation of relational algebra (see Chapter 5). We shall generally assume at least this level of hardware support throughout this section.

Device Categorization

The classification that follows is based on one given by DeWitt and Hawthorn [8.34], who distinguish four kinds of device:

- processor-per-track (PPT)
- processor-per-surface (PPS)
- processor-per-disk (PPD)
- multi-processor-cache (MPC)

DeWitt and Hawthorn use the term "processor-per-head" (PPH) for what we have here called PPS; however, we prefer our term as a more accurate characterization of this kind of device. Let us now examine each of the four categories in turn.

1. Processor-per-track (PPT) devices

This class of device can be regarded as an upgraded form of the fixed-head disk (Fig. 8.5). Another term used for this category is "cellular-logic devices" [8.29]; this term refers to the fact that there is hardware logic (a microprocessor) for each individual "cell" (storage element, that is, track). Every track thus has its own dedicated processor, and all processors can perform the same search operation in parallel, so the entire device can be searched in a single revolution. Examples of devices in this category include the Context-Addressed Segment-Sequential Memory CASSM [8.36, 8.37], from the University of Florida, and the Relational Associative Processor RAP [8.39–8.44], from the University of Toronto.

2. Processor-per-surface (PPS) devices

Just as the PPT category can be viewed as an upgraded fixed-head disk, so the PPS category can be regarded as an upgraded form of the moving-head disk (Fig. 8.4). There is one processor per surface; hence the amount of data that can be searched on one revolution is one track per surface (that is, one cylinder), and moving the processors from one cylinder to another requires a seek operation. As a consequence of this latter point, indexes or other locator mechanisms are still desirable with this kind of device.[1] Such a device formed part of the so-called Database Computer [8.46–8.49], from Ohio State University. The Content Addressable File Store (CAFS) from ICL [8.50, 8.51] also appears to have some PPS characteristics, though in other respects it falls into the PPD category (see below).

3. Processor-per-disk (PPD) devices

The PPD category uses conventional moving-head disks with a conventional disk controller, but interposes a *filtering processor* between that disk controller and the channel to apply the search logic and eliminate data that does not qualify (see Fig. 8.6). As with the PPS category, therefore, indexes or other conventional locator mechanisms are still desirable with this kind of device. The PPD approach has the advantage of providing the functionality of the PPT and PPS approaches (but not of course the performance) at much lower cost; it clearly reduces the volume of data sent to the host. IDM [8.14] falls into this category.

4. Multi-processor-cache (MPC) devices

This last category is rather different from the first three. As described, each of the first three categories suffers from certain obvious inefficiencies. Consider, for example, the first category, the PPT category, in which the entire device can be scanned on each revolution. Since it is probable that many distinct relations will be stored on the device, and since each search will really be interested in only one of those relations, most of the processors will actually be doing unproductive work most of the

---

1. With a PPT device, by contrast, no such mechanisms are necessary; but note the implication that record-type and similar "descriptor" information must be explicitly represented as part of each stored record in a PPT device, in order to support hardware searches on the basis of record-type (etc.) as well as on the basis of data values. In practice such additional fields will probably be required in other types of device as well. The Database Computer, for example, stores the relation-name with every stored tuple and the attribute-name with every stored attribute-value [8.47]. The stored database can thus occupy considerably more storage than in a conventional system.

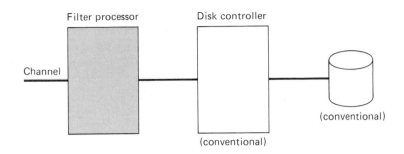

Fig. 8.6 The processor-per-disk category.

time. Or consider a PPS device, which can search one cylinder per revolution. If any part of that cylinder contains data that is known not to be of interest—for example, if the relation to be scanned is less than a cylinder in size—then, again, some of the processors will effectively be idle during the scan of that cylinder. Thus, the parallelism inherent in the design of those devices cannot be fully exploited much of the time. MPC devices, by contrast, represent an attempt to make genuine use of parallel execution, both within an individual query and across multiple distinct queries.

Instead of applying search logic directly (or conceptually) to data "on the disk," as the other three categories do, MPC devices introduce an intermediate level of cache storage between that logic and the disk (see Fig. 8.7). The cache storage has a capacity equal to n pages of disk data, where n is the number of microprocessors. Before a microprocessor can operate on any page of data, that data must first be read from the disk into an available page slot in the cache. There is no fixed relationship between processors and page slots in the cache—any processor can be switched to any one of those slots at any time. Thus, different processors can be operating on the same or different data pages at the same time. Moreover, those processors need not all be executing the same instruction at the same time. Together, these two features provide the basis for achieving the "genuine" parallelism referred to above. The precise allocation of processors to queries can be determined dynamically; at one time, all processors might be working on the same query together, at another time they might be working on several different queries simultaneously. Examples of MPC devices include DIRECT [8.52, 8.53], from the University of Wisconsin, and EDC [8.56], from the Electrotechnical Laboratory of Japan. The EDC device is interesting, providing as it does a working example of a system based on magnetic bubble storage.

Performance

Having presented our categorization of the various device types, we now proceed to examine their relative performance characteristics. For purposes of comparison (and following reference [8.34]), we introduce a fifth category, CS ("conventional sys-

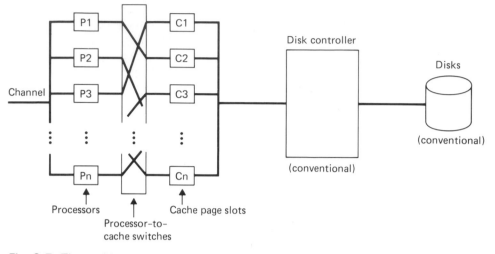

Fig. 8.7 The multi-processor-cache category.

tem''). A CS "database machine" consists of a stand-alone host processor, running a conventional software DBMS such as INGRES or System R. Note: We should mention at this point that the amount of buffer storage available in the host is a critical performance factor. The trend in today's systems is toward larger and larger main memories, and hence toward larger and larger database buffer pools. Given a large buffer pool at its disposal, a conventional software DBMS can achieve very satisfactory performance under many circumstances. It is probably this fact more than any other that makes the database machine a somewhat doubtful proposition. But let us continue with our discussion.

First we consider four classes of query, ranging from fairly simple to quite complex, and discuss in a very intuitive manner the performance that we might expect from a PPS kind of device (that is, an "upgraded moving-head disk") on each class. The purpose of that discussion is merely to give some idea of the factors that are relevant to performance issues in an associative disk environment. We then present the results of some more analytical comparisons of the five device categories, taken again from reference [8.34].

The four classes of query we consider are as follows:

1. Simple inquiry (for example, "What is the city for supplier S4?")
2. Batch report (for example, "List all parts by color")
3. Complex intrarecord query (for example, "List all parts that either have color = red or have weight > 10 and city = London")
4. Join query (for example, "List details of parts supplied by supplier S1")

■   *Class 1* (simple inquiry). For category PPS, this class of query involves one seek to get to the right cylinder (we assume that the relevant index search or hash has already been done), plus one (associative) scan or read of that cylinder. For category CS, it also involves a single seek (again assuming that the index search or hash has already been done) plus a single scan or read of the appropriate track within that cylinder. Net result: Performance on CS and performance on the associative disk are identical.

■   *Class 2* (batch report). Suppose the required data occupies n cylinders. For category PPS, then, we have n seeks plus n (cylinder) reads. For category CS, we have n seeks plus $20n$ (track) reads, assuming 20 tracks per cylinder. In both cases the data must then be sorted. In practice it is likely that the sort operation will dominate everything else, so the net result is that performance on the associative disk is only marginally better than that on CS.

■   *Class 3* (complex intrarecord query). As with the previous class, a scan of the entire relation is required, but the number of records returned is likely to be comparatively small. Thus, even if a sort is required, we may assume that the time it takes is insignificant (main storage sort). So the figures are: n seeks plus n reads (PPS), n seeks plus $20n$ reads (CS). Net result: The associative disk shows a marked improvement over CS for this class of query.

■   *Class 4* (join query). Here matters are not very clearcut. Precise figures depend heavily on details of the algorithms used to implement the join, and it is difficult to make any definitive statements. Indications are that the associative disk should outperform CS on "very hard joins" but that CS may outperform the associative disk on "easy" ones [8.1], but it is difficult to make this statement more precise.

Thus, a tentative conclusion from these four examples is that associative disks may well be useful for what is sometimes characterized as "the library search problem"—that is, the complex intrarecord query—but that for other kinds of query they provide a level of performance that at best is only marginally superior to that of a conventional system. Let us now examine the work of reference [8.34] to see to what extent this tentative conclusion is borne out by analysis.

The work reported in [8.34] proceeded as follows. First, three classes of query were identified—selection queries (corresponding to our Class 1 above), join queries (our Class 4), and aggregate function queries such as "List total quantity supplied of each part" (no correspondence in our classification above). Then, formulas were derived representing the total execution time for each category of machine (CS, PPT, PPS, PPD, and MPC) on each class of query. Finally, each of those formulas was evaluated for a wide variety of parameter values (for relation size, predicate selectivity, etc.), and the results were tabulated and analyzed. We do not go into details of the analysis here, but rather content ourselves with discussing some of the most interesting conclusions as presented in [8.34].

■   *Selection queries.* Categories CS and PPD both performed quite well if an appropriate index existed; in other words, judicious choice of indexes can make CS a perfectly adequate "database machine" for this class of query, although PPD was better by a factor of approximately 50 percent. If no index existed then PPS was the winner. MPC was no better than PPD despite its considerable additional complexity (and cost). Interestingly, PPT was not significantly better than PPS, except in the particular case where there was no index and the hit ratio was quite low; hence, considering the complexity of the device, it appeared that PPT was not really cost-effective, even when used for the class of operation for which it was specifically intended.

■   *Join queries.* PPT, PPS, and PPD all performed very badly on this class of query. The basic problem is that the device is not able to carry out a join operation per se; instead, the host machine must decompose the join by tuple substitution into a sequence of selection operations. Unfortunately, it is frequently the case that a sort/merge algorithm is the best implementation for a given join query. MPC did outperform CS, but not dramatically so (MPC was typically twice as fast as CS); the basic problem here is that the join algorithm is intrinsically sequential in nature, so that the parallelism of MPC was of no particular help.

■   *Aggregate function queries.* The results in this case were less easy to interpret. MPC was the clear winner (an order of magnitude better than CS in most cases), but tended to deteriorate as the number of subrelations to be aggregated increased (that is, as the GROUP BY became more selective, in SQL terms), until it was actually worse than CS. PPT, PPS, and PPD all outperformed CS (but, once again, not dramatically so) when the number of subrelations was small, but very quickly became much worse than CS. Overall it seemed as if, once again, CS was as good as anything.

We conclude our discussion of associative disk performance with a brief note on another aspect of performance, namely storage capacity. The capacity of a typical associative disk is necessarily quite limited. CASSM, RAP, and RARES, for example, all have an upper limit of about ten million bytes [8.7].[2] It is thus unlikely that the entire database would be stored on associative disks, unless it was quite small, because the cost would be prohibitive. In most cases, therefore, the bulk of the database will continue to be stored on conventional moving-head disks (as suggested in Section 8.1); if the system includes any associative disks in addition, then they will probably be used as a cache between the conventional disks and the main processor. Thus associative disks might be seen as providing another level in the well-known "storage hierarchy." We shall have more to say on this topic in the next section.

---

2. See reference [8.41] for some ideas for overcoming this limitation in the case of RAP.

8.4   CONCLUSIONS

We have now discussed both the dedicated backend machine approach and the associative disk approach in some detail. (We remind the reader that the two approaches
are not mutually exclusive.) The fundamental reason for introducing a database
machine of either kind is to improve system performance; however, as we have
shown, it is by no means clear that any such improvement will actually be obtained
in practice, except in certain special cases (for example, the "library search"
application). It is true that there may also be some other advantages, such as
improved security, which might be more important to some installations than any
concomitant loss in performance. In general, however, it does seem that the case for
database machines remains unproven, and that for most applications a totally conventional approach is at least adequate and may well be the most cost-effective.[3]

So where does this leave us? In the remainder of this section we indicate briefly
some possible areas or applications in which the use of some kind of database
machine may in fact pay off. The first of these, the storage hierarchy, has been mentioned in passing several times earlier in the chapter. Again the possibilities are not
mutually exclusive and could be used together in the same system in a variety of
combinations.

Storage hierarchy

The concept of a storage hierarchy is not new. Current systems already provide at
least two levels of storage (main storage and disk), and more usually three (main
storage, disk, and tape). Sometimes there will also be a fast cache in the CPU, over
and above the bulk main storage, or a mass storage archival device in addition to the
moving-head disks. Typically, each level of the hierarchy is cheaper (per bit), larger
(in capacity), and slower (in direct access to any given item), than the level above it.
Storage hierarchies are designed to take advantage of the "90:10 rule," which (in
this context) states that 90 percent of accesses go to 10 percent of the data (that is,
most applications exhibit considerable "locality of reference"). The idea is that the
most frequently accessed data will be near the top of the hierarchy, occupying fast
but expensive storage, while the rest is near the bottom, occupying slow but cheap
storage. Of course, a Storage Hierarchy Manager is also needed, to keep track of
where data is and to perform the necessary "staging" (that is, moving data up and
down the levels as necessary).

---

3. This is a good opportunity to refute the often-heard suggestion that relational systems, in
particular, require some kind of hardware breakthrough if they are ever to achieve satisfactory performance. That suggestion is simply untrue. There is absolutely no inherent reason
why a relational system that is implemented on perfectly conventional hardware should perform any worse—or indeed any better—than any other kind of system. See reference [8.57].

We have already suggested (Section 8.3) that an associative disk may have to serve as a cache between main storage and conventional disks, at least if the database is fairly large. In addition, some researchers have strongly advocated the use of a "genuine" hardware associative memory as a cache, that is, as an additional level of the hierarchy, appearing immediately below the main storage level; see, for example, references [8.32, 8.55].

Catalog and index support

The reader will recall from Section 8.1 that one of our original objectives was to do away with the need for catalogs, indexes, and similar pointer-based locator mechanisms. The reader will also recognize that this objective has not been achieved, except in the case of the PPT device (and that device has problems of its own, one of which is the fact that a lot of control information has to be stored directly with the data, as indicated in Footnote 1). Note, however, that access to indexes and the like is by definition (a) associative and (b) very frequent. It therefore seems worth investigating the possibility of placing this information in a dedicated associative disk or other associative memory of its own. Such an architecture is proposed by Kerr [8.33], for example.

Text search

We have assumed throughout this book (and its predecessor, Volume I) that the database is "formatted"—that is, that it exhibits a highly regular structure. Such an assumption is appropriate for many applications; but there are also certain "text search" or "information retrieval" applications, in which the database contains (for example) scientific abstracts or other textual information, and the overall structure is much less regular. Queries against this kind of database tend to be quite complex—for example: "List title, author(s), date, and publisher for all papers on database machines." Such a query requires the system to scan long text strings, looking for occurrences of substrings such as "DATABASE MACHINE" or "ASSOCIATIVE DISK" or "CELLULAR LOGIC". Associative disks may prove useful in such applications [8.31].

REFERENCES AND BIBLIOGRAPHY

8.1 M. R. Stonebraker, E. Wong, and L. A. Rowe. Distributed Data Base Management Systems and Data Base Machines: Lecture notes from a course presented by The Western Institute in Computer Science, sponsored by The University of Santa Clara, Santa Clara, California (August 1981).

8.2 *Proc. 3rd Workshop on Computer Architecture for Non-Numeric Processing. ACM SIGARCH* **6,** No. 2; *ACM SIGIR* **7,** No. 1; *ACM SIGMOD* **9,** No. 2 (May 1977).

8.3 *Proc. 4th Workshop on Computer Architecture for Non-Numeric Processing. ACM SIGARCH* **7,** No. 2; *ACM SIGIR* **13,** No. 2; *ACM SIGMOD* **10,** No. 1 (August 1978).

8.4 *Proc. 5th Workshop on Computer Architecture for Non-Numeric Processing. ACM SIGIR* **15,** No. 2; *ACM SIGMOD* **10,** No. 4 (March 1980).

8.5 IEEE Computer Society. *Computer* **12,** No. 3: Special Issue on Database Machines (March 1979).

8.6 D. K. Hsiao. "Data Base Machines Are Coming, Data Base Machines Are Coming!" Guest Editor's Introduction to [8.5].

8.7 D. K. Hsiao. "Database Computers." *Advances in Computers,* Vol. 19, Academic Press (1980).

8.8 G. A. Champine. "Four Approaches to a Data Base Computer." *Datamation* **24,** No. 12 (December 1978).

An introductory paper. The "four approaches" are

1. backend processor for a host (as described in Section 8.2);
2. intelligent peripheral control unit (that is, associative disk);
3. storage hierarchy (as described in Section 8.4);
4. network node (that is, database machine serving multiple hosts).

8.9 F. J. Maryanski. "Backend Database Systems." *ACM Comp Surv.* **12,** No. 1 (March 1980).

A tutorial on the "dedicated conventional machine" approach. Several prototype systems are described: XDMS [8.11], Cullinane's IDMS backend prototype, two Kansas State University systems, and GE's MADMAN system.

8.10 M. R. Stonebraker. "Operating System Support for Database Management." *CACM* **24,** No. 7 (July 1981).

8.11 R. E. Canaday, R. D. Harrison, E. L. Ivie, J. L. Ryder, and L. A. Wehr. "A Back-End Computer for Data Base Management." *CACM* **17,** No. 10 (October 1974).

8.12 T. Marill and D. Stern. "The Datacomputer—A Network Data Utility." *Proc NCC* **44** (May 1975).

The Datacomputer is a database machine of the "dedicated conventional machine" variety (DEC PDP-10 plus conventional disks and mass storage). It is intended to serve as a node in a heterogeneous network of computers (ARPANET); in fact, the distributed system SDD-1 (see Chapter 7) is built on top of a network of Datacomputers. The Datacomputer DML is a set-level language (comparable to QUEL or SQL) called Datalanguage.

8.13 Software AG. The Database Machine (product announcement, 1980).

8.14 Britton Lee, Inc. IDM 500 Intelligent Database Machine (product announcement, 1980).

8.15 J. P. Armisen and J. Y. Caleca. "A Commercial Back-End Data Base System." *Proc. 7th International Conference on Very Large Data Bases* (September 1981).

Describes a backend machine called MIX, scheduled for commercial availability late in 1982.

8.16 C. T. Watson and G. F. Aberle. "System/38 Machine Data Base Support." In IBM System/38 Technical Developments: IBM Form No. G580-0237 (1978).

The IBM System/38 is a "database machine" only inasmuch as it is a general-purpose computer that was designed throughout to provide integrated operating system and database management support. It provides a single-level store (there are no I/O instructions as such—all I/O is done "under the covers" by the system), and a very high-level machine instruction set that includes direct (microcoded) support for certain database objects such as indexes.

8.17 G. F. Amelio. "Charge-Coupled Devices for Memory Applications." *Proc. NCC* **44** (May 1975).

8.18 J. E. Ypma. "Bubble Domain Memory Systems." *Proc. NCC* **44** (May 1975).

8.19 W. Anacker. "Superconducting Memories Employing Josephson Devices." *Proc. NCC* **44** (May 1975).

8.20 A. K. Gillis, G. E. Hoffmann, and R. H. Nelson. "Holographic Memories—Fantasy or Reality?" *Proc. NCC* **44** (May 1975).

8.21 W. C. Hughes, C. Q. Lemmond, H. G. Parks, G. W. Ellis, G. E. Possin, and R. H. Wilson. "BEAMOS—A New Electronic Digital Memory." *Proc. NCC* **44** (May 1975).

8.22 L. J. Laub. "Optical Mass Storage Technology." In [8.4].

8.23 G. P. Copeland. "What If Mass Storage Were Free?" In [8.4].

This paper has little to do with "database machines" per se. However, it is relevant to the topic, inasmuch as it is certainly concerned with the impact of new hardware technologies on database system architecture in general. It describes the problems associated with deletion, much along the lines of the paper by Schueler [6.7], and claims that those problems could all be overcome under the limiting-case assumption that mass storage is free. It then suggests that optical disk technology comes one or two orders of magnitude closer to this hypothetical ideal than conventional storage, and moreover is inherently more reliable. It concludes that optical disks are therefore much more suited to future database requirements than are magnetic disks or tapes, and that the availability of this new medium may cause a radical rethinking of the architecture of those future systems.

8.24 K. Kannan. "Magnetic Bubble Memories—A State-of-the-Art Review." Ohio State University: Dept. of Computers and Information Science Technical Report (March 1976).

8.25 K. Kannan. "Electron Beam Addressed Memories—A State-of-the-Art Review." Ohio State University: Dept. of Computers and Information Science Technical Report (April 1976).

8.26 K. Kannan. "Semiconductor Memories—A State-of-the-Art Review." Ohio State University: Dept. of Computers and Information Science Technical Report (July 1976).

8.27 H. Chang. "Bubbles for Relational Database." In [8.3].

Presents the logical design for a bubble chip dedicated to relational operations. The paper shows how all of the operations of the relational algebra can be implemented in terms of such chips. It also considers the technical and economic feasibility of such a design, and discusses the possibility of implementation using existing technology. Reference [8.28] explores this last point in some depth.

8.28 H. Chang. "On Bubble Memories and Relational Data Base." *Proc. 4th International Conference on Very Large Data Bases* (September 1978).

See [8.27].

8.29 S. Y. W. Su. "Cellular Logic Devices: Concepts and Applications." In [8.5].

Traces the development of cellular-logic devices from simple keyword retrieval machines, through character string manipulation machines, to the kinds of machine intended specifically for database management that were categorized as PPT devices in Section 8.3. The paper then gives a detailed description of CASSM [8.36, 8.37] as an illustration of this kind of device. (CASSM appears to be the first such device designed specifically for database management.) The author points out that, although the question of hardware search has been thoroughly investigated in such devices, problems of system recovery, security control, error recovery, and concurrency control (etc., etc.) have not been adequately addressed.

8.30 D. C. P. Smith and J. M. Smith. "Relational Data Base Machines." In [8.5].

Describes some designs for associative disks that are specifically intended to support relational structures and relational operations. The machines described include CASSM [8.36, 8.37], RAP [8.39–8.44], RARES [8.45], and CAFS [8.50, 8.51]. Of these, RARES is a paper-only design; prototypes of CASSM and RAP were built, but only CAFS is currently available as a commercial product. (A few other paper-only designs, including some that use alternative hardware technologies such as bubble memories, are also discussed in outline.) Note: CASSM provides direct support for hierarchies as well as for relations.

8.31 L. A. Hollaar. "Text Retrieval Computers." In [8.5].

8.32 P. B. Berra and E. Oliver. "The Role of Associative Array Processors in Data Base Machine Architecture." In [8.5].

An associative array processor is a device that provides a genuine hardware implementation of associative memory and corresponding access operations. The paper discusses the use of such a processor as a staging device between the main processor and database bulk storage. Three different system configurations are given, and timing data is provided for each. A detailed proposal based on these ideas is presented in [8.55].

8.33 D. S. Kerr. "Data Base Machines with Large Content Addressable Blocks and Structural Information Processors." In [8.5].

The "large content addressable blocks" of the title of this paper refer to associative disks, and the "structural information processors" are small, specialized associative processors for storing, accessing, and maintaining "structural information" such as indexes and catalogs. The paper advocates a database machine architecture (essentially the architecture of the Database Computer [8.46–8.49]) that incorporates such components. It also gives numerous very clear examples of how associative disks function.

8.34 D. J. DeWitt and P. B. Hawthorn. "A Performance Evaluation of Database Machine Architectures." *Proc. 7th International Conference on Very Large Data Bases* (September 1981).

8.35 D. L. Slotnick. "Logic Per Track Devices." *Advances in Computers,* Vol. 10, Academic Press (1970).

The paper that introduced the idea of the associative disk.

8.36 S. Y. W. Su and G. J. Lipovski. "CASSM: A Cellular System for Large Data Bases." *Proc. International Conference on Very Large Data Bases* (September 1975).

8.37 S. Y. W. Su and A. Emam. "CASDAL: CASSM's Data Language." *ACM TODS* 3, No. 1 (March 1978).

CASSM is a PPT device (the prototype implementation used a fixed-head disk). It provides direct support for hierarchically structured data. The authors give their reasons for choosing a hierarchical model, and present numerous examples of their user-level language CASDAL. The most notable feature of that language is that it does not include a join operator; instead, it provides two operators called "match" and "mark," both directly supported by the hardware. "Match" allows the user to identify those rows in one table that have the same values for some specified field as selected rows in another; "mark" allows the user to mark rows satisfying some specified condition for further processing (by setting certain mark bits stored with the row on the disk). The paper also describes the CASSM hardware and the CASSM hardware-level instructions (not in complete detail), and shows by example how a CASDAL program can be compiled into such instructions.

8.38 G. J. Lipovski. "On Imaginary Fields, Token Transfers and Floating Codes in Intelligent Secondary Memories." In [8.2].

An analysis of certain design features of CASSM [8.36, 8.37] and RAP [8.39–8.44], with corresponding suggestions concerning the architecture of future associative processors.

8.39 E. A. Ozkarahan, S. A. Schuster, and K. C. Smith. "RAP—An Associative Processor for Data Base Management." *Proc. NCC* 44 (May 1975).

RAP (now called RAP.1) is one of the earliest and best-known PPT devices. The prototype implementation used CCD shift registers for storage. RAP was specifically designed to support relational databases. Each stored relation occupies one or more tracks on the device (no track can contain data from more than one relation); each track contains, in order, a relation-name, a set of attribute-names, and one or more tuples of the relevant relation. Tuples can be "marked," as in CASSM. The paper shows how the RAP instruction set uses those tuple markings, and hence how typical user-level queries can be implemented in terms of those instructions. One noteworthy feature of RAP is its direct support (via a hardware "set function unit" positioned between the RAP controller and the individual track processors) for the functions COUNT, SUM, AVERAGE, MAXIMUM, and MINIMUM.

8.40 E. A. Ozkarahan, S. A. Schuster, and K. C. Sevcik. "Performance Evaluation of a Relational Associative Processor." *ACM TODS* 2, No. 2 (June 1977).

Describes the relational operations supported by the RAP hardware and contrasts the RAP support with a conventional (index-based) software implementation. Analytic models of the two approaches are presented, and some detailed performance comparisons are made for the case of medium-to-large databases and low-selectivity transactions (less than 3 percent of records selected from a database of 100,000 records). The figures show a significant advantage for the RAP approach.

8.41 E. A. Ozkarahan and K. C. Sevcik. "Analysis of Architectural Features for Enhancing the Performance of a Database Machine." *ACM TODS* **2,** No. 4 (December 1977).

Discusses two extensions to the basic RAP device for improving performance in specific situations. The two extensions are "multiprogramming" and "virtual memory."

- Multiprogramming allows simple, fast queries not to have to wait while slow, complex queries are being processed. In effect it allows two streams of queries, a high-priority stream and a low-priority stream, to be processed simultaneously, although the device is actually dedicated to a single query on any given revolution. The support for this form of "multiprogramming" involves an extra set of mark bits with each stored tuple and duplicate marking logic in each track processor.

- Virtual memory support allows RAP to support databases that are larger than the basic device capacity. It works by assigning two tracks to each storage cell. At any given time, one of those tracks is connected to the search logic, and the other is being used as a buffer to a conventional I/O controller, which can (for example) be loading data into RAP from bulk storage.

8.42 S. A. Schuster, H. B. Nguyen, E. A. Ozkarahan, and K. C. Smith. "RAP.2—An Associative Processor for Data Bases." *Proc. 5th Annual Symposium on Computer Architecture* (April 1978).

Describes some revisions to the original RAP design [8.39]. The major revisions were as follows: (1) The RAP.1 controller was replaced by a general-purpose computer; (2) the design of the cell memory was changed to match the capabilities of new storage technologies instead of being constrained by conventional disk technology; and (3) a new instruction set was designed with (in particular) extended marking functions. A RAP.2 prototype was built in 1977 with a PDP 11/45 as host, a PDP 11/10 as controller, and two million-bit CCD memory cells. The paper also describes some additional enhancements, not yet implemented, that could form the basis of a possible "RAP.3" design.

8.43 P. J. Sadowski and S. A. Schuster. "Exploiting Parallelism in a Relational Associative Processor." In [8.3].

The enhancements to the original RAP design [8.42]—in particular, the use of new technologies, such as bubbles, for the cell memories—lead to a variety of possibilities for improving performance. This paper shows how partitioning relations across memory cells instead of storing one relation per cell (as in RAP.1) provides considerable improvements through increased parallelism. Analytic and simulation results are given in support of this demonstration.

8.44 T. M. Ozsu and E. A. Ozkarahan. "SYNGLISH—A High Level Query Language for the RAP Database Machine." In [8.4].

SYNGLISH is a "very high-level query language based on the semantic structure of natural English sentences." Some examples of SYNGLISH queries are as follows:

1) What are the names of employees?

2) What are the names of employees with salary > salary of employee who manages them?

3) Count the employees who work in department = "toy".

(Update statements are also supported.) The paper describes an operational translator for compiling SYNGLISH statements into RAP assembler language.

8.45 C. S. Lin, D. C. P. Smith, and J. M. Smith. "The Design of a Rotating Associative Memory for a Relational Database Management Application." *ACM TODS* **1,** No. 1 (March 1976).

Describes the design of RARES (Rotating Associative Relational Store), a PPT device that was however never actually built. RARES was specifically intended to support a high-level software query optimizer such as SQUIRAL (see Volume I). Its major distinguishing feature is its "orthogonal" storage layout, in which tuples are stored bit by bit *across* the tracks instead of serially along the tracks (as is more usual). The advantage of this arrangement is that it can support a high output rate for selected tuples, even when those tuples must be transmitted in a certain sort order (the SQUIRAL optimizer is designed to eliminate unnecessary sort operations, but sometimes sorting is essential). It also means that the microprocessors associated with each R/W head require considerably less private working storage than in other PPT designs.

8.46 R. I. Baum and D. K. Hsiao. "Database Computers—A Step Towards Data Utilities." *IEEE Transactions on Computers C-25,* No. 12 (December 1976).

The term "data utility" in the title of this paper merely refers to a large, on-line, concurrent-user database system. This paper outlines the problems of providing such a system with conventional software, particularly the performance problems inherent in providing adequate security and integrity controls. It discusses associative disks such as CASSM and RAP, and then goes on to describe the architecture of the Database Computer (DBC). Unlike those other devices, the DBC is intended to be a "total solution" to the problem of building a database system (see annotation to reference [8.47]). The paper concludes with some suggestions concerning the future architecture of database computers.

8.47 J. Banerjee, R. I. Baum, and D. K. Hsiao. "Concepts and Capabilities of a Database Computer." *ACM TODS* **3,** No. 4 (December 1978).

As explained in the annotation to reference [8.46], the Database Computer (DBC) represents one of the most thorough designs for a database machine to date—it does not limit itself to just one aspect of the total problem, such as hardware support for the selection operation. It is intended to serve as a dedicated backend to one or more general-purpose frontend machines. As such, it consists of a group of interconnected, functionally specialized hardware devices, with a comparatively small supporting software DBMS. Those devices include (a) a mass memory for storing the database itself, with corresponding associative search logic; (b) a structure memory for storing directory information, again with corresponding associative search logic; (c) a security filter processor, which is responsible for enforcing a wide variety of authorization constraints (the DBC is unique among database machine proposals in the importance it attaches to data security); and (d) a command and control processor, which directs the operation of the entire system. It is suggested that the mass memory should be implemented using PPS-style associative disks; the structure memory would preferably be implemented using bubble or CCD technology [8.33].

8.48 J. Banerjee and D. K. Hsiao. "The Use of a Database Machine for Supporting Relational Databases." In [8.3].

Describes how SQL statements could be mapped into DBC operations and takes a brief look at performance questions (that is, performance of DBC vs. performance of a software DBMS on those SQL statements). See [8.49] for more on this latter topic.

8.49 J. Banerjee and D. K. Hsiao. "Performance Study of a Database Machine in Supporting Relational Databases." *Proc. 4th International Conference on Very Large Data Bases* (September 1978).

8.50 R. W. Mitchell. "Content Addressable File Store." *Proc. Online Database Technology Conference,* Online Conferences Ltd., England (April 1976).

Describes CAFS, an associative searching device commercially available from ICL. Multiplexed data from up to 12 disk tracks is passed to CAFS, which applies selection criteria to that data and filters out unneeded records before passing the rest to the host machine (it can also filter out unneeded fields from those records that do qualify). The selection conditions can be quite complex and can involve (for example) nested Boolean expressions. Also, the device can handle several distinct searches simultaneously, thus providing parallel execution of several distinct user queries.

8.51 E. Babb. "Implementing a Relational Database by Means of Specialized Hardware." *ACM TODS* **4,** No. 1 (March 1979).

Describes two extended versions of the basic CAFS device [8.50]. The first extension involves the use of a one-bit-wide direct access memory, the "single bit array store"; the second involves multiple such stores, together with hash-addressing to access those stores. The paper shows how each of these extensions can help in the implementation of projection and join operations. In the case of projection, CAFS will transmit only non-duplicate tuples to the host; the bit array stores are used to remember whether a tuple identical to the current tuple has already been transmitted. In the case of join, CAFS does not actually handle the entire operation itself; instead, it passes participating tuples from the first relation to the host, using the bit array stores to remember values of the join attribute from those tuples as it does so; it then uses those remembered values to select participating tuples from the second relation and passes those in turn to the host; and the host then computes the actual join. In both cases, therefore, the effect of the hardware extensions is to reduce the amount of data to be sent to the host and thus the amount of processing to be done by that host.

8.52 D. J. DeWitt. "DIRECT—A Multiprocessor Organization for Supporting Relational Data Base Management Systems." *Proc. 5th Annual Symposium on Computer Architecture* (1978).

As explained in the body of the chapter, DIRECT is an MPC device. In its implemented form it consists of a PDP 11/45 host, a microprogrammed PDP 11/40 controller, a set of CCD memory modules, a set of PDP 11/03 processing units, and a crossbar switch to interconnect the memories and the processors. The paper presents the rationale for the MPC design. Early systems such as XDMS [8.11] were "single instruction stream, single data stream" (SISD) devices: They could handle one search (instruction) at a time, and could examine one stream of data from the database at a time. Later systems such as RAP [8.39–8.44] and CASSM [8.36, 8.37] were "single instruction stream, multiple data stream" (SIMD) devices: Although still limited to one search at a time, they could examine multiple portions of the database in parallel. The inefficiencies inherent in SISD and SIMD devices were sketched in Sections 8.2 and 8.3. Hence, devices like DIRECT support a "multiple instruction stream, multiple data stream" (MIMD) architecture, in which multiple searches can be executed in parallel against multiple portions of the database. That architecture permits parallelism both within and across user-level queries. See [8.53] for details of how such parallelism is exploited in DIRECT.

8.53 D. J. DeWitt. "Query Execution in DIRECT." *Proc. ACM SIGMOD International Conference on Management of Data* (May 1979).

8.54 D. E. Shaw. "A Relational Database Machine Architecture." In [8.4].

8.55 E. J. Oliver and P. B. Berra. "RELACS: A Relational Associative Computer System." In [8.4].

See [8.32].

8.56 S. Uemura, T. Yuba, A. Kokubu, R. Ooomote, and Y. Sugawara. "The Design and Implementation of a Magnetic-Bubble Database Machine." *Proc. IFIP Congress 1980.*

Describes an operational prototype device called EDC based on "electronic disks" (bubble memories). EDC fits into the MPC category (like DIRECT); however, its "disks," being electronic, have the property that each "track" can be independently started or stopped at any time, because the rotation is electronic, not physical. Stored relations are partitioned across the memories of the device. A high-level language called EDCL, based on relational algebra, is compiled into EDC primitive operations, which are then interpreted by a microcoded control program and dynamically distributed to the controlling logic for each memory.

8.57 W. F. King, III. "Relational Database Systems: Where We Stand Today." *Proc. IFIP Congress 1980.*

An evaluation of the progress made in relational systems over the ten years immediately following the publication of Codd's original CACM paper in 1970, with the emphasis on pragmatic and implementation aspects. (King was the leader of the System R project throughout much of its life.) The paper is divided into three sections: Original Motivations, Relational System Performance, and Future Directions. In the first section King assesses (favorably) the achievements of implemented systems to date with respect to Codd's original six objectives for relational systems:

- provide a high degree of data independence;
- serve as a common data model for a wide variety of users;
- support set-level application programming;
- simplify the task of the DBA;
- provide a solid theoretical foundation;
- provide a basis for inferential systems.

In the second section of the paper, King discusses, specifically, the performance lessons to be learned from System R. The results obtained with that system demonstrated very clearly that "exotic hardware (associative memory, etc.)" is *not* required in order to achieve good performance in a relational system.

In the third section, King addresses (among other things) the role of "intelligent" (that is, associative) disks. He suggests that such devices are useful only for applications requiring complex searches of nonindexed data (in other words, "library search" applications); they are not applicable to typical database applications at all. He also considers the backend machine approach (a software DBMS running in a backend processor, possibly augmented with some kind of associative hardware); here again there seems to be very little performance advantage compared with a conventional system. Reference [8.49] is cited in support of this position.

In addition to database machines, the third section of the paper also discusses desirable functional enhancements to today's systems (multiple data model support, program conversion techniques, distributed systems with location and replication transparency, and semantic integrity control).

8.58 M. R. Stonebraker. "MUFFIN: A Distributed Data Base Machine." University of California at Berkeley: Electronics Research Laboratory Memo No. UCB/ERL M79/28 (May 1979).

MUFFIN stands for "Multiple Fast or Faster INGRES." It is intended as a distributed database system in which certain nodes are database machines, that is, comparatively conventional processors dedicated to database functions (other, nondedicated nodes may also have some portion of the database stored locally). A MUFFIN system consists of a number of "pods," interconnected via a low-speed communication network. Each pod consists of a set of "A-cells" and a set of "D-cells," interconnected via a high-speed local network. An A-cell is a conventional machine (A stands for application), and runs application programs, a conventional operating system, and the Distributed INGRES software. A D-cell is an "ideal" database machine, that is, a processor dedicated to database management and running only one program, namely a pared-down version of INGRES (see the subsection on "Backend software" in Section 8.2). Note that to the A-cell version of INGRES the system looks just like a normal distributed system, except that the query optimizer must be aware of the difference in speed between inter- and intra-pod communication.

As the paper states, the foregoing design bears little resemblance to that of other database machines. Several arguments are presented for rejecting those other approaches. The MUFFIN approach, by contrast, treats database machines as a special case of distributed databases, and thus reduces the database machine issue to a previously unsolved problem.

Index